# REEL
# BLACK
# TALK

# REEL BLACK TALK

## A SOURCEBOOK OF 50 AMERICAN FILMMAKERS

Spencer Moon

*Foreword by George Hill*

**GREENWOOD PRESS**
Westport, Connecticut • London

Library of Congress Cataloging-in-Publication Data

Moon, Spencer.
    Reel Black talk : a sourcebook of 50 American filmmakers /
Spencer Moon ; foreword by George Hill.
        p.   cm.
    Includes filmographies, bibliographical references, and index.
    ISBN 0–313–29830–0 (alk. paper)
    1. Afro-American motion picture producers and directors—United
States—Encyclopedias.   2. Afro-American motion picture producers
and directors—United States—Interviews.   I. Title.
PN1998.2.M66   1997
791.43'0233'02573—dc21          96–47539

British Library Cataloguing in Publication Data is available.

Library of Congress Catalog Card Number: 96–47539
ISBN: 0–313–29830–0

First published in 1997

Greenwood Press, 88 Post Road West, Westport, CT 06881
An imprint of Greenwood Publishing Group, Inc.

Printed in the United States of America

The paper used in this book complies with the
Permanent Paper Standard issued by the National
Information Standards Organization (Z39.48–1984).

10 9 8 7 6 5 4 3 2 1

**On the cover, clockwise from top**: Melvin Van Peebles, photo courtesy of Shelley Bonus;
Ayoka Chenzira, photo courtesy of Andre Harris; Neema Barnette; William Greaves, photo
courtesy of Deane Folsom.

# CONTENTS

# FOREWORD: NINETY-PLUS
# YEARS OF FILMMAKING

As early as 1899, African Americans were involved in the industry of film-making. William Foster of Chicago got his colored filmmakin' thing started in 1913. Oscar Micheaux, our premier filmmaker, took directing, writing and producing to a higher level with the release of his first film in 1918. Micheaux directed more than forty films between 1918 and 1948, a feat that remains unequaled in Black film history. In the early years, Black filmmakers had to go from theater to theater collecting their share of the box office receipts after each screening.

Since those early years, hundreds of African American producers and directors have exercised their creativity. I'd say this work by Spencer Moon is long overdue. A dynamic volume, it speaks to the passion these women and men have for their chosen profession. Moreover, Moon's diligence bursts off each page and is indicative of his love for them, their cinema and their filmmaking abilities. A filmmaker himself, Moon takes us "on location" and looks into the minds and hearts of his subjects, capturing for the first time in literary history what it involves to bring forth this type of entertainment in an industry that has consistently denied people of color their rightful place and status.

Multitudinous images have been stamped on celluloid by the filmmakers presented herein. Their representations of who we were, what we are, who we be, who we is and that which we may become are available for our children's children and will bear witness to the colored/Negro/Black/African American cinema of the twentieth century.

As we move rapidly into the next century, I hope that many more filmmakers will follow in the footsteps of Oscar Micheaux and bring forth the dreams, the love stories, the positive reflections of who we are. My children, your children and generations of unborn Black babies await this triumph. They deserve nothing less. The "in the hood" films, the sexist comedies and nasty language films, are passé.

Micheaux's films were dramas. He produced no comedies and only one full-blown musical. He had talented, beautiful women as his leading ladies; they included Evelyn Preer, Edna Mae Harris, Bee Freeman and Ethel Moses. Micheaux's wife, Alice Russell, worked with him, first managing their book distribution company and then later with their film production, becoming the *first* African American female producer. Micheaux generated greater box office revenue by featuring women in his films. The same approach works today. One need only look at the success of *Waiting to Exhale* (1995).

O ye Blackmen of strength and vision: The time has come for you to open wide every door in the industry to Black women in all arenas as actresses and behind the cameras as filmmakers. Our women have paid their dues, just as we men have. Let us not march into the next century knowing that we did not do that which was just and responsible. We can make the future a better world. Black women have a gift to give, a delightful and much-needed perspective to share. We do not succeed until Black women succeed.

The legacy on these pages will last as long as the films do. This book allows each filmmaker to speak in his or her own words. That does not happen on the silver screen, because making a film is a collaborative effort among the director, the cinematographer, the actor or perhaps all of the above. Of course, every film has the director's stamp on it, his or her hand in it, his or her name in the credits. But it does not always speak to what is deep inside, to what makes the film tick. It does not reveal why a director decided to do a particular film in the first place. It is *this book* that presents the true voice of the director; and the passion of these directors is exemplified herein.

George Hill, Ph.D.

## ON GEORGE HILL

Archivist, historian and journalist, George Hill has authored nineteen books including *Blacks in Hollywood, Airwaves to the Soul, Black Action Films* and *Ebony Images*. He has pioneered the exhibiting of movie posters on a variety of ethnic genres: Seventy Years of Black Cinema, American Indians on the Silver Screen,

Black Women in Film, and Fifty Years of Hispanic Cinema. His exhibits on film music include Jazz at the Movies, Soul Music Cinema, Country Music Movies, Hollywood Hip/Hop and Celluloid Rock.

# PREFACE

The success of this book will make it possible to assay the over 125 African American and diaspora filmmakers on whom I have a working file today. With a little thought and research, you may realize that in terms of numbers this work represents only the tip of the iceberg. Some filmmakers are lucky enough to make a living at their craft; many are not. Independently made films produced outside the Hollywood system are no less important or interesting.

## HISTORY

The movie industry in Hollywood was started by a group of independent filmmakers who fled competition in New York and New Jersey, the early U.S. film center. These filmmakers—mostly immigrants—entered the business as small competitors against the larger companies started by the likes of Thomas Edison and George Eastman. Edison and his group had started the Motion Pictures Patents Company, a consortium of film studios. These men saw the profits to be made in the fledgling film business and were not going to let upstart companies of immigrants stop them or their money-making interests. So the small companies were literally run out of town, many by force and violence. They moved to California to take advantage of the better weather for shooting and the physical distance from the competition. Those independent filmmakers started the Hollywood system of filmmaking.

In terms of Black cinema, the following high points are significant:

*1898* Newsreels show the all-Black 9th Cavalry marching. They helped Teddy Roosevelt in his famous charge up San Juan Hill.

*1910* African Americans Peter Jones and Bill Foster make comedies in Chicago.

*1917* Race movies constitute the African American community's response to the revisionist, reactionary and racist *Birth of a Nation* (1915). Race movies are written, produced, directed and distributed by and star African Americans. Race movies present Black people in positive perspectives, and their success prods many White producers to make race movies. From 1917 until the late forties, several hundred race movies were produced and marketed; subsequently integration during the early fifties killed the market for independently made films from and for the Black community. Black film stars who had achieved minor successes in race movies got bit parts in Hollywood films in the late forties and fifties.

*1923* The first short-subject sound film is produced by Lee DeForrest, starring African Americans Noble Sissle and Eubie Blake. They sing one original song and one cover tune, three minutes in length (available on *The African American Cinema, Volume II*, distributed by the Library of Congress/ Smithsonian home video series). Sissle and Blake were progenitors in theater. They co-wrote the first all-Black show on Broadway in 1921, *Shuffle Along.* Their short subject was produced before the Al Jolson feature film *The Jazz Singer* was released in 1929.

*1950* Sidney Poitier begins a two-decades-long reign as the pre-eminent African American film star in Hollywood films. By the end of the seventies he has gone from box office star to the director's chair, by choice. His talent, box office appeal and success as director is significant considering African American cinema today.

*1971* *Sweet Sweetback's Baadasssss Song*\*\* and *Shaft*\*\* are released. Hollywood-financed Black cinema of the seventies, later called Blaxploitation, begins.

*1978* *The Wiz*\*\* is financed and produced by Berry Gordy of Motown Records. The film costs millions to produce and is a financial flop. Its financial failure is used by the major Hollywood studios as a reason to discontinue making Black cinema through the Hollywood style of filmmaking and distribution.

*1986* *She's Gotta Have It*\*\* is released—the Black cinema renaissance begins.

*1991* A peak year when nineteen feature films are produced, directed, and written by *and star* African Americans. Not since the seventies have so many

Black-cast feature films been released in the United States. Several were produced and financed outside the Hollywood system.

*1996* *People* magazine's "Hollywood Blackout" article creates national response. The article shows through interviews and statistics the paucity of Black participation behind the scenes. Through statistical analysis, the article demonstrates the lack of significant participation by African Americans as producers (who can green-light movies), line-producers, directors, writers and technicians. Jesse Jackson, Whoopi Goldberg and Quincy Jones stand divided about the progress of African Americans in the Hollywood style of production. This in turn creates a national focus on jobs and the practices of labor unions and craft guilds.

The April 29–May 5 "Black in America" issue of the *New Yorker* magazine broadens the popular press's—and thereby overall popular—opinion of the Black experience in America.

## CONTEXT AND POWER

African American participation in the development of the film (and later, television) industry parallels the dominant culture's history. Our history is no mystery. There is a process of contextualization that must be understood before one can fully appreciate Black cinema produced by and starring African Americans. The question of whose standards of filmmaking are to be used in this discussion is important, and the answer is obvious. By international world cinema standards, the African American tradition rivals the cinema from anywhere else in the world.

The filmmaking experience for African American filmmakers can be a schizophrenic one. If we don't aspire to make films through the Hollywood system, the response to our work (sometimes from our own community) is less than serious. So a dichotomy exists: Do we make films through Hollywood, or do we follow our own independent vision? This book presents a cross-section of filmmakers from both camps and some who work in both arenas.

Cinema by its nature is Darwinian in scope; only the strong survive. At the time of the writing of this book, the country is divided along racial lines—bolstered by institutionalized racism. There are clear political, social and economic factors to Black existence in America today. This is even more pronounced in the costly business of filmmaking and distribution in America, which is controlled by a lowest-common-denominator and/or commodifying Euro-centric system. Yet despite this fact, there exists a clear and viable alternative network of production and distribution outside this control mechanism.

Black cinema should be seen in international terms. The emerging video distribution alternatives have made it possible for just such a perspective to emerge. Distribution, as you will read, is a critical issue for Black filmmakers in Hollywood and elsewhere. When the programs have some place for more local, regional, national and international exhibition besides those traditionally run by Hollywood, then an important juncture will have been reached.

The power of media today is clear to me. Under a California Arts Council, Artists-in-Residence grant, I co-taught a video production class in the San Francisco county jail system for three years. My partner, another filmmaker, taught the nuts and bolts of video production; my focus was on teaching media literacy, film history, consciousness and Black history. In teaching incarcerated individuals (both men and women) about how media works and about Black history and consciousness through documentaries and other cinema, I saw how media can both help and hurt our society. Many of those incarcerated, mostly misdemeanor and felony violators, said that once they understood how media had instilled values and ideas in them (i.e., the "programming" they had received), they understood its effect on them and the way they presented themselves to the world outside the walls of jail. Obviously, more than programming had led many of these individuals to their time in jail. But it is clear that part and parcel of what made them who they were at the time of our class was negative programming: images of African Americans in stereotypical, demeaning and comedic roles.

Currently, in teaching this same curriculum to junior college students, I find that their responses, though more articulate, are strikingly similar to those of the jail inmates. But the junior college students can do something that the inmates could not: change their immediate circumstances by watching media more consciously, articulating their dissatisfaction to local and national media through phone calls and letters of complaint, being more conscious in their movie-going habits and seeking out work by independent filmmakers.

## ABOUT THIS BOOK

For purposes of this book, I have chosen filmmakers most of whom make their living at their craft. This is the first book in which Black filmmakers themselves share their filmmaking experiences from the African American perspective. This is the first time that an African American has written such a book on the Black filmmaking experience. My effort is not to ghettoize their work but to show the diversity, depth and breadth of Black filmmaking whenever possible from a very personal perspective. These filmmakers are indeed products of their environment. As America is slowly and maybe not so surely learning, it is a very diverse and nonmonolithic experience to be Black in America.

The book is also an attempt to honor and recognize for a new generation some of the historic filmmakers who laid the foundation for the current crop of Black filmmakers—both Hollywood and independent. But it is not a comprehensive overview; it serves only as an introduction to the filmmakers profiled.

The choice of who was to be included in the book was based on my own personal perspective. I felt the need to include a variety of filmmakers stylistically; the breakdown is as follows:

- Interviews: 54% (27)
- Women: 14% (7)
- Historic filmmakers: 12% (6)
- Los Angeles: 50% (25)
- San Francisco: 10% (5)
- Not California: 28% (14)
- Narrative/feature film genre: 40% (20)
- Potpourri—work in a variety of genres: 18% (9)
- Documentary: 18% (9)
- Television: 6% (3)
- Animation: 4% (2)
- Experimental: 2% (1)

There are forty-four chapters on fifty filmmakers. There is some overlap of categories. One example: women and Not California.

The *Gallery of Greats* calendar and honorees are mentioned many times. See the chapter on Madeline Anderson* for a complete explanation of the *Gallery of Greats* event, program and honorees.

Readers should not get hung up on dates. They are included in the text where appropriate. Dates for directors and their work on episodic television are not included. With the proliferation of additional networks, coupled with syndication, many of the shows listed can be found on some network, some affiliate or some cable system channel today.

The publisher asked me originally to include the dates of birth for filmmakers included in the book. Many directors have asked that I not print their date of birth, and I have honored this request. Several said they did not want to contribute to ageism in addition to racism in the industry, so they declined to tell me their date of birth. Therefore, only the dates for historic filmmakers have been included.

The idea for this book grew out of my relationship with George Hill, who wrote the Foreword. George inspires me still. This book is a labor of love, loss and memories. I am sure all the filmmakers would say their work is intended for as wide an audience as possible—they are artists first. Their ethnic heritage is simply part of what makes them unique. One of my goals in writing this book was to demonstrate that there is more film and video work available *of interest* than you are seeing in the movies, on television or at the local video store. In addition to telling about who is who, the book will tell something about what is where. I hope you enjoy reading the book, and I hope it opens the doors of perception to new horizons in film and video.

## NOTE

An asterisk (*) indicates that an individual appears as an entry in this book. Two asterisks (**) indicate that a film is available on home video—see Appendix for sources.

## SOURCES

### Books

Cripps, Thomas. *Slow Fade to Black: The Negro in Film 1900–1942.* New York: Oxford University Press, 1993.

Dennis, Denise. *Black History for Beginners.* New York: Writers and Readers Publishing, 1984.

Gabler, Neal. *An Empire of Their Own: How the Jews Invented Hollywood.* New York: Doubleday, 1988.

Hill, George, and James Robert Parish. *Black Action Films: Plots, Critiques, Casts and Credits for 235 Theatrical and Made-for-Television Releases.* Jefferson, NC: McFarland, 1989.

Hughes, Langston, and Milton Meltzer. *Black Magic: A Pictorial History of Black Entertainers in America.* New York: Prentice-Hall, 1967.

### Magazines

Gordon, Lewis R., et al. "Race and Racism in the Last Quarter of '95: The O.J. and Post O.J. Trial and the Million Man March—A Symposium." *The Black Scholar* (Oakland, CA) (25), no. 4 (1996), p. 37–59.

Hertzberg, Hendrik and Henry Louis Gates, Jr. "The African American Century." *The New Yorker* (72), no. 10 (April 29 and May 5, 1996), p. 9–10.

Lambert, Pam, et al. "What's Wrong With This Picture?: Exclusion of Minorities Has Become a Way of Life in Hollywood." *People* (New York) (45), no. 11, (March 18, 1996), p. 42–52.

# ACKNOWLEDGMENTS

I would like to thank the following individuals for their part in helping me create this book: my mother, Florence Edna Moon Finley, and her friend James Jackson; my relatives and family in Talladega (Alabama), Atlanta, Detroit, and New York City; Louise Connors, her daughters and extended family; Denise Maunder; Bonnie Boren; George Hill; my agent, Amy Kossow of the Linda Allen Agency; Alicia Merritt and Greenwood Publishing; scholars I've known and admired: Ed Guerrero, Albert Johnson, Herb Boyd, Amiri Baraka and Don Bogle; the students and staff of City College, San Francisco; my friend and educator, Ivan Kovacs; my friend and legal counsel, Sherry Gendelman; the artist Robert Ellis-Lee; the Marshall brothers, Pluria and Rudy and Rudy's wife, Ruth; Fernando Exposito and Jim Harrison; my friend Kenn Graddick; the spirit that was the Hancock House in Detroit, Michigan, and those who were part of that spirit and remember it still; the filmmakers who gave me interviews; the filmmakers in the book whose lives and work inspired me; those who accepted me and encouraged me along the way; those who rejected me and discouraged me along the way; my Black ancestors, on whose shoulders I stand; and finally the Holy Spirit that inhabits my body and gives me consciousness.

# THE
# FILMMAKERS

William Alexander. *Illustration courtesy of R. Ellis Lee.*

# WILLIAM ALEXANDER

## BACKGROUND

William Alexander (1916–1991) is remembered as a versatile film pioneer. He was born in Missouri and grew up in Colorado. Athletically inclined, Alexander played football in high school and was a gymnast in college. He attended the Colorado State College of Education, now the University of Northern Colorado. After leaving school Alexander found work with the National Youth Administration, a federal agency led by the well-known Black-rights activist Mary McLeod Bethune. Alexander left Colorado for Washington, D.C., in 1941. In December of that year America entered World War II. Alexander secured work with the Office of War Information, making films related to Negro affairs. Because of the war effort, veteran filmmakers were teamed with novices. Alexander worked with a Hollywood veteran by the name of Emmanuel Glucksman. The team also included novice Black producer Claude Barnett. Together this team created the first Black-oriented newsreels, which were distributed under the title *All-American News*.

## WORLD WAR II AND NEGRO WAR EFFORTS

*All-American News* were essentially propaganda films, because America needed Negro participation to win the war. Alexander co-produced, narrated and did man-on-the-street interviews for over forty newsreels. These historic newsreels were some of the best and first consciously produced, positive film images of Black people other than the race movies that had originated some two decades earlier. Scenes depicted everyday acts such as the daughter of famed boxing great Joe Louis playing the piano, as well as writer Ann Petrey receiving a $2,400 prize for her novel *The Street*. The newsreels also featured footage of the all-Black 92nd Infantry Division. By Alexander's own estimation, these newsreels reached over nine hundred Black theaters nationwide.

The most widely distributed film on Blacks during World War II was *The Negro Soldier*. It was part of a series entitled *Why We Fight* produced by Frank Capra. In addition to showing in America, the film was shown in the European and Asian theaters of war. Carlton Moss, an African American, wrote the script for this film and appeared in it.

## INDEPENDENT PRODUCTION

After the war Alexander founded the Associated Producers of Negro Motion Pictures. He also founded his own company, Alexander Productions. His production manager, Harryette Miller, remembers that Alexander knew how to raise capital and get productions executed once they were conceived. By 1946 Alexander had enough money to make four films, including two musical short subjects: *Vanities* and *Rhythm in a Riff*. His feature films were *The Highest Tradition* and *Rhythm in a Riff*, whose alternate title was *Flicker Up*. In 1947 Alexander made a film with heavy-weight champion Joe Louis entitled *The Fight Never Ends*.

Alexander was a solid, independent and prolific filmmaker. In the fifties he produced a series of newsreels for the Black audience entitled *By-Line*. As an independent journalist he covered the Organization of African Unity's deliberations on the civil war in Biafra. In 1960 he produced a twelve-part series for the ABC television network on seven newly liberated and African-governed states. In addition to his documentaries he made several feature films, including one in 1974 based on a novel by William Bradford. This film, *The Klansman*, featured Richard Burton.

Alexander was the recipient of prizes at the Cannes Film Festival, and he received a United Nations award for his documentary work.

## FILMOGRAPHY

### Producer

#### *Selected Short Subjects*

*All-American News*, 1945. Newsreels designed to present positive images of Negroes to encourage their involvement at home and in battle in World War II.

*Vanities*, 1946. This short featured singer Joesfred Portee, a dance number by Audrey Armstrong and impressions by Charles Keith. *Rhythm in a Riff,* 1946 (alternate title, *Flicker Up*). This film featured crooner extraordinaire, Billy Eckstein. Other performers were Babe Wallace, Sarah Wallace, Garfield Love, Ray Moore, Ann Baker and Hortense Allen.

*Open the Door, Richard,* 1947. A comedy skit by the comedian Dusty Fletcher. The film's title later became the basis for a hit song with the same title.

*Jivin' In Bebop',*\*\* 1947. A musical short that featured Dizzy Gillespie and his big band with vocalist Helen Humes. This film introduced the then-new jazz music sensation, be-bop, to mass audiences. Gillespie's band at that time included such notable jazz soloists as Milt Jackson on vibes, James Moody and Benny Carter on reeds. Songs featured in the film included *Oop Bop Sh'Bam, Bob a Lee-ba* and *He Beeped When He Shoulda Bopped.* Co-directed by Spencer Williams.\*

*Boogie Woogie Blues*, 1948. Another musical, featuring Hadda Brooks singing and playing piano. Songs included *Don't Take Your Love from Me* and *I'm Tired of Everything But You.*

### Feature Films

*The Fight Never Ends*, 1947. Boxing heavyweight champion Joe Louis and a very young and unknown actress by the name of Ruby Dee starred in this film. Louis had made his debut in a film made nine years earlier called *The Spirit of Youth*. In this second film, Louis played himself. The film also had a brief appearance by the always-melodious singing sensations the Mills Brothers.

*Souls of Sin*, 1949. Written and directed by Powell Lindsay, who was also part of an ensemble cast. The cast featured Billie Allen, Bill Chase, Savannah Churchill, William Greaves,\* Louis Jackson, Charlie Mae Rae, Emory Richardson, Jessie Walter and Jimmy Wright. Churchill played a vamp called Regina who leads Dollar Bill (played by Wright) to destruction. In addition, the story follows the lives of three men (including Wright) in Harlem trying to overcome poverty. One man's life is ruined by crime; the other two succeed despite the odds against them. Savannah Churchill was known for her hit record *I Only Want to Be Loved by You*. In this film she introduced a song called *The Things You Do to Me.*

*The Klansman,*\*\* 1974, 112 min., color. Directed by Terance Young. The film starred Richard Burton, Lola Folana, Lee Marvin, Linda Evans, Spence Will-Dee, Lucianna Paluzzi, Cameron Mitchell and O.J. Simpson. Critically and financially this was the least successful of Alexander's films given its budget, cast and contemporary production values.

## SOURCES

Bogle, Don. *Blacks in American Films and Television*. New York: Simon & Schuster, 1989.

Hill, George, and James Robert Parish. *Black Action Films*. Jefferson, NC: McFarland, 1989.

Kisch, John, and Edward Mapp. *A Separate Cinema: Fifty Years of Black-Cast Posters*. New York: Farrar, Straus and Giroux, 1992.

"Obituary," *New York Times*, December 6, 1991, p. B16.

Simpson, Donald. "Black Images in Film: The 1940's to the Early 1960's," *Black Scholar* (21), no. 2, 1990, p. 20–27.

Time-Life Books, eds. *African American Voices of Triumph: Creative Fire, A Tradition of African Art, Filmmaking, Music, Literature, Visual Arts*. Alexandria, VA: Time-Life Books, 1994.

# MADELINE ANDERSON

## BACKGROUND

Being a pioneer is never easy. Madeline Anderson thought in her days grow-ing up in Lancaster, Pennsylvania, that she would be a filmmaker—a surprise to her family and friends. "People equated filmmaking with Hollywood, and everyone knew a Black girl couldn't aspire to be a Hollywood producer." She was encouraged to pursue another interest—teaching.

Anderson has put the two together and is the *first* African American female independent filmmaker in the United States to produce a television series and have it air nationally. She became executive producer of *The Infinity Factory (1978)*, which aired on PBS. It taught 8- to 12-year-olds the everyday usage of mathematics. Anderson worked for four years as an in-house pro-ducer and director for the Children's Television Workshop (CTW). She produced a dozen or more short films and two half-hour documentary-style teaching films for parents and teachers. For *The Infinity Factory* (in addition to being executive producer), Anderson produced twenty-three 3-minute films, and produced and directed eighteen magazine-length (7- or 8-minute long) documentaries, ten of which she edited. She started making films as a civil rights activist to inform and encourage people to act.

## INDEPENDENT PRODUCTION

Anderson's first independent film was *Integration Report, One* (1960). She described what it was like to make *Integration Report, One*.

Madeline Anderson

This film taught me that you can't be an independent filmmaker unless you know how to do it. To do all of it. From making that film, I got into editing as a career path in filmmaking.

Richard Leacock was a mentor when she was just beginning in independent production. Later, he became her business partner and together they formed Andover Productions. They produced two film series: *Bernstein in Europe* and a science series for Educational Services for MIT. Anderson supervised each series from production through editing.

## RACE AND GENDER ISSUES

Have your gender and race affected your work?

When I first started out there was the catch-22. You could not work in the industry unless you were in the union. You could not become a union member unless you had a job. Most of the unions at the time were father-son unions. All the fathers were White. So that posed a problem in my getting into the union. I was able to get into the editors union only after threatening not to sue the production company I had worked for as an editor for a year and a half. I started out with Richard Leacock at Andover Productions as a production manager, then later became a producer. When I left, I got into the editors union after that. I made *Integration Report, One*, and then worked on *The Cool World* with Shirley Clarke. I freelanced after that and got on the staff at National Education Television.

I really didn't let gender and race issues bother me. I knew I would have trouble with both. I was determined to do what I was going to do at any cost. I kept plugging away. Whatever I had to do, I did it. A lot of it was gritty hard work, taking a lot of nonsense and bad behavior from people. I was determined I was going to work in this field. I worked mostly with White men. I saw them doing things and I knew I could do those same things as well or even better. So I was not going to let that stand in my way. I expected it; I expected what I had to go through. It wasn't easy, but I made up my mind that I was going to do it.

## UNIQUENESS

Anderson was asked to describe her unique contribution to filmmaking.

I've done more educational and social documentaries than many of the other independent filmmakers, but I think it leans heavily in educational films.

Anderson worked for National Education Television (NET) for five years as an associate producer, writer and editor before it became WNET-TV, New York City's first public television station. She also said that her work on the pioneer series *Black Journal* was as an editor, associate producer and writer. The beginnings of *Black Journal* at NET were initiated by Alvin Perlmutter, who became the show's executive producer. Anderson requested that she be assigned to the program once it began development and production. *Black Journal*'s staff was all White in the beginning except for Anderson; that was in 1968. However, later more Black staff were hired. The host of *Black Journal*, Lou Potter, was a Black writer from Chicago. In 1969 William Greaves* was brought in as a part-time host for the program, and even later the small but burgeoning Black staff asked for and got a Black executive producer. Greaves was named to that position. Within a year the program not only had a mostly Black staff but had won an Emmy for its efforts.

Anderson left NET and produced, directed and edited her film *I Am Somebody* for the hospital workers union, Local 1199. Anderson also worked as an in-house producer/director for *Sesame Street* and *The Electric Company* for the CTW.

> Around 1975 I took a leave of absence to form my own company, Onyx Productions. I did a film for the Ford Foundation called *The Walls Came Tumbling Down*. It was a filmed report of the projects that they funded that year. This film was on a public housing project in St. Louis, Missouri. The tenants became their own landlords. I continued to work for CTW and did a half-hour film in Portuguese called *Sesame Street Is Everywhere*. I did some 16mm films for the New Jersey Board of Higher Education. Although I left the staff of CTW, I remained available to them and they used my services.

During this period Anderson also taught, lectured and was director of the Broadcast Funding Division for Howard University at WHMM-TV. She was involved in the original start-up operations for the station.

Anderson had spent time in the Middle East working for CTW.

> After I came back from the Middle East I took time off, and in 1990 I got serious about ministry. I had been volunteering with the Catholic Church. I tried to figure out how to combine my volunteer work in the church with my filmmaking skills. There was a position that opened with the diocese Office of Black Ministry. The work of the organization is cultural, social and religious. They have programs that teach people of African descent our history, traditions and achievements in the church. After two years I was able to make a videotape.

I produced an adult education video. It is titled *Ol' Time Religion*. I am now the director of the Office of Black Ministry.

## GALLERY OF GREATS

Our initial interview with Anderson was conducted during the time she was being inducted into the *Gallery of Greats*. The *Gallery* is a calendar produced annually by Miller Brewing Company to honor African Americans in various fields. Proceeds from sales of the calendars go to Black charities. In 1991, Miller chose Black filmmakers as the honorees with proceeds going to the Thurgood Marshall Education Fund. Events held in Los Angeles included the unveiling of the original portraits used for the calendar, with the artist Louis Delsarte present. Many of the calendar honorees attended the three days of events. Those honored included Anderson, St. Clair Bourne,* Charles Burnett,* Kathleen Collins-Prettyman, Ossie Davis, William Greaves,* Charles Lane, Spike Lee,* Oscar Micheaux,* Michelle Parkerson,* Melvin Van Peebles,* and Spencer Williams.*

When we asked Anderson if she was surprised to be selected for the *Gallery of Greats*, she said:

> When I looked at it in context, I wasn't; I was one of the early female filmmakers. I'm very pleased and honored. When you make the kind of films I make, you don't get famous. For many years many people (who saw my work) never knew I was Black. I am pleased that my work is being recognized, even though it's not feature films. Usually those are the people who get the honors.

## ADVICE FOR ASPIRANTS

Her words to aspiring filmmakers are:

> Be prepared. If the opportunity comes and you're not prepared, then it's a wasted opportunity. A lot of the things I've done, I could not have done unless I was prepared.

## FRUSTRATION

When asked to describe her biggest frustration as a filmmaker, she replied:

> Every independent filmmaker's frustration is raising money. Particularly the films I make. There is a message that has to be put out there.

The potential for film and television to get the message out there and to change things hasn't even been scratched yet.

## RENAISSANCE

What do you think of the Black film/video renaissance?

I think it's great. More people of African descent are being given an opportunity to express our experiences in the United States and our achievements. We're trying to get others to know us as people, as human beings. I think some of these films have crossover appeal. I am also concerned that films be well made. I wouldn't want us to go through the period of exploitation of our images on film again, as we saw in the seventies. I think that now there is a real opportunity to express ourselves honestly. Whenever we do something, we're always limited by what we can do. I think that now there is a greater opportunity to do what we want to do. A lot of the younger filmmakers are taking good advantage of that.

## BEYOND HOLLYWOOD

Do you think independent production and distribution outside the Hollywood system is a viable artistic and business venture?

I think it's viable artistically. In terms of business, I don't think it's moved as well as it should have. I think people shy away from the kinds of films we make outside the Hollywood system. There is a real change in the filmmaking world now. People tend to devalue films made outside Hollywood—more so in our community than in others. We don't seem to have a real art community yet, but it is growing.

## UNIQUENESS AND ADVICE FOR ASPIRANTS (1996)

Have your views about what makes you unique as a filmmaker changed since we last spoke five years ago?

I really don't think I'm unique. I have a great passion about anything that I do. That's what drives me.

Has what you want to tell young people who want to get into the business changed since we spoke about this subject five years ago?

I'm preparing to do a seminar for high school students. The emphasis is on being prepared. For high school students it's about being prepared for college, because so many things are happening to us as a people and there is a need to be prepared to take advantage of educational opportunities that are out there. There are forces working to take away those things that we have gained. If you are not prepared, you're not going to be able to take advantage. Our lives are more controlled than ever. In order to break that control, you need to be able to see beyond what people are trying to do. This is another reason you have to know your history. If you don't know your history, you don't know what's happening. In the sixties, seventies and eighties, we got opportunities for education. Now our opportunities are being infringed upon. Now young people are not going to be able to take advantage of these opportunities, because many of them don't realize what's being taken away from them. They don't know what was out there. My advice is the same, even more so: be prepared.

## THE FUTURE

What do you hope to accomplish in the future?

I think I haven't even made a dent in what I want to accomplish as a filmmaker.

## SELECTED FILMOGRAPHY

### Producer/Director

*Integration Report, One*, 1960, 20 min., 16mm. A survey film on civil rights.

> I was very excited and filled with so much hope. I saw that film as the first of many reports; thus its title. This film exemplified why I became a filmmaker: because as a child I was never taught any of our history, except the slave history. We were never taught contemporary Black history. So at one point I wanted to be a teacher to teach our history. Somewhere along the way I was looking for a better way of teaching. Making *Integration Report, One* was about the civil rights movement. I thought this was it. *Two* and *Three* and *Four* never came because people with money weren't interested in teaching us our history. It was very difficult to raise money for further films.

*I Am Somebody*, 1969, 30 min., 16mm, WNET-TV. A documentary on a strike by the Charlotte, North Carolina, hospital workers. Hospital workers Local 1199B got support for its efforts from the Southern Christian Leadership Conference, the national AFL-CIO and the New York chapter of hospital workers Local 1199. The

114-day strike included mass marches, police violence, arrests and a boycott of Charlotte's White merchants. In the end, right won over might. A powerful record of Black workers fighting for the same pay as their White counterparts, who earned more before the strike.

> With this film I thought the social documentary was a way to go, because of public television's interest in these kinds of films.

*The Walls Came Tumbling Down*, 1975, 30 min., 16mm. Ford Foundation, client.


### Executive Producer

*The Infinity Factory*, 1978, 52 shows, 30 min., CTW. Designed to teach 8- to 12-year-olds how to use math; shown on 256 PBS stations.


### Senior Producer

*Al Manaahil*, 1987, in Arabic, 65 shows, 30 min., CTW. Shot, edited and shown in Saudia Arabia.

> I traveled back and forth about every six weeks for more than a year to produce these shows. I was called the senior producer. What I did was everything. I supervised the production and post-production. The techniques were similar to the style and technique of *The Electric Company*. It was a series on literacy specifically for Arabic-language countries, teaching children 7 to 14. The program also taught women the language of the Koran. I did the same thing that I did with the Portuguese film, which is another reason I was hired. I wrote the script in English; it was then translated and I memorized the script so I could produce, direct and edit without really having to learn the whole language. I had translators there to help. I was teaching as well as producing. They had a lot of state-of-the-art equipment, but they did not fully know how to use all this video equipment. I worked with all-male crews. This was very touchy. I had to learn their traditions and protocol. I had to know how to behave according to women's behavior in their culture—because when you're teaching, the first thing is respect. I became the mother figure, because mothers are harmless. They used to call me teacher. At first there was a little hostility, a little resentment. After they saw that I could help them and knew what I was doing, they became friendly and cooperative. I was there as the sole CTW representative during post-production. The way I got along was to be respectful of their traditions and customs. I got along very well. It was a good experience.


### Producer/Director/Editor

*Ol' Time Religion*, 1990, 30 min., video. Its content is a seminar that Anderson's diocese does every year called Praise Him.

**Assistant Editor/Assistant Director**

*The Cool World*, 1964, 125 min., 35mm, color, Cinema 5 release. Produced by Frederick Wiseman and directed by Shirley Clarke.

> I met Shirley at Andover Productions. She was part of a group that called themselves the Filmmakers group, which included Graham Ferguson, Willard Van Dyke, D.A. Pennebaker and Richard Leacock. After Andover Films and the Filmmakers group had broken up, Shirley wanted to develop a longer film, a feature. She asked me to work on it with her. The way I feel about the film now is that, I think it was an honest film. It wasn't a romantic idea of who the young people were in the film. That's how they were. Some of the young actors in the film were from gangs or were friends of gang members. I think Shirley tried to do a good job of telling the truth about what was going on at the time. I think it was one of the best films at that time of the genre.

## BIO-CRITICAL REVIEW

"*The Cool World* is a remarkably controlled un-exploitive motion picture on its own. . . . Is worthy of being known more than just [as] a footnote in film history."—George Hill and James Robert Parish, *Black Action Films*

## AWARDS

Association of Independent Film and Video Makers, Life Achievement Award, 1985

Black Filmmakers Hall of Fame, Inductee, 1993

*Gallery of Greats*, Inductee, 1991

Sojourner Truth Festival of the Arts, Woman of the Year, 1976

## EDUCATION

Studied at Millersville State Teachers College, Pennsylvania

New York University, B.A. Psychology

## SOURCES

Interview by George Hill and Spencer Moon, January 1991; follow-up interview, Spencer Moon, June 1996.
Hill, George, and James Robert Parish. *Black Action Films*. Jefferson, NC: McFarland, 1989.

Neema Barnette

# NEEMA BARNETTE

## BACKGROUND

To be a Black woman who is working very successfully in a predominantly White male domain is a tribute to determination and talent. Neema Barnette, an award-winning director, talked about her mentor, Vinette Carroll, the first and one of the few (at that time) Black woman directors in theater on and off Broadway. Carroll later became the *first* Black woman to direct live television. Carroll was one of Barnette's instructors as a graduate of the New York City High School of the Performing Arts.

> I would watch Ms. Carroll directing other students on my lunch hour. My father was a jazz musician, so I liked that movement, that choreo-poem. I was influenced by the early seventies Black theater movement. It was contemporary and combined music, dance and drama. Ms. Carroll was the first director that I saw formulate that concept.

While acting in high school, Barnette had won the Diana Sands Acting Award (named for the talented Black actress who appeared in the 1961 film *A Raisin in the Sun*\*\*). She described the experience of winning that award as pivotal and special because of her love and respect for Sands's work. When Vinette Carroll formed the Urban Arts Corps, she asked Barnette to be a part of that theater company as an actress. Members of the company taught in the community. One of Barnette's summer jobs during college was teaching and directing drama at the Harlem YMCA.

Directing was fun because you could do everything. You could put your two cents in everything: music, movement, set design, etc.

## LEARNING, UNIQUENESS AND STYLE

Barnette reflected on what she learned that has helped her work as a director:

Looking back now, Performing Arts High School was really a finishing school for me. It gave me discipline, it made me enjoy my art. After my father died, and growing up in a single-parent working-class family in Harlem, that experience (high school) really helped me.

When asked to describe what makes her unique as a director, Barnette said:

I have my own style. Anyone who would screen my work and look at every one of its pieces, you could see some of me in there. In the movement and, really, a love for life. A deep interest in the drama of life. The rhythm of people, particularly Black people. My positive outlook on life and people. My sense of understanding comes out in my work.

Her style was imprinted in the American Playhouse production of *Zora Is My Name*.

I changed that production around three hundred and sixty degrees. I hired a set designer, a choreographer, a costume designer. I wanted to mix classic and contemporary. Which is how I like to go. When you do a historical piece and add a sense of modern to it, it makes people today far more interested in watching it. If you're given poetic license to do that—theater and multimedia mixed together.

## PRODUCTION

Barnette described her experience on productions in general:

On everything I do, I have a battle. Because I have my own vision and I do things my own way. I have to be true to what I see in my head. People aren't used to it, because it's not what they're used to looking at. If I put my name on it, it has to be mine. "Mine" meaning a combination of the entire production team. I'm a director who respects my crews. I'm nothing more than a reflection of my crew and cast, whoever they may be. I enjoy every job that I do. I enjoy creating. As a director, you have a lot of control. It is difficult sometimes. I work hard; I like to generate excitement. I like to work with people who believe in what they're doing. Not just waiting for a paycheck. I don't like to waste my time.

## THE INDUSTRY AND GENDER ISSUES

When asked whether part of her challenge in working is as a woman in a predominately male area, Barnette gave an emphatic Yes! She added:

I relish it. I go with it instead of fighting it. The stereotypes of women directors don't work with me. I'm not a bitch or hard-core or demanding. I find challenges for my cast and crew, and when we meet the challenges together we find common ground. As long as you go into a situation knowing what you're doing, that's your strength. But I'm sure being a woman has had a lot to do in some instances with my opinion not being respected or believed. Or that the public will like it. That's why I love the public so much. I'm what you would call a grass-roots director. The proof is in the work. If your work is good, then what's the problem? The problem has to be racism and sexism. It's like raising a child. You take a deep breath. You know in the long run it's got to be worth it, or you're going to get kicked in the behind.

## SISTERHOOD

We asked how she regards her relationship with other Black female directors.

It's very important. It gives me a lot of inspiration. It gives me someone to talk to. Especially when we begin to have similar experiences with the same organizations. We communicate on this. Our story is a different story. I've been trying to get other Black female independents to come out to Hollywood. These women are very important to me. Euzhan Palcy, Ayoka Chenzira* and Julie Dash.* We have a very strong support system. For example, I attended the *Gallery of Greats* program to see Michelle Parkerson.* When I made *Sky Captain*, Michelle and I used to tour together. The support system is strong.

Barnette talked about Julie Dash and the release of her first feature film, *Daughters of the Dust*** (1991).

Julie is going to need a lot of support when that opens. She knows that she has it from us. If I hadn't been inside the system, I could not have shared my experience with Ayoka Chenzira on a project she was shopping out here in Hollywood. We told her to take her script back from the studio and do it herself. Now she's shot it. I'm an independent who works in Hollywood. We share the same goals, the group of us. When you've been in the streets making movies and you don't have two cents, you come from a different mindset than someone who works in Hollywood only. You know how important sisterhood and comradeship is. We're still all struggling. We don't do the things yet that many other really successful Black directors do, but we all seem comfortable where we are.

When I work on independent projects and in Hollywood, I try to bring as many of those people in as I can because we understand each other. I've spoken to television executives on many occasions about these women, when I've been told they were looking for other Black directors. It boils down to politics. But like Nina Simone said, "You're young, gifted and Black." Some of the Black stars I work with remain true to themselves, and yet the television executives can't get rid of them because of ratings and their popularity. Television is not a director's medium. In my battle it's the written word against the visual elements I direct and see how that matches up. The result counts. As a Black woman, you have to prove yourself. I've tried to keep the community as a priority and Hollywood as secondary. That's what has kept me going. That's one reason I admire Marla Gibbs (*227* and *The Jeffersons*); she has a foundation set up in the community. You have to build a base in the community.

I'm proud of where I came from. My first real job in filmmaking was given to me by Bill Greaves* in 1976, as an associate producer. You need to trust in your instincts as an artist. Out here in L.A. we need to get more Black filmmakers involved in self-production and self-producing. I cannot wait for the phone to ring. I have projects I'm developing. I'm not into grants. I'm in no rush to produce my independent projects. My husband is an actor who went back to New York to go on tour in *Malcolm X* (a play). We don't believe in waiting for others to provide for us. Once they see what your message is, they can get in the way and distort it and hurt it. We need to get together out here in Hollywood. We could be a strong group if we got together.

## RENAISSANCE

What do you think of the Black film/video renaissance?

I'm happy to see this renaissance. As far as the doors being opened, until we get our own distribution it will always be a rush of a few projects, some excitement, and then that will die down. There are some makers of color who are about [doing] what they feel is pure entertainment. The bottom line is that film is a very strong political tool. Even though you're entertaining, it's saying something—whatever you want to say as a filmmaker. I don't know if I'll see it in my lifetime, that Hollywood will hand over money that we give them through goods and services, to Black filmmakers to tell reality-based or balanced stories about Black folks. We're their hidden agenda. I think as long as they can make us remain their hidden agenda, they will do so. It is up to us to break that mold. No matter what color you are, you always find in Hollywood that you're part of the latest hype. If one kind of film comes out and it's a small success, they want to get a lot of those kinds of films. With the success of *Waiting to Exhale*** (1995), they (Hollywood) wanted to do a lot of Black female–oriented stories. They are doing them, but there aren't any Black women directing or writing them. Now we have more carbon copies of original pieces. People like the Hudlins, Matty Rich,* Darnell Martin, Julie Dash or Euzhan Palcy—it shouldn't be an issue for any of them to make several films, because we're used to working with low budgets anyway. Their films have proven that they make money. Why don't they have more opportunities to make films? It doesn't make sense. I don't see a lot of hope unless we do our own thing.

## BLACK STUDIOS

That response spurred me to ask why the Black Hollywood community's more successful movers and shakers had not created a Black version of the DreamWorks SKG production concept. (DreamWorks SKG is a production company founded by film and media industry titans Steven Spielberg, Jeffrey Katzenberg, and David Geffen.)

I think our people are asleep. Why should I read in the *Hollywood Reporter* about White filmmakers making films on Black history subjects? That's *my* history. We wonder why; we want to know why. Film is an elitist business, and Black people are new at elitism. It would be nice even on a small level if Black people in the industry talked to each other about the business.

## BEYOND HOLLYWOOD

Do you think independent production and distribution outside the Hollywood system is a viable artistic and business venture?

Yes, I think it is viable and profitable. Examples for us to look at include the Independent Filmmakers Project. They have created small but reasonable and manageable money sources for independent production. There are some stories where the money needs to come from our community in order for them to be told properly. I talked with Carl Franklin* recently about telling the real stories of our history, instead of getting a recoding of history by others. It is important that we create work that can be left as a legacy of truth. We have to do it for ourselves.

## ADVICE FOR ASPIRANTS

What can you tell young aspiring filmmakers?

Young people need to know how rough it is. You don't necessarily need Hollywood to tell a story you have a passion about. If you have a passion for a story, you can find many ways of telling it. It doesn't have to be through the system. The system is decentralizing now. It's decoding and it's being recoded. There is a lot of room for young people with new ideas and new vision to pop up wherever you are and still make it happen. It's not about the surface; film is forever. Put something on the screen that means something. I think there is a good future for young people.

## UNIQUENESS (1996)

Have your views about what makes you unique as a filmmaker changed since we last spoke?

I think I'm no more unique than any other storyteller. My passion will continue to burn until I can tell the truth. Until I can at least tell the truth. Because the images that I see are not the images that are real to me.

## STUDIO CONTRACT AND THE FUTURE

In 1992 Barnette signed a three-picture production contract with Columbia Pictures. I asked her what happened with the deal.

Frank Price, who helped us get the deal, left Columbia. So the new executives there are not as interested in working with us currently. If you don't have people at a studio that you can pitch your ideas to who are interested in your ideas and can relate to it, it becomes useless. These people have their own agenda, and you can't blame them. We need more people in positions of power with agendas like ours—a broader spectrum of creative people who can increase their creative loop and not narrow it. Right now it's very narrow.

What do you hope to accomplish in the future?

I'd like to create a workshop for young Black women who want to create movies. I'd like to develop very multitalented filmmakers who can go out there and deal with anything. Filmmakers who know how to survive and have stories that must be told. Be able to share my experiences, the pitfalls and glories, with them. Hopefully to open the doors so that experiences of other Black women filmmakers—like Julie Dash and Debbie Allen and myself have gone through—will help the next generation; that's really what it's about. That is a goal I'd like to achieve in the next five years. To have my own little space to keep turning over new people. One of the prerequisites will be for each one to teach one. I want to be a part of making sure that this set of talent is stronger and understands what they're getting into. The more prepared they can be, the stronger they'll be, the better they'll be.

## FILMOGRAPHY

Barnette's comments in this filmography were made during the follow-up interview in 1996.

### Producer

*To Be a Man*, 1984, 30 min., 35mm, ABC after-school special. Directed by Cliff Frazier.

### Director

*One More Hurdle: The Donna Cheek Story*, 1984, 30 min., video, NBC after-school special. The story of the first Black equestrian rider in the 1984 Olympics.
*The Silent Crime*, 1984, 30 min., 16mm film and videotape, NBC. A prime-time documentary on domestic violence.

#### *Independent Film*

*Sky Captain*, 1985, 65 min., video. A drama that featured Lynn Moody, Lawrence Hilton Jacobs and Bernie Casey. Written, produced, directed and edited by Barnette.

Tells the story of a young Black teenager, played by Ernest Harden, who is suffering psychological collapse following the death of his single-parent mother.

*Are You with Me?*** 1990, 16mm. Produced by AIDS Film, New York. A documentary on AIDS as it affects the African American community; focuses on mothers and children.

*Spirit Lost*, 1995, 35mm, United Image Entertainment. Produced by Tim Reid, featuring Leon, Regina Taylor and Cynda Williams. A ghost story about a spirit who lurks in an old house and tries to control the husband of a young couple.

*Cuttin' the Mustard*, 1996, 35mm, color. This independent feature film, being executive-produced by Barnette and her company, Harlem Lite Inc. Productions, is in pre-production as of the writing of this book. Reed McCants, her husband, is writing and directing this film.

## Television Movies

*Better Off Dead*,** 1993, 35mm, Lifetime Cable. Featuring Tyra Farrell and Mare Winningham. Produced by author/activist Gloria Steinem. A White neo-Nazi female convict accused of killing a Black policeman is later defended by a Black female lawyer.

> It was a very spiritual production for me because of the nature of the film. The producers let me switch the roles from the way it was originally cast. We put Tyra Farrell, an African American actress, as the attorney and Mare Winningham, a White actress, as the bad girl. It was a really good film to work on and it had a large Black crew of technicians. For me this film proved to the powers that be that we can do our work no matter what the nature of the story.

*Shattered Dreams: The Kathryn Messenger Story*, 1993, 35mm, CBS. Featuring Tyne Daly, Lisa Silverstone and Gerald McRaney; shot on location in Charlotte, North Carolina. In 1951 in Florida a White farm couple is harassed and later arrested for befriending some Black people.

> Telling a White sharecropper's story from a Black perspective. A lot of that came out in the way I shot it and the music I picked to accompany the film. The way I paced the editing. Working in the South and feeling the roots of your ancestors, you feel a lot down South.

*Sin and Redemption*, 1994, 35mm, CBS. Featuring Richard Grieco, Ralph Waite and Cynthia Gibb. This telefilm was distributed in Europe as a feature film.

*Godspeed*, 1994, Showtime Cable. Featuring Louis Gossett Jr.

*Run for the Dream: The Gail Devers Story*, 1996, 105 min., 35mm, Showtime Cable. Featuring Louis Gossett Jr., Robert Guillaume and Charlayne Woodward. Gossett also worked as co-executive producer for the telefilm. This is the true story of Olympic champion Gail Devers and the physical and emotional challenges she overcame to win an Olympic Gold Medal in 1992 in the 100 meter sprint. Devers won two Gold Medals in the 1996 Olympics: one in the 100 meter sprint, and another as part of the 4 by 100 meter relay team.

It was great to work with Lou again. He is definitely one of our warriors. A brilliant talent. He comes with that silent sense of history that a lot of Black actors come with that you feel in the subtext of the film's story.

Telling the story of Gail Devers, a young Black female hero who is alive while you're telling her story. . . . It is not too often that we get to tell the story of young Black women, whose strength and courage persevere beyond ordinary circumstances. We have so many young Black women who do that on a daily basis, but we don't often have the opportunity to put it down forever on film. I was very happy to be able to tell her story within the structure.

*Close to Danger*, 1996, 35mm, Reicher Entertainment. This telefilm is to be released first in Europe as a feature film and then later to be shown on American network television. Featuring Rob Estes and Lisa Renner.

## Episodic Television

*A Different World*, NBC; *China Beach*, ABC; *Cosby Mystery Hour*, NBC; *The Cosby Show*, NBC; *Diagnosis Murder*, CBS; *Frank's Place*, CBS; *Hooperman*, ABC; *It's a Living*, ABC; *The Robert Guillaume Show*, ABC; *Royal Family*, CBS; *The Sinbad Show*, NBC; *What's Happening, Now*, Columbia Television, synd. Directing this program in 1987 made Barnette the *first* African American female to direct an episode of situation comedy for television.

I felt part of the failure of *The Sinbad Show* on NBC was, they were trying to put a new fresh talent in an old mold. This is a new day; you can't do the same old thing with these new comedians. Working with Sinbad was a sheer joy. He is very supportive. When you work with Black artists that have your back [that protect you from a knife-in-the-back] it is very important, particularly for Black directors. I'm sure some of the other Black directors in episodic television will tell you that we don't get the respect—even from our own Black stars, initially—as they give the White directors. We have to just stand there and take it until they realize that we're going to light them better, we're going to give them more attention. Yes, you did have more close-ups.

## Television Specials

*Different Worlds: A Story of Interracial Love*, 1993, 30 min, 16mm, CBS. Featuring Duane Martin and Noelle Parker. Two teens witness the slaying of a classmate at a convenience store. Despite their different backgrounds (he is Black, she is White), they come to know and later love each other. Their friends and family cannot understand what they share and learn about difference.

I took this job because I wanted to show what I could do in a more compact format. I got work on my first movie of the week special based on the strength of this production.

*Zora Is My Name*, 1989, 90 min., color, video, PBS American Playhouse. The production features an all-star cast: Ruby Dee, Oscar Brown Jr., Lou Gossett Jr., Paula

Kelly, Roger Mosley, Beah Richards, Count Stovall, Lynn Whitfield and Flip Wilson. The story takes the life and words of the late author/cultural anthropologist Zora Neale Hurston and creates a unique meld of yesterday and today. Hurston wrote about the American South from her unique Black female perspective. She chronicled the periods from the twenties to the fifties and also managed to explore the myths and folklore of Haiti. The setting for the story is the past, but the context is today. The director uses minimalist sets and expressionistic lighting with period costumes. Barnette has taken this woman's life and words and brought a renewed sense of vigor and a deeper understanding of the timeless qualities to her work. The ensemble works very well together and re-creates the different periods in Hurston's life, filling them with special meaning by their performances.

> I feel very happy about this work today. Last year Julie Dash,* Carl Franklin,* St. Claire Bourne* and I were selected to go to Hong Kong for an African American film festival. In Hong Kong they had a book and film list, and one of the pieces they were studying was this program. I met some young brothers and sisters there, and they said it is used in their schools as curriculum material. A lot of libraries are using it. It is a very different kind of piece on Zora. The piece itself was well worth doing. My experience on *Zora* was not so dissimilar to the experiences I continue to have, particularly when I'm working on a Black project. Especially when you're dealing with people who are working within the realm of character that they've created about Black folks. You come in and try to create some sense of reality. As a result, there is always more difficulty when you're doing stories about us.

### Music Videos

Eric Gable, *Hard Up*
Aretha Franklin, *Think*
Chris Stanley, *Universal Love Song*
Stevie Wonder, *Don't Drive Drunk*

### Commercials

Classic Coke, *Barber Shop*, Burrell Advertising, Sun Light Pictures, 1988.

### Theater

*The Blue Journey*, 1982, Public Theater of New York. Written by Oyamo; produced by Joseph Papp.
*Tamer of Horses*, 1987, Los Angeles Theater Center. Written by Bill Mastersione.
*The Talented Tenth*, 1989, Manhattan Theater Club, City Center, New York. Written by Richard Wesley.

## BIO-CRITICAL REVIEW

*Better Off Dead.* "The best telemovie that Lifetime Cable channel has ever done."—
  Jon Burlingame, *Flint Journal*

————. "One of those rare television movies that is as complicated as life."—Marion Gambel, *Indianapolis News*

————. "The movie delivers on its challenges."—Irv Letofsky, *Hollywood Reporter*

*Different Worlds: A Story of Interracial Love.* "A sensitive look at the multitude of barriers that prevent human connections between ethnic and racial groups."— *Los Angeles Times*

————. "It's amazing the amount of story this *CBS Schoolbreak Special* manages to cram into one hour. Why can't telefilms be this good?"—Linda Renaud, *Hollywood Reporter*

*Run for the Dream: The Gail Devers Story.* "This movie works, score 7." (Out of possible 10 highest rating.)—*TV Guide*, "Hits and Misses"

*Shattered Dreams: The Kathryn Messenger Story.* "It packs a mule kick. A-."—David Hiltbrand, *People*

————. "This first-rate production brings some unexpected lustre to the network movie genre."—*Daily Variety*


## AWARDS

American Film Institute, Directing Workshop for Women, Directing Fellow, 1984

Delta Sigma Theta Sorority, Lily Award, Outstanding Images in Black Media, 1988

*Better Off Dead*
  Cable Ace Award, Best Film, 1994

*China Beach*
  Black Filmmakers Hall of Fame, Honorable Mention, Television Special, 1991

*Cosby Mystery Hair*
  Peabody Award, 1995

*The Cosby Show*
  Monitor Award, Outstanding Directing, Comedy, 1990

*Different Worlds: A Story of Interracial Love*
  Directors Guild of America, Nomination, 1993
  Humanitas Certificate, CBS Schoolbreak Special, 1992

*Frank's Place*
  Directors Guild of America, Nomination, Best Direction, Comedy Series, 1988
  NAACP Image Award Nomination, 1988

*One More Hurdle: The Donna Cheek Story*
  Emmy Award Nomination, 1985
  NAACP Image Award, 1985

*The Silent Crime*
  American Women in Radio and TV Award, 1986
  Emmy Award Nomination, 1984

*Sky Captain*
  Atlanta and Chicago Film Festivals, Winner, 1984
  Whitney Museum, New American Filmmakers Award, 1984

*The Talented Tenth*
  Adelco Award, Outstanding Directing for Theater, 1989
  DeLeo Award, Best Directing, Off-Broadway Play, 1990
*To Be a Man*
  Emmy Award, 1985
*What's Happening, Now*
  NAACP Image Award Nomination, 1987


## EDUCATION

High School of the Performing Arts, New York City

City College of New York, B.A., literature

New York University School of the Arts, M.F.A., theater


## SOURCES

Interview by George Hill and Spencer Moon, January 1991; follow-up interview,
    Spencer Moon, July 1996.


### Newspapers and Magazines

Burlingame, Jon. *Flint Journal* (Flint, MI), January 12, 1993, p. 44.
Garmel, Marion. *Indianapolis News*, January 14, 1993, p. 30.
Hiltbrand, David. *People*, December 20, 1993, p. 13.
Letofsky, Irv. *Hollywood Reporter* (Los Angeles, CA), January 12, 1993, p.
Renaud, Linda. *Hollywood Reporter*, April 7, 1992, p. 14.
*Daily Variety* (Los Angeles, CA), December 17, 1993, p. 68.
*Jet* (Chicago, IL), June 3, 1996, p. 43.
*Los Angeles Times*, April 7, 1992, p. 15.
*TV Guide*, June 1996, p. 49.

# ST. CLAIR BOURNE

## BACKGROUND

No matter what business you are in, mentors are cherished and appreciated luxuries. Many times the mentor relationship in media makes the difference for new Black filmmakers. Arthur Baron, St. Claire Bourne's film instructor at Columbia University, told him he would recommend him to William Greaves,* who as executive producer of the first national Black public affairs program, *Black Journal*, organized a training program around a corps of young Black filmmakers. This training ground helped establish some successful and important careers. In 1968–1971 St. Clair Bourne was part of the staff. He described it as a major time in his life.

Another important influence on Bourne's work as a filmmaker was his father, a journalist by profession. Bourne Jr.'s own beliefs led to his being arrested at a sit-in in 1963. He saw the Peace Corps as an alternative to the frustration he felt, and he joined in 1964. Bourne's experiences in the Peace Corps from 1964 to 1966 in Lima, Peru, working on a community newspaper left vivid images in his mind about the relationship of media to social change. Consequently his work has shown a marked preference toward films that deal with issues about changing cultural and political trends.

## CAREER PHASES

Bourne looks at his work as a filmmaker in phases. On *Black Journal* he produced about twelve pieces and described the work as slightly innovative

St. Clair Bourne

television journalism. Then he moved into the narrative documentary style. He cited several of his films—*Let the Church Say Amen* and *The Black and the Green*—as good examples of this style. *In Motion: Amiri Baraka* was cited by Bourne as a work that stretched his ability in the narrative documentary style. He feels that his film *Langston Hughes: The Dream Keeper* represents the most advanced and refined example of this narrative style.

Bourne describes himself as a "cultural guerrilla fighter," someone who is opposed to the capitalist system but must figure out how to live and survive. His work has been shown worldwide. He was honored with a retrospective of his work in Brazil, and to date he is the *only* African American filmmaker so honored.

During the last several years he has produced about one film a year. As an independent he discovered that you can't depend on one project alone, financially or emotionally. Having more than one project in development and, later, production is a way of keeping the money flowing. His recent international linkage and travel has brought him into contact with Black British film/video collectives in the United Kingdom. A recent U.K. production by Julian Mayfield was a byproduct of Bourne's *Langston Hughes: The Dream Keeper*. The film by Mayfield, entitled *The Long Night*, is a drama as opposed to Bourne's documentary portrait. Bourne acted as co-producer for this work. There was controversy surrounding the Mayfield work because it dealt with Hughes's private life. The family objected and had it suppressed in some cities, such as New York. Bourne has gone on record as supporting the film and its producer. He believes that the importance of independent filmmakers supporting each other is immeasurable.

Bourne is developing a project that deals with an interracial group of expatriate Vietnam vets living in Scandinavia, and he hopes to get some of the funds through his contact with the Black British filmmakers. When shooting his documentary on Langston Hughes in Senegal, he used the production team of the great African filmmaker Ousmane Sembene. Bourne is optimistic about continuing the international linkage of Black filmmakers.

**AFTER SPIKE LEE**

We discussed the growing climate for Black productions in the United States. Bourne thinks Spike Lee* has helped to create an environment in which there is more interest in work by and about Black people on the mass market and feature-film level, whether independently produced or produced in Hollywood. Bourne is continuing to make documentaries, but most of his projects in current development are feature films. He would like to see independents produce "more culturally correct films about Black people. I want these works to also get the access to distribution they deserve."

During his production of *Making of "Do the Right Thing,"* Bourne said he learned a valuable lesson.

> It showed me that somebody could make a political film that has good production values and the people will come; it was theory before, but I got to see it close up. I made the film *Making of...* to see if this youngblood could make a statement in the Hollywood context and get it out; he pulled it off.

This film was a departure from Bourne's usual documentary subject matter. *Making of...* was his first work on a mainstream popular subject, whereas he described his prior films as being about culturally correct political people. This film was unique because it had a theatrical release in fifty-two cities as well as exhibition in festivals all over the world, including the Munich Film Festival, Hawaii Film Festival, Amiens (France) Film Festival, Turino (Italy) Film Festival and Blacklight (Chicago) Festival. It has also won more than a dozen awards. Bourne says, "I try not to get involved in awards; I try to develop the work. Someone else can market the work."

### UNIQUENESS

When asked what makes him unique from other filmmakers, Bourne said that he has produced documentaries that

> define Black people as they themselves would define themselves and stretched the documentary style. Creating the narrative documentary. Narrative documentary is basically structured in narrative story form with an identifiable cast of characters. But they are real people. Shooting cinema verité and then editing so it tells a story. Other people have done that, but that is what makes me unique.

### *GALLERY OF GREATS*

In 1991 a dozen Black filmmakers where chosen by Miller Brewing Company for its *Gallery of Greats* calendar. Bourne felt that his selection for the *Gallery of Greats* was significant

> because it is an accumulation of information of significant Black artists in one place, and it is being done in the corporate mainstream. It is something I am somewhat uneasy about; but the information will be available to the larger community, and it does not distort what anybody says or has done, and the money that is made goes to Black people.

## POLITICAL CLIMATE (1995)

Bourne thinks the political climate since our original interview has changed.

> Because of the swing to the right politically and its effect on funding, I cannot continue to make a living doing documentaries. Spike Lee has taken the audience to the big screen. People look for truth now in features, where once they looked at documentaries. I'm working on a feature. Besides this feature in development, I'm continuing to produce documentaries. I'm developing a documentary on pan-Africanism, with the funds coming from the actor Wesley Snipes. He called me up one day and said he was familiar with my work and wanted to produce this documentary.

St. Clair Bourne attended the Toronto International Film Festival, New York's Independent Feature Film Market, the Carthage Film Festival and Sundance Film Festival with his latest work *John Henrik Clarke: A Great and Mighty Walk*. Bourne directed the feature-length non-fiction film, and actor Wesley Snipes was executive producer and narrator.

The subject of Bourne's film, controversial scholar and activist John Henrik Clarke, was the leading proponent of an Africentric view of history and culture. A vocal critic of Eurocentric education, Clarke designed the Black and Puerto Rican Studies Program at the City University of New York and until his retirement was an influential professor at Hunter College. *John Henrik Clarke: A Great and Mighty Walk* explores the background and philosophy of this influential figure, and includes interviews with Clarke, along with rare archival footage and photographs. Lou Potter is the screenwriter and Kimiko Jackson serves as producer. The score for the film was composed by Kipper Jones with additional music by two legendary musicians, percussionist Max Roach and saxophonist Yusef Lateef.

Said Bourne,

> Because of Wesley Snipes's involvement in the film, we had an unusual melding of big Hollywood production values with the sensibility of a personal and very independent documentary. It was exciting but strange to have resources to interview Clarke on a soundstage with two cameras, a 24-person crew and caterers.

Bourne also was a co-producer of the critically acclaimed HBO Pictures dramatic feature *Rebound* with Don Cheadle, James Earl Jones, Forest Whitaker and Clarence Williams III.

As an educator/consultant, some of the groups and organizations Bourne has worked for include Cornell University, UCLA, World Black African

Festival of Arts and Culture in Nigeria, American Film Institute, Rockefeller Foundation, Los Angeles Film Exposition, New York State Council on the Arts, and the Film Fund.

## SELECTED FILMOGRAPHY

### Producer

*Black Journal*, 1968–1971 (Staff Producer). The following titles were made for *Black Journal: The South Black Student Movement; Malcolm X Liberation University; Souls Sounds and Money; Paul Robeson; Sickle Cell Anemia; Afro-Dance; The Nation of Common Sense*. Television magazine–length works of under 30 minutes per title.

*Let the Church Say Amen*, 1973, 58 min., documentary. Describes the travels of a young Black student, who is preparing to be a minister, through the southern United States. Filmed in Atlanta, Georgia, the Mississippi delta countryside and the city of Chicago, the program shows the Black church from an inside point of view and how it affects everyday Black life in both urban and rural America.

*Val Verde*, 1978. Documentary about a vanishing Black resort town. Produced for KCET-TV, PBS.

*The Black Police*, 1980. Documentary study of attitudes among Black police officers. Produced for KCET-TV, PBS.

*Big City Blues*, 1981, 28 min., CBS Cable, documentary. A new look at an old American musical form—the blues. Filmed in Chicago, the capital of urban blues culture, the film mixes scenes of the city with musical performances and interviews with people connected with the blues. Featuring Jim Brewer, Son Seals, Queen Sylvia Embry and Billy Branch, the film entertains with music and also informs new audiences about the full range of contemporary American culture.

*America: Black and White*, 1981, NBC White Paper Special Report (Field Producer). Documentary on the state of race relations in the Reagan administration.

*In Motion: Amiri Baraka*, 1982, 58 min., documentary. This work is about a major spokesperson for the Black consciousness movement in America and a major figure on the American literary and political landscape from the late fifties to the present. The program was developed with an extra sensitivity for audiences that might not be familiar with contemporary American political history. Baraka's writing symbolizes the political and cultural evolution of mid-century America in both artistic expression and content. Therefore, although this program is provocative, it is also accessible and informative.

*The Black and the Green*, 1983, 45 min., documentary, PBS. Because of pressure from sources inside PBS, this program never aired. After completion, its content was deemed objectionable. The program is a journey of discovery by five African Americans as they travel to Northern Ireland. The group attempted to find out the truth behind the headlines and sought out common elements in that situation and the Black movement in America. A film about human rights, social change, the role of religion and, specifically, the Irish conflict—from the unique perspective of Black

American observers. These travelers have seen a Northern Ireland that is not reported in the mainstream media.

*On the Boulevard*, 1984, 28 min., drama/narrative. Featuring Gloria Charles and Lawrence Hilton-Jacobs, a bittersweet love story about relationships and how they can be affected by the economics of employment.

*Langston Hughes: The Dream Keeper*, 1986, 58 min., documentary. Part of the PBS series *Voices and Visions*, a documentary series on American poets. The program is a loving look at an American poet-laureate. The piece chronicles Hughes's part in the Harlem Renaissance as well as his body of work. It is a mix of cogent interviews contrasted with readings of Hughes's work by himself and others. The program does much service to the man, to his art and to the American literary milieu. It bears repeated viewing, giving the viewer new and different insights each time.

*Gullah*, 1988, 60 min., film, documentary. Produced for the *National Geographic Explorer* series. A film about the impact of tourism and development on local people and their African-based culture in the South Carolina Sea Islands.

*New Orleans Brass*, 1989, 60 min., film, documentary. Produced for the *National Geographic Explorer* series. Explores the brass band's traditional culture in New Orleans and the people who created it.

*Making of "Do the Right Thing,"* 1989, 60 min., documentary, First Run Features. Documents the making of Spike Lee's* feature film, *Do the Right Thing*, in the Black community of Brooklyn, New York.

*Will to Win*, 1995, BBC series. Bourne produced two one-hour documentary segments for this six-part series, which examines the political impact of the Black athlete in international sports. He produced the titles *Myth and Reality* and *Breaking Down Barriers*.

*Heritage of the Black West*, 1995, 60 min., National Geographic Society. An examination of the past and contemporary presence of African Americans in the American West. Narrated by Roscoe Orman ("Gordon" of *Sesame Street*).

### Feature Films in Development

*Exiles and Allies.* A drama based on real events of the Vietnam War, when the Swedish government offered refuge to American war resisters and deserters as part of a national anti-war policy. This story follows five young American war resisters from their arrival to their last bitter days in Sweden. The resisters and deserters were treated like heroes by the Swedish anti-war movement until the end of the war. Then, no longer holding propaganda value, they were abandoned by the government. Disillusioned and desperate, many of these men turned to crime for survival. Their odyssey became a national scandal. Production is set for summer 1996. Co-producer is Cinetofon, a Swedish film production company. Additional funds committed by the Swedish Film Institute.

*The Bride Price.* A contemporary romantic thriller set in Senegal about a romance between an African American Peace Corps volunteer and an African holy man's daughter.

*Deacons.* A story of love and strained friendship over the role of Black armed self-defense during the civil rights period of the sixties in the American South.

### Executive Producer

*A Question of Color*, 1993. Produced and directed by Kathi Sandler. A film essay on the impact of slavery on African American beauty standards and skin color discrimination within the Black community. Produced and broadcast on PBS. Winner for Best Cultural Affairs Documentary, Prized Pieces, National Black Programming Consortium, 1993.

*A Portrait of Max*. Produced by Delores Elliot and directed by Sam Pollard. A musical documentary about the legendary percussionist and composer Max Roach. Filmed in California, New York and Milan, Italy. Currently in post-production.

### Co-Producer

*The Long Night*, 1990, drama, b/w, film. Based on the Julian Mayfield novel of the same name. A fictional account of the life of Langston Hughes. In addition to Bourne's film and this one, a third film (also fiction) on Hughes's private life is called *Looking for Langston*, by British director Isaac Julian.

### BIO-CRITICAL REVIEW

"Through his work, Bourne has formulated an alternative platform of discursive authority that contests the ground and limits of 'minority programming.' "—Clyde Taylor, "Program Notes," *New American Filmmakers Series*

### SELECTED AWARDS

*Gallery of Greats*, Inductee, 1990

*America: Black and White*
   Monte Carlo Film Festival, Nymphe d'Or, Best Documentary, 1981

*Big City Blues*
   Black Filmmakers Hall of Fame, First Prize, Music, 1981

*Black Journal*
   Emmy Award, Staff Producer, 1970
   Excellence in Broadcasting, John Russworm Citation, 1970

*In Motion: Amiri Baraka*
   Global Village Documentary Festival, First Prize, 1984

*Langston Hughes: The Dream Keeper*
   Black Filmmakers Hall of Fame, First Prize Overall, 1988
   San Francisco International Film Festival, First Prize, TV/Cultural Documentary, 1988

*Let the Church Say, Amen*
   International Film and TV Festival, New York City, Bronze Award, 1973

National Black Programming Consortium, 1996
6th Oscar Micheaux Award

Retrospectives of Bourne's work have been shown at the Whitney Museum of American Art, New York; the Kennedy Center, Washington, D.C.; and the Cineclub Botafogo, Rio de Janeiro, Brazil.

## EDUCATION

Syracuse University, B.S., political science/journalism.

## SOURCES

Interview by George Hill and Spencer Moon, January 1991; follow-up interview, Spencer Moon, June 1995.
Taylor, Clyde, curator. "Program Notes," *New American Filmmakers Series, Exhibitions of Independent Film and Video*. New York: Whitney Museum of American Art, 1988.

# CHARLES BURNETT

The interview on which some of the material in this chapter is based was conducted after Burnett's film *To Sleep with Anger* (1990) had been released, marketed and distributed with lukewarm financial success.

## BACKGROUND

Burnett, who was born in Mississippi, described his parents as principled. They made sure that the children were fed first in his family, and they felt that manners and courtesy were important life skills. Grandparents were influential as well. His early years in the South, albeit brief, were filtered through the eyes of his grandmother, who helped him put things in perspective regarding segregation.

By the time he was 3 years old, Burnett's parents had moved from Mississippi. His father was a career man in the military and was stationed in Southern California; they moved to Los Angeles, where his mother found work as a nurse's aide. Burnett graduated from Fremont High School and then enrolled at Los Angeles Community College in electronics courses. Later he decided to change his career orientation. Having grown up in the Watts South Central section, he saw friends getting into trouble. He described the need to tell the stories of those who did not make it out of the neighborhood as part of his motivation for wanting to be a filmmaker. His formal training in filmmaking was at UCLA. Influences on his work include Russian novelists, the writer James Agee, the Dutch documentary filmmaker

Joris Ivens, and the British documentary filmmaker Basil Wright. Wright's *Song of Ceylon* (1934) and his belief in a humanistic approach to filmmaking made Burnett take the entire process of filmmaking more seriously.


## FILMMAKING

Burnett sees filmmaking as a constant struggle. The work is twenty-four hours a day; you live and breathe the work. Also, the people in the business are different. Because there is a lot of money involved in the process of filmmaking, the business attracts people with a certain mentality related to issues of power and ego. Burnett is not sure if the most "mature" people are attracted to filmmaking.

Burnett's work can be described as social realism. As a filmmaker he admires neo-realist films. Filmmaking for him begins with the story, which should have a message and take on a certain form. Burnett thinks that film has the potential to confront issues that would over time create a better society.


## UNIQUENESS

In the sixties, art was seen as a means of social change and a tool; this sensibility has influenced his work, Burnett said. It is difficult to change this influence because it is so much a part of his character, and he always wanted to express things for which he felt an affinity. He feels that Hollywood representations don't present his experience of the real world or create an environment in which people can survive. Burnett's desire is to make films that show the humanity and universality of the Black experience. Action and violence for their own sake when so many dollars are involved in production are not easily justifiable, in his perspective. He is troubled by issues such as homelessness and its pervasiveness in contrast to the ease of obtaining money to make a film. The average Hollywood film budget of $20 million he considers a lot of money. People need to be accountable for their work; there should be some redemptive factor involved in spending such vast amounts of money. It should not be spent just for the sake of entertainment. Burnett sees himself as a storyteller. Entertainment is a secondary consideration; automatic, in some sense. He wants to be involved in something that will make him feel challenged, not ashamed.

Burnett has regard for his wife and family and does not want to further add to the "pollution factor" of some films already in existence. Because of his background and how he grew up, Burnett does not want young people to experience the negative influences that he did. He believes that certain sensitive aspects of life are taboo for films.

*GALLERY OF GREATS*

Burnett was self-effacing regarding an honor received near the time of our interview. He felt that the *Gallery of Greats* honor he received in 1991 should have gone to those more deserving, considering that historic film-makers such as Oscar Micheaux* and Spencer Williams* were among those honored. Burnett felt that people like Carlton Moss, an early documentary filmmaker, were equally deserving of this honor. "Sometimes the battles of the independent filmmaking process overwhelm you, so that when someone calls and says, 'Congratulations, you've just been honored,' it is hard to realize this is happening."

## L. A. REBELLION

During the late seventies and early eighties, there were a significant num-ber of African Americans enrolled in the film programs at UCLA. This group of filmmakers, men and women, helped each other and worked on each other's films. After a volume of work produced by this group had re-ceived national as well as international recognition outside the Hollywood mainstream, the name "L.A. Rebellion" was given to them and their work. Burnett was an integral part of the group. Other filmmakers in the group were Julie Dash,* Ben Caldwell, Haile Gerima, Pam Jones, Larry Clark, Alile Sharon Larkin, Monona Wali, Billy Woodberry and Barbara McCullough (to name just a few). Their inspiration for filmmaking was the antithesis to the Hollywood films of the seventies. Their weekly screenings and discus-sions concerned the very nature of filmmaking and the social, political, psy-chological and economic factors affecting Black people in their everyday lives, essentially living under a system of apartheid.

In January 1986 noted Black film theorist/educator Clyde Taylor of Tufts University curated a program of films by this group. Taylor was the origi-nator of the expression "L.A. Rebellion"; with the 1986 program at the Whitney Museum of American Art, New American Filmmakers Series, he codified these filmmakers' historic place in American cinema. Taylor said in his program notes, "As Black independent film work is given closer scrutiny, the L.A. movement will be recognized as an indispensable part of its devel-opment."

## DISTRIBUTION

Burnett felt that distribution is crucial: All it takes is one person who doesn't have confidence in the film in distribution, and the film won't be marketed properly. Samuel Goldwyn Company admitted that it had little money to spend on *To Sleep with Anger*, a film that many agreed merited better handling (Kendall, 1994).

## SELECTED FILMOGRAPHY

### Director/Cinematographer

*Several Friends*, 1969, 16mm, color. Young friends must come to grips with growing up and facing adulthood.

*America Becoming*, 1990, 60 min., 16mm, color, documentary. We visit six American cities and delve into the lives of ethnic Americans (Hispanic and Asian). We see these ethnic groups who as migrating immigrants are part of what America is becoming, a nation as varied and colorful as a quilt. Their interactions with African Americans and the established White community are analyzed; questions are raised, with some answers—but all done quite objectively.

### Cinematographer/Screenplay

*Bless Their Little Hearts*, 1973. Directed by Billy Woodberry. A beleaguered Black family coping with urban America—compelling, insightful Black drama. A very well done first feature film by Woodberry. Burnett's script is dramatic without being stereotyped or overwritten.

*The Horse*, 1973, 14 min., 16mm, color. The emotional reactions of several men and a boy to the shooting of a sick horse.

*Killer of Sheep*, 1977, 84 min., 16mm, b/w. The daily life of a slaughterhouse worker who lives in south central Los Angeles. A simple story but a truly complex film. There is an allegorical nature to this tale of a working man who slaughters animals to earn money for his daily nourishment and the deadening effect it has on his spirit.

### Director/Cinematographer/Screenplay

*My Brother's Wedding*, 1984, 120 min., 16mm, b/w. A drama about a man who is forced to choose between attending the funeral of a friend and his brother's wedding.

### Director/Producer/Screenplay

*To Sleep with Anger*,** 1990, 101 min., 35mm, color, Samuel Goldwyn Company. Burnett reflected that a little more time and a little more money could have made a difference in the outcome of this work. Actors received shares of the film's profits, instead of salaries commensurate with their skills.

The Independent Feature Project (an organization set up to encourage, promote and support non-mainstream feature film production) held a panel discussion in Los Angeles on the making and marketing of *To Sleep with Anger*. Participants included executives of Sony Pictures, Edward Pressman Film Corp., and Samuel Goldwyn Jr.

Studios, producers and marketers of the film; Danny Glover, co-star and co-producer of the film; and Charles Burnett, the film's writer/director.

The original script was written for public television. After the script was read, the ensuing discussion between Burnett and public television led Burnett to withdraw the work. In the meantime, Caldecot Chubb called and asked Burnett what he was working on. Chubb read the script and wanted to raise the money to film it. They spent the next two-and-a-half years fundraising. Through various contacts they brought Danny Glover on board for a featured role and obtained a commitment from him to help co-produce the film. Edward Pressman and other executives got involved, and the film was produced. The final budget raised was $1.5 million.

The Black community was never made fully aware of the power or impact of this extraordinary film, so that it never found the audience it richly deserved (Hill and Moon, *Blacks in Hollywood*, 1991).

## Director/Screenplay

*The Glass Shield*,** 1994, 105 min., 35mm, color, Miramax Films. On a $3 million budget, Burnett has fashioned a very well made detective story. The focus is on John Eddie Johnson, the first Black officer in an all-White Southern California sheriff's department. Michael Boatman as Officer Johnson and Lori Petty as Officer Fields, the only ally he has against the old boy network, are very good. They convey the terror of police battling police literally for their very lives. The film is based on the true story of a Black officer who worked in Orange County, California. The adage "truth is stranger than fiction" is apropos. Burnett's neorealist style presents the compelling story of a Black officer who finds corruption in a department rife with bigotry and arrogance of power. His stand with only one other officer, the female (also an outcast), against a police department and a system that breeds cronyism and lying is valiant and courageous. One of the best films ever to tackle the issues of police abuses of power, racism and a system that breeds corruption. Recommended viewing. The cast also features the rapper Ice Cube in a very good role. Cube shows with this role that he was no "one-film wonder" in *Boyz N The Hood*.**

## BIO-CRITICAL REVIEW

*To Sleep with Anger.* "One riveting piece of filmmaking that opens a perceptive window on African Americans."—Sterlinda Barrett, *Accent/L.A.*

———. "Initially pretends to be commonplace, but that is an illusion. A very entertaining, complex film. His most accomplished work to date."—Vincent Canby, *New York Times*

———. "This picture transcends racial stereotypes, with an acute evocation. It is a spellbinder."—Richard Corliss, *Time*

———. "The latest film by Charles Burnett is droll, visionary, alarming, ironic, and deeply moving all at the same time—and so far, I'm talking only about the images under the opening credits."—Stuart Klawans, *The Nation*

———. "A testimonial to the resilience and solidarity of the family and, though it doesn't come right out and say so, specifically the black family."—Ella Taylor, *Los Angeles Weekly*

## EDUCATION

Los Angeles City College, A.A., electronics
UCLA, School of Theater Arts, B.A., film emphasis
UCLA, School of Theater Arts, M.F.A., film emphasis

## SELECTED AWARDS

American Film Institute, Maya Deren Award for Independent Film and Video Artists, 1991
Friends of the 1991 Black Oscar Nominees, Special Recognition

*The Horse*
   Oberhausen Film Festival, Second Prize, 1978
*Killer of Sheep*
   Berlin International Film Festival, Critics Prize, 1981
   Houston International Film Festival, Silver Award, 1980
   National Film Registry, Library of Congress, 1991
   U.S. Film and Video Festival, First Prize, Feature Film, 1982
*To Sleep with Anger*
   National Critics Poll, Best Screenplay, 1990
   Spirit Awards, Best Director and Best Screenplay, Independent Feature Project, 1990
   Sundance Film Festival, Special Jury Prize, 1990

## GRANTS AND FELLOWSHIPS

Guggenheim Foundation Fellowship, 1980
MacArthur Foundation Fellowship, 1988
National Endowment for the Arts, 1985
Rockefeller Foundation Fellowship, 1988
UCLA, Louis B. Mayer Grant, Most Promising Thesis Project, 1977

## SOURCES

Interview by George Hill, January 1991.
Independent Feature Project, panel on *To Sleep with Anger*, recorded by George Hill, February 1991.

## Books

Famighetti, Robert, ed. *The World Almanac and Book of Facts: 1996*. Mahwah, NJ: Funk and Wagnalls, 1995.

Harris, Erich Leon. *African American Screen Writers Now: Conversations with Hollywood's Black Pack*. Los Angeles: Silman-James Press, 1996.

Hill, George, and Spencer Moon. *Blacks in Hollywood: Five Favorable Years, 1987–1991*. Los Angeles: Daystar Press, 1991.

Kendell, Stephen D. *New Jack Cinema: Hollywood's African-American Filmmakers*. Silver Springs, MD: J.L. Denser, 1994.

Klotman, Phyllis Rauch. *Screenplays of the African American Experience*. Bloomington: Indiana University Press, 1991.

Time-Life Books, ed. *African-American Voices of Triumph: Creative Fire, A Tradition of African Art, Filmmaking, Music, Literature, Visual Arts*. Alexandria, VA: Time-Life Books, 1994.

## Newspapers and Magazines

Barrett, Sterlinda. "To Sleep with Anger, Charles Burnett's Magical Tour of Black Los Angeles," *Accent/L.A.*, November, 1990, p. 23.

Burnett, Charles and Charles Lane. "One on One," *American Film* (Los Angeles), August, 1991, pp. 40–43.

Canby, Vincent. "Enter a Demon with a Winning Smile," *New York Times*, October 5, 1990, p. B3.

Corliss, Richard. "Blood Bonds," *Time* (136) No. 17, October 22, 1990, p. 63.

George, Lynell. "The Long Distance Runner: Charles Burnett's Quiet Revolution," *Los Angeles Weekly*, October, 1990, p. 20.

Klawans, Stuart. "To Sleep with Anger," *The Nation*, November 5, 1990, p. 537.

Taylor, Clyde. "The L.A. Rebellion: New Spirit in American Film" *Black Film Review* (2), No. 2 (Spring, 1986), pp. 20, 24–27.

Taylor, Ella. "Seeing Double: To Sleep With Anger Weds Magic and Logic," *Los Angeles Weekly*, October, 1990, pp. 21–23.

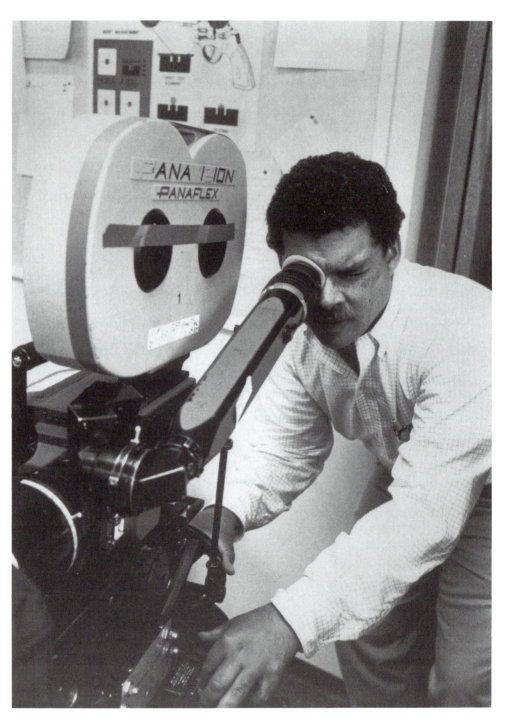

Roy Campanella II

# ROY CAMPANELLA II

## INTRODUCTION

Filmmaker Roy Campanella II is currently developing two prestigious mini-series for television. The first is *Harlem*, a two-part miniseries for Showtime. Campanella will also produce and direct from his original screenplay. The film tells the story of how Harlem became America's Black Cultural Mecca. It is an epic family saga covering the years from 1900–1935. In addition, Campanella is developing a miniseries for ABC titled *All God's Children*, based on the Pulitzer Prize-winning non-fiction signature piece written by Fox Butterfield, depicting the origin of violence in America.

An auteur who carefully divides his time between producing and directing independent and mainstream projects, Campanella is a connoisseur of classic world cinema. "Ingmar Bergman was my first exposure to a deep examination of the human condition. This type of examination needs to be done from other cultural perspectives too," says Campanella. "There is room in the African American cinema movement for someone to examine our relationships in the same introspective and intimate manner as Bergman did. I have some projects that explore our situation in that way."

In addition to the two miniseries, Campanella is developing four original features and one project that he has acquired the rights to, *Mr. Sister*. Films in development include: *Tonight at Noon*, *Phat Pockets*, *The Company We Keep* and *Kiss the Sky*, a dramatic film focusing on three teens as they overcome the limitations of poverty and despair to change their lives and the high school they attend.

Following the route of many contemporaries since the early days of film and television, Campanella garnered invaluable training before launching a career in cinema, always combining his artistic sensitivities with his African American sensibilities. "I have found that, just like a jazz musician who likes to practice his craft by doing a lot of studio work, TV also gives me the chance to sharpen my abilities as a director because you are constantly faced with different kinds of creative choices. And at the same time, it has offered me a chance to earn a good livelihood."

Over the years, Campanella has certainly honed his writing/directing talent in both the television and film genres. Combined with his creative ambitions is a close familiarity with routes to financing sources and production: his mandate now is to create a financially successful product with direct appeal to black audiences, which according to industry specialists, accounted for more than $1.4 billion at the box office in 1995. Campanella, who always divides his time between mainstream and independent narrative low-budget features, is currently raising financing for *Deep Like the Rivers*, his screen adaptation of the novel *Not Without Laughter* by Langston Hughes.

Along with Charles Burnett* and Julie Dash,* Campanella is also associated with Directors' Circle Filmworks (DCF), an independent film and production company he founded with the objective of producing high-quality films budgeted at $6 million and under. Although his brainchild, Campanella makes it clear that DCF is an umbrella company for talented, independent filmmakers. The Filmworks' philosophy centers on the creation of a circle of independent talents who contribute to and benefit artistically and financially from the synergistic environment.

From a marketing perspective, DCF plans to create a niche for its films within the black audience segment, although its product will ideally possess entertainment values able to transcend cultural differences the same way many black musicians transcend them. According to Campanella, "The real problem we face is that the players who control the production financing are not concerned with catering to different tastes. If targeted correctly, the audience is there: the black community has the spending power to generate a massive buying capability."

"African Americans represent almost 15 percent of the population with a spending power of over $300 billion," says Campanella, "yet a cohesive social development was never allowed, and attempts to disenfranchise those African Americans trying to build constructive economic enterprises still goes on. One of the ways to perpetuate this is through the image, not just on television, but in the press, on stage, on the radio and in advertising. We have been hungry for our real image, which is one of the reasons why I feel interest in black films has grown."

Campanella is one of four African Americans to ever receive the prestigious Directors Guild of America award. He won for the highly acclaimed 1991 PBS/Wonderworks television movie *Brother Future*. This drama about an inner-city Detroit teenager who travels back in time to 1822 and experiences slavery is highly popular among Black teens. Campanella also received honors from the Columbia International Film Festival and the National Black Programming Consortium for *Brother Future*. Over the years, Campanella's work has garnered awards from other organizations including the Black Filmmakers Hall of Fame and the Los Angeles Black Media Coalition. His highly acclaimed CBS movies of the week, *Body of Evidence* and *Quiet Victory: The Charlie Weydemeyer Story*, were both rated above-average by Leonard Maltin in his *TV Movies & Video Guide* (1996 edition).

After graduating with honors from Harvard, Campanella, who is the son of Roy Campanella, the renowned Hall of Fame catcher who played for the Brooklyn Dodgers in the 1950s, continued his education—obtaining a Master's of Business Administration at Columbia University, where he was also awarded the Louis G. Cowan Award for Excellence in Management. Campanella started his professional career in the industry as a director-cameraman and editor at WGBH-TV in Boston. He followed this position with an association with CBS, initially as a film and videotape editor, then as a production executive for CBS Entertainment. After leaving CBS, Campanella began working as an independent writer, producer, and director. Since then, his directing credits have grown to include series such as *Brewster Place*, *Falcon Crest*, *Frank's Place*, *Homefront*, *I'll Fly Away*, *Knot's Landing*, *Life Goes On*, *Sonny Spoon* and *Wiseguy*, among other programs.

Campanella's professional affiliations include: the Directors Guild of America, Writers Guild of America, the National Association of Black MBA's, Producers Caucus, Academy of Television Arts & Sciences and Independent Feature Project/west.

## CAREER

I'd like to get you to talk about the different aspects of your career.

Over a period of time you develop a perspective that helps you to define and focus on your work. I believe one's career is like a river. The creative currents of my work as a director, writer, and producer within episodic, long form television, independent films, documentaries, and commercials flow together like a river. This business can sometimes rob people of their perspective.

Any special highlights for you?

Fortunately what I'm working on right now is a highlight. I'm writing an original two-part miniseries called *Harlem*. It's an epic family saga that starts in 1900 and goes to 1935. It explores the movement of African Americans into Harlem at the turn of the century. The Black migration from the South to the North, the Harlem Renaissance, World War I, the birth of the jazz age, prohibition, the numbers business in Harlem, and the battle for that business between Black numbers bankers and Dutch Schultz, the decline of the Harlem Renaissance, and the beginning of the Great Depression. All of this is conveyed through the personal intimate story of a family. The Harlem I'm creating addresses the true dimensions of that community and its growth into a Black cultural mecca. It depicts key historical figures, such as W.E.B. DuBois, Marcus Garvey, Madame C. J. Walker, Langston Hughes, and Zora Neale Hurston. It will air on Showtime.

## BLACK FILM/VIDEO RENAISSANCE

What do you think of the Black film/video renaissance?

That's a question that's worthy of a book. I'm always glad to see us working and creating. Without passing judgment on the actual films, when you look at this period in perspective it's hard to say it's a renaissance. The high point was 1991 in terms of numbers of feature films released. If that lasted for five years and not one I'd say it's a renaissance. The fact that it peaked so quickly, that we only had that volume for a short period of time, says to me it was a fortunate, but highly unusual confluence of forces. The ratio of artists to activity is not even close to renaissance proportions.

## UNIQUENESS

What makes you unique as a filmmaker?

The distinctive qualities I have as a filmmaker are in two complementary areas. In terms of my approach to material it's all consuming. I immerse myself in the material in a manner that I think is very distinctive. *Brother Future* is a perfect example. I didn't just take what was available in terms of the slave era material. I did a tremendous amount of my own research, which I shared with the various key creative departments on the production. I also prepare a backstory for each character. In terms of style and technique, I create a visual design for each project. It is very important that content determines form, that substance determines style. That does not happen often today. But in every picture I've done—each camera set-up, each scene, each sequence and the overall piece—my guiding vision was that the substance would dictate the style. So I know why I place my camera in certain positions. All too often today style is ahead of substance. It's unfortunately one of the influences that comes from music video and commercials, in which selling is more important than communicating— than telling a meaningful story. I see myself as a story-teller, and I think the story has to dictate how it's told. Those are the two distinguishing characteristics of my work.

What can you tell young people who want to get into the business?

Make sure that you really want to do it. There is unfortunately a heavy sauce of supposed glamour that covers up what can be a foul and rancid business. I love filmmaking and that is what has sustained me. If you cannot bring a great deal of love and commitment to it, then you should choose some other line of work. I also feel, based on conversations with many of my colleagues, that a lot of people who say they want to get involved in film in certain capacities today, have not looked at all the opportunities in the film industry. We have areas of the business where there aren't any of us. There are key craft areas like the camera department, props, special effects, editorial, production design, and producing where we could be better represented. There still is unfortunately a real need for entrepreneurial producing types to come along and package pictures—put together the financing.

## BEYOND HOLLYWOOD

Do you think independent production and distribution outside the Hollywood system is a viable artistic and business venture?

I think so. As we approach the twenty-first century, there are a number of avenues that are available to us that are on the periphery of the massive media conglomerates. The market that we have to serve, in particular the core market, is not an exceptionally large one in terms of how to reach it, but it's a very lucrative market. The studios have instituted over the years a strategy of using our popular and talented Black actors in buddy pictures or star vehicles. Basically these are comic book movies. There is nothing wrong with those kinds of pictures, in general, but we need a diverse selection of movies. The strategy has been to apply this same block-buster mentality to the Black audience. There's an alternative, whole world of creativity and African American story-telling that's being left out. The financial parameters of what we can do could, if orchestrated properly, fit within the marketplace, create a niche, and be viable. The budgets of many of the pictures that

I'm talking about in this alternative area would be six million dollars or less. The release pattern of these alternative movies would be more of a platform- or road-show type. The core audience would be nurtured. The audience would be catered to so that the media buy in terms of advertising for that picture would be very sensitive to their tastes.

## BLACK HOLLYWOOD

His response spurred me to ask why a Black version of the DreamWorks concept was not put together.

Clearly the potential is there. The potential is also there for us to have our own national association of filmmakers, in which we come together and pay a small amount of dues and for those individuals who don't have health care so they'd be covered. I'm covered by the Directors Guild and the Writers Guild. There are a lot of brothers and sisters who have been out there for twenty or thirty years and don't have health coverage. There are a number of very creative scenarios that could play themselves out over the years. We have an unfulfilled historical mandate.

## INDEPENDENT FILMS

Campanella describes the disposition of his early independent films.

Most of my early independent work is available through Directors' Circle Filmworks. It's been exhibited, shown on television and in festivals around the world.

## FILMOGRAPHY

### Producer/Director/Writer

*Straight, No Chaser*, 1972, 30 min., 16mm. "This was done while I was a student at Harvard." The film's title comes from jazz composer Thelonius Monk's tune of the same title. This documentary film explored life in Harlem. This very personal work features interviews with a family he had known for years.

*Pass/Fail*, 25 min., 1978. Explored the dreams of a documentary filmmaker.

*The Thieves*, 1979, funded by the American Film Institute

*Impressions of Joyce*, video. A work done as an artist-in-residence for Channel 13 in New York, WNET-TV. An experimental narrative.

### Executive Producer/Director

*Rites of Passage: The Making of "JoJo Dancer,"* 1986, 12 min., Columbia Pictures, shown on HBO. A documentary on the making of the Richard Pryor film *JoJo Dancer Your Life Is Calling*.

### Producer/Director/Co-writer/Co-editor

*Passion and Memory*, 1986, 56 min., shown on PBS. An exceptional documentary that chronicles the lives of Lincoln Perry (Stepin' Fetchit'), Dorothy Dandridge, Hattie McDaniel, Bill Robinson and Sidney Poitier.

> An adaptation of Don Bogle's book *Toms, Coons, Mulattoes, Mammies and Bucks*, a documentary. It examines the African American experience in the films of Hattie McDaniel, Bill Robinson, Stepin' Fetchit', Dorothy Dandridge and Sidney Poitier.

## TELEVISION MOVIES OF THE WEEK

### Producer/Director/Co-writer

*Body of Evidence*, 1987, CBS. Featuring Margot Kidder, Barry Bostwick, Tony LoBianco, Caroline Kava, Jennifer Barbour and David Hayward. A suspense thriller concerning a wife who suspects her husband might be a serial killer. TV critic, *L. A. Times*

> *Body of Evidence* came about when I was examining a lot of Hitchcock's work. François Truffaut interviewed him extensively. In Hitchcock's film *Suspicion*, he wanted to have Cary Grant actually be the killer but the studio wouldn't let him. I started thinking, wouldn't that be interesting to have a piece about a woman who marries a murderer? I coupled that with a curiosity, which has since become national, about serial killers. *Body of Evidence* deals with a forensic pathologist who is a serial killer. It's violent, but it is also a pattern of antisocial behavior that hadn't been explored an awful lot, it terms of drama. I created a fictional New England town in Calgary, Canada where we shot the piece, which was a challenge. I co-wrote the story, produced and directed this piece. That represents one of the few times that an African American has done that for a network television movie of the week. If you look over African American involvement in terms of creating the story, producing and directing the picture, that combination is rare. Maybe two or three other people have done it in the history of television that are African American. It is rare because we are not given that many opportunities.

### Director

*Quiet Victory: The Charlie Wedemeyer Story*, 1988, CBS. Featuring Pam Dawber, Michael Nouri, Bess Meyer, Peter Berg, James Handy, Dan Lauria and Grace Harrison. Campanella states, "I was a director for hire on this film. I was very interested in the story. Critically it did well and the ratings were good.

The movie is a docudrama about a football all-star who develops Lou Gehrig's disease. Despite disability, Charlie Wedemeyer became a successful high school coach albeit wheelchair-bound and unable to speak.

## INDEPENDENT PRODUCTION

*Brother Future,*** 1991, 120 min., 16mm, PBS, *Wonderworks* series. The film features Phill Lewis, Moses Gunn, Vonetta McGee and Frank Converse. It's a time-travel tale of an inner-city Black youth who gets hit by a car and wakes up in nineteenth-century slave-holding South Carolina.

> It was a huge battle to make this film. I was a director for hire starting out, then basically took over the whole project creatively. The film came to me as a poorly written screenplay. It had great potential because the essence of the story was rich. An inner-city kid time travels back to 1822 and experiences Denmark Vesey's slave insurrection—that's rich. In the original story, the treatment of the lead character was demeaning. He was a buffoon; you laughed at him and not with him. By the time he learned the lesson at the end, you didn't care. I was faced with the dilemma of accepting the assignment and trying to make it into the piece it should be or just walking away and letting them hire some hack that would come in and do their bidding. That happens much too much. I decided there would be a lot of satisfaction if I can turn this around into a piece that Black youth, in particular, and all youth in general can benefit from. That turned out to be a very satisfying experience. We won awards from the Directors Guild of America, Columbus International Film Festival, and the Black Programming Consortium.

## EPISODIC TELEVISION

### Director

*Brewster Place*, ABC; *Codename: Foxfire*, NBC; *The Colbys*, ABC; *Dallas*, CBS; *Dream Street*, NBC; *Falcon Crest*, CBS; *Frank's Place*, CBS; *Hawaiian Heat*, CBS; *Hooperman*, ABC; *Hotel*, ABC; *Jesse Hawkes*, CBS; *Knight Rider*, NBC; *Knot's Landing*, CBS; *Life Goes On*, ABC; *Lou Grant*, CBS; *Mancuso, FBI*, NBC; *The Marshal*, ABC; *Our House*, NBC; *Simon and Simon*, CBS; *Snoops*, CBS; *Sonny Spoon*, NBC; *Wiseguy*, CBS.

### Producer/Creative Consultant

*227*, NBC. Campanella optioned Christine Houston's play *227* on which the television series is based. Campanella, the author, and Marla Gibbs worked together on creating a television program of the play. Campanella worked on the television series pilot as co-producer with Marla Gibbs, the series's star, and the show's producer Bill Boulware. His lucrative five-year (pay or play) contract permitted him to pursue his other creative interests while being credited as a consultant for the run of the series.

## COMMERCIALS

### Director

Tide, Saatchi and Saatchi Agency; baseball, Coca-Cola, *Profiles in Accomplishment* (featuring Bill Cosby and Jayne Kennedy).

## SCRIPTS

I asked him about three scripts he let me read as samples of his abilities as a writer. These works are all original scripts in development, and I asked him what stage of development each was in.

**"The Company We Keep:"** It's going through a re-write, fairly soon. I've teamed with a couple of Black female executives at Warner Records for this production, Allison Gabrielle and Tracy Nicole Richards.

**"Deep Like the Rivers:"** We still have the rights to the Langston Hughes novel *Not Without Laughter*. We're putting together independent financing to do it.

**"The First:"** This is a screenplay about Jackie Robinson from 1945, when he played with the Kansas City Monarchs, to 1947, when he broke the color barrier in baseball by playing with the Brooklyn Dodgers.

## BIO-CRITICAL REVIEW

*Body of Evidence.* "Crackerjack tale, above average."—*Leonard Maltin's 1997 Movie and Video Guide*

*Brother Future.* "Remarkable, funny and poignant. Sensitive direction."—*Los Angeles Times*

"Funny, poignant, and thought-provoking, A−."—*Entertainment Weekly*, Jeff Unger

*Quiet Victory: The Charlie Wedemeyer Story.* "Inspiring drama, above average."—*Leonard Maltin's 1997 Movie and Video Guide*

**EDUCATION**

Harvard University, B.A., anthropology (with honors)

Columbia University, M.B.A.


**SELECTED AWARDS**

*Pass/Fail*
> Black Filmmakers Hall of Fame, Best Drama and Best Picture, 1978


**Individual**

Los Angeles Black Media Coalition, Outstanding Technical Achievement Award, Directing, 1988

Directors Guild of America (D.G.A.) nomination


**SOURCES**

Interview by Spencer Moon, September 1996.


**Books**

Maltin, Leonard, ed. *Leonard Maltin's 1990 Movie and Video Guide*. New York: Penguin Books, 1990.


**Newspapers and Magazines**

"Another Star Emerges from the Campanella Family, but This One Is a Hollywood TV and Film Director." *Ebony*, September 1982, pp. 69–72.

Archerd, Army. "Just for Variety." *Variety*, May 1996, p. 2.

Campanella, Roy II. "Persistence of Vision: Surviving in the Film World." *Millimeter*, June, 1987, pp. 55–58.

Clark, Michael. "Box Seat with a View: The Double Play of Merchant to Ivory to Campanella." *Shoot*, October 1995, p. 107.

Chu, Dan and Lois Armstrong. "Roy Campanella Jr. Begins a Hit Streak of His Own as Director of TV Films." *People*, May 1986, pp. 141–42.

"Campanella Jr. Enters Pact." *Los Angeles Sentinel*, September 1991, p. 21.

*Los Angeles Times* (4/6/91).

Tavares, Elspeth. *Business of Film*, May 1992, p. 99.

# AYOKA CHENZIRA

## BACKGROUND

Can you tell me about your background and how you decided to become a filmmaker?

> I was one of those children who was raised to be an artist. I got exposure to the arts at an early age. The piano, the cello, dance lessons, going to the opera and the theater, and movies regularly. My mother, who is an educator, has always had the spirit, creativity and tenacity of an artist, and the support was not there for her to pursue a career in the arts. So I got much of her desires in this area. My mother has extremely artistic sensibilities. She made all of my clothes, which was terrible growing up. No child wants designer clothes. The consequence is I can't shop today because the clothes don't compare. She had strong interests in dance and music, but because of a lack of support for her interests, I received the benefit of her ambitions. I look back and see this is a very different way to grow up. Most American parents don't want their children to be artists. That was never an issue in my mother's household.

## COMPANY BUSINESS

Chenzira talked about the genesis of her company, Red Carnelian, and her business partner.

Ayoka Chenzira. *Photo courtesy of Andre Harris.*

A red carnelian is a stone. The version I like best reminds me of blood—an essential life force. When I was looking for a name for the company, things just came together psychically and spiritually for me. Red Carnelian started in 1992 as a d.b.a. [start-up company before incorporation] and went to a corporation in 1993. Barbara Chirinos had seen my work and asked me if she could volunteer for a while. She had a strong background in sales and a personality that worked well with mine. Her people skills are excellent. Together we are building Red Carnelian. She wanted to learn the business side of filmmaking; I really needed someone. I've traveled a lot around the world with film. People all over the world still called and wrote me letters; I quite frankly could not keep up with the day-to-day responses that I needed to do. I'd never thought about the idea of bringing in a partner and training someone, although I had worked with numerous people informally and many contract employees over the years. I thought, well, why not? and it's worked out fabulously. Barbara started out with a business background and went into insurance and the health care field, moved into theater and then into film. So what she brings to the company is an incredible business sensibility. She is used to managing a lot of people—excellent people skills and a real focused administrator.

## RACE AND GENDER ISSUES

Have your gender and race helped or hindered your success as a filmmaker?

I wouldn't really describe it as either. I see things as much more integrated than that. I think that timing has a lot to do with choices, options, availability. I think that when people choose to make race, class and gender an issue, it is. When they choose not to, it is not. Overall, the industry—meaning Hollywood and the five men who own everything—does not have a lot of interest in works created by women and people of color. Black women are rarely considered specifically unless they already fall into a category that corporate culture understands and sees as profitable. This seldom happens.

## ENDORSEMENT

In Chenzira's press kit is a full-page letter of endorsement from the well-known actress Ruby Dee. How did you get Ruby Dee to endorse your film catalogue?

I've known Ruby for a long time; she has followed my career and was familiar with my work. She has been a great supporter of my work and vice versa. She is a brilliant performer. She presented me with my SONY Innovator Award at the awards ceremony. We connect on many levels. I needed her help and she was generous.


## RENAISSANCE

What do you think of the Black film/video renaissance?

Frequently when people talk to me about Black film, what they're really talking about is Hollywood cinema, which is all they usually know. They want to know how come I don't do that. But I do make some distinctions. Part of why I make distinctions is because my background as a maker is very much tied to the independent film scene. This is coming at a time when money for independent work from places like the National Endowment for the Arts, state and local arts funds, the foundations and public television is decreasing. I make distinctions because in the Hollywood arena you do not have for the most part singularity of vision—meaning that directors, just by the structure of the contract, are hired hands. If you are a hired hand, then somebody is your boss. In the Hollywood system, there are a lot of people who are your boss. I think the rule now is up until about two weeks on the set you can be fired, even from your own movie. These things can be buffered according to what your attorney has negotiated. You are providing a product, and it is all very tied to Wall Street. So I think the public is seeing more Hollywood product designed for shareholder profit only, not necessarily independent films.

I would not necessarily describe the work that's being produced in Hollywood as Black film. Bringing in a Black director and confining their creativity as well as defining their creativity is a problem. Bringing in a crew that in some cases is still struggling to properly light our skin tone range in one shot is a problem. It's of the same concern as African filmmakers who get French money and are required to have a French director of photography. This explains why a lot of the African films look alike.

In terms of visual concepts and language, it becomes much more of a collaborative experience around trying to birth this film baby primarily so that it will have some value on Wall Street. I'm not saying that it's a system that people shouldn't be involved in; only I don't describe that as Black filmmaking or independent filmmaking because I think that the voice of the maker is critical. Being able to have an arcing [non-traditional] philosophy of story and a way to carry out the vision that is not shaped by ancillary products is important. In the independent community, you have a better sense of where Black America is when you look at the work that is unencumbered by those choices that are critical to the profit margins of corporate culture.

## BEYOND HOLLYWOOD

Do you think independent production and distribution outside the Hollywood system is a viable business venture?

I think it absolutely can and will be. We are on the ground floor and all of these things take time. Timing is important. It is inevitable that it will happen. I think smart, savvy venture capitalists will get on board. It is absolutely critical that we have theaters and home video distribution, that we participate and help shape dreams, encourage people to question and reevaluate, to conquer fears, to have fun, to tell truths.

## UNIQUENESS

What makes you unique as a filmmaker?

I don't know that I am a unique filmmaker. I'm simply a person who is both inspired and frustrated by life. But always hopeful. The subtotal of all of my experience, which is similar to some people and a hell of a lot different than other people. I know that I will continue to make films. That I will continue to find a way to bring the visions that are in my head to the screen, and to continue to develop an audience for my work. I also work to help other independent filmmakers work. I've got stories to tell. I want to tell them. I have incredible tenacity and determination, and I continue to get them out there. I enjoy making the invisible. I believe that wonderful things happen when you testify to the brilliance and stupidity of the human spirit.

How do you see your portfolio of work?

Eclectic. My works are like my children. There are things that you love about them; there are quirks about all of them. I am proud of all my films and the experiences they have created for me.

## ADVICE FOR ASPIRANTS

What can you tell young people who want to get into the business?

Try to be well informed and tenacious, because no one cares if you make a film or not. It wasn't like that fifteen or twenty years ago. Now everybody wants to make a film. I don't care if it's the butcher, the lawyer, the dentist, the doctor, the stripper—everybody wants to make a movie because it is associated with fame and fortune. Your little film, you will have to want it and care about it more than anything because finding other people to support your little film may not be as easy as you think. Know that it is an art form and it is a business, and don't let businesspeople and other nonbelievers tell you that art is ineffective. Usually people are not good at both. This means you have to know where you want to be, where you stand in all of this.

Most young people I know want to be directors. Directing requires excellent people skills, which a lot of people don't have. They may know where to move the camera, but they don't know how to talk to the actors, how to get a performance, if we're talking about narrative work. If you want to go to Hollywood, you have to surround yourself with the tools that are going to make that happen: lawyers, agents, managers, a personal trainer. Going to the right parties, being seen, being considered hot. Maybe you don't want to do that; maybe you want to do work that is experimental in nature and show it underground, that's a possibility too. It may mean if you make that choice you may work two or three jobs. So it depends on what you're looking for. The way that I work is very much like a novelist, a painter or a choreographer.

**THE FUTURE**

What do you hope to accomplish in the future?

I want to be able to tell the stories that I want to tell. Option other people's work and help them produce. For our company, Red Carnelian, to be a studio capable of production, distribution and exhibition. I'm very much interested in digital exhibition and a home video component.

What else is in development after *Alien Card* is completed and in distribution?

More animation, more narrative work and a soap opera.

**FAMILY**

I have a daughter who is sixteen and I have been married for eighteen years. What's interesting is watching my daughter, who has also grown up as an artist but has a very strong business sensibility. She has been making some public service announcements, and one of them got nominated for an Emmy. There really is another generation. When I see her going to the movies and having clear critical skills in place, it's a very interesting thing to witness. Her name is Haj Chenzira-Pinnock. The whole household is supportive of one another's interests and talents. It is an interesting Black household where you have artists. The environment is extremely supportive, and the unusual is more the rule than the exception.

Ayoka's husband (and sometime collaborator) is Thomas Osha Pinnock.

My husband, Thomas, was a lead dancer with the Dance Theater of Jamaica. He came to the United States on a Martha Graham dance scholarship. His background is as actor, dancer, choreographer. He has traveled extensively with his one-person show. He is an award-winning screenwriter and my best friend.

## SELECTED FILMOGRAPHY

### Producer/Director

*Sylvilla: They Dance to Her Drum*, 1979, 25 min., 16mm. Researcher; script; director, second camera: Ayoka Chenzira. A documentary portrait of Sylvilla Fort, who was the training link between the Katherine Dunham and Alvin Ailey periods of dance.

> This is very personal work about my dance teacher; she died before the work was completed. It is the only documentary on this woman who is the link between Katherine Dunham and Alvin Ailey. She died five days after an incredible tribute to her was done on my birthday. After she died, I couldn't make films for a long time. Then I thought I would only make films about Black people who were dying.

*Hairpiece: A Film for Nappyheaded People*, 1984, 10 min., 16mm. Script, co-editor, art work and animation: Ayoka Chenzira. A satire on the question of self-image for African American women.

> Comes out of the question of self-image for Black women living in a society where beautiful hair is hair in the wind that lets you be free. I am amazed that Black men still wear shower caps comfortably. I still am amazed that women sit and have their hair chemically straightened. As a personal choice, I understand it. It is still incongruous to a lot of other development issues. The why of it always implies a negative. The context is generally "to fix"; why is kinky hair seen as broken?

*Secret Sounds Screaming*, 1985, 30 min., video. Research and music: Ayoka Chenzira.

> It is about sexual assault, a documentary on sexual abuse of young people. This is my first completely independently produced project.

*Five Out of Five*, 1986, 3 min., 16mm. Editor: Ayoka Chenzira.

> Produced for New York Women Against Rape (NYWAR), a not-for-profit group that wanted to do a music video for young people around issues related to sexual assault.

*On Becoming a Woman*, 1986, animation. Producer, animations sections only: Ayoka Chenzira. A series designed to teach young girls about sex.

> Produced as part of a four-hour series for the National Black Women's Health Project. I was hired to produce the animated part of the series. It's a mother-daughter series teaching girls about sexuality as well as sex as it relates to birth control.

*Boa Morte*, 1988, 60 min., 16mm. A documentary shot in Brazil on the Sisterhood of Boa Morte, founded for the purpose of buying African women out of slavery. *Boa morte* means "good death."

> This was shot in Brazil about a Black women's organization involved in buying Black women out of slavery. The oldest member that I met at that time was 120 and the youngest member was 80 years old. The experience is worthy of a book. Juanita Anderson was producer and co-director.

*The Lure and the Lore*, 1989, 20 min., Hi-8 video. Editor and second camera: Ayoka Chenzira. Thomas Osha Pinnock, a Jamaican performance artist, captures the immigrant experience in dance and words.

> The first work I produced in the new Hi-8 video medium. It was a way of testing the equipment's potential and its possibilities for production. It aired as part of a public television series called *New to America*, on immigration. The series host was Edward James Olmos.

*Zajota and the Boogie Spirit*, 1990, 18 min., 16mm animation. Researcher, writer, camera, editor, additional art work/animation, character choreographer: Ayoka Chenzira. An animated journey of the history of African Americans from the shores of Africa to the Caribbean and the Americas.

> I brought in an animator from Ghana. I have a strong interest and background in dance. The piece grew out of Black American people feeling uncomfortable about being good at dancing. Not only good at, but something that has been critical in our lives. Dance has been used to bring rain, celebrate the birth of children, help with the harvest, seek the approval of gods, and as a survival tool. This film comes out of that philosophy. It began with a large historical element that was juxtaposed against the dance. However, I painfully discovered that too many people don't know history. The film was reworked for a young adult audience.

*Pull Your Head to the Moon: Stories of Creole Women*, 1992, 12 min., 16mm. Screen adaptation: Ayoka Chenzira. Collaboration with director/performance artist David Rousseve. Produced for *Alive TV*.

> That was originally done for the public television series *Alive TV*. I was asked to take a wonderful two-hour stage piece and make it a 12-minute film. One of my favorite pieces. I think we pulled off the transformation.

It is the story of a young man struggling to deal with the loss of a lover. He is aided by his grandmother, who recounts her tragic loss of a loved one in the early nineteen-hundreds on a plantation in Louisiana. David and I went on to work on other projects. He is brilliant and I am nourished by his work. We shot in Louisiana and New York.

*Williamswood*, 1992, 15 min., Hi-8 video. Editor: Ayoka Chenzira. A performance/ drama featuring the choreography of Hubert Lepka; produced for Austrian television.

This is a work I was hired to direct. A television company in Austria called and asked me if I wanted to direct an experimental film. They had seen some of my work on dance. They had a company whose technique is very physical. They work with tractors on stage and they climb on buildings, they do aerial work. It's a very different kind of piece. I asked to bring a director of photography. They agreed and I took Ronald Gray, who shot *Alma's Rainbow* and *Pull Your Head to the Moon*. Even when I got off the plane I didn't know what the piece was supposed to be about. There was no script. It is a fantasy piece. I would never have been hired to do a work like this in the United States, not only because of the nudity involved, but Black directors here are hired for Black-themed work. Whereas when I went to Austria, they were looking at my creative talent.

*MOTV (My Own TV)*, 1993, 54 min., 16mm, Hi-8 video and Super 8mm film. Screenplay by Thomas Osha Pinnock. Produced for the Independent Television Service for its five-hour dramatic series *TV Families*. A bittersweet story about the love between an African American woman and her Jamaican husband and the fantasy and tragedy that result. Shot in ten days, edited in twenty-one days.

Produced as part of a family series for public television, but we own the copyright to this work.

*Alma's Rainbow*, 1993, 88 min., 35mm. Screenplay: Ayoka Chenzira. A female rite-of-passage, romantic comedy drama.

I could write a book on the response to *Alma's Rainbow*. The film took a long time to make. I raised all the money independently. Distributors came and looked at the film, and there was a real split between what the men thought about it and what the women thought about it. The response by women has been overwhelmingly positive. The response by men, who write the checks, was that it was not an action piece. There was no Black pathology; there was no movie point of reference for three Black women driving a story. They also see that it is not a linear narrative in the tradition of exposition, climax and resolution. The editing and story-telling is based on the emotions of the characters. This is something that women understood and men did not. We found a distributor who was not interested in selling it only to twenty-something White guys in the suburbs. Unfortunately, the arrangement with the distributor and our company did not work out; we did get the film back, however, unencumbered. This film grows out of mothers being afraid of their daughters' own budding sensuality.

*Snowfire*, 1994, 7 min., Hi-8 video and 2¼" slides. Writer, producer, director, director of photography and music: Ayoka Chenzira. Produced for AIDS Films as part of its four-part series *Positive: Life with HIV*. This work was the series' only dramatized story. The story of a Jamaican man coming to grips with his son being gay and his death by AIDS.

> Part of the AIDS Film series. There was a four-hour series on AIDS done for public television. The series was called *Positive: Life with HIV*. The Independent Television Service contracted AIDS Film here in New York City to hire forty filmmakers from around the country to do small segments on some issue around AIDS.

*Sentry at the Gate: The Comedy of Jane Galvin-Lewis*, 1995, 58 min., Hi-8 video. Director, producer and director of photography: Ayoka Chenzira. A character comedy of Jane Galvin-Lewis portraying seven irreverent characters who parody mainstream and popular American culture.

> At my company, Red Carnelian, we decided that we wanted to do a couple of things. Aside from beginning to option other people's works and continuing to do my own works, we wanted to begin to highlight people who we thought were talented or interesting in some way. We would put our resources behind them and create a production that would be nationally and internationally available. The comedienne Jane Galvin-Lewis is someone whose work I've admired for a long time. Her comedy is very smart, political; and it's character comedy. She has a range of interesting characters and she is funny and hard-edged without being "in the street" in terms of profanity. We found her, pitched the idea to her, put the company's resources behind her and created this piece. We got some support from the National Black Programming Consortium, who saw the work-in-progress, liked it and gave us some finishing funds.

*In the Rivers of Mercy Angst*, 1996, 25 min., Hi-8 video and 2¼" slides, computer-generated. A woman struggles to free herself from the Keeper of Memory in this surreal odyssey.

> The lead actress is someone that my husband found in the subway. *Snowfire* and *In the Rivers of Mercy Angst* mark a departure in my kind of film desire, both in terms of creating and turning out some creative differences, seeking to do work that is experimental, affordable and controllable. I had been looking for a style that allowed me to blend what I do in animation with some computer styles that I'm interested in, along with my own sense of narrative story-telling. These two works mix Hi-8 video and 2¼" slides, which are then computer-manipulated for a narrative story. The still photography part of them is shot in the same way that you do for a narrative story film. So you end up with about two thousand stills to create the time that you need. It is new and I'm enjoying it.

### Director

*Alien Card*. A work-in-progress; screenplay by Thomas Osha Pinnock.

We're hoping to shoot it in fall 1997. *Alien Card* is about three Jamaican immigrants coming to America looking for the American dream. It is going to be a 35mm feature film.

## BIO-CRITICAL REVIEW

"Her works are visually beautiful, inspirational and entertaining. Through her vision we witness the pain and beauty of the Black experience in a way that encourages hope and love. We need this."—From the desk of Ruby Dee

"As one of the few Black females to have written, directed and produced a 35mm feature film for theatrical release, let alone preside over her own film company, her achievements speak for themselves. (Her company) Red Carnelian . . . is a necessary entity filling a void manufactured by a selective Hollywood."—Clarissa Cummings, *Brooklyn Advocate*

## SELECTED AWARDS, GRANTS AND HONORS

American Film Institute

Jerome Foundation

Mayors of New York and Detroit, honors for contributions to independent Black cinema

National Endowment for the Arts

New York State Council for the Arts

SONY Innovator Award, 1991

Sundance Institute

## EDUCATION

New York University, B.A.

Columbia University, Teachers College, M.A.

## WORK

Chenzira is director of the B.F.A. degree program in film and video at City College, New York; she is a tenured associate professor.

## SOURCES

Interview by Spencer Moon, June 1996. Some program descriptions and Ruby Dee
    letter supplied by filmmaker.
Cummings, Clarissa. "Red Carnelian Opens Doors for Black Film Art," *Brooklyn
    Advocate* (Brooklyn Women on the Move issue) (4), no. 4 (April 1996), pp.
    4, 6.

Francee Covington

# FRANCEE COVINGTON

## BACKGROUND

Francee Covington has worked in television production since 1968. Her experience includes work for WCBS-TV, New York; ABC Sports, New York; WBZ-TV, Boston; British Broadcasting Company (BBC) and Ghana Broadcasting Company (GBC); KGO-TV (ABC); KQED-TV (PBS); and KPIX-TV (CBS) in San Francisco. She has also produced programs in Spain and Australia. Her duties and responsibilities have included writer, reporter and producer. She has produced investigative-quality work in long- and short-form documentaries covering a wide range of topics for television. In 1987 she founded her own company, Francee Covington Productions. Her clients have included AT&T, Pacific Bell, Pacific Gas and Electric, the San Francisco Symphony, the State of California and recently the San Francisco Black Coalition on AIDS.

She is part of a group of Black women entrepreneurs in the San Francisco area that dates back to Mary Ellen Pleasant, one of the first and most outstanding Black businesswomen in San Francisco from about 1862 to 1890. Pleasant owned land, boarding houses and a laundry service and was a staunch abolitionist who supplied money to John Brown.

Covington says she is continuing a long tradition of African American business owners in San Francisco and what she is doing is not new territory. Our interview was conducted in her suite of offices in an African American section of San Francisco called the Fillmore District.

## CORPORATE PRODUCTION

Is there any of your work you'd like to comment on?

A lot of people don't like to do corporate work. I love to do corporate work. After producing a popular local television series and having it canceled, I decided to set up my own business. I finally realized after going through a series of exercises with a highly paid career consultant that, indeed, I didn't want to change careers; I just wanted to change who I was working for. That's when I started my production company, on February 2, 1987. I had the company working out of the back bedroom of our house initially; within a year I opened an office.

We started with corporate clients. I very much enjoyed working with corporate clients because I learned something new about business each and every day. Narrowcasting to a captive audience. These productions were done in documentary style, infotainment style, entertainment style. Sometimes with all of the cast and crew we would be up to forty people easily—actors, extras, crew, original music. Nicely budgeted projects. Corporations within their corporate communications divisions usually have state-of-the-art equipment. They purchase satellite time to talk to their offices worldwide. They have the latest and the greatest. More often than not, it is better than what you would find at your local broadcast operation. I've produced many hours of corporate productions.

## NEW PERSONAL PROJECT

Describe your current very personal project, *Soul to Seoul*.

*Soul to Seoul* is a project that came about as a result of the frictions that exist between the African American and the Korean American communities. 1994 was the first year of a student exchange program with African American students from San Francisco. A commissioner of the San Francisco Redevelopment Agency thought it would be a great idea when we opened the Yerba Buena Gardens arts complex in San Francisco. A beautiful memorial is contained within the complex to Dr. Martin Luther King Jr. San Francisco has a sister city relationship with many cities around the world, and Seoul, Korea, is one of them. This commissioner sent word to Seoul (she is herself Korean American) that it would be very nice if the government in Seoul could send some token of esteem for Dr. King for the opening of the Gardens and the memorial. What came back was, "We will sponsor five African American students to study at one of our most prestigious universities." It was all expenses paid: tuition, airfare, room and board and some spending money. So I thought this is concrete evidence that people are trying to overcome these recent animosities. The relationship between African Americans and Koreans is traditionally a friendly relationship. The reason I wanted to do this project was to remind people of that.

I grew up spending summers and major holidays in North Carolina with my grandparents, Samuel Lee Thompson and Lillie Mae Thompson. My uncle served in the Korean War. As I was growing up I was surrounded by Korean artifacts—the fisherman and his wife, village scenes, and photographs of my uncle and his Korean dates. When he came home I remember quite vividly these jackets that the men wore that had the map of South Korea. The city of Seoul was represented by a star on the maps. I wasn't even in the double digits as a child, and I was fascinated by these things. I always knew there was a place called Seoul and a place called Korea, even though at that time I would not have been able to point it out to you on a map of the world. So, coupled with the fact that African Americans to this day, who are in the Eighth Army serving in Korea, risk their lives to ensure that Korea remains a sovereign nation, it is something that Koreans should not forget, and it's something that African Americans should be reminded of. Along with the fact that the darlings of the Seoul Olympics of 1988 were Florence Griffith-Joyner and Carl Lewis, two African Americans. The explosion in the number of immigrants that have come to the United States from Korea over the last fifteen to twenty years is what has led to this friction.

I wanted to be able to show people that there are attempts being made on both sides to understand our respective communities, and I wanted to shine a light on that effort. I spent a lot of my own money doing this project. I need to raise money to finish post-production. We did have a couple of grants that came in. Becthel-Seoul gave us a grant; a division of Samsung gave us a grant. My aunt Mary Ellen Phipher-Kierton in Brooklyn, New York, gave me some money. She lives right there in the heart of where the animosity toward Korean grocers was vented. She thought this was so important that she gave me some money. So the program has been shot, and I need to get funds to finish it.

## TELEVISION PRODUCTION

I asked Covington to tell me about her career in television and how it prepared her for corporate production as well as her own independent productions.

I first started in the number-one market with the number-one station, WCBS-TV, as an intern while finishing my undergraduate degree. I was able to work in news, operations, programming. That training and experience are the foundation of my work as producer. I made friends there that I have until this day.

## UNIQUENESS

Describe what makes you unique as a producer.

I don't think I am unique. I think I'm just one of many solid, hard-working producer/directors. I wish there were more of us now, especially with the explosion of more channels available to people. It would really be nice if there were more product being turned out that reflected our stories and our lives. That is what's sorely missing. We only have so many producers currently working in the field. What they can generate is only a few projects, a few shows. On the other hand, if we had hundreds working in this medium it would be better. I don't really see that as competition, but as another avenue for African Americans to produce our stories so they can be seen and heard.

## ADVICE FOR ASPIRANTS

What can you tell young people interested in the business?

The first thing you have to do is finish your college education. That is critical. I don't care how bright or talented you are; you need that degree. That degree gives you options. That is what everyone needs in order to make a life that they are happy with. Get your degree and concentrate on your writing and communication skills. Learn to be able to make complex issues easily understood by a mass audience. Those are the skills that are needed. If you want to be a director, directors direct, producers produce, writers write. So if I meet a young person and they say, "I want to be a director," I say, "What have you directed?" Even if you have to play Mickey Rooney, "I've got a barn, let's put on a show," that's what you're supposed to be doing. Getting those chops. Not waiting by the phone until someone gives you this grand opportunity. Because you won't be ready. You have to practice and practice until you find your own voice. Finding your own voice in video and film is just like finding your own voice as a writer. So that when people read your work or hear your work, they go, "Oh, I see, this is in the style of . . ." It becomes your signature.

## THE FUTURE

What is it you hope to accomplish in the future?

I want to continue doing good work. I want to do better work. I want
to continue to grow. I want to work with people who are senior to
me, so I can learn from them before they retire. I would like to learn
more. I see myself going more into multimedia. I see myself looking
to the future at an academic career. This is really a field for young
people. I enjoy it tremendously. When you are called to compete with
people who are less experienced, therefore less expensive, that's something. I should move the way my life moves naturally. I'm not getting
younger, I'm getting older. I should move toward a place where being
older is an asset, and I think I'll find that in academia.

## PERSPECTIVES

The recorder was stopped and then restarted when we discussed some
other aspects of the Black filmmaking experience.

In doing writing and field research as well as acting as associate producer for the KQED-TV, PBS, series on aging called *Over Easy*,
hosted by Hugh Downs, I interviewed lots of seniors. Many of the
seniors I interviewed for the show were White. More often than not
I was asked if I knew a Black person they knew once upon a time in
their lives. The producer and I laughed when we discussed this White-
people-who-think-all-Black-people-know-each-other syndrome.

Another different example of the color issue is from the corporate
side while working for Pacific Gas and Electric. They started a new
video campaign and had a producer whom they badgered to no end
about this Covington woman who was so good, and he had to use me
to produce this new material. He had that look of surprise when he
discovered I was Black—but so was he, and we laughed when we discovered that no one on the corporate side bothered to tell him that I
was Black. As it turned out we worked together for years, and quite
well. What I try to do is establish a working relationship over the
phone. So that by the time they meet me and discover that I am Black,
my competence makes that a nonissue.

I try every day to do the best that I can. Even though every day the
work can be all-consuming, I really feel privileged to be doing this.
When I think about what we've gone through as a people from slavery
to now, I feel an obligation to do my best. I feel an obligation to work
on some pro bono projects. Because when the sun went down on the

slaves and they looked to the future, they must have said this is not going to be the state of Black people always. I have to move that process along a little bit—both in how we are portrayed, and in the things that I do. I also have to move things along with those people that I might be working with. Right now I have two interns working with me. I think they're going to be really good. I'm a little hard on them—with love, of course. I want them to be good, and they've got what it takes to be good. I always try to include some historical perspective when I can, even in doing the corporate work. It is essential to let people know about our history in the building of the West and the country, which is contrary to popular press images.

## SELECTED FILMOGRAPHY

### Producer

*Story of a People: The Gospel According to . . .* , 1987, 60 min., video. Part of the nationally syndicated series *Story of a People*. Executive-produced by Robert Dockery Jr., the series is a documentary portrait of the African American experience. This particular episode featured performances and interviews with gospel greats such as the Reverend Edwin Hawkins, Tremaine Hawkins, Albertina Walker, the Reverend Al Green, Denise Williams, the Winans and the Barrett sisters and was hosted by Robert Guillaume.

> The producer, Robert Dockery, called me late one Saturday evening. It was midnight in New York. He called because he had gotten my name from Carol Munday-Lawrence, another African American woman writer/producer/director. Carol had recommended me to produce this particular episode. As it turned out, she wrote the script for this show and I was hired as field producer. We began working immediately. They already had air dates for this episode of the series, so we began work to meet those air dates. I worked a few months on the series. I traveled to Philadelphia, Los Angeles, Chicago, Detroit, Indiana. We were all over. It was involved and produced on a pretty tight production schedule because of the impending air dates.

*Ikebana: Vol. 1. The Ohara School*,** 1991, 60 min., video. Featuring Fay Kramer, president emeritus of Ikebana International, joined by Suiyo Fujimoto, grandmaster of the Ohara School.

*Ikebana: Vol. 2. The Sogetsu School*,** 1992, 30 min., video. Featuring Soho Sakai of the Sogetsu School, with commentary by Fay Kramer, president emeritus of Ikebana International.

*Ikebana: Vol. 3. Techniques for Longer Lasting Cut Flowers*,** 1993, 30 min., video. Featuring Fusako Seiga Hoyrup, president of the Wafu School and instructor at San Jose City College.

Ikebana is my hobby. Ikebana is the art of flower arrangement. It has been my hobby now for a little more than a decade. I have my teaching credential in Ikebana. I am a fourth grade, which means bottom-rung, teacher of the Sogetsu School. I've had my credential about three years. I really enjoy it a lot. It has even helped me with my directing. The way I look at things in the frame now is very different than when I looked at them before I studied Ikebana, because with Ikebana we have what's known as a bird's-eye view. This bird's-eye view is taken from the top of the arrangement. The bird's-eye view helps you to create a sense of depth in whatever it is that you're creating. So you're looking at the foreground, the middle ground and the background. It has been a wonderful exercise for me. It helps me to see all that is going on in all parts of the frame and how people are approaching the work.

My school of training is the Sogetsu School. This school is considered the more avant-garde school of Ikebana. Ikebana has more than six hundred schools, according to the secretary of education for Japan. A school is a style, just as you have many styles of music. You have classical European, rock, rap, jazz, etc. Sogetsu is a type of flower arranging under Ikebana. It's very calming and very soothing. I discovered Ikebana during a very stressful period in my life. To relieve stress I would go to my basement workroom at home and create one arrangement after another. During this period initially the house was filled with flower arrangements. Ikebana was very helpful.

It also has been very instrumental in me looking at my life—in terms of aging and the past, the present and the future. You don't only arrange flowers, you arrange branches and inorganic material. When you look at a flower or some greenery, you are looking at the inherent beauty of that thing. Not whether it is a bud or a fresh flower. Things that are dying or passing away can also be quite beautiful. In any stage of development you can find beauty in something. Now that I'm maturing, this is very good for me.

Let this be a lesson to people: Do not let your hobby take over your business. That's how the video series came about. I should have kept them totally separate. I wanted to do a series of Ikebana tapes. I was able to get the on-camera assistance of several very esteemed women Ikebana instructors. We've received excellent reviews for the series, but I have not been able to promote it as widely as I would have liked. I'm not a marketer of special-interest videos. A lot of people were aware of the tapes. We get fan mail every now and then. It is the one thing that has made this company of mine truly international. We've had sales in Canada, Japan, England, Singapore, Hawaii, Hong Kong; they've been sold everywhere. So that's very nice. When people look at them, they really like them. People order and say they like the different volumes and ask if I have any new volumes, and I have to say no. The others have to make some money first.

*Reality Check*, 1996, three 30-min. programs, video. The programs were designed to foster AIDS awareness in the African American community. Each show emphasized safe sex and prevention messages in an entertaining and informal format. Broadcast over KMTP-TV, Channel 32, San Francisco. Cablecast over twenty-six additional cable systems in the greater San Francisco Bay Area.

## BIO-CRITICAL REVIEW

The reviews for Volume 1 of the *Ikebana* series have been uniformly excellent.

"Reading a book on the art of flower arrangement is far less informative than watching an expert do it and explain it as they proceed. That plus excellent camera angles make *Ikebana: The Ohara School* an excellent method of instruction."—Dick Tracy, *Sacramento Bee*

"One is most certainly tempted to try creating an arrangement after watching this presentation. The technical quality is professional."—Fay Weinstein, *Florists' Review*

"The format of the program is formal and easy to follow. This should be an attractive purchase for public libraries."—Barbara Hornic-Lockard, *Library Journal*

## PUBLICATIONS

Covington has published articles in major newspapers in New York and San Francisco, and essays in books and magazines.

## SELECTED AWARDS

*Africa*
>   Black Filmmakers Hall of Fame, First Place, Public Service Announcement/Commercial, 1995.
>   Emmy Award Nomination, Sojourner Truth Foster Care Agency, Outstanding Achievement Public Service Announcement, 1993/4.

*Bill Summers*
>   Black Filmmakers Hall of Fame, First Place, Music, 1981.
>   CEBA (Communications Excellence to Black Audiences) Award of Merit, 1981.
>   Emmy Award Nomination, Outstanding Feature Segment, 1979.

*The Card Game*
>   Black Filmmakers Hall of Fame, Honorable Mention, Public Service Announcement/Commercial, 1991.

*Morgan Horse*
>   National Commission on Working Women, Women at Work Broadcast Awards, Third Place, Television News Feature, 1983.

*Samoans*
>   CEBA (Communications Excellence to Black Audiences) Award of Merit, 1980.
>   Emmy Award Nomination, Outstanding Achievement, Documentary Program Series, 1980.

*2,000 Years of Nigerian Art*
   Emmy Award Nomination, Outstanding Achievement Public Service Announcement, 1980.


## EDUCATION

City College of New York, B.A., political science and history

University of Ghana, West Africa, all coursework completed for master's degree, African studies


## SOURCES

Interview by Spencer Moon, March 1996.


### Books

Jackson, George F. *Black Women Makers of History: A Portrait*. Oakland, CA: GRT Book Printing, 1985.


### Newspapers and Magazines

Hornic-Lockard, Barbara. "Video Reviews," *Library Journal*, May 15, 1993, p. 110.
Motamedi, Beatrice. "Black Inc., Against the Odds," *San Francisco Business* (25), no. 5, May 1990, p. 1.
Tracy, Dick. "The Good Life," *Sacramento Bee*, July 11, 1992, p. 14.
Weinstein, Fay. "Video Review," *Florists' Review* (Topeka, KS), September 1992, p. 72.

# JULIE DASH

## BACKGROUND

Julie Dash began filmmaking in an after-school program during high school. The program was sponsored by the Studio Museum of Harlem. In college Dash majored in psychology. She was later accepted into the film studies program at the Leonard Davis Center for the Performing Arts in the David Picker School of Film at City College of New York. She produced her first film while still an undergraduate; it was a promotional film for the New York Urban Coalition entitled *Working Models of Success*. She received an undergraduate degree in film production and moved to Los Angeles, where she attended the Center for Advanced Film Studies at the American Film Institute. During her tenure there she worked as an intern on production of the television series *Roots*. Her second film, *Four Women*, grew out of that training. She enrolled in the University of California, Los Angeles, for graduate study. Her thesis work, *Diary of an African Nun*, was based on a story by the Pulitzer Prize–winning author Alice Walker.

While in Los Angeles Dash worked for a time as a board member of the Motion Picture Association of America. She was one of six board members whose job it was to rate more than 350 films each year for theatrical distribution in the United States. During this time Dash completed her film *Illusions*. It was designed as the first segment of a planned series of films on the lives of Black women.

## FIRST FEATURE: *DAUGHTERS OF THE DUST*

The film that brought Dash national and international recognition was her first feature-length film, *Daughters of the Dust*. Prior to the film's national distribution, I had an opportunity to talk to her and the film's cinematographer, A. J. Jafa. The opportunity for the interview was a special preview screening in Oakland, California, organized and presented by the Black Filmmakers Hall of Fame in April 1991. This screening was the *first* screening of the completed film to a large Black audience.

### A. J. Jafa, Cinematographer

I spoke with Jafa first. He talked about working with Dash on a project they had completed after *Daughters* entitled *Praise House*. *Praise House* was completed as part of the Public Broadcasting Service series *Alive from Off Center* (now *Alive TV*). Jafa described his experience with Dash and her critique of his work as a cinematographer. She gave him certain critiques that made him later want to work with other women directors in order to gauge the validity of her critiques. Jafa said he learned a lot on *Daughters of the Dust* but wouldn't call it a fun experience. Jafa encouraged Dash to make *Daughters of the Dust* into a feature film instead of the originally planned short subject. Jafa felt he contributed to the social, political and psychological levels of the film. He encouraged and led discussions about what making a Black film means. He also discussed the film's editing, music, dialogue, art direction, aesthetics and overall concept. He encouraged Dash to use Black artists in some positions, people with no prior film experience but with the requisite artistic and building skills to make things work. He felt that every aspect of the film's process should be interrogated to make the work a truly independent Black vision, to make the work not just original but aboriginal, to deconstruct cinema and rebuild it in an Africentric vision.

### Production and Content

The film is about the Geechee culture, people who live off the southern coast of the Carolinas and Georgia. They have their own dialect and language, called Gullah. Their traditions and idioms are very tied to the West African experience. Even the scenes of people eating and what they are eating are culturally specific. The company had the assistance of a scholar who translated lines into the Gullah idiom for more authenticity. The scholar also coached the actors in the Gullah dialect.

To help in creating characters for the film, Dash gave each character an astrological sign. Before rehearsals for shooting took place, Dash gave each actor a background biography of their character to read. She saw each character as representing an African deity. She gave each actor information for further research on the characters. The rehearsal lasted for only a few days.

The story is a universal rite of passage: The younger generation always strives to move forward, always wants more than their parents had. There will be a struggle, a tug and then separation. It is universal in all cultures, this rite of passage.

## Finances and Distribution

Finances for *Daughters of the Dust* came from the National Endowment for the Arts and the Fulton County, Georgia, Arts Council. With only partial funding, about 35 percent of the film was shot. From that footage a trailer was made to continue fundraising. At a conference of Third World Women in Cinema at the Sundance Institute in Utah, the trailer was screened. A representative of public television's *American Playhouse* saw the trailer and contracted to provide final funding and make the work a feature-length film. Filmmakers under this agreement with public television have a window of opportunity to find theatrical distribution, and after the theatrical run is completed the work goes to public television for several years of airing.

Because of the film's content and style, fundraising was difficult. Dash said there exists a fear of Black people using their culture to make statements in code. This is a modern variation on the fear that led slaveholders to take the slaves' drums away.

## Aesthetics

Dash said that the film was shot in a jazz-like style, an improvisational modality. A memorable moment occurred during production when a sand storm hit during the shooting of a key dramatic scene. There was the incongruity of a sunny day with clouds of sand as they shot on a beach. It was seen as an omen by certain members of Dash's crew, who considered it as representing the spirits of the past visiting the film that deals with the historic experiences of Black people.

## Audience Response

In the question and answer session immediately following the film's screening, Dash described a fifteen-year-long odyssey of writing, researching and producing *Daughters of the Dust*. The film was shot in twenty-eight days and edited over a year. It was shot on several islands off the coast of South Carolina. The crew was 90 percent Black. Dash described the inspiration for the film as coming from her father's side of the family, which is from Charleston and the sea islands of South Carolina. She sees these islands as having the heaviest African retention in this part of the twentieth century and as a sacred ground for the Black diaspora experience. The Oakland, California, audience gave Dash an overwhelmingly positive response.

Dash thinks the positive audience response was because of the fact that people see the film as refreshing, totally different, totally new, something they weren't privileged by before. It resembles nothing they've seen on television, in motion pictures or books; most people know very little if anything about the Geechee culture. The general audience is tired of seeing the same old thing, over and over again.

### Television Interviews

In a television interview on *Live from L.A. with Tanya Hart*, Dash spoke of the obstacles she encountered to get this work distributed. Conflicts arose even after many awards and generally positive audience response. The main conflict was between what the powers that be (i.e., that control distribution) want audiences to see, and what the film actually shows. Not until distribution was achieved and the film was sold out for every performance at every theater where it opened did Hollywood begin to call her. Dash said that she made this film for the African American audience. She wanted to touch on issues related to women and the family from the Black diaspora perspective. The offers from Hollywood have been for Dash to direct mostly derivative work, and she has thus far declined those offers. She feels she has her own stories that she wants to tell unencumbered.

Cheryl Chisholm (director of the Third World Film Festival, Atlanta, Georgia) asked Dash questions immediately following the public television premier of *Daughters of the Dust* in 1994. Dash described it as a special film, a celebration of the African American woman. She described herself as on a mission to redefine how Black people and women see themselves on screen. She wanted to reflect the perspective and view of an African American woman looking at other African American women. To achieve this, there was a very conscious and nonstandard camera placement: placing the cameras so shots reflected an interior position; holding close-up shots and deliberately letting them run longer on screen (something not usually done in editing), especially on faces of Black women.

### UNIQUENESS

Dash talked about what makes her unique as a filmmaker. She described herself as a "film missionary," on a mission to do stories about African American women and their experiences. She also said her mission is to show experiences that she was never able to see as a child watching television. Reading the works of Black female authors such as Toni Morrison, Toni Cade Bambara and Alice Walker had caused a major shift in her thinking.

With their respective voices and characters, the Black female authors exemplified the real things that Dash knew and talked about with her friends. She shifted from an interest in documentary filmmaking to a desire to tell stories in the dramatic form like those she had read by Black female authors.

## ADVICE TO ASPIRANTS

Dash said that aspiring filmmakers should not be afraid of their own voice. Young filmmakers should tell the stories they want to tell and are in their gut. "Don't let anyone ever tell you it is not interesting and there is no audience for your work. There is always an audience for your work, and there will be someone that you're going to move by what you do. Go ahead and be bold; don't be derivative." Most independent filmmakers who survive are serious about their art and craft. It is not easy or glamorous. Young filmmakers may find themselves working for years on the same project to see it through to completion.

## FILMOGRAPHY

### Producer

#### *Short Subjects*

*Working Models of Success*, 1973, 16mm, documentary.

*Four Women*, 1975, 4 min., 16mm, b/w. An experiment with stylized movement and dress, expressing the spirit of Black women from Africa to America.

*Diary of an African Nun*, 1977, 13 min., 16mm, b/w. A young African novice is consumed with a religious and cultural conflict expressed through an interior monologue.

*Illusions*, 1983, 34 min., 16 mm, b/w. A drama reminiscent of Oscar Micheaux's* stories of light-skinned Black people passing for White. That issue is at the heart and soul of this film set in the postwar forties. The Black person in question is a woman working for a film studio. At the fictional offices of National Pictures, the heroine moves back and forth from the Black world to the White world, with neither one suspecting her chameleon-like life. Lonette McKee portrays the lead as Mignon Dupree, a motion-picture studio executive.

*Breaking the Silence: On Reproductive Rights*, 1988, video documentary.

*Phyllis Wheatley*, 1989. YWCA industrial short.

*Preventing Cancer*, 1989. Industrial short for Morehouse School of Medicine.

*Relatives*, 1990, Super 8mm. Made for television.

*Praise House*, 1990, 27 min., video, color. Dash described the work as a narrative dance work. It features the dance ensemble of the Urban Bush Women.

*Lost in the Night*, 1992. Music video for Peabo Bryson.

*Feature Films*

*Daughters of the Dust*, 1992, 113 min., 35mm, color, Kino International. Written and co-produced by Julie Dash. Co-producer and cinematographer, A.J. Jafa. Dash acknowledges that the films of Spencer Williams* were a historic antecedent and influence. Her intent was to make a work similar to his films, which she described as dramatic work with a religious and ethnographic quality. The film was shot in all-natural light and with reflectors only. Costuming and hairstyles of the turn-of-the-century era in which the film is set were duplicated and authenticated by scholars and experts on the period. One of the techniques used is that of a talking drum, an African percussion instrument, on the soundtrack. The drum repeats over and over a rhythmic cadence, the expression is "remember me, remember my name, take me wherever you go." This technique is described by Dash as a way to remember your ancestors. Dash wants this, her first feature, to be remembered in twenty years as the beginning of something new in authentic Black cinema.

## BIO-CRITICAL REVIEW

*Daughters of the Dust*. "Reminiscent of Bergman and Antonioni, yet definitively African American."—Gene Seymour, *New York Newsday*
———. "Crisp, sensitive direction in putting together a moving work about a simple but proud people immersed in a distinct culture as they try to touch their own spirits."—Clifford Terry, *Chicago Tribune*
———. "The film is an extended, wildly lyrical meditation on the power of African cultural iconography and the spiritual resilience of the generations of women who have been its custodians."—Stephen Holden, *New York Times*
———. "Dash engenders a strong and resilient community of women, the portrait so fluid and striking that the after-image vividly persists."—Lynell George, *Los Angeles Times*

## EDUCATION

City College, New York, B.A., film production
UCLA, M.F.A., film production

## AWARDS

*Daughters of the Dust*
American Film Institute, Maya Deren Award, 1992
Black Filmmakers Hall of Fame, Black Filmworks Festival of Film and Video, Best Film, 1992; Oscar Micheaux Award, 1991
CEBA Award, 1991
Certificate of Appreciation, first feature length film in theatrical distribution by an African American woman, Maxine Waters, Member of Congress, 29th District, California, 1992
Coalition of 100 Black Women, Cadance Award, Trailblazer, 1992

Sundance Film Festival, Best Cinematography, 1991
Women in Film, Special Merit Certificate, Crystal Award, 1992
*Diary of an African Nun*
Directors Guild of America, Student Film Award, 1978
National Black Programming Consortium, Best Producer and Best Drama, Prized
Pieces, 1979
*Four Women*
Miami International Film Festival, Women in Film, Gold Medal, 1978

## GRANTS

American Film Institute, 1981

Appalshop Southeast Regional Fellowship Grant, 1988

Fulton County Arts Council Grants, 1988, 1987

Georgia Endowment for the Humanities, 1988

John Simon Guggenheim Memorial Foundation Grant, 1981

National Endowment for the Arts, Individual Artist Grants, 1985, 1983, 1981

Rockefeller Intercultural Fellowship, 1989

## SOURCES

Interview by Spencer Moon, April 1991.

### Books

Acker, Ally. *Reel Women: Pioneers of the Cinema, 1986 to the Present.* New York: Con-
tinuum, 1991.
Cole, Janis, and Holly Dale. *Calling the Shots: Profiles of Women Filmmakers.* Kingston,
Ontario: Quarry Press, 1993.
Dash, Julie, with Toni Cade Bambara and bell hooks. *Daughters of the Dust: The
Making of an African American Woman's Film.* New York: New Press, 1992.
Harris, Erich Leon. *African American Screen Writers Now: Conversations with Holly-
wood's Black Pack.* Los Angeles: Silman-James Press, 1996.
Klotman, Phyllis Rauch, ed. *Screenplays of the African American Experience.* Blooming-
ton: Indiana University Press, 1991.

### Newspapers and Magazines

George, Lynell. "Daughters of the Dust." *Los Angeles Weekly,* March 1992, p. 13.
Holden, Stephen. "The Past through Tomorrow, Julie Dash Enobles the Old Ways."
*New York Times,* January 1992, p. 14.
Seymour, Gene. "Daughters of the Dust." *New York Newsday,* January 1992, p. 35.
Terry, Clifford. "Daughters of the Dust." *Chicago Tribune,* January 1992, p. 23.

### Television

*Live from L.A. with Tanya Hart* (BET Cable), 1992.
*Screen Scene* (BET Cable), 1992.

# IVAN DIXON

Ivan Dixon described his father's influence on his life:

> All the experiences that went on before caused everything that I think now. So my life and work are totally influenced by it, I think. My father was an entrepreneur. I watched him turn a little candy store into a self-service grocery store, over the years. He later started a bakery. The major competition prevented us from getting salt, essential in baking. We tried to get supplies in New Jersey for a time. They stopped those wholesalers from supplying us; eventually we went out of business. It reminds me of how movie entrepreneurs like (Oscar) Micheaux* did in the segregated market with his films; he cornered the market. . . .
>
> My father taught me that it was important to be honest and it wasn't important to be honest because somebody else would think you were dishonest; what mattered was you would know you were dishonest. The point is what kind of self-respect you have.

## PERSPECTIVE

His perspective, he feels, has not kept him from accomplishing what few have done in the industry.

I believe I've worked as much or more than some people who acceded to others' demands and attitudes. By going my own way, I think I've worked as much as anybody.

When pressed to elaborate, he said:

Some of it is what I know about my craft, and I think some of it is respect for someone who has his own personal point of view. A sense of personal worth is something that other people will respect; it seems to me that's just as important.

## ACTING CAREER HIGHLIGHTS

Dixon graduated from North Carolina Central University and then accepted a scholarship to Case Western Reserve University in Cleveland, Ohio. His studies in drama led to teaching on the staff of Karamu House, a cultural center in Cleveland. He came back to New York City to study drama at the American Theater Wing, where his classmates included James Earl Jones and Mel Stewart. Dixon landed off-Broadway roles in *A Wedding in Japan* and *A Land beyond the River*.

When he decided to pursue work in Hollywood, he got work as double and stunt-double for Sidney Poitier in several of Poitier's first films, *Edge of the City*, *The Defiant Ones* and *Something of Value*. He continued acting in theater and appeared in *The Cave Dwellers* and the original cast of *A Raisin in the Sun*—the Broadway production and the film version as well. The latter film role led to many more film acting assignments, including *Car Wash*, *A Patch of Blue*, *Porgy and Bess* and the critically acclaimed *Nothing But a Man*.

Dixon carved out a solid career in television by acting in over two hundred productions, including *Twilight Zone*, *I Spy*, *The Fugitive*, *Ironside*, *CBS Playhouse*, *The Defenders*, *Studio One*, *The Mod Squad*, *The Chrysler Theater*, *It Takes a Thief* and *The Name of the Game*. He is most remembered for his recurring role on the situation comedy *Hogan's Heroes* (CBS, 1965–1971), where he played the radio operator Sergeant Kinchloe.

## DIRECTING

In the process of creating a successful acting career, Dixon also created an opportunity for himself to direct. *Hogan's Heroes* became his graduate school in directing. He was on the set everyday for five seasons and observed more than a hundred shows. He talked with the editor and got to edit some film. He talked with the cameraman, Gordon Avil, who gave him his personal time on weekends when he found out that Dixon really wanted to learn about directing. Prior to Dixon's work on *Hogan's Heroes*, James Goldstone let him observe him directing the then-popular series *The Eleventh Hour*, a drama about two psychologists. He got into acting because, he says, "It was something I could do, but directing was always my ambition."

His first directing assignment came in theater at the Mark Taper Forum, where he directed an all-star cast in a benefit performance of Jean Genet's *The Blacks*. It got good reviews. One day Bill Cosby saw him on the studio lot and asked him when he was going to direct his (Cosby's) series. Subsequently he directed Bill Cosby's television special and, later, his first weekly television series, *Bill Cosby* (NBC, 1969–1971). In 1979 Dixon directed *Harris and Company*, the first network Black-cast drama. The program featured former football great Bernie Casey. In *The Complete Directory to Primetime Network TV Shows: 1946–Present*, the authors have said of this short-lived series, "an unusual attempt to build a dramatic series around a loving, caring Black family."

## IVAN DIXON PLAYERS

Dixon wants young people to remember that efforts in Hollywood to integrate the screen began with the early pioneers, such as Oscar Micheaux* and the Johnson (George and Noble) brothers. His own political and organizing efforts dating from 1961, as well as the Negro Actors for Action, helped to integrate television. Dixon is not forgotten at North Carolina Central University, where the Ivan Dixon Players (the resident student drama company named in his honor) continue to graduate aspiring young talent.

## THE FUTURE (1995)

Dixon has left filmmaking and is currently the owner of a radio station in Hawaii. The station KONI-FM has an adult contemporary format and is the number-one rated station on the island of Maui. It is a 24-hour, 50,000 watt station. Dixon enjoys the business world and would like to continue his efforts as an entrepreneur. He has followed his own conscience and made a difference. His goal for the future is continued success as an entrepreneur.

## FILMOGRAPHY

### Director

#### Feature Films

*Trouble Man*, 1972, 99 min., Twentieth Century Fox. Dixon wanted to do certain historic and positive-image films. *Trouble Man*, the first feature he directed, was a studio-initiated project.

I had to do something to prove I could make a (theatrical) film to go to backers and say, "Now, Twentieth Century Fox gave me a couple million dollars to do a film for them; maybe you can invest some money in me to do a film that I really want to do." During that time they were doing those Blaxploitation kind of things. The Blaxploitation genre consisted of a black male, with a certain physical strength, not much mental strength, beating up on "chuck." At the same time screwing everything that he could. There was a lot of open sex and violence in these films. That was the key. They made a lot of money. They appealed to the prurient interests of the young Black audience at the time. The part that was the key to drawing Black audiences was the violence toward "chuck," because that's what a lot of people were feeling very strongly at that time. And not so much in a covered-up manner anymore, because of the sixties and what was going on in the sixties.

This anger and this bitterness was being felt by a lot of people, and it was coming out. It was time to let it come out and be uncovered and be seen. In the film *Shaft*, when Richard Roundtree hits the guy and knocks him through the window, Black males cheered. I understood all that. That's what was very appealing about all those films at the time: Melvin Van Peebles's* film, *Sweet Sweetback's . . .* (1971); the Black woman's films, *Coffy* (1973) and several others like it; the Black superheroes, *Black Samson* (1974), etc. *Trouble Man* was written by John D.F. Black, the same guy who wrote *Shaft*. He left MGM, the producers of *Shaft*, and wanted to do another *Shaft* kind of film to make another killing for himself. They hired me to make the film.

It featured Robert Hooks and has an excellent and very "listenable" score by the late Marvin Gaye.

I couldn't make it like they wanted it made. I couldn't make the sex scenes. When we auditioned for the Black female lead, a number of ladies made me extremely proud when they refused to do it because of the sex in the script. Those ladies came in and very strongly defended themselves and their own dignity. On the other hand, those ladies never did any or very few films. The people who really stand for something are the ones who are really destroyed by this business in many respects. Those people who are whores in another sense, or even sophisticated and sneaky whores—both males and females in this racket—are the ones who seem to make it, in terms of making a good deal of cash. None of the Blacks in this business have any economic security. It is our own fault. That has to do with our inability to do our own films and reach our own audience.

*The Spook Who Sat by the Door*, 1973, 102 min., United Artists. After Dixon's earlier film experience, he decided he wanted to direct a film based on material he chose. He chose the then best-selling novel *The Spook Who Sat by the Door* by Sam Greenlee. Dixon and Greenlee co-produced the film; Greenlee wrote the script and Dixon directed. Dixon said, "If you're capable of making a film, that's no chore. That's a wonderful experience to have." In terms of this film, "You couldn't believe the obstacles that were put in our way." He raised the initial capital of $750,000 from friends and business associates and got the movie started. United Artists put up money to complete the film and took control of it. The film was poorly distributed and made no money. When discussing *The Spook . . .* he said, "I got to do one film that showed where my mind was." He regards the distribution process for theatrical features as being as treacherous as a minefield.

> They (distributors) will make deals when you've got something that appeals to them, and that's understandable. But they will not support something that they feel kind of awkward about.

He cited a film by Charles Burnett,* *To Sleep with Anger.* He described this as another community-based film that did not receive adequate or appropriate distribution.

> There is a lot in that film that distributors don't understand, don't like, are afraid of. . . . They don't feel that they ought to support it because it appears to be running against their grain, philosophically, socially. So they kind of avoid it. It is not all their fault. This film was running in a local movie house and the Black audience was not there. The Black audience also has a certain kind of responsibility to the filmmaker who is trying to do something that is really meaningful to them. Friends said they went to see the film and two people were in the audience. On the other hand, films that run against the Black grain of middle-class Black standards get protested. But when you go to see the film, the theater is full. It's crazy, but it's really true. The distributors don't know how to deal with a serious Black film anyway. The young filmmakers coming along, if nothing else, make what I tried to do valid.

*The Spook . . .* stands as a staunch political, no-holds-barred, positive Black cinema achievement. It takes a stand for Black Nationalism by force. A Black man after much brown-nosing and resistance wins admittance to the CIA. He toms for five years to learn all he can. He then goes back to the Black community, mentally and physically ready. He trains a street gang into an effective guerrilla army strong enough to take on the police and the army and rob banks with cool efficiency. A startlingly militant film, made in the height of the move by major studios to push Black films of any ilk; a positive affirmation of the strength of unity.

A scene of great poignancy is one in which a biracial brother makes an impassioned speech for all biracial people that leaves no room for compromise:

> Cause we is all niggas' man, jus' yella' thas' all, we is all niggas', and some nigga' blacker'n' me is gon' kill me for my part in this, so um' ready to give my life man cause it's all our struggle.

The film is a valuable primer on Black cinema politics, post–civil rights sixties, and on Black unity. It is considered by many as one of the best albeit little-seen and hard-to-find films of Black cinema.

> Of all the over two hundred shows (films and television) I have directed, this is the film I am most proud of having done. There are only a couple of things of over thirty-five years in this business that I am sincerely

proud of. *Nothing But a Man* as an actor and *The Spook . . .* as a director. Like most directors of episodic television, we do a lot of shows. I've made a very good living in episodic television as a director. But to do something that's meaningful and fulfilling—that's totally different.

His work on this film and the resultant conflict with the United Artists parent company, Transamerica, found Dixon unemployed and unemployable for a time. His friend Cleavon Little subsequently helped him get work as a director after interceding on his behalf with producers of *The Waltons*. He felt some of his strongest work in series television was in this series, "because this middle-class southern White family was similar in their lifestyle and values to my own." He later directed over a dozen shows in the nine-season hit series.

### Episodic Television

*A-Team*, NBC; *Airwolf*, CBS; *Apple's Way*, CBS; *Baa Baa Black Sheep*, NBC; *Bionic Woman*, ABC; *Bill Cosby Show*, NBC; *Bret Maverick*, NBC; *Delvecchio*, CBS; *Downtown*, CBS; *Eddie Capra Mysteries*, NBC; *Get Christie Love*, ABC; *Greatest American Hero*, ABC; *Hardy Boys*, ABC; *Harris and Company*, NBC; *Hawaiian Heat*, ABC; *Houston Knights*, CBS; *In the Heat of the Night*, NBC; *Julia*, NBC; *Khan*, CBS; *Legmen*, NBC; *Magnum P.I.*, CBS; *McCloud*, NBC; *Mod Squad*, ABC; *The Nancy Drew Mysteries*, ABC; *Nichols*, NBC; *Palmerstown, U.S.A.*, CBS; *Palms Precinct*, CBS; *Richie Brockleman*, NBC; *Righteous Apples*, PBS; *Rockford Files*, NBC; *Room 222*, NBC; *Scarecrow and Mrs. King*, CBS; *Shaft*, CBS; *Snoops*, CBS; *Starsky and Hutch*, ABC; *Tales of the Golden Monkey*, ABC; *Ten Speed and Brownshoe*, ABC; *Trapper John, M.D.*, CBS; *The Waltons*, CBS; *Women of Brewster Place*, ABC; *Wonder Woman*, CBS.

Dixon feels that in terms of episodic television,

> as a director, for your show to be considered for an Emmy, you have to submit that show for an Emmy. I just don't believe in that. I believe that if I've got to say, "I think this is worth an Emmy," then what is the award about? Is it a contest between me and the other people? I don't agree with that philosophy. If the producers and the Academy see a show and it's well directed and worthy of an award, then they should put it up for an award. I've never submitted for an award. You have to do it yourself. They don't self-nominate for the Oscars.

### Television Movies

*Perry Mason: The Case of the Shooting Star*, NBC; *Love Is Not Enough*, NBC; *Percy and Thunder*, TNT.

### Television Specials

*Bill Cosby Special*, NBC; *Counter Attack: Crime in America*, ABC; *Frederick Douglass*, ABC; *Sty of the Blind Pig*, PBS.

## BIO-CRITICAL REVIEW

"A noble pioneer who on more than one occasion has plowed new ground in his fight for a more humanistic and realistic portrayal of blacks in movies, a struggle that has contributed significantly to a turn-around in the severe stereotyping of blacks in films."—Black Filmmakers Hall of Fame, *Program Catalogue*, Inductee Essay

## AWARDS

Black Filmmakers Hall of Fame, Inductee, 1980

Friends of the Black Emmy Nominees, Black Pioneer Award (first recipient as director), 1980

*Car Wash*
  NAACP Image Award (actor), 1969

*Final War of Ollie Winter*
  Emmy Award Nomination, Best Actor in a Dramatic Special, 1967

*Hogan's Heroes*
  NAACP Image Award, Best Actor, 1969

*Magnum, P.I.*
  NAACP Image Award, Director, 1984

*Nothing But a Man*
  First Negro Arts Festival, Dakar, Senegal, Best Actor, 1967

*The Spook Who Sat by the Door*
  NAACP Image Award, Director, 1974; Producer, 1974

*Trouble Man*
  NAACP Image Award, Director, 1972

## MEMBERSHIPS

Academy of Motion Picture Arts and Sciences

Academy of Motion Pictures, Executive Committee of Foreign Films

Black Filmmakers Hall of Fame

Directors Guild of America

Directors Guild of America, Western Council

Screen Actors Guild of America

## SOURCES

Interview by George Hill and Spencer Moon, January 1990; follow-up interview, Spencer Moon, May 1995.

Brooks, Tim, and Earle Marsh. *The Complete Directory to Primetime Network TV Shows: 1946–Present*. New York: Ballantine Books, 1992.

*Program Catalogue*. Oakland, CA: Black Filmmakers Hall of Fame, 1980.

# BILL DUKE

## BACKGROUND

When you first meet Bill Duke, you are taken by his 6-foot, 4-inch domineering presence and his demeanor. If you recall his film work, where he has portrayed a variety of forceful characters, then you are struck by the contrast between those characters and Duke as a person. He is soft-spoken and gentle, in contrast to his imposing muscular frame.

Truly a gentle giant, Duke was the first member of his family to go to college. His parents had hoped for a medical profession for their son, so he enrolled in a program to study medicine and also took a speech and drama class. After a year, he knew this was where he wanted to be. Duke's undergraduate study of acting was under the tutelage of Lloyd Richards, one of the first Black directors in television. Richards was at Boston University when he worked with Duke. Richards, who currently heads the Yale drama department, helped Bill get into New York University and obtain his first acting job in the Negro Ensemble Company. Duke acknowledges Richards as his mentor.

Duke's parents worried that he had chosen a career where the odds of success for Black people were stacked against him. He describes the many years he spent learning and practicing his craft as lean.

## DIRECTING

Eventually Duke moved from acting to directing. He says he never earned more than $3,000 in a year, including unemployment, while learning his craft in New York. He has directed more than thirty off-Broadway plays and worked for some well-known producers and theater companies. Among them are Joe Papp, Woody King Jr., the Mark Taper Forum and the Los Angeles Actors Theater. His move to Los Angeles resulted in work as an actor, teacher, writer and director. Duke taught acting for more than a decade; now it is a hobby. He has been featured in over two dozen films.

As a disciplined actor and director, part of his focus comes from practicing and teaching transcendental meditation. His vegetarian diet is a part of that discipline. Duke has taken a Sanskrit concept—*yagya*, which means "all work done in the name and spirit of evolution"—as the name for his production company, Yagya Productions. In 1983 a nearly fatal airplane crash changed his perspective on what is important in life; he realized he needed to change his focus from the *transitory* to the *immediate moment*. As an extension of his deep understanding about what is important, he has started his own foundation, the Reach Back Foundation. Through it, young people get to apprentice on his films.

Duke also understands the nature of the business and how it affects Black people. One of his favorite quotes is from Malcolm X: "No matter how good a football player you are, if the game is baseball you better have a bat."

Duke has probably directed more episodic television than many directors in Hollywood. He admires Sidney Poitier, Paul Robeson and the director Frank Capra. He also enjoys the renewed kinship and camaraderie he has found with other Black directors, young and veteran alike (including the Hudlin brothers* and Melvin Van Peebles*) and the sense that, as he puts it, "if they don't stand together, there is no way they're going to survive." He believes Black directors could very easily be "the flavor of the year." He is concerned about what's going to happen to Black directors; he sees the need for them to have some understanding of the industry. He does think there is a small glimmer, something there now that is beginning to grow.

## FILMOGRAPHY

### Director

#### *Short Subjects*

*The Hero*, 1979.

#### *Feature Films*

*A Rage in Harlem*,** 1991, 110 min., 35mm, color, Miramax Films. The interview with Duke came at a time when he had completed production of his first theatrically released feature film, *A Rage in Harlem*. Duke insisted that 90 percent of the crew have minority heads of departments—a first for many. He argued that if they don't get an opportunity, how can they become heads of departments?

Duke's excitement about his new film was evident. He described the director as being like a symphony conductor, the script like sheet music. "So you have to hire the best actors to get the most out of the script." There is a commonality in his vision as a director, although he is not always able to execute it. He tries not to let his training get in the way of an organic approach to directing. What he chooses to talk about is an expression of his humanity. "Black people have to talk about their humanity. There are so many attempts to dehumanize Black people." He wants to make films about the human condition that transcend racial stereotypes, films that speak about the nobility of the human spirit.

We asked Duke to describe the greatest joy of having his first theatrically released film. His immediate response was the cast: having people do the film because they care for him as a director and as a person. People took salary cuts to do this film. Without the support the cast gave him, he said, he never could have made this film. Danny Glover came to the set a week before having surgery on both knees and both feet; he sat down in his scenes because he was in such pain walking. Robin Givens, Duke said, is one of the most giving actresses he had ever worked with. He said it is rare to work with an ingenue actress who is serious about the craft, and she was. He didn't think that people understood that actors go inside to bring up "stuff that people go to their psychiatrist to forget. Actors hurt themselves to give you a person you believe on that screen."

The film was produced with a $9 million budget. It presents two parallel love stories between opposites; it features Robin Givens, Forest Whitaker, Gregory Hines and Danny Glover. The film is set in Harlem of the fifties.

Chester Himes, one of the most popular Black authors to be translated to screen, wrote the original novel. This is the third Chester Himes story to reach the screen. The first two were *Cotton Comes to Harlem*** (1970) and *Come Back Charleston Blue*** (1972). The former was directed by Ossie Davis, and the latter by Mark Warren.*

Gregory Hines said in an *Ebony* magazine article that he grew up in Harlem in the fifties, so he knew what Chester Himes was writing about. Himes was a great writer, and it is rare that a vehicle like this comes along. The film has two messages: Black love is beautiful, and Black women are beautiful. The film was shot in Cincinnati during the summer of 1990. The contemporary section of Cincinnati was chosen because it most closely resembled Harlem of the fifties. The director and stars spoke with *Arts and Entertainment*, a cable television magazine show, about the film. Hines remembers being 10 years old in 1956, the time frame of the film. He remembers how exciting it was as a child to be in Harlem. It was a place where everything was seemingly beginning, where everybody came. An interesting period and an extremely interesting location. This is the first Black-cast film shot in Cincinnati, and people from the Black neighborhood were utilized as extras.

*Deep Cover,*** 1992, 112 min. 35mm, color, New Line Cinema. An action thriller featuring Laurence Fishburne as an undercover cop who uses a drug-dealing attorney (Jeff Goldblum) to bring down a major supplier. A tough, suspenseful story. Fishburne and Goldblum deliver excellent performances. Clarence Williams III is a standout as part of the supporting cast.

*Cemetery Club,*** 1993, 107 min., 35mm color, Touchstone Pictures. Featuring Olympia Dukakis, Ellen Burstyn, Diane Ladd, Danny Aiello, Lanie Kazan and Bernie Casey.

*Sister Act 2: Back in the Habit*,** 1993, 100 min., 35mm color, Touchstone Pictures. Featuring Whoopi Goldberg, Kathy Najimy, Barnard Hughes, James Coburn, Maggy Smith and Mary Wickes. A sequel to *Sister Act*,** 1992. These two films show that Duke is emerging from the Black-director-as-director-of-Black-genre-films-only syndrome. Both films are a mix of comedy and drama.

### Television Movies

*The Killing Floor*,** 1984, 118 min., color, Orion Home Video. A compelling story of a Black sharecropper who leaves the South for work in Chicago. He finds work in the slaughterhouse along with bad working conditions and low wages. His efforts at union organizing, the end of World War I and racial tension lead to violence. This film was not picked up by a theatrical distributor, despite being chosen for the Critics' Week at the 1985 Cannes Film Festival. The cast featured Damien Leake, Alfre Woodard, Clarence Felder and Moses Gunn.

*Johnnie Mae Gibson: F.B.I.*, 1986, 100 min., color, CBS. The dramatic story of the *first* Black female FBI agent. It is based on Ms. Gibson's true story. Featuring Lynn Whitfield, Howard Rollins Jr. and Richard Lawson.

*The Meeting*, 1989, 90 min., color, PBS *American Playhouse*. A dramatic rendering of a fictional meeting between Martin Luther King Jr. and Malcolm X. Featuring Dick Anthony Williams as Malcolm X, a role he had played in the NBC television movie *King* (1978). *The Meeting* also features Jason Bernard as Dr. King.

*A Raisin in the Sun*, 1989, 210 min., color, PBS *American Playhouse*. This is the 30th Anniversary presentation of the historic play by the late Lorraine Hansberry. The original play was the *first* play written by an African American woman to be produced for the Broadway stage. It is as relevant today as it was yesterday. It was the first Broadway production to focus on the Black family and become a success. This rendering has some scenes that were not part of the original production; they address African nationalism, Black pride, ghetto conditions and racial incidents. They were considered too militant for the 1959 theatrical presentation. Robert Nemiroff was executive producer, and Hansberry's husband carefully supervised the overall aspects of production for television. Featuring Esther Rolle, Danny Glover, Starletta DuPois, Kim Yancey, Lou Ferguson, Stephen Henderson, Kimble Joyner, Helen Martin, Joseph C. Phillips, Ron O.J. Pearson, Charles Watts and John Fiedler.

### Episodic Television

*Amen*, NBC; *Berrengers*, NBC; *Cagney and Lacey*, CBS; *Call to Glory*, ABC; *Crime Story*, NBC; *Dallas*, CBS; *Emerald Point, N.A.S.*, CBS; *Falcon Crest*, ABC; *Fame*, MGM, synd.; *Flamingo Road*, ABC; *Helltown*, NBC; *Hill Street Blues*, NBC; *Hunter*, NBC; *Knots Landing*, CBS; *MacGruder and Loud*, ABC; *Matlock*, NBC; *Starman*, CBS; *Trauma Center*, ABC; *Twilight Zone*, CBS.

### Actor

### Selected Films

*Menace II Society*, 1993; *Bird on a Wire*, 1990; *Street of No Return*, 1989; *Action Jackson*, 1988; *No Mans Land*, 1987; *Predator*, 1987; *Commando*, 1985; *American Gigolo*, 1980; *Car Wash*, 1976.

*Selected Television*

*Benson* (ABC); *Charlie's Angels* (ABC); *Kojak* (CBS); *Mannix* (CBS); *Palmerstown, USA* (CBS); *Starsky and Hutch* (ABC).

## BIO-CRITICAL REVIEW

*Cemetery Club.* "Duke has now become a director to watch in Hollywood, a director of more than Black experience films."—Tim Hughes, *Wave Newspaper Group*

*Deep Cover.* "Director Bill Duke maintains a powerful momentum without rushing past the picture's cruel truths and despairing humor."—Julie Saloman, *Wall Street Journal*

———. "Duke's masterful handling of dialogue gives individual scenes a fresh, off-hand intensity."—Carter Harris, *Bay Guardian*

———. "Says something real about the times, and I suspect it's a picture that will last."—Mick LaSalle, *San Francisco Chronicle*

*The Killing Floor.* "Impressive drama. Above average."—*Leonard Maltin's Movie and Video Guide, 1995*

*The Meeting.* "A fascinating exercise in speculative theater, featuring stellar performances."—Howard Rosenberg, *Los Angeles Times*

*A Rage in Harlem.* "Meets one's expectations for the comedy and drama of black American life that Himes wrote with such panache. Duke keeps his cast sufficiently keyed up to give the film a lively authenticity."—Armond White, *Emerge*

*A Raisin in the Sun.* "Every bit as accomplished and perhaps more vivid than its theatrical counterpart."—Sylvie Drake, *Los Angeles Times*

———. "Even though the play is programmatic, the themes are handled with delicacy and poise."—David Gritten, *Los Angeles Herald Examiner*

*Sister Act 2.* "Bill Duke, who has directed much smarter films, is less at fault than the Up with People script."—Caryn James, *New York Times*

## SELECTED AWARDS

*The Hero*
   American Film Institute, Best Young Director, 1979
   Houston Film Festival, Gold Award, 1980

## BILL DUKE PUBLICATIONS

Bill Duke, *Heroes: A Black Family Picture Album* (New York: Thunder Mouth Press, 1993).

*Bill Duke's 24 Hours L.A.*, n.p., n.d.

## EDUCATION

Boston University, B.A., theater

New York University, Tisch School of the Arts, M.F.A.


## MEMBERSHIPS

American Film Institute, Board of Directors, Alumni Association


## SOURCES

Interview by Spencer Moon and George Hill, January 1991.


### Books

Maltin, Leonard, ed. *Leonard Maltin's Movie and Video Guide, 1995*. New York: Penguin, 1994.


### Newspapers and Magazines

"A Rage in Harlem," *Ebony*, January 1991.

Drake, Sylvie. "Raisin in the Sun," *Los Angeles Times*, February 1, 1989, p. 22.

Gritten, David. "Raisin Retains Its Power on Playhouse," *Los Angeles Herald Examiner*, February 1, 1989, p. 21.

Harris, Carter. "Deep Cover," *San Francisco Bay Guardian*, April 15, 1992, p. 41.

Hughes, Tim. "The Cemetery Club," *Wave Newspaper Group*, April 7, 1993, p. E1.

James, Caryn. "Answering a Call for Help from the Convent," *New York Times*, December 10, 1993, p. B7.

LaSalle, Mick. "Cop Thriller Set in Surreal Sleaze," *San Francisco Chronicle*, April 15, 1992, p. E1.

Modderno, Craig. "Two Hats," *Movieline*, April 1990, p. 29.

Rosenberg, Howard. "Raisin in the Sun," *Los Angeles Times*, May 3, 1989, p. 21.

Rugoff, Ralph. "Actor-director Bill Duke," *Premiere*, July 1990, p. 47–48.

Saloman, Julie. "A Cop Thriller," *Wall Street Journal*, April 16, 1992, p. 23.

Sorrell, H. L. "A Triple Threat Talent," *Players*, May 1991, p. 20–23.

White, Armond. "Survivin' Uptown: A Comedic Look at What It Took," *Emerge*, March 1991, p. 47.


### Other

*Arts and Entertainment*, A&E Cable-TV, 1991.

*Internet Movie Database*, 1996.

# JAMAA FANAKA

## WHAT'S IN A NAME?

Walter Gordon, the son of Robert Lee Gordon and Beatrice Gordon, revealed why he became Jamaa Fanaka:

> I had seen a film called *Cooley High* directed by Michael Schultz,* who
> is a Black person. But because of his name I thought he was Jewish; I
> didn't know until later that he was Black. When I found out that fact,
> I was even more excited and thrilled about the film and the filmmaker.
> I wanted to make sure that nobody would make the mistake of thinking
> my film was by a White person. That was what spurred me at UCLA
> to change my name to Jamaa Fanaka. As a matter of fact, my under-
> graduate degree has "Walter Gordon" on it and my graduate degree
> has "Jamaa Fanaka" on it.

The origin and meaning of his name came through his university studies.

> I went to the African language department and got a Swahili dictionary.
> *Jamaa* means "togetherness," "family" and "cohesiveness." *Fanaka*
> means "success" and "progress." Through togetherness we shall pro-
> gress and succeed.

## BACKGROUND

Few African American filmmakers have directed six feature films in less
than a decade. Fanaka talked about how he came to filmmaking.

Jamaa Fanaka

When I was growing up, I loved films. I never even thought about being a filmmaker. My original gift and love was writing. I used the G.I. Bill and went to Compton College. I used my grades and experience and got a scholarship to UCLA, where I was enrolled to study script-writing. Regardless of your study in the UCLA film school, you have to make a film called Project 1—a Super 8mm film. My film was a takeoff on the Faust legend. It was well received at UCLA.

After that experience, the directing bug hit me. My Project 2 was a feature film. They said at school, "That cat is crazy. He's got to be crazy; the average Project 2 is about 10 minutes." I was at a university; I was seeking knowledge. The best way to learn about making a feature film is to make a feature. It's about gaining confidence. No matter how good or how bad a finished feature film is, the fact that you make it is an accomplishment.

Once something is articulated on film, it will live forever. I can imagine in the year 2550 they will look at Black cinema circa 1970–1990. The one who is on top now may not be seen that way by future generations. Vincent Van Gogh died on the bottom, and now his work is heralded. I would love to see what happens five hundred years from now, when they look at my features and the work of my contemporary Black filmmakers.

## THE INDUSTRY

When probed about his thoughts on the industry, Fanaka had one pet peeve especially.

I think the shame of this industry is the Indigo Films project. Columbia Studios gave Richard Pryor and his Indigo Films company $40 million and after two years they gave the money back, saying they couldn't find any Black filmmakers. They had the power and money to make any film they wanted, and they didn't make one. Jim Brown (athlete/ actor/activist) was about to make a film and they fired him. I can't believe we didn't rise up in arms over this. That's unforgivable.

Fanaka also felt that Black people in business need to gain the confidence of their own community.

For many years when Black people opened businesses, people would say, "Where is the White man that he's fronting for?" We have become our own man, in many respects. That's the only way we're going to get around those kind of hoaxes like Indigo.

Fanaka has other concerns about opportunities, or seeming opportunities.

> Always be skeptical of anything that they're going to give us. They
> will say we're having this contest or this government program. Black
> people will come up with these great ideas, and they steal them. They
> mix it up with this and mix it up with that so it's partly disguised. The
> average Black person, even when they steal ideas from us, is so afraid
> to do anything. They have us afraid of so-called blackballing, when
> we're blackballed already and don't even know it.

## UNIQUENESS

When asked to describe what makes him different as a filmmaker, Fanaka
spoke candidly:

> The only thing that makes me similar to other Black filmmakers is our
> color. I'm just so proud to be of the same race as people like Spike
> Lee,* Robert Townsend,* Charles Lane and the Hudlin brothers.*
> We're going to take over film, like we took over music. Spike Lee is
> the Jackie Robinson of filmmakers. There were a lot of good film-
> makers before Spike Lee, and now there are a whole lot after. Just like
> there were many great Black baseball players before Jackie Robinson
> and many great Black baseball players who came after Jackie. But he
> was the one who got us recognized, and look at how well we're doing
> now in baseball, basketball and football. There was a guy named John-
> son in the old Negro leagues who was a slugger. I consider myself a
> slugger. I just want to be myself. It is very difficult to be yourself once
> you get amalgamated into this society. They start to pigeonhole you
> and predict you. I love my independence. I'm individualistic. I want to
> be my own man. I like these new guys, however. You can't argue with
> success; a lot of White people don't like what Spike Lee has done and
> is doing.

## ADVICE FOR ASPIRANTS

> Always have the next script ready. Always have one ready that you want
> to do real bad. You don't want to be in a position of having a hit film
> and they say, "What do you want to do next?" and you stutter for 15
> minutes. Be right on it like Spike (Lee) is. I love that in him.

## ACTIVISM (1995)

Fanaka's work to make change and create a more receptive environment
in Hollywood for himself and other Black filmmakers led him to found a
new group.

About a year and a half ago I helped to co-found a group called the African American Steering Committee of the Directors Guild of America (DGA). The reality is that people generally believe that African American filmmakers have made giant strides. In fact, the exact opposite is the case. We have made all of the signatories of the DGA agreement obligated to submit quarterly statements. These statements tell us about every job opening in the industry, breaking down the figures on who filled the job and what the race is of each person. Those figures, submitted quarterly, reflect that we have lost ground in the last ten years. We have one agreement at the Disney Studios for a director training program for people of color. I would prefer to be a lot more aggressive than we are.

People are afraid, and rightly so. The industry has the power to blackball you. They have a list at the networks, and if you're not on that approved list of directors you can't get work. The only person to go public with that list was Sheldon Leonard, a well-known White producer (*The Danny Thomas Show*, *The Andy Griffith Show*, *Gomer Pyle, U.S.M.C.*, *The Dick Van Dyke Show*, *I Spy*, to name a few of his many hits). He went to CBS with his agent and pitched the idea of the subsequently produced *I Spy* reunion television movie. He said he had an Oscar-winning writer to do the script; they pulled out their list and said he wasn't on their list of acceptable writers. This list has been in existence for ten years and everybody knows about it. Sheldon Leonard is the first and only person to go on record that he suffered as a result of this list.

## FILMOGRAPHY

### Director/Producer

### *UCLA Undergraduate Student Work (1971–1973)*

*A Day in the Life of Willie Faust, or Death on the Installment Plan*, 20 min., 8mm film.

> My Willie Faust sold his soul to the devil for drugs. I wrote, produced, directed and starred in this film, with my wife and daughter playing the wife and daughter of the fictional character.

*Welcome Home, Brother Charles*, 105 min., 35mm, color, Crown International Pictures (retitled and released as *Soul Vengeance*). A returning Black Vietnam vet is outraged by how he finds life back in the hood. Fanaka described his first feature-length work: "It's an art film, really."

### *UCLA Graduate Thesis Film*

*Emma Mae*,** 1976, 100 min., 35mm, color (alternate title, *Black Sister's Revenge*). A teen-age Black girl from Mississippi comes to live with her cousins in Los Angeles.

Emma Mae (Jerri Hayes) goes from a young girl with just plain common sense to one who learns the ways of the street. She changes her family and her community. When she finds her true self through sacrifice, she also learns she has talent and the ability to lead and organize. Under her leadership an unproductive community becomes a productive one with a community-run business, a car wash. A politically and socially sensitive film on what Black people can do to transform themselves and their lives and community with a little grit, sweat and togetherness. The performances are uneven, but the story is well told and stands the test of time.

> My graduate thesis was another feature made with grants from UCLA Black studies, the American Film Institute and the Rockefeller Foundation. The finished negative cost about $250,000. I'm very proud of this work. It was based on an older cousin I grew up with down in Mississippi whose real name was Daisy Lee. I grew up in Jackson, an urban area. Daisy Lee lived in a rural area. She would stay with us during summer months when we were children. She defended my brother and me from harm and could beat boys her own age. I liked that feeling of family and protection. It became archetypal in my mind, and *Emma Mae* is the resultant script. Daisy Lee is dead now. She'll now live forever, thanks to this film. This film is about the maturation of a young woman and her love for self and family.

### Feature Films

*Penitentiary I*, 1979, 99 min., Gross Distributing.

*Penitentiary II*, 1982, 103 min., MGM/UA.

*Penitentiary III*, 1987, 91 min., Cannon.

Leon Isaac Kennedy is Martell ("Too Sweet") Gordone in all three films. All three are 35mm, color.

> The *Penitentiary* films are about the fact that no matter what we're faced with, each individual has the possibility to rise above his circumstances. I tried to make a different film with each one of these, although I had some of the same characters in each film. I tried to put them in certain situations and develop themes that were different. Too Sweet (the protagonist in each film), the allegorical character, represents the best in everyman and how he reacts to abnormal situations. He is reacting normally to an abnormal situation. *Penitentiary III* was well received critically, and it did well overseas in terms of box office. It was not, however, a bona fide hit in the United States. It shows that no matter what, I know what I'm doing when it comes to making a film. As an example, Robert Townsend's film *The Five Heartbeats*, a film I love, was a box office failure. Now that doesn't mean it was a bad film. Just because a film is a financial success doesn't mean that it's a good one, either. I've grown with each film I've made.

*Street Wars*,** 1992, 94 min., 35mm, color.

> This movie came about because my two favorite types of films as a kid were gangster films and World War II aerial dog-fight films. I loved

Bogart and Cagney, but my favorite was John Garfield. When I compare, say, a James Dean to Garfield, he seems affected. I think Garfield was a tremendously strong actor. His acting technique showed the dichotomy between right and wrong and good and bad was so black and white. All Black people love gangster films. We introduced the word "Bogart" as a verb. We like him so much, it became part of our language. "Man, what are you trying to do, Bogart me?" So I decided to combine the gangster genre with the aerial dog-fight genre. I thought this would be something that had never been done before—a Black gangster film with a ghetto air force.

My parents invested their life savings in *Penitentiary I*. When it was a hit, they made a lot of money. They said, "Look, the money we made on *Penitentiary* you can use to make *Street Wars*. We're with you all the way, son." They celebrated a fiftieth anniversary; I'm so proud of my parents.

The story I shot is about a gangster who considers himself very smart. He also knows behind every great fortune there is a great crime. We as Black people have always taken negatives and made positives out of them anyway. This young gangster sends his younger brother to one of the best schools in the region. Using ultra-light aircraft while in school, our hero learns to fly. The young brother during a summer break before entering West Point visits his older brother. His older brother while he is visiting is killed right in front of him. So the challenge is whether to take over the legitimate business that his brother started with drug money, or go on to West Point. He decides to teach the loyal and straight employees how to use ultra-light aircraft armed with Uzis to attack the dope and crack houses in the community—a ghetto air force. The public loves this; the younger brother gets the girl and flies off into the sunset. It's a drama, it says something about the milieu. Each film has its own validity. This film is one I refused not to make. This film shows a lot more hope.

The dues I paid from making *Penitentiary I* to *Street Wars* have made me a better person. I think I'm a mature radical. They say those who have the gold, rule. I accept that, but I won't accept the tyranny of the gold. When it gets tyrannical, I'm going to stand up—except now I'm going to do it with a lot more diplomacy. There is nothing I ever did on planet Earth that I'm ashamed of. I'm not saying everything I ever did was good; I'm not saying I didn't make mistakes. If I was going to be ashamed of it, I didn't do it.

Fanaka talked in a subsequent interview (in 1995) about the distribution for *Street Wars*:

*Street Wars* is one of my biggest disappointments. As a matter of fact, I have a lawsuit going right now. The distributor released the wrong version. They distributed a work-in-progress version. I called the mistake to their attention at least four months prior to the release of the film. They said it was too late, they couldn't make changes. I said it's not too late. They ignored me and released a version with inferior sound and other technical problems inherent in a work-in-progress print. Despite that, it could have done better had they released the version I wanted. It has only had one national theatrical release, and that was in St. Louis. It is now on home video, still with the wrong version.

## BIO-CRITICAL REVIEW

*Penitentiary I.* "One of the most expressive movies of the year. His work transcends the primitivism of the sex and violence seen in his film."—Tom Allen, *Village Voice*

————. "Too vital and personal to be a copy of anything."—Kevin Thomas, *Los Angeles Times*

George Hill and James Robert Parish, *Black Action Films*

*Penitentiary III.* "The underlying theme of achieving one's goal by focusing on one's inner strength creates a totally incongruous juxtaposition. The film leaves you wondering, as it also entertains and there is a very honest message."—George Hill and Spencer Moon, *Blacks in Hollywood*

## EDUCATION

UCLA, B.A. (summa cum laude), motion picture and television

UCLA, M.F.A., theater arts

## AWARDS AND GRANTS

American Film Institute grant, 1973

Ford Foundation grant, 1970

Mayor of Los Angeles, Hon. Tom Bradley, Commendation to Jamaa Fanaka for his dedicated efforts and outstanding contribution as a writer, director and producer, 1982

New York State Council for the Arts grant, 1976

Rockefeller Foundation grant, 1971

UCLA Black Studies grant, 1975

UCLA Chancellor's grant, 1974

## FILM FESTIVALS

American Film Institute/Los Angeles Film Festival, 1993

Cannes Film Festival—Director's Fortnight, 1982

d'Amiens Film Festival, Amiens, France, 1980

Florence International Film Festival, Italy, 1985

Milan Film Festival, Italy, 1977

New American Filmmakers, Los Angeles, 1979

Rotterdam International Film Festival, Holland, 1986

San Francisco International Film Festival, 1981

## SOURCES

Interview by Spencer Moon and George Hill, March 1991; follow-up interview, Spencer Moon, July 1995.

Hill, George, and James Robert Parish. *Black Action Films.* Jefferson, NC: McFarland, 1989.

Hill, George, and Spencer Moon. *Blacks in Hollywood: Five Favorable Years, 1987–1991*. Los Angeles: Daystar Publishing, 1992.

# CARL FRANKLIN

## BACKGROUND

Carl Franklin grew up in a tough neighborhood. His escape came through a scholarship to the University of California at Berkeley, playing football. After friends suggested drama as a way to fulfill an English requirement in college, he found an unexpected niche in drama. By the time he graduated, alumni suggested he try to pursue his acting ambitions in New York. He found work in both New York and Washington, D.C., in regional theater. His big break came when he began working with the New York Shakespeare Festival, which was run by Joseph Papp.

Franklin got his first work in film by accident. He accompanied a friend to an audition and found that he himself got work in the project instead of his friend. His screen debut was in the film *Five on the Black Hand Side* (1973), directed by the African American filmmaker Oscar Williams. After moving to Los Angeles, Franklin acted in and had recurring roles on several television series: *Caribe*, a police drama that featured Stacy Keach; *Fantastic Journey*, a science fiction series that featured Roddy McDowell; and *McLain's Law*, a police drama that featured James Arness.

## DIRECTING

The turning point from acting to directing came after Franklin felt a certain disillusionment with acting; he felt he had lost the killer instinct needed for auditions. In 1986 he was accepted into the American Film Institute master's program. Part of his apprenticeship in filmmaking included working for a time with the legendary filmmaker Roger Corman. Corman's low-budget, maverick style of filmmaking instilled certain values in Franklin's personal style of production.

## SELECTED FILMOGRAPHY

### Director

*Punk*, 1988, American Film Institute master's project. The story concerns a 9-year-old Black child from south central Los Angeles. The young child is not sure how to grow up to be a man. His mother, a single parent, is doing her best to help his development. The story takes a shocking turn when the young boy kills a child molester. Featuring Don Cheadle.

*Full Fathom Five*,** 1990, 82 min., 35mm, color, Concorde Films. A Roger Corman production.

*One False Move*,** 1992, 105 min., 35mm, b/w, IRS Releasing. A realistic thriller reminiscent of film noir. A trio (Michael Beach, Billy Bob Thornton and Cynda Williams) does a drug robbery, stealing a large quantity of cocaine and leaving murder and mayhem in their wake. On the run they are pursued by two Los Angeles detectives and a Southern sheriff. Featuring Bill Paxton, Cynda Williams, Billy Bob Thorton and Michael Beach. Budget was $2 million.

*Devil in a Blue Dress*,** 1995, 101 min., 35mm, color, Columbia Tristar. Based on series of books by Walter Moseley following one Ezekiel Rawlings. Moseley co-produced the film and Franklin wrote the screenplay, featuring Denzel Washington, Don Cheadle and Jennifer Beals. Very good action/drama set in the postwar forties.

### Television

*Laurel Avenue*,** 1993, 180 min., HBO Cable network miniseries. Contemporary drama that focuses on the realities of life in a Black American family. Honest and realistic, it is also entertaining and moving in its portrayal of a Black working-class family. Produced by Paul Aaron and Charles S. Dutton. Story was written by Paul Aaron and Michael Henry Brown, screenplay by Brown. Shot on location in Minneapolis, Minnesota. The program features Mary Alice and Mel Winkler.

## BIO-CRITICAL REVIEW

*Devil in a Blue Dress*. "More than a satisfying mystery. It's a fable about a Black man thrown into a white ocean and learning how to swim."—Mick LaSalle, *San Francisco Chronicle*

———. "A beautifully designed and acted period piece, fragrant with atmosphere and taut with uncertainty."—Paul Reidinger, *San Francisco Weekly*

*Laurel Avenue*. "Superbly acted by a cast of non-stars and tautly directed by Carl

Franklin, *Laurel Avenue* is an honest but not exploitive, affirmative without sappy television uplift."—Richard Zoglin, *Time*

———. "*Laurel Avenue* is a flavorful, moving and wonderfully acted drama spanning one weekend in the life of the Arnett family of St. Paul, Minnesota."—Joyce Millman, *San Francisco Chronicle*

———. "This is one family story that begs to be continued."—John J. O'Connor, *New York Times*

*One False Move.* "Franklin has enough sense to let the small detail matter as much as the big. What could have become a tense little low budget thriller thus becomes distinctly more than that."—Derek Malcolm, *Guardian Weekly*

———. "The movie is awfully good for what it is—an intelligent crime thriller that combines gritty, violent realism with the more stylized manner of the old *film noir*."—Julie Saloman, *Wall Street Journal*

———. "This new filmmaker could work well with other types of material and on a much more ambitious plane. Thanks to the thoughtfulness and promise he displays this time, he undoubtedly will."—Vincent Canby, *New York Times*

## EDUCATION

University of California, Berkeley, B.A., history and drama

American Film Institute, Los Angeles, M.F.A.

## SELECTED AWARDS

*One False Move*
  Independent Spirit Award, Best Director, 1993
  Los Angeles Times Critics Association, New Generation Award, 1993
  National Board of Review, Ten Best Films of 1992

## SOURCES

### Books

Brooks, Tim, and Earle Marsh. *The Complete Directory to Primetime Network TV Shows: 1946–Present.* New York: Ballantine Books, 1992.
Kendall, Steven D. *New Jack Cinema: Hollywood's African American Filmmakers.* Silver Springs, MD: J.L. Denser, 1994.

### Newspapers and Magazines

Correction. Maslin, Janet, "New Director Pits Dividends in Conventional Story," *New York Times,* July 17, 1992, p. B3.

LaSalle, Mick, "Denzel's Black and Blue Film Noir," *San Francisco Chronicle*, September 29, 1995, pp. C1, 12.

Linfield, Susie, "A False Move that Paid Off," *New York Times*, August 9, 1992, p. B3.

Malcolm, Derek, "Debut That Puts Not a Foot Wrong," *Guardian Weekly* (U.K.), April 18, 1993, p. 32.

Millman, Joyce, "HBO's Real World *Laurel Avenue* Avoids Cliches of Black TV Families," *San Francisco Chronicle*, July 9, 1993, p. D1 & D4.

O'Connor, John J., "Two-part Portrait of a Black Working Class Family," *New York Times*, July 9, 1993, p. B6.

Saloman, Julie, "An Intelligent Crime Thriller," *Wall Street Journal*, July 16, 1992, p. 32.

Zoglin, Richard, "No Easy Solutions Here," *Time*, July 12, 1993, p. 21.

# WENDELL FRANKLIN

## BACKGROUND

Wendell Gordon Franklin was born in 1916 to parents who were in show business. His mother was a performer in two of the leading traveling Black-cast musicals from the twenties, *Stepping High* and *Shuffle Along*. The stage was the most popular form of entertainment at that time, involving African Americans. Because of the nomadic lifestyle involved in touring shows like those mentioned, Franklin's parents let a couple who were friends adopt young Gordon. The couple owned and ran a hotel, a restaurant and a nightclub. So Mr. and Mrs. Henry James Franklin adopted Gordon when he was 2 years old and officially changed his name to Wendell Gordon Franklin. Later the Franklins hired young Wendell's mother as a nurse for him, a position she held until he was 7 years old. Franklin's mother died at a young age.

Because his adopted parents owned the Bronx Hotel in Los Angeles, Franklin was exposed to performers and music at an early age. The death of his adopted father by age 13 left him with deep remorse. Growing up, his classmates included the former mayor of Los Angeles, the Honorable Tom Bradley. (Later in Franklin's career, Mayor Bradley gave him a special recognition during the Directors Guild of America's Fiftieth Anniversary celebration. Bradley acknowledged that as kids he and Franklin had both had dreams as youngsters, and here they stood, having realized some of their dreams.)

## SKILLS DEVELOPED

Franklin's religious upbringing in the Black church provided opportunities for him to help organize and present programs for the community and family. Franklin remembered the early days of African American involvement in motion pictures. He recalls one Ben Carter, who became the first Black casting agent in Hollywood. If you were Black and wanted work as an extra in films, Carter was the man to know. Franklin also recalls going to Grauman's Chinese Theater in the thirties to see the opening for the film *Trader Horn* (1931). This film and its live pre-film stage show performance of costumed African Americans dancing wildly (the film was set in Africa) left a vivid impression on the teenage Franklin. He and other African Americans still had to sit in the segregated balcony.

Franklin grew up at a time when African Americans owned more than a dozen movie theaters in Los Angeles—unlike today, when the fact that the opening of former basketball star and AIDS activist Magic Johnson's multiplex cinemas was much heralded because it seemingly ushered in a new era of African American movie theater ownership. How quickly and conveniently our history is forgotten! In fact, from the thirties through the forties African Americans attended, owned and operated over four hundred theaters—not including those that allowed mixed patronage (Whites on the main floor, Blacks in the balcony). Just as the social economics of integration helped bring about the demise of race movies, it did the same to the need for Black-owned and -operated theaters.

Franklin worked as an extra in films in 1936. He saw his first live theater performance when the famed African American Lafayette Players repertory company traveled to Los Angeles from their home in New York City. Distinguished Lafayette Players included Evelyn Preer, Edward Thompson, Cleo Desmond and Clarence Muse. Preer later found fame as part of Oscar Micheaux's* repertory film company. Muse made films from the early sound era until the late seventies. He is remembered through the Clarence Muse Youth Award, presented by the Black Filmmakers Hall of Fame of Oakland, California. Cleo Desmond later provided the first serious study of theater for Franklin. Franklin also worked with a local radio deejay, Joe Adams, on KDAY-AM. This contact led to Franklin's first efforts at organizing and producing large performance events.

Franklin, Adams, Edward Deeson and Frank Jackson (the latter two were cosmetic and beauty entrepreneurs) rented the Philharmonic Auditorium and came up with the concept of doing a benefit for cancer research. They enlisted the aid of Walter Winchell, at the time a nationally known syndicated columnist, and produced the event to raise money for the Damon Runyon Memorial Fund for Cancer Research. They called their event "Dream in Silhouette" and had Redd Foxx, Lionel Hampton, Benny Carter and the Hall Johnson Choir as a stellar cast. The initial benefit was such a success that they later produced several more performances in and around Los Angeles, including a version that came to the Oakland, California, Civic Auditorium.

## THE PLUNGE INTO SHOW BUSINESS

Marriage, the birth of his son and military service put Franklin through the paces of serious responsibility. He continued his talent for organizing live performances in the service. He produced entertainment shows for the servicemen, both Black and White, despite the lack of integration in the armed forces. While in the service he attended college in Virginia, studied drama and became serious about show business. After completing his service and getting a divorce, he went to New York to try his hand in theater. His first real job in show business involved going on as a stand-in for a dancer who was ill. His performance was so bad that he got fired. He went home to Los Angeles dejected. After searching around for work, he applied with the help of Black community resources for a job at NBC. He was shocked when he was hired as an assistant to the parking lot supervisor.

## NBC AND HISTORY

After spending over a decade getting to know the stars who worked at NBC on a first-name basis, Franklin got promoted to parking lot supervisor. One day he mustered the courage to ask for—and then get—the job of stage manager for television production. He said, "I kept pushing to be a stage manager; this was like asking for the holy grail." He was the second African American stage manager in television history. The *first* African American television stage manager by several months was Fred Lights at NBC in New York, who worked with Dave Garroway and the *Today* program. Among the many NBC shows Franklin subsequently worked on was *The Nat King Cole Show*. On that show he worked with the *first* African American cameraman, Sidney Provost.

Franklin had to overcome hostility from White technicians who were reluctant to take cues from a Black man. He got in trouble with directors on more than one occasion because White technicians moved more slowly than necessary when he gave them cues. One of the worst experiences in Franklin's television career happened on the popular program *Queen for a Day*. The host, Jack Bailey, screamed at Franklin for touching White participants in the program—one of his responsibilities involved tapping people on the shoulder to cue them to go on-stage. To mollify Bailey, Franklin had to tap the stage floor next to the White participants as a substitute cue for actually touching them.

## THE NEW DIRECTORS GUILD OF AMERICA

As a working television stage manager, Franklin was a member of the Radio and Television Directors Guild. He was in the right place at the right time when the Motion Picture Directors Guild merged with the Radio and Television Directors Guild. Thus, in 1960 at age 44, Franklin became the *first* African American in the now-merged guild for radio, television, and motion picture directors: the Directors Guild of America.

## OPPORTUNITY CALLS

The phone rang and they said, "This is George Stevens Productions." I said, "You're kidding!" They said, "We want an assistant director. You're a member of the Guild; would you accept work on *The Greatest Story Ever Told?*"

George Stevens was in pre-production on his epic, *The Greatest Story Ever Told*, when he asked the Guild if there were any Black assistant directors. The Guild said there were none. Stevens decided he wanted a Black assistant director for this film, which dealt with issues of tolerance and Judeo-Christian ideals. A special meeting of the Guild was held, and Franklin was present as he was voted to the position of assistant director in the Guild.

Stevens was well aware of what he had done; he saw that the results of hiring a Black assistant director had produced more headlines nationally than his cast itself, which was an international and all-star cast. Franklin worked on this film and made history by doing so. The naysayers voiced their opinions, but Stevens would have none of it. One technician even quit in disgust rather than work with Franklin. The film went on to national and international success.

Franklin was gratified not only for the opportunity but because the film itself had a multi-ethnic cast of stars and extras that included many African Americans in on-screen roles. Now he was making motion picture history and doing a job he loved. Franklin worked for many months on location in Utah. For the film's premier, Stevens did a benefit screening with the proceeds going to the Freedom March. Dr. Martin Luther King Jr. attended the premier, along with Franklin and many other members of the Black community. Franklin's church also had a special screening in his honor, at which he got the red-carpet treatment for his participation in making this classic religious film.

## VOTED TO NEW POSITION

By 1962, Franklin was voted to a second assistant director position with the Guild. After many productions, he was hired by Haskell Wexler for his docudramatic work (*Medium Cool*, 1969) that defined the social and political experience in this country during the sixties. Franklin was first assistant director for this film. He felt that the three directors with the most lasting impact on him as a person and as a filmmaker were George Stevens, William Wyler (with whom he worked on *Funny Girl*) and Haskell Wexler.

## FEATURE PRODUCTION

Franklin directed only one feature film *(The Bus Is Coming)*; its producer was Horace Jackson. Franklin had helped with a Guild-sponsored screening of an earlier feature film effort entitled *Living between Two Worlds*, which was produced by Jackson. Despite the limited release of that effort, Franklin admired Jackson and his courage in breaking through to the threshold of feature film production.

## AWARD CEREMONY

In 1988 Franklin accepted an award from the Los Angeles Black Media Coalition for his nearly forty years of pioneering efforts. In his acceptance speech he castigated the media power structure and praised the Black technicians who were working in the industry. He decried the fact that in 1988 the employment of African Americans behind the cameras of film and television production was at one of its lowest points since he had entered the industry in 1960. He lauded those African Americans whose work made it possible for stars in front of the camera to look good, even though they themselves went unrecognized by the general public. As we now know from the *People* magazine article of 1996 (Lambert, Wright, Brailsford, et al., 1996), this indeed was not only true then but is still very true: Little if any progress related to hiring Black technicians in the film and television industry has occurred since 1988.

The award Franklin received was named in honor of William Foster, a pioneering Black filmmaker of silent films. The program notes describe the award as one that "recognizes individuals whose daring efforts and trailblazing contributions have helped to make it possible for others to succeed in the entertainment industry." Amen to that. During Franklin's retirement, he was a consultant to the Directors Guild working on special projects. He died in 1994.

## SELECTED FILMOGRAPHY

### Director

*The Bus Is Coming*, 1977, 109 min., 35mm, color, William Thompson International. Produced by Horace Jackson. K-Calb (spell it backwards) Productions. According to financial reports in *Variety* and the *Hollywood Reporter* from 1977, this independently made feature film produced for less than $300,000 had grossed over $12 million and receipts were still coming in. Franklin and his producer saw little if any of these profits because, as Franklin described, the distributors kept two sets of books. Franklin even went so far as to initiate litigation over this financial issue, but to no avail.

## Assistant Director

### Films

*Kitten with a Whip*, 1964, 83 min., directed by Douglas Heyes.

*McHale's Navy*, 1964, 93 min., color, directed by Edward J. Montaigne.

*The Night Walker*, 1964, 86 min., directed by William Castle.

*Art of Love*, 1965, 99 min., color, directed by Norman Jewison.

*The Greatest Story Ever Told*, 1965, 141 min., color, directed by George Stevens.

*The War Lord*, 1965, 123 min., color, directed by Franklin Schaffner.

*Gambit*, 1966, 109 min., color, directed by Ronald Neame.

*Incident at Phantom Hill*, 1966, 88 min., color, directed by Earl Bellamy.

*Madame X*, 1966, 100 min., color, directed by David Lowell Rich.

*Munster Go Home*, 1966, 96 min., color, directed by Earl Bellamy.

*Three on a Couch*, 1966, 109 min., color, directed by Jerry Lewis.

*Enter Laughing*, 1967, 112 min., color, directed by Carl Reiner.

*Who's Minding the Mint?* 1967, 97 min., color, directed by Howard Morris.

*Funny Girl*, 1968, 155 min., color, directed by William Wyler.

*Strange Bedfellows*, 1968, 98 min., color, directed by Melvin Frank.

*Gaily, Gaily*, 1969, 107 min., color, directed by Norman Jewison.

*Medium Cool*, 1969, 110 min., color, directed by Haskell Wexler.

*Model Shop*, 1969, 95 min., color, directed by Jacques Demy.

*Omen II*, 1978, 107 min., color, directed by Don Taylor.

### Episodic Television

*The Bill Cosby Show*, NBC; *Eddie Fisher Show*, NBC; *Ellery Queen*, ABC; *Farraday and Son*, NBC; *George Gobel Show*, NBC; *The Green Hornet*, ABC; *Harris and Company*, NBC; *It Could Be You*, NBC; *Matinee Theater*, NBC; *McMillan and Wife*, NBC; *The Monroes*, ABC; *The Name of the Game*, NBC; *Peyton Place*, ABC; *The Racket Squad*, synd.; *The Tammy Grimes Show*, ABC; *This Is Your Life*, NBC.

### Television Specials

*Martin Luther King*. Eli Landau produced this documentary in tribute to Dr. Martin Luther King Jr.

**Stage Manager**

*The Jerry Lewis Show; The Nat King Cole Show; Queen for a Day; This Is Your Life—* all NBC.

## BIO-CRITICAL REVIEW

*The Bus Is Coming.* "Seems like just what the doctor ordered in this day of stalled inter-racial understanding."—Dan Knapp, *Los Angeles Times*

———. "Story line, which approaches its premise honestly, in straightforward narrative."—*Variety*

## SELECTED AWARDS

Black Filmmakers Hall of Fame, Special Recognition, Oscar Micheaux Award, 1987

Brotherhood Crusade, Special Leadership Award, 1986

Directors Guild of

America Golden Jubilee, Citation, 1986

Los Angeles Black Media Coalition, Outstanding Technical Achievement Awards, Special Award, William Foster Award, 1988

## MEMBERSHIPS

Directors Guild of America

National Association for the Advancement of Colored People, a past president of the Beverly Hills/Hollywood chapter.

## EDUCATION

Attended Washington and Lee University, Lexington, Virginia

## SOURCES

### Books

Brooks, Tim, and Earle Marsh. *The Complete Directory to Primetime Network TV Shows: 1946–Present.* New York: Ballantine Books, 1992.

Davis, Zeinabu. *Wendell Franklin.* Los Angeles: Directors Guild of America, 1995.

Maltin, Leonard, ed. *Leonard Maltin's Movie and Video Guide, 1995.* New York: Penguin, 1994.

McNeil, Alex. *Total Television Including Cable: A Comprehensive Guide to Programming from 1948 to the Present.* New York: Penguin, 1991.

Sampson, Henry T. *Blacks in Black and White: A Source Book on Black Films.* Metuchen, NJ: Scarecrow Press, 1995.


### Newspapers and Magazines

"Bus Is Coming," *Variety*, April 1977, p. 67.
Knapp, Dan. "Black Filmmakers Take Gamble on *Bus Is Coming*," *Los Angeles Times*, April 1977, p. 53.
Lambert, Pam, Lynda Wright, Karen Brailsford, et al. "What's Wrong with This Picture? Exclusion of Minorities Has Become a Way of Life in Hollywood," *People* (45), no. 11 (March 18, 1996), pp. 42–52.
*Los Angeles Black Media Coalition, Outstanding Technical Achievement Awards Program Catalogue.* Los Angeles: October 1, 1988.


### Other

*Screen Scene* (BET Cable), April 1992.

# WILLIAM GREAVES

## BACKGROUND

William Greaves began the process of becoming a filmmaker as a small boy who loved drawing pictures late at night, much to the annoyance of his parents. By the time he had reached his teens, he had won many honors for his accomplishments as an artist. He later enrolled in City College of New York and became a dancer with an African dance troupe. His love of the stage led to work in the American Negro Theater. He appeared in productions with Sidney Poitier and Frederick O'Neal. His career in the theater flourished when he was selected by Lee Schubert to appear in one of his original productions. Greaves later appeared in the original *Finian's Rainbow*. By 1948 he was a member of the New York Actors Studio, where he participated in productions with Marlon Brando, Julie Harris, Anthony Quinn, Shelley Winters, Ben Gazarra and Rod Steiger. One of his first feature film roles was in *Lost Boundaries*.

Once Greaves decided to become a filmmaker, he distinguished himself while working in Canada for the acclaimed National Film Board. For six years he learned every aspect of filmmaking. Regarding his decision to become a filmmaker, Greaves says,

> As a young Black actor, the Uncle Tom parts I was sometimes asked to play revolted me and I invariably turned down this kind of role. I was also continually assaulted by images of Black people on the movie screen that were not only unacceptable but insulting. I saw what was

William Greaves. *Photo courtesy of Deane Folsom.*

happening to older Black actors like Canada Lee, Paul Robeson and Gordon Heath—the games that were being played with their careers— and I decided to get behind the cameras, where I could control what appeared on the screen. I was determined and full of energy; and despite assertions that it was a ludicrous idea for a Black man to pursue a career as a director and producer of motion pictures, I was fairly confident that I would succeed.

## BLACK JOURNAL

Greaves elaborated on his early experiences with one of the first magazine format programs for television, *Black Journal*, where he began as co-host and became executive producer. The program was originally conceived and produced by Whites. For a time there was no Black participation in the decision making and creative control of the show. Madeline Anderson* was an editor on the program and for a time the *only* Black person on staff of this groundbreaking and important program.

I was one of the early co-hosts of the show. I had made over eighty films prior to coming to *Black Journal*. During the tumult of the sixties there was a need to transform this program into a Black-controlled show. It was ludicrous to have a series about the Black experience controlled by White producers. The other Blacks on staff were in assistants' jobs. They (the other Black staff) agitated to have a Black executive producer. I made the Black assistants into producers and directors. We then proceeded to do authentic productions for NET.

Later, NET became WNET-TV, one of the first Public Broadcasting System stations. Greaves described how he helped to organize many Black producers from around the country into the National Black Producers Association. Tony Brown was elected president of the group. Brown's association with Greaves in this group led Greaves to propose that Brown replace him as host when he left *Black Journal*. After *Black Journal* lost its funding, Brown made the concept into *Tony Brown's Journal*, now the longest-running African American public affairs program in television history.

## INSPIRATION AND INFLUENCES

In an interview conducted while Greaves was being inducted into the *Gallery of Greats*, he commented that

I've been inspired by a number of filmmakers. I was inspired by people outside of film. One draws from the social, cultural and political environment in which one moves. All of that is processed in my computer and comes out the other end.

He talked about having met some of the people who inspired his work.

As a young actor I met Satyajit Ray (famed East Indian director) and studied with Elia Kazan and Lee Strasberg. I worked in the films of William Alexander, who was important to me as a role model. I worked with Louis de Rochemont (director of *Lost Boundaries*, 1949). All of these people were very influential in my thinking, in terms of having personal contact with them.

## ADVICE FOR ASPIRANTS

Greaves went on to describe himself and to admonish aspiring filmmakers:

I'm one of those individuals who gravitate toward knowledge, information, expansion of my consciousness. . . . Watch out for mental and psychological slavery; watch out for unwittingly serving the interests of the oppressor in the way in which you control the images and representations of your people. It is not enough to control the images; the images must be controlled by someone who is conscious. Keep in mind the negative and deleterious effect the control of these images can have on people, our people and White people. White people have been lulled into a state of arrogance, by Uncle Tomism. A lot of it has been our unwitting contribution to the arrogance of White people. It has led to behavior both domestically and internationally that can get our country into a lot of trouble.

Aspiring young Black producers have to become aware of the powerful role that the media plays in impacting, structuring and liberating or enslaving the consciousness of an audience. An aspiring Black producer should focus in on the whole business of excellence—the excellence of the craft, the ideas, the work habits. When the work is made, it is a reality; it is an indestructible one that will last for quite some time. The nature of the Black experience is such that we do not get that many opportunities to make films. Every film we make is a central player in what happens to us at the next stage of our incarnation on this continent.

Greaves has done much more than just succeed. He has produced, written, directed, shot and edited over two hundred films. His work has been in the documentary, industrial and feature film genres.

In addition, Greaves's films have won over eighty international awards—

a record for Black independent filmmaking. He has been called the dean of independent filmmakers, of the modern era, by the author Donald Bogle. Many of Greaves's productions are available directly from the filmmaker.

## SELECTED FILMOGRAPHY

### Producer

*Selections from "Black Journal,"* 1960s, 60 min. Greaves is the *first* Black producer to win an Emmy. *Black Journal* is notable for having provided the opportunity for many independent Black filmmakers to work on a nationally syndicated production. Filmmakers who worked on segments for the program include Madeline Anderson,* Stan Lathan* and St. Claire Bourne.*

*The First World Festival of Negro Arts*, 1966, 40 min., b/w. A documentary shot in Dakar, Senegal, it is the official record of the convening of artists and intellectuals from throughout the African diaspora to celebrate African art and culture.

*Symbiopsychotaxiplasm . . . Take One*, 1968, 90 min. An experimental feature. Selected by *Variety* magazine at the conclusion of the 1991 International Feature Film Market as one of the top five films among the 300 films shown.

*Still a Brother: Inside the Negro Middleclass*, 1968, 90 min., b/w. A documentary in which members of the Black middle class address their position in contemporary American society and their views on the Black underclass.

*Ali, the Fighter*, 1971, 60 min. Documentary of the Muhammad Ali and Joe Frazier fight. Docutainment shot in cinema verité style about the historic first fight between these two great Black boxing legends.

*From These Roots*, 1974, 30 min., b/w. Documentary for the Schomberg Center for Research in Black Culture, narrated by Brock Peters with music by Eubie Blake. The film is a study of the Harlem Renaissance of the twenties from a social, political and cultural perspective.

*Bustin Loose*, 1981, 94 min., Universal Studios. Feature film with Cecily Tyson and Richard Pryor. William Greaves was executive producer. One of Pryor's best performances on film. Pryor and Tyson take a busload of emotionally disturbed children cross-country from Philadelphia to Seattle.

*Booker T. Washington: The Life and the Legacy*, 1983, 30 min. Docudrama with Maurice Woods and Al Freeman Jr.

*Frederick Douglass: An American Life*, 1985, 30 min. Docudrama.

*Black Power in America: Myth or Reality?* 1986, 60 min, PBS. Documentary with Franklin Thomas, Clifton Wharton Jr., Dr. Mary Berry, Arthur Ashe, Mayor Tom Bradley, Eleanor Holmes Norton and Don King.

*The Deep North*, 1988, 60 min., WCBS. Documentary on racism.

*That's Black Entertainment*, 1989, 60 min. Documentary on the history of early Black cinema.

*Ida B. Wells: A Passion for Justice*, 1989, 60 min. Showcases Greaves's talents. A little-known champion of human rights is shown within an accurate historical perspective. The oversight by history in not telling this brave woman's story is rectified by this fascinating and revealing biographical portrait of an early feminist and Black rights advocate. Features Toni Morrison reading words written by Ms. Wells and narrating Wells's story. Since its release the work has won over twenty-two film festival awards. It is the most popular title that Greaves distributes through his company. It has proven popular with women's groups, journalism departments, Black studies groups and groups dealing with issues of racism and violence. Greaves explains that not only does this work present positive images,

> Operationally it details a modus operandi for people who want to get into political activism. They learn from this film how to attack problems on a global level—through the press, lectures, going beyond rhetoric to economic boycotts. To use our clout internationally as a people.

*A Tribute to Jackie Robinson*, 1990, 18 min. Made for the Jackie Robinson Foundation.

*Resurrections: Paul Robeson*, 1990, 60 min. Pilot for cable television featuring Moses Gunn.

### *Work-in-Progress*

> My current work-in-progress on Ralph Bunche (1903–1971) when finished will be a three-hour special titled *Ralph Bunche: An American Odyssey*. Bunche was the primary mover in the United Nations hierarchy with respect to decolonization of the world. While he was working with the U.N., close to a billion people of color regained the right of self-determination throughout the world. He was the only person involved in the Arab-Israeli conflict to get all sides to sign an armistice agreement. That has yet to be duplicated as a feat. Because of that he won the Nobel Peace Prize. We don't only make films; we make blueprints for the Black community for actualization and self-realization and for the full democratization of the United States.

## BIO-CRITICAL REVIEW

"Greaves packs great meaning into small, essential details. Providing both private and public amplitude makes Greaves' documentaries uncommonly rich. Best of all, for a filmmaker-historian like Greaves, this method makes his vision timeless."—Armond White, *City Sun*

"Greaves, in addition to being an important historical force, has produced an impressive and surprisingly diverse body of work, both in approach and subject matter."—Adam Knee and Charles Musser, *Film Quarterly*

## SELECTED AWARDS

Association of Independent Video and Filmmakers Award, 1986

Black Filmmakers Hall of Fame, Inductee, 1980

First Actors Studio Award, 1980

*Gallery of Greats*, Inductee, 1991

*Black Journal*
  Emmy Award, 1969/70

*Ida B. Wells: A Passion for Justice*
  Black Filmmakers Hall of Fame; Independent Film, Video and Screenplay Competition Awards: Third Place, Overall Competition; Winner, Documentary Category, 1991
  National Urban League Award, 1990

## SELECTED ADDITIONAL HONORS

King Memorial College, Doctor of Humane Letters

Listed in the following: *Who's Who among Black Americans; Who's Who in the World; Who's Who in America*

National Endowment for the Arts, Panelist

National Endowment for the Humanities, Panelist

## SELECTED MEMBERSHIPS

American Federation of Television and Radio Artists

Directors Guild of America

Screen Actors Guild

Writers Guild

## SOURCES

Interview and follow-up interview by Spencer Moon, January 1991; June 1995.

### Books

Bogle, Donald. *Blacks in American Films and Television*. New York: Simon & Schuster, 1988.

### Newspapers and Magazines

White, Armond. "Greaves' Film Essays Capture Memorable Moments." *City Sun*, April 17–23, 1991, p. 19.
Knee, Adam and Charles Musser. "William Greaves, Documentary Film-Making and the African American Experience." *Film Quarterly* (45), no. 3 (Spring 1992), pp. 13–25.

Henry Hampton

# HENRY HAMPTON

## BACKGROUND

Henry Hampton's company, Blackside, Inc., is one of the most successful independent documentary film companies in the country. Founded in 1968, three years after Hampton marched from Selma to Montgomery in that historic march with the late Dr. Martin Luther King Jr. and thousands of other civil rights activists, Blackside is also one of the nation's oldest minority-owned production companies. Over the past 25-plus years, Blackside has created and produced more than forty commercial, industrial, educational and documentary programs. Clients for its productions have included Capital Cities Communications, J. Walter Thompson, Digital Equipment Corporation, Harvard Business School, the Robert Wood Johnson Foundation and agencies of the federal government. Corporate sponsors for its productions have included Lotus Development Corporation, the Melville Corporation, General Electric, Raytheon and Toyota.

Hampton founded his company after working for the Unitarian Church in Boston as a press official. His objective in securing contracts with companies such as Digital Equipment Corporation, Bank of New England and the Social Security Administration was to complete his assignment of producing films that trained and educated employees and constituencies of these companies. However, his major objective was to train Black people in film production.

By 1980 his company had over two dozen employees and was doing nearly $2 million a year in business. To keep this momentum going, Hampton decided that his future lay in creating major projects that could sustain his staff and would have some social-political impact. Those projects included the development of several major series of programs.

Those series were *Eyes on the Prize*, a documentary history of the civil rights movement; *The Great Depression*, a story of how Americans responded to the greatest crisis in this century; *America's War on Poverty*, a history of the origins and implementation of this social battle plan; and *Breakthrough: The Changing Face of Science in America*, profiles of twenty contemporary African American, Latino and Native American scientists and engineers making inroads in biology, astronomy, physics, mathematics and other scientific disciplines.

## BODY OF WORK

Hampton described his work in general.

I think that almost all of my work has been aimed at trying to inform the general American community, but in particular African Americans. I really believe that television and film remain some of the most powerful instruments in our society. They have not been used to help confront the various difficulties and barriers that African Americans must face. We've gone through a period where there are missing pages in our history. I say "missing pages" because of all those people who have contributed to our culture that we don't know about. I continue to be surprised after having spent almost thirty years doing research on our history for the programs I produce. It is very important to me to go beyond the simple re-telling or exploration of African American history. It is important to look at the deep themes that have driven our participation in America.

### Eyes on the Prize

He described the work that brought him to national and international prominence.

*Eyes on the Prize* put us on the national map, although we had been in business for twelve years before that program was finished. This program was an attempt to look at history that people had walked over before. I think we brought to it a unique perspective. We put it into a story context. That period, which seemed sort of spontaneous and not connected, became the result of a long strain of history that began to make sense to people. We built movements and individuals took on leadership; the kind of power that happens when people overcome obstacles; the kind of freedom that occurs in the spirit—all those were elements that I think made this work different from the other films that had been made about the civil rights movement.

In a full-page ad in *Variety* magazine (March 1990), Hampton expressed his thoughts on his experience with *Eyes on the Prize*.

After twelve long but rewarding years, we've accomplished many things and reached our most ambitious goal—to reinvigorate a productive dialogue across the country on issues of race and democracy. Rarely in a lifetime are you given a chance to touch the history of a people and a nation in such a way. It has been our privilege.

### Training

Hampton talked about another important component of his work.

We have always felt that it was our responsibility to train people, to prepare them to go out and compete for their own vision, to have people be prepared to produce high-quality material. They in turn can then take on other elements of the story of the African American experience.

### UNIQUENESS

Hampton described what makes him unique as a filmmaker.

I think part of what makes me unique is that I operate more in a team fashion than many filmmakers. I've become very good at organizing teams of producers and core personnel to make better films that live up to my vision. The work is shared over time. That is what has allowed me the opportunity to produce multi-part programs so successfully. This method allows work to be produced in a timely fashion, whereas a single filmmaker would take much longer to produce the same results. I insist that on our productions we have multiple points of view based on sex and gender. It does not mean that there isn't a strong thread of advocacy in our work. We create an environment where strong points of view are brought together. My success over the last twenty-eight years is due to our work approach and methods. We make certain that we maintain very high standards of production and research quality. We also reflect a lot of different people's points of view.

## ADVICE FOR ASPIRANTS

He gave advice to aspiring filmmakers.

I get half a dozen job-related query letters a week. I get letters not only from a lot of African American youth but White, Latino and Asian. They have been intrigued by media most of their lives. There aren't any easy places where most of them can go to get past the first stage. Many of them go on to film school and come to us after that. One of the elements of our work is, we use people in very responsible roles. There is a fair amount of carrying and "go-fering," but they also are given a chance to be part of story sessions and documentary reviews; they are allowed to have their say. They're listened to, and it works both ways. It reinforces the notion that points of view are a powerful addition to our work even when they are young people, and they bring those different perspectives to the process.

## THE FUTURE

We asked what Hampton hopes to accomplish in the future.

Twenty years ago I realized you could make a good living making documentaries. It is, however, a tenuous living because of the vagaries of the marketplace. I began a conscious plan to invest in real estate and media properties, which I thought would give me a base and would make me less dependent entirely on foundations and grants to survive. Those investments have served me well. It has provided me with true independence. It is important for young people to know that there are real possibilities out there for them. I'm developing some work in the fiction area. Story development is a problem of every documentary filmmaker, so that is certainly an area I will be exploring in the future—works of fiction and feature films.

## FILMOGRAPHY

### Executive Producer

*Code Blue* (1982). A half-hour film produced for the National Institute for Health designed to recruit minority physicians.

*Nighttrain*, 1989. An innovative use of television to present content about the minority community of Boston and to train African Americans for jobs in business. The television series aired over five Boston commercial stations.

*Take These Keys* (1989). Produced for the Harvard Business School. A short film about the leader of the Hough Development Corporation in Cleveland and the attempt to build again after the riots of the sixties.

*The Great Depression: 1929–1941, A Television History*, 1994, PBS. The untold story of how Americans responded to the greatest crisis to confront them in this century. A testament to courage, perseverance, and the American spirit. Through eyewitness accounts and archival film footage, it relates the extraordinary times that changed millions of lives and our nation forever. Nine one-hour programs.

*Malcolm X: Making It Plain*, 1994, PBS *American Experience* series. A two-and-a-half-hour biography of Malcolm X. Produced and directed by Orlando Bagwell.

*Breakthrough: The Changing Face of Science in America*, 1995, PBS. This series profiled twenty contemporary African American, Latino and Native American scientists and engineers breaking new ground in biology, astronomy, physics, mathematics and other disciplines. Intimate biographical portraits chronicled the rewards and special challenges confronting people of color who choose a life in science. A rare view into the personal side of science. Six hour-length programs.

*America's War on Poverty*, 1995, PBS. This series explored the origins of America's War on Poverty and how attitudes toward race—as well as faith in the accessibility of the American dream—shape the battle plan. A five-part series of one-hour programs.

### Creator/Executive Producer

*Eyes on the Prize*, *I* and *II*, 1990 and 1992, PBS. Fourteen one-hour video documentaries on the civil rights movement in America from 1954 to 1985.

As important as what happened to the people of the civil rights movement yesterday is what they are doing today. A companion book to the first series was written by Juan Williams with the *Eyes on the Prize* production team. The book briefly describes people chronicled in the work and what they are doing today. For example, Rosa Parks has moved to Detroit and is an honored guest at many civil rights events. John Lewis is a congressman from Georgia. Andrew Young, former mayor of Atlanta, was recently a member of the Atlanta Olympic Committee. Robert Moses is now a Mac-Arthur Foundation award winner and a mathematics instructor in elementary school. Constance Baker Motley is a U.S. District Court judge. Thurgood Marshall became a Supreme Court Justice. Martin Luther King Jr. won the Nobel Prize and is honored annually with a national holiday. Clearly, the civil rights movement changed the nature of society and politics in the United States, providing Black people in particular a stronger social and political voice.

### BIO-CRITICAL REVIEW

*Eyes on the Prize*. "More than merely superb storytelling, this is essential history and mandatory viewing."—Howard Rosenberg, *Los Angeles Times*

———. "One of the most distinguished documentary series in the history of broadcasting."—Ed Siegel, *Boston Globe*

―――. "A fabulous work of art. And of history, sociology and humanity."—David Bianculli, *New York Post*

## SELECTED AWARDS

Charles Frankel Prize, 1990

Corporation for Public Broadcasting, Ralph Lowell Award, 1993

Harvard University, Loeb Fellowship, 1977

Heinz Family Foundation Awards, Arts and Humanities, 1995

Lyndhurst Fellowship, 1989

Massachusetts Civil Liberties Union, Roger Baldwin Award, 1987

Massachusetts Cultural Council, Commonwealth Award, 1993

National Conference of Black Mayors, Tribute to a Black American Award, 1992

Unitarian Universalist Association, Holmes-Weatherly Award, 1989

*America's War on Poverty*
   Columbus International Film and Video Festival, Bronze Plaque (2 programs); Honorable Mention (1 program)
   Worldfest Houston, Grand Award

*Eyes on the Prize, Parts I and II*
   Emmy Award, 1990 (3), 1992 (3)
   Oscar nomination, 1990
   Peabody Award, 1990 and 1992

*Eyes I* (1990)
   Alfred I. duPont–Columbia University Awards, Gold Baton TV Critics Association, Best Program of the Season
   American Film and Video Festival, Emily Award (Best of Festival)
   *Time* magazine, Best Documentary of the Decade
   *TV Guide*, Best Documentary of the Year

*Eyes II* (1992)
   Alfred I. duPont–Columbia University Awards, Silver Baton
   CEBA Award of Excellence
   NAACP Image Awards, nominated for Best Variety Show Special
   National Association of Black Journalists, First Place, Documentary, Award of Excellence
   National Black Programming Consortium, Historical Documentary, Runner-Up

*The Great Depression* (1994)
   Alfred I. duPont–Columbia University Awards, Silver Baton
   Cine, 4 Golden Eagles
   Emmy Award (also, 3 nominations)
   National Black Programming Consortium, Community Choice Award
   New York International Festival, Silver Medal

*Malcolm X: Making It Plain*
   Cine, Golden Eagle
   Emmy Award, News and Documentary Research

National Black Programming Consortium, Prized Pieces, Second Place
New York Association of Black Journalists, GRIOT (highest award)
Peabody Award, Biography

## PUBLICATIONS

Henry Hampton and Steve Fayer (Sara Flynn, ed.), *Voices of Freedom: An Oral History of the Civil Rights Movement* (New York: Bantam Books, 1990).

Beginning in 1968 Blackside developed and produced several major educational projects, including *Studies in the History of Black Americans* (Silver Burdett, publisher) and *The Black Chronicle*, a meticulously researched edition of a black newspaper chronicling African American history from the colonial period through 1954 (Holt, Rinehart and Winston, publisher).

## EDUCATION

Washington University, St. Louis, Missouri, B.A., pre-med and English literature

## MEMBERSHIPS

Carol DiMaiti Stuart Foundation

Childrens Defense Fund

International Documentary Association

Massachusetts Film Advisory Board

Revson Foundation, Trustee

## SOURCES

Interview by Spencer Moon, June 1995.

### Books

Williams, Juan, with the *Eyes on the Prize* production team. *Eyes on the Prize.* New York: Penguin, 1987.

### Newspapers and Magazines

Bianculli, David, *"Eyes on the Prize," New York Post*, March 1990, p. 31.
DeMarco, Darcy, "Keep Your Eyes on Henry Hampton, Creator Readies *Eyes on the Prize*," *Black Film Review* (3), no. 3 (Summer 1987), pp. 14–15.
Rosenberg, Howard, *"Eyes on the Prize," Los Angeles Times*, April 1990, p. 23.
Siegel, Ed, *"Eyes on the Prize," Boston Globe*, March 1990, p. 24.
*Variety*, March 1990, p. 35.

Hobart Whitaker Harris

# HOBART WHITAKER HARRIS

## BACKGROUND

In order to achieve even a modicum of success, Black filmmakers sometimes have to go through extraordinary circumstances. Black doctors know that their training and sensitivity to the medical concerns of our community have helped make a critical difference in terms of health care for Black people. Hobart Harris is in an unusual position because he is a doctor who has a serious commitment to filmmaking, a doctor/filmmaker.

When I first met Harris in 1991, he was enjoying the success of having co-produced the Grand Prize Film at the 1990 Sundance Film Festival, *Chameleon Street*. The film was written, produced, directed by and starred his older brother, Wendell B. Harris Jr.* At the time of our first interview, Hobart Harris was completing his medical training at the University of California, San Francisco. He is clearly not one to let grass grow under his feet. He has produced, written and directed a second feature film that is very much an autobiographical work, *Diary of a Blade*. The narrative feature film examines the life and times of a medical resident in training. Harris is currently an associate professor of surgery at the University of San Francisco, San Francisco General Hospital, Department of Surgery. He has held this position since July 1994.

Our first interview focused on *Chameleon Street*, coming off the success of Sundance. The interview, in its original content, was much longer and more detailed about the production and marketing of that project. The questions and responses I chose to include for purposes of this book when compared to his comments in 1996 show a progression in Harris's thinking as doctor/ filmmaker. He is a very astute, articulate and sincere physician and artist.


## UNIQUENESS

What makes you and your brother unique as filmmakers?

It would take me some time to sit down and give you very precise, very specific illustrations, but I think my brother and I share some of the same artistic sensibilities. And while all Black folks growing up in America have a shared experience and a shared or common vision or perspective on the world, there are still very unique takes on that perspective and very unique responses. Just as it's absurd to assume all Black filmmakers would be alike, the opposite side of that coin is that they're all intrinsically or inherently different or unique. It's a very interesting question as to what makes us different from a Spike Lee* or the Hudlin brothers.* There are certainly creative decisions that they have made in their work that I wouldn't have made.

Where does the difference come from? I'm not sure, other than to say two people encountering the same set of circumstances will respond differently. I've trained in medicine and I'm completing my training in general surgery, so I've gone through a long road that has been inundated by natural sciences and math and so forth. I've always had a certain creative desire. My brother and his work and our interactions have always helped me to express a lot of that creatively, and he's always nurtured and fostered that.

As children we'd make movies, we'd watch movies. I was watching credits as soon as I could read. My brother would quiz me incessantly on films; he has an encyclopedic mind when it comes to the fine arts. He is a much more focused, some might say obsessed, person with the arts. For me it has become a facet of my life as I've grown and I see myself trying to chart where my professional life is going to go. The medical training now is beginning to phase out, and it's time to execute the profession, not just train for it. So to some degree I think my brother brings a much finer appreciation of the arts in general, of the history of film; and when he writes, he writes from that base. I think it would be hard to find anyone, Black or White, who's better educated in the arts than my brother.

I bring in all modesty a certain clarity, a certain type of logic, if you will. I mean, when I read his work I'm the one who's always trying to make sure that there's good continuity, that there's a type of flow or stability, a certain linkage that I like to see in a work. I think that's a reflection of my training in the basic sciences, which tends to want to fill in all the gaps to explain things, to show the interrelationships of events and occurrences. My training as a physician certainly had some impact on the medical scenes and an effort to make them realistic.

But I see similarities between myself and Spike Lee in terms of what may motivate us, and I think that fundamental motivation is to have the opportunity to tell stories as we see them and tell the truth—as opposed to being a consumer of these falsehoods, of these misconceptions, of these inaccuracies about what it is to be Black. Black folk are as diverse, as heterogeneous, as any people on the face of the earth. We would all laugh at some of the same jokes. I mean, we're all going to laugh at *Dolemite* (a trickster comedy character on records and, later, in films created by Rudy Ray Moore during the seventies). That's going to have a uniquely funny aspect to Black folks; but at the same time there's going to be something unique to my experience, having grown up in Michigan, the son of a physician trained in medicine, that even my brother won't share.

## ADVICE FOR ASPIRANTS

What would you say to aspiring young film students and filmmakers?

I see myself as, at best, an infant in this business. So you have to take what I have to say with a grain of salt, at least be cognizant of where I'm coming from and what stage I'm at in my own development. But I think you have to have that desire, that inner commitment and need to produce, to express yourself. I think you have to develop a sense of self, sense of confidence, sense of what it's going to take to satisfy yourself and always hold that really close. Because not just in film, but in so many endeavors, people are going to have a variety of agendas that they are going to present to you. Many of which may not contribute to you in a positive way. The more self-contained you are, the greater ability you have to reflect and come to some personal level of comfort and satisfaction, to know when you've pleased yourself; when you have done what is satisfactory to you, the more you will be able to weather the storm.

Certainly, you've got to encourage people to do what they want to do. I think it was Benjamin Mays (Black educator, president of Morehouse College, 1940–1967), I'll paraphrase him because I won't be able to quote him exactly; he says something to the effect that the great tragedy of life is not that you don't achieve your goal but that you have no goal to achieve. I'm saying to set your goals and go after them. It's more important that you be involved in the process, that you be focused, that you be directed, that you be trying, than that you ultimately achieve whatever it is. Because as soon as you achieve it, then you're on to something else. At least that's the way my life has been. There's very little time savoring laurels of any one particular event. Sundance is a prime example. It was great that night and the next day; but as everything passed, the new struggle became more apparent. Pretty soon Sundance was a pleasant memory, but it was no longer the main mission at hand.

## RENAISSANCE

What do you think of the Black film/video renaissance now, having done two feature films in the last five years? (This question was asked in 1996.)

Unfortunately, I'd say that fundamentally I'm disappointed. Because for the most part the filmmakers who seemed to have the greatest opportunities in terms of the scope and magnitude of the projects they have been able to get made have seemingly—and it may be due to forces I'm not aware of—pandered to some of the lowest elements. In terms of entertainment, in terms of aspects of society. In many ways I see the vast majority of films by Black directors as simply having redefined the 21st-century Black exploitation event.

I think most of the films are extraordinarily limited in scope. They are on average not particularly intelligent. From my perspective, they tend to be a modern-day minstrel show. I'm speaking specifically of the Hollywood-funded feature films of greater than a few million dollars' budget. There are particular filmmakers that I find to be the most flagrant abusers, whom I choose not to name. There are some notable exceptions. I think Charles Burnett* makes very challenging, very interesting, independent features. I think Julie Dash* has done some excellent work. I think Spike Lee continues to be the most prolific and challenging of Black film directors. I think Carl Franklin* is an excellent filmmaker. For reasons that I'm sure have a lot to do with what is perceived to be commercial in Hollywood—and perhaps as a result of other forces that I'm either personally unaware of or that these filmmakers simply cannot overcome, or choose not to overcome—the vast majority of the "body of work" that has resulted from this Black renaissance in film is from my point of view worthy of being discarded and burned.

## BEYOND HOLLYWOOD

Do you think independent production and distribution outside the Hollywood system is a viable artistic and business venture?

I think that the explosion of the video market, and explosion of independent film that occurred in the early eighties, has clearly dissipated. The large spate of the independent film production companies has gone the way of the dinosaur. By and large, the avenues that were available to create unique, independent African American film are smaller now than five years ago. However, there has been a proliferation of film festivals. You can go on-line on the Internet and find festival after festival after festival; film festivals small and large have become businesses. They have become mechanisms that communities use to attract tourism, mechanisms that various organizations and cities use for a variety of agendas. I question how much of that agenda is focused on developing emerging and unique talent, i.e., African American talent. There will be individuals who make an impact in festival venues. One should be realistic and be prepared to pursue alternative methods well beyond the Hollywood mainstream for distribution and promotion.

## UNIQUENESS (1996)

Have your views about what makes you unique as a filmmaker changed since we spoke in 1991?

Right now, in 1996, there are two things that come to mind that I think distinguish me as a filmmaker from others. I am extraordinarily secure and moderately successful in an entirely different career. This allows me a certain intellectual/artistic/economic freedom that I don't think other filmmakers may have. As a direct consequence of that, I am only drawn toward stories that are representative of the complexities, intelligence and diversity of the African American experience. The two films that I have been involved with have complex characters; they tend to be intelligent characters, and the struggles and issues they confront, while having universality and commonality to the human struggle, are above the stereotypes of the Black experience that have heretofore been presented.

## ADVICE FOR ASPIRANTS (1996)

Having produced two feature films in the last five years, what can you tell young people who want to get into the business now?

Do everything they can to become skilled as a writer, director, actor—whatever aspect of the industry they're interested in pursuing. They should continually refine their craft. They should develop a sense of inner confidence and a sense of artistic quality and sensibility that they are secure with. Because the struggle is ever-present, on-going, and will never dissipate; so they must be thoroughly and absolutely committed. Be unwilling to accept no for an answer; to have a decent chance for bringing a creative concept or creative vision to fruition.

## THE FUTURE

What do you hope to accomplish in the future?

I hope to become a better filmmaker. There is a lot of room for personal growth; hopefully, that will occur. I continue to pursue interesting and complex stories that are entertaining. I like dramas, mysteries and comedies. Whatever the genre is, I like them to be layered and complex. I hope to become more skilled at producing just that sort of film.

What's in development after this project [Producer/Director of *Diary of a Blade*] gets distributed and marketed to your satisfaction?

I have written a rough first draft of a feature film based in large part on an incident of euthanasia. The screenplay still needs work.

## FILMOGRAPHY

### Producer/Director

*Chameleon Street*, 1990, 92 min., 35mm, color. Executive producers, Helen B. Harris and Hobart Harris. The screenplay was written by and starred Wendell B. Harris Jr.* in the lead role. See the chapter on Wendell Burks Harris Jr. for more information about this production.

*Diary of a Blade*, 1995, 96 min., 35mm, color. Written by Hobart W. Harris. The director of photography, Bruce Schermer, worked in the same capacity on the now-infamous *Roger and Me* by Michael Moore. Schermer was the second unit and camera operator for the first unit on *Chameleon Street*. Dan Lawton, a producer on this film, was a producer on *Chameleon Street*. Helen B. Harris, the associate producer for the film, was co-executive producer of *Chameleon Street*. She is the mother of Wendell and Hobart Harris. The youngest Harris brother, Charles B. Harris, was the still photographer for this film and a production assistant and still photographer for *Chameleon Street*. Just as "the family that plays together stays together," apparently the family that makes movies together creates a legacy for generations to come.

The creative impetus and drive behind the film was my experience training as a surgical resident. That experience gave me the emotional push or desire to commit to celluloid what I felt was a different perspective on the process of surgical training in medicine in the United States compared to what is normally portrayed in film and on television. It began with taking a desktop computer along with me, when I committed myself to a 6-week, 24-hour-a-day, 7-day-a-week stint as the chief resident of the Trauma Service at the San Francisco General Hospital in November 1992. During those 6 weeks I committed myself to taking daily notes on my experiences, having anticipated that this would be an extraordinarily stressful but also fervent period in terms of being filled with a lot of dramatic situations and events.

From those notes, the diary/journal that I maintained over the six weeks, I was able to begin roughing out a narrative drama based in large part on those actual experiences. Then, over the subsequent year and a half or so I polished the script, revised it and began putting together the actual pre-production of what I determined early on would be a low-budget, independent feature film. I wasn't interested in trying to sell it to Hollywood. I wasn't interested in trying to go through that very detailed and usually time-consuming process of trying to get a major producer, a studio or talent interested in the project. I had a very limited window of opportunity in terms of my personal career and life to get this work produced. If it was going to be produced, the independent route was going to be the most efficient way.

So then I essentially used contacts that had been developed in the southeastern Michigan area during the production of *Chameleon Street* and identified a producer and cinematographer, began fundraising and eventually pulled together the budget and the crew. So when I arrived in Flint, Michigan, in January 1994 I was able to hit the ground running. The pre-production had been finished, the script had been broken down and it was a question of casting, getting locations, rehearsing and preparing to shoot. It was a 17-day shoot, shooting almost daily; we enlisted the services of local businesses in Flint, Michigan, which was critical. The year before I had contacted the local city hospital, which was going to be essential. If they were not willing to support this project, allow me to actually film on the premises, there was no way I was going to be able to re-create the environment of a hospital in a realistic fashion with essentially no budget. We would shoot in the hospital, usually beginning around 3:00 in the afternoon and shoot until midnight or 1:00 AM, when things were most quiet in the hospital, then vacate. Post-production took another year and a half.

Where did you get the money for production?

Most of it was raised through friends and colleagues in medicine—fellow residents and surgeons I had come to know during my training process—and then a few family and personal contacts outside of the medical community. The budget was a little over a hundred thousand dollars. There were approximately eighteen investors. Outside of myself, no one invested more than two thousand dollars on an individual level. The average was between five hundred dollars and a thousand dollars. That represents about half the budget. I came up with the other half, which was my own money.

*What stage of distribution is the film in now?*

I've sent the film to a variety of festivals, and we've won one prize already through this process. The next scheduled festival is in December in New York, the Contemporary Films of the African Diaspora Festival. My goal is to have the New York screening be a boost to the film's marketability. After that, depending on the response, to arrange some San Francisco theatrical exhibition. Then to try cable television, perhaps the Independent Film Cable network. Luckily, with a low-budget film like this we don't have a tremendous budget to be recouped. As a result, I can be more flexible and patient in trying to carefully place the film. It is a film that does not age rapidly. The environment and the time frame are by no means readily identifiable.

What difficulty we've encountered in marketing is because of what I feel was my greatest success with the film: breaking the mold of traditional representation of physicians and medicine in film and television. The film is unlike any other film on the subject of medicine. I say that not just because it's my film; that's what I've been told by others like John Pierson, considered one of the gurus of independent filmmaking in the United States in the past decade. He said it was unlike anything he had ever seen before. As a result you are swimming upstream to audiences, and it's even worse for critics and/or festival programmers. I actually think that most of them are not particularly secure with their own film sensibilities. So when they see things that are very different, they may in fact have more difficulty than the average viewing public in terms of being able to evaluate and assess entertainment value. Festival programmers feel more constrained by the need to correlate and compare film A to previously screened films, whereas the film-viewing public can simply take a film at face value. When we've screened it to audiences, including an audience of a thousand people in Flint, Michigan, and about a hundred people in Oakland, California, the response has been overwhelmingly very, very positive. People have enjoyed the film; there has been a lot of enthusiasm. They see that there is a fair amount of comedy and drama in the work. For me as a filmmaker, the audiences got it.

Harris's parting comments on the production of *Diary of a Blade*:

One of the things I can't underscore enough is how much support I received from the community of Flint, Michigan. We established alliances through the support of the local Chamber of Commerce. A variety of businesses provided us with services, meals, costumes; the local hospital, the hospital employees. Some of the hospital employees were part of the ensemble cast. One of my associate producers was part of the hospital staff. That support made me want to at least share the first public screening with them and perhaps raise a little money for their on-going mission in the delivery of health care services. We scheduled a benefit premier in Flint. The proceeds were shared by the Hurley Medical Center and the Flint Area Educational Foundation.

## BIO-CRITICAL REVIEW

*Diary of a Blade.* "The film's realism is also its strength, and Harris is at ease enough to provide his story with the levity it needs to be entertaining and insightful. Rated \*\*\* good."—Ed Bradley, *Flint Journal*

## EDUCATION

Harvard College, A.B. (magna cum laude), biology

Harvard Medical School, M.D. (cum laude), medicine

Harvard School of Public Health, M.P.H., general studies

University of California, San Francisco, general surgery residency

## AWARDS

*Chameleon Street*
  Sundance Film Festival, Grand Jury Prize, 1990
*Diary of a Blade*
  Black Filmmakers Hall of Fame, Second Prize, Feature Film Category, 1996

## SOURCES

Interview and follow-up interview by Spencer Moon, May 1991; August 1996.
Bradley, Ed. "Debut Film Makes Point with Realism and Honesty," *Flint Journal*,
    September 14, 1995, p. B4.
Woods, Michael D., comp. *Afromation: 366 Days of African American History*. Omaha,
    NE: Mykco Communications, 1996.

Wendell Burks Harris Jr.

# WENDELL BURKS HARRIS JR.

## BACKGROUND

Wendell Harris's fascination with films and the movie-making process began at an early age. He attended the nationally known Interlochen Arts Academy in Michigan for his high school degree. He later attended the Juilliard School of Drama in New York for his undergraduate degree in fine arts. At Juilliard he studied with John Houseman (co-founder with Orson Welles of the Mercury Theater). During the early eighties he produced, directed and acted in a series of radio programs that received local, regional and national distribution. In 1983 he read a newspaper account of William Douglas Street, a Black con artist who was a master impersonator. The story so intrigued him that he met the man and did a series of video interviews that were adapted into a narrative screenplay.

## FIRST FEATURE FILM: *CHAMELEON STREET*

I first met Wendell in 1991 prior to the San Francisco opening of his first feature film, *Chameleon Street*, and did an initial interview. Many quotes are from that interview, except where noted.

### Doug Street

In 1991 I asked Wendell, What made Doug Street a character you'd want to write about?

What I immediately saw when I read the first article on Doug was his ability to act, and act convincingly. That's the test of an actor: Does the audience believe? Part of the addiction that Doug has to the act of impersonation is the moment when he looks into somebody's eyes and he can see that he is pressing the right buttons to make them believe his performance. That's maybe the purest part of the high he gets from impersonating, because he certainly doesn't look for money. In fourteen years he made less than $4 thousand from the impersonations.

Where is Doug Street today (in 1996)?

I can't tell you the exact prison. When we last spoke (1991) he was out, because he had been released in 1989. Doug was of great assistance to us during the production of the film.

## Process

How did you write the script? Describe a little bit of your process.

A bit of my process can be described by saying cigarettes, 16-hour writing stints, a lot of coffee, sometimes espresso, and a lot of bone-cracking. I continually crack the neckbones and also the spine. Writing is really a situation where you sit down alone in a room with four walls and you go over and over and over. For me, the process in *Chameleon Street* was even more prolonged because it took us four years to raise the money. During that four-year period I was determined to make some use of that time beyond just making presentations to potential investors. So it was a block of time that eventually led to twenty-eight separate revisions of the script. The process was one of perfecting and polishing and letting the thing grow over a four-year period. That's time which I don't always expect to have. I really kind of look askance when people suggest that you shouldn't spend more than a certain allotted number of weeks on writing a screenplay; that if you start writing for a year or two years, you are doing detrimental harm to the screenplay. Anybody halfway sane can spend four years on a script and make it better, than if they had spent one year.

## Investors

Initially, I thought that when we began searching for funds, these prominent Black businessmen who really have the funds to do it would be the ones. It turned out to be the guy down the street that you've known for twenty years that invests $25 thousand. Yes, we couldn't have done *Chameleon Street* if we had not had the substantial number of Black investors that we had. We were selling $25 thousand shares in a limited partnership. We did have a few White investors. The majority were Black. The people who ended up investing were not those that I initially thought would invest. The ones who ended up investing were the ones who had known my family, my parents who have been in Flint, Michigan, since 1951. The majority of them never even read the script.

Would you talk today (1996) a little bit more about the film's finances?

The investors all got their money back with one exception: Dr. Wendell B. Harris Sr. and his wife, Helen, my parents. The investment that they had put into the budget, we are still not totally clear yet in terms of their investment. Although we have given them back two-thirds of it. Everyone else who invested in the film got their money off the top.

## Sundance

How did you feel when you won the award at the Sundance Film Festival?

I felt elated, I felt vindicated, I felt validated and I felt very hopeful. At that moment, what I envisioned was a very quick distribution on a national level. While accepting that award from Willem Dafoe and Danny Glover, the program M.C.s, with my mother [Helen] and brother (Hobart), we all thought the same thing—that within three weeks we would be in every state in the union. None of us were aware that we had more than a year of hard distribution negotiation to go through, not to mention legal problems.

## Distribution

How did you deal with the fact that it wasn't snapped up immediately by a distributor?

I began writing. I wrote three screenplays back to back in a little over a year after Sundance. After Sundance, I first went out to Hollywood and had a lot of meetings. After none of those jelled into anything palpable, I returned to Michigan and began writing. I wrote a script about the current drug scene in the United States, a comedy script, and then began to work on a script about the life of Joe Louis, the great heavyweight champion boxer.

How has ancillary nontheatrical distribution gone? (1996)

Academy Video has released *Chameleon Street*, and everything was fine until 1994 when they went bankrupt. So now I'm constantly searching for video copies of *Chameleon Street*. As Donald Bogle (noted Black author/scholar/educator) warned me in 1994, Black authors and Black filmmakers always need to keep copies of their work. They are always at risk; the next thing you know, they are collector's items.

### Success or a Facsimile

Have you had the kind of success you had hoped for with *Chameleon Street?*

I can definitely say every time the film is seen that's a success, because there's always such a great reaction. I can't overemphasize the need to be committed to your vision. If you make a feature film and commit six years of your life to it, as well as most of your family's money and individuals' investments, and if you have less than an immediate return on those investments, then the critical response becomes one of your major rewards. I've have no complaints about the film being misunderstood or savaged by critics; in fact, it's been quite the opposite. I've always been kind of amazed that after entering the public arena, I have no complaints about journalists or media so far. It's not because *Chameleon Street* was universally praised, because the critics who wrote about it understood the intent of the film. The audiences who have seen the film have gotten the intent of the film. This was true if I was observing an audience in Venice, in Africa or wherever. People get the film. So the issue becomes one of distribution. *Chameleon Street*'s distribution was minuscule, given the potential of distribution. I'm constantly hearing from people who have seen the film or just rented the film. Because the film never opened in several hundred theaters nationwide, it was at a complete disadvantage. I cannot say that the distribution of *Chameleon Street* was adequate, let alone what I had hoped for.

### RENAISSANCE

In 1991 I asked, Do you think the current Black cinema renaissance has a future?

Yes, definitely. For the first time in the history of cinema, Black auteurs are making themselves known. By definition an auteur is not a hired hand of a studio, but an artist with a vision. Whether it's Jean-Luc Godard or Spike Lee,* the films will get made. That's why we have a different cycle this time around, different than the cycle of *Superfly*, *Troubleman* and the so-called Blaxploitation period.

What do you think of the Black film/video renaissance? (1996)

Institutionalized racism is synonymous with Hollywood. While you may find it difficult to point a finger at an individual, that's the nature of institutionalized racism; it is still an impediment. Because of institutionalized racism, people of Michael Moore's (*Roger & Me*, 1989) or Quentin Tarantino's (*Pulp Fiction*, 1994) racial complexion preclude this concern. They don't have to make any kind of strategy, nor do they have to deal with the impediments that institutionalized racism present for Black producers, writers and directors. Having said that, look at what takes place: Any White director is virtually assured the opportunity to fail once, fail twice, fail three times and still come back. Many of the Black directors are in the same kind of position that Melvin Van Peebles* found himself in after the revenues *Sweet, Sweet Back . . .*** started to come in. Or they are in the same position that Oscar Micheaux* found himself in during the late thirties when he was losing his actors to the Hollywood sponge. The point is that it's still the same monster. Perhaps the monster's toenails have been filed down somewhat, perhaps the monster's been doused with some water. The monster is still there.

What if we had arbitrarily cut off Alfred Hitchcock when his first two films came out and they didn't stop the world? They had lackluster box office sales. If he had been cut off, there would be no Hitchcock legacy. If he had been cut off in those early days before he had a grasp of the medium, let alone whatever he had achieved had been solidified, there would be no American career of Hitchcock.

There is not that elbow room in Hollywood for Blacks to stretch, learn, move, or even, for that matter, have assignments that go beyond a certain circumscribed stereotypical bent. For example, when I signed with Jerry Weintraub in October 1992 to direct a science fiction film for Warner Brothers, I was told at the time that this was a history-making deal. This is what the White executives at Warner and throughout Hollywood told me. They said I would be the first Black male director/writer of a science fiction Hollywood opus. I was told at the same time by Black Hollywood executives and Black Hollywood attorneys, the day I signed to do the deal was also the day the deal was destined to go into turn-around (i.e., be shelved). How did they know this? They knew the system out there and when things were status quo and when things were not.

## UNIQUENESS

What makes you unique as a filmmaker?

What a personal question. Absolutely nothing except what makes me unique as a person. My own personal experience, personal obsessions, my own personal vision, my own personal drive, my own personal destiny. Like a flower unto itself, alone. I think that I've met very few people who are as obsessive as I am about film. I've met a lot of obsessive people, but very few that I thought of as constantly "out there." I mean, everything I think, say, do is somehow related to film. When I dream at night, I dream about film. I've had this passion since I was 4, when I saw a black-and-white film on the television my father had in his office. I didn't know at the time what I was watching, but I knew in an instant that the concept behind this vision was remarkable. I later learned that the film I was watching was James Cagney in *Public Enemy* (1931). I didn't understand the word "film" at the time, but I did comprehend that people together had arranged action, character and music and you could show it again and again. That's probably the central revelation of my life, so far at least.

I asked Harris in 1996 if his views on what makes him unique as a filmmaker had changed since 1991.

A cook cooks food; a painter paints paintings; a filmmaker makes films. Before you actually get to the point of making the film, there is the art of the deal. Whatever color you are, you have to go through those steps and that's understood. But when you are working and not making as many films as you would care to make, because you are having difficulty in getting the autonomy you want as well as the funds you need, then you learn not so much about new aspects of whatever it was that you thought makes you unique. That doesn't change. What changes is your take on what you thought you could take in the first place. What changes is your attitude toward your own caliber, your own ability to stick with it until there is no stuck left.

## INDEPENDENT PRODUCTION

In the 1996 follow-up interview, Harris described his production company, Prismatic Images, Inc., for me.

It is a Michigan-based corporation with an office in Los Angeles, Prismatic West, to gather the necessary financial backing in the Los Angeles arena that is available. The Los Angeles staff includes associate producers Vincent Boccio and Phil Darius Wallace. Both Vincent and Phil are working to solidify the contracts that are so prevalent out there, such as production and distribution or companies. They are also gathering the financial base of the company.

Certainly the experience of *Chameleon Street* taught us that the independent filmmakers put all their effort, finances and time into a finished work and then go with their hands out to a distributor who will hopefully put up the money for prints and advertising. Because of the situation with *Chameleon Street*, we are very much interested in putting together financial structures that include prints and advertising in order to secure a solid distribution deal. With the finances in place, the independent filmmaker has options in deciding who will distribute as opposed to asking and negotiating and having an evaluation made on what they think and how much they (the distributor) will put in. The purpose of Prismatic West is to supplement all the artistic work into a marketing strategy.

## BEYOND HOLLYWOOD

Do you think making independent feature films and marketing outside the Hollywood system is still viable?

It's more viable today than at any other time. But that doesn't mean it's still not a struggle.

## ADVICE FOR ASPIRANTS

What would you say to young aspiring filmmakers?

Get out. I remember when in the last twenty-five years I've gone to innumerable film seminars, film symposiums, meetings and panel discussions. So many times, filmmakers who had achieved something would be speaking about the difficulties of the business. How if you could find something else to do, perhaps you should do it. I always said, "What jerks. Come on, just give us the information, don't tell us not to get into film. We know what we want." Now, at this stage, I would seriously say to make sure it's what you want to do. I think if it's not what you want to do and you think it is, you'll know it pretty soon. Because it is such a crucible of finances, ego, whims, you end up spending your life and energy just on the mechanics and the art itself virtually takes care of itself. Since you must wear so many hats, you have to be so many people. Whether you want to be involved in the business side or not, you don't have a choice, you've got to. There are so many obstacles that unless you've got that bite-the-bone-to-the-bullet attitude, you really might as well do something else.

When asked to update his comments to young people, Harris said:

Take the old adage, "show business." It should really be categorized as "business show." Take that to heart enough to understand that the marketing of the product is going to demand a huge amount of attention. You don't have to be an actor/writer/director to need to pay attention to your deals. Even if you are acting and only acting, or writing and only writing, whatever you do in the business you're going to have to deal with the marketing of yourself. You look at all the artists and how they deal with the problem of marketing themselves, with or without the added complexity of marketing a Black artist. You look at Vincent Van Gogh, who could not sell anything while he was alive. Now, of course, he is the avatar of 20th-century post-impressionism. This is exactly the situation that drives men and women mad unless they put some coherent emphasis on how they are going to attack this marketing mountain. I would only add that the business side of it is something to be paid the same caliber attention that an artist pays to acquiring their technique. Vincent Van Gogh should have had someone like Roseanne Barr to talk with. If he could see how this woman has used her genius to market her neurosis, then he would understand the crux of the issue. Whether you're Salvador Dali, James Baldwin or William Shakespeare, you're marketing your neurosis. Be scientific about it.

## FILMOGRAPHY

### Director/Actor (Co-Star)

*Collette Vignette,*\*\* 1986, 4 min., video. In the 1996 follow-up interview, Wendell described his first significant award-winning artistic screen endeavor.

The material for the final cut of this project was culled from twenty-four hours of interviews with Collette Haywood when she was 18 years old and at the height of her teenage sensibilities. She was so effective, she later got a featured role in *Chameleon Street*. This film (*Collette Vignette*) allowed her to display her unique outlook and her ability to tell the truth. The concept grew out of me asking her questions hour after hour on a wide range of topics; from her comments on the television series *Perfect Strangers*; her ambition of being the mother of the next Dr. Martin Luther King Jr.; her take on Blacks in cinema; her take on the meaning of menstruation; and ad infinitum.

What has happened to the distribution of this work?

> Initially, for the first several years after it won the Grand Prize in the competition, it was given over to the American Film Institute (AFI). They had complete control over the work during that period. During that period it was shown by the AFI on various venues available to them through cable television, and also sent out as part of their promotional packet, etc. Now that we have the distribution rights back, we are going to handle its redistribution but at the moment we have not placed it. As synchronicity would have it, I had a conversation today with representatives from Showtime and HBO cable networks. They both are interested in looking at *Collette Vignette* as part of a package of short subjects that they will be running.

## Director/Screenplay/Actor (Starring as Doug Street)

*Chameleon Street*, 1990, 98 min., 35mm, Northern Arts Entertainment. Executive producers, Helen B. Harris and Hobart Harris, Wendell's mother and brother, respectively. His father, Wendell B. Harris Sr., served as medical consultant for the hospital scenes. His younger brother, Charles, served as production assistant and still photographer.

The story is about William Douglas Street, who impersonated a variety of people including a Harvard graduate doctor, a *Time* magazine writer, a French foreign exchange student at Yale University, and a civil rights lawyer. As a doctor he performed over three dozen hysterectomies, all of which were successful. Street later served time in jail for his chicanery. In the film, Street's first operation is a very funny scene. He is shown preparing for the operation by sneaking into the men's room with a medical book tucked in the back of his pants under his white doctor's smock to bone up on physiology.

Can you describe some memorable production moments?

> The masquerade-ball sequence, which required seven days to shoot, was memorable. We had three separate camera units working simultaneously. I was in a make-up room being made up for the scene. They had put together a video relay system that showed me what was going on. I directed from the back of this make-up room. The evening of the fourth day when the beast mask was being taken off my face by the make-up man, it unfortunately also started taking off layers of skin. The adhesives used to make the mask adhere to my skin was as damaging to the face as what they put on to take it off. I went home that night and looked in the mirror and thought my face looked like the final *Portrait of Dorian Grey*. That was memorable.
>
> Every part of the film was memorable to a large degree. That was because it was so exciting to see something that you had put together over a four-year period and then see it, on a $2 million budget, be infused with life as you had envisioned it. That's always the tragedy of Frankenstein. He's not sorry that he succeeds; he's sorry from a cosmetic standpoint that his creation is horrible to see. In the same way raising

the body of *Chameleon Street*, I was really glad to see that all of the right colors were in place and it was what we had envisioned creating in the first place.

## Writer/Director/Actor

### Radio

*Black Biography*, 1981–1982, audiotape, 24-program series, each 15 minutes in length. Wendell described some of the production details of his radio work:

> We handled living and deceased Black historic personalities. For the show on the Black western pioneer James P. Beckwourth, I portrayed Beckwourth. For someone like Julian Bond, we would actually have the tape of their voice. We had individual sales to radio stations around the country, as well as selling a large number of shows to army surplus stores around the world. We also marketed extensively to libraries and schools around the country.

*The Casebook of Key-Lloyd Johnson*, 1981–1982, audiotape, 13-program series. Wendell talked about this program and the two radio series and the valuable lesson he learned as producer:

> This series was marketed originally only in Flint, Michigan, and later Detroit, Michigan. The story behind both of these radio series is that we produced them for about $150 thousand and later were offered $380 thousand by IBM to purchase both series. For foolish reasons, we turned that offer down. For those who do produce radio or otherwise and get an offer of twice what you spent to produce it, take the money. We learned a very valuable lesson there.

## Actor

### Selected Theater

All roles for Juilliard School of the Arts, main stage production:

*The Cherry Orchard*, performed the role of Firs.

*The Crucible*, performed the role of John Proctor.

*Hamlet*, performed the title role.

*Uncle Vanya*, performed the role of Telygin.

Also performed over two dozen lead roles between high school and college combined.

## BIO-CRITICAL REVIEW

*Chameleon Street*. "Mr. Harris demonstrates that he's a triple-threat new filmmaker of original and eccentric talent."—Vincent Canby, *New York Times*

————. "Wendell Harris' performance as (Doug) Street is remarkable—a tour-de-force capturing the many nuances of a displaced man finding a bogus place in life and then being displaced again when he is exposed. The script is intense, literate and involving, each scene designed to probe Street's oddball personality to greater depths."—John Stanley, *San Francisco Chronicle*

————. "The film is an auspicious debut for Harris, who transforms a pat television docudrama into an examination of why a man of [Doug] Street's intelligence needs to pretend to be someone else, and why others are so ready to believe him. In telling the story of this impostor's rise and fall, *Chameleon Street* addresses issues of race, economics, sex, anger and pride."—*San Francisco Sun Reporter*

## AWARDS

*Chameleon Street*
 Dakar Film Festival, Senegal, Festival Honor Award, 1992
 NAACP Image Award, 1991
 Sundance Film Festival, Grand Prize, 1990

*Collette Vignette*
 Sony/U.S. Visions Video Contest, Grand Prize, 1986 (Judges included Francis
   Ford Coppola, Levar Burton, Justin Bateman, Tom Shales, Whoopi Goldberg)

## EDUCATION

Interlochen Arts Academy, Michigan, high school diploma (with honors)
Juilliard School of Drama, New York, B.F.A.

## MEMBERSHIPS

American Federation of Television and Radio Artists

## SOURCES

Interview and follow-up interview by Spencer Moon, May 1991; May 1996.

### Newspapers

Canby, Vincent. "*Chameleon Street*: A Man Compelled to Be Anyone Else," *New York Times*, March 24, 1991, pp. B1, B4.
"Chameleon Street Now Playing at Lumiere," *San Francisco Sun Reporter*, June 26, 1991, pp. 31–32.
Stanley, John. "Actor/Writer/Director: A True 'Chameleon' Newcomer Tells Tale of Real-Life," *San Francisco Chronicle*, June 16, 1991, p. 10.

Reginald Hudlin

# REGINALD AND WARRINGTON HUDLIN

The initial interview with both brothers took place in 1991. They were being given the Clarence Muse Youth Award by the Black Filmmakers Hall of Fame in Oakland, California. The follow-up interview was with Reginald.

## BACKGROUND

The current Black film renaissance has helped open the door for several filmmakers. This is the case for the Hudlin brothers. Reginald says that because of his relationship with Spike Lee,* when producers would chase Spike with films and ideas, he referred them to Reginald. As a result of the search for new Black directors, Reginald's first feature, *House Party*** (1990), was produced. He and his brother Warrington had already established themselves as producers and directors of their own independent productions. Columbia Pictures paid Warrington to produce and direct the film *The Making of "School Daze"* (1987), a promotional production on Spike Lee's second feature film. In addition, Warrington and Reginald had been responsible for helping to create the Black Filmmaker's Foundation. This organization was first a distributor of independently produced film and video by African Americans, and now an organization for networking African American film/video makers.

When the opportunity came to make the dynamic leap, the brothers were both ready to produce and direct one of the most successful first feature films by Black talent for a Black teen audience in quite a while. Reginald's college thesis film became the feature film *House Party*. The film has grossed $26 million in theatrical release to date, says Reginald. When talking to Reginald about his relationship with his brother and their joint filmmaking efforts, thoughts of two earlier brothers who left a legacy of films—the Johnson brothers, George and Noble—come to mind. In 1916 the Johnson brothers formed the Lincoln Motion Picture Company in Los Angeles, California.

## SUCCESS OF *HOUSE PARTY*

In our initial interview, we asked why the film *House Party* had been so successful.

> Any movie that's successful is because people see it multiple times. The thing that distinguishes a movie that makes a lot of money, a mega-hit, is the repeat viewings.
>
> There is this White guy in Indiana who has seen it thirty-two times. A friend was visiting this guy in Indiana and saw this guy watching this tape of *House Party*. Not all thirty-two times were on tape, he said. He said if you actually count tape, it gets into some really obscene number. My friend said he knew the guy who made *House Party*. The White guy didn't believe him, so they called me. And he told me it's his favorite movie. He is a young adult in his twenties who is plugged into what the film is saying. Not the target demographic, by any means.
>
> It shows that when you make a movie that you believe in, people respond. It has very Black humor in the cultural sense but all people get into it. It exceeded its demographic, which was teenagers. Once adults got into theaters and saw the brilliant performance of Robin Harris, they realized it was a film for them as well.

Why did you choose not to do *House Party 2*** and *House Party 3***?

> In terms of career planning, we felt it was important for us to constantly do different kinds of films. America already says you're a Black filmmaker and poses certain limitations. But then to say you're a Black filmmaker who only does teen hip-hop movies is another box. So to completely shatter those kind of preconceptions, I decided that the next film is going to be a science fiction musical comedy.

## INFLUENCES

When probed to mention cinematic influences on his work, Reginald said:

Certainly, filmmakers like Steven Spielberg, George Lucas, that kind of pure entertainment. Then you have a guy like Terry Gilliam with that anarchistic imagination. Then you have the Hong Kong filmmakers like John Woo, masters of the action genre. John Ford, particularly his film *The Man Who Shot Liberty Valence* (1962)—I just keep going back to that movie. Frank Capra, Preston Sturges, Akira Kurosawa, I could go on and on.

## OPPORTUNITIES

After the success of *House Party*, the Hudlin brothers signed an agreement with Tri-Star Pictures to develop motion pictures and with NBC to develop television programs.

In early 1991 a joint press conference was held by the Black Filmmaker's Hall of Fame and the Black Filmmaker's Foundation. The purpose was to announce that for the first time in two decades, more than a dozen films by Black directors were being released later in 1991 and that audiences should support those films.

After the brothers' relationship with Tri-Star Pictures ended, they signed another production agreement with Twentieth Century Television in 1993.

How is the relationship with Twentieth Television going?

Our relationship with them ended a year ago. But as soon as that relationship ended, their movie division called me to do the film *The Great White Hype*.

Are you having the kind of success or opportunities for production and distribution that you had hoped for in your relationship with these large companies?

We have very mixed feelings about it. It's nice to have someone underwrite your overhead and all that. When you're not working in the same genre over and over, it's hard to have a relationship with those large companies. One project may excite one studio and another project they may have no interest in, it would be perfect for another studio across town. What has sort of happened is, we have films in development in five different studios. That has proved to be more successful for us than being tied contractually to one studio or company.

## UNIQUENESS

As the Johnson brothers were progenitors of race movies, the Hudlins are part of the new Black cinema renaissance. Reginald described what makes him unique as a filmmaker.

I think there is a consistent theme in our work. My approach has always been to make a film that I have not seen before. I try to make films from my personal perspective. It is tied not only to my race but to the fact that I'm from the Midwest. I wanted to make films not set in Harlem or Watts, but in a small town. I wanted to deal with contemporary youth culture—not in every film, but certainly in *House Party*. My student film version of *House Party* was done before there were any popular films on the hip hop subculture. Meaning not just the rap music but the dancing, the clothing, that whole attitude. By the time we began production of the feature version of *House Party*, there still had not been a film from the perspective of the typical young person involved in this subculture as opposed to stars. The response from young people has been, "This is my life"; "I can relate to this." I've had 50-year-old White people who said the same thing. When you are so specific, you plug into a universal that a lot of people can relate to. What makes each individual perspective of each Black filmmaker unique is what they draw upon. I'm from East St. Louis, statistically the Blackest city in the United States—95% Black population. The culture is very rich there. We consistently draw on those East St. Louis cultural roots to inform our filmmaking. Those sets of experiences and appreciations are filtered also by the fact that our college years were spent in Ivy League schools. Those two things in balance give us a perfect reference point. You see, a film works on a lot of different levels simultaneously. It can be very high-brow, with a lot of arcane information that slips in on one level. Then there are other things that are totally R' and B' (rhythm and blues).

When questioned in 1996 regarding what makes him unique as a film-maker, Reginald said:

There is this schism in the Black community where there is a very strong anti-intellectual sentiment. I call it ghettocentricity. At the same time, there are a group of artists and thinkers that really want to build on the kinds of gains that we made in the sixties, in terms of really stretching out and breaking the bounds of what is considered traditional Black culture. The problem is, these two directions have very little interaction, and I think that's disastrous. I feel that my work is able to bridge those two groups. In bridging those two groups my work plugs into a very broad appeal, across boundaries of race and age. After you look at my latest film, you have to ask what is the commonality of the films. I think it is the combination of high and low culture. It satisfies a huge chunk of the audience regardless of class, age or race. I don't see a lot of other filmmakers doing that in the same way.

The parents of the Hudlin brothers (their father is an insurance executive and their mother is an educator) helped them to create their success today. Their parents believed a quality education was important. They believed that two young Black men could study filmmaking at two of the best Ivy League schools in the country.

## ADVICE FOR ASPIRANTS

What can you tell young people interested in the business?

I usually tell them to quit. Usually if you tell people to quit and they do it, then they shouldn't have been in the business in the first place. This is a process of elimination. But for those who are really determined to move forward, get your craft together first of all. It drives me crazy when so many people don't have a knowledge of film history. When we asked them about international cinema, like Costa-Gavras, Jean-Luc Godard; it's like, who? No sense of style. So you need that first and foremost. For people of color, the poison that is holding us back is self-hate. Until you really start to think about that and how that affects your life, it's really hard to live up to your full potential.

## THE FUTURE

What do you hope to accomplish in the future?

Just looking at the next five years, I would like to create a bigger body of work. Making more movies. The trick is to make more movies and to make them good movies. That's my immediate focus—to have more product out there. To not have long gaps between projects. It's hard, because I'm constantly trying to make quantum leaps in terms of subject matter. The long-term goal is to build some kind of institution that makes it possible for the next generation of filmmakers to totally smoke my work. No question about that. To me, when you look at forms of Black expression, the most artistically successful is music. The challenge is to get as articulated, as varied, as complex as Black music. In terms of the expression of the human experience.

When we spoke in 1996 about his plans for the future, Reginald said:

I'm trying to develop films in as many different genres as possible: science fiction, comedy, action, fiction, horror and historical genres for both feature films and television.

## FILMOGRAPHY

### Directors/Producers

*House Party,*\*\* 1990, 98 mins., 35mm, color, New Line Cinema. Written and directed by Reginald Hudlin and produced by Warrington Hudlin. Featuring the rap group Kid'N'Play, Full Force, Robin Harris, Martin Lawrence, Tisha Campbell and A.J. Johnson. Cameo appearance by George "Funkadelic" Clinton, leader of the band "Parliament-Funkadelic," the godfather of funk and party music. Marcus Miller composed the film's score, which featured hip hop music by Kid'N'Play and Full Force, to name a few. (Miller has won Grammy awards for his talent as music producer. This includes work with Miles Davis, Luther Vandross and David Sanborn.)

   *House Party* is an urban musical comedy. It takes its direction from earlier Hollywood films that go back as far as the Andy Hardy series, the Henry Aldrich comedies, the beach blanket movies, the Elvis musicals, and films like *Stormy Weather* (1943). Its humor is accessible to the average filmgoer. Some of the Black humor seems toned down, and as a result this film has a broad audience appeal. The story is of a teenager who breaks his word, after being grounded by his father, not to attend a party. The resultant comedy of errors is nicely paced and edited, with some refreshing performances by Christopher Reid, Martin Lawrence and Tisha Campbell. Reginald commented on the film's production:

> We knew after the first week of production that you could make a lot of *House Partys*. There was a general feeling on the set that you could make *House Party 2* through *10*. They could all really be funny. People enjoyed these characters; you wanted to see what would happen to them the next day and the next day. As Warrington said, I didn't want to keep doing that all my life, as fun as that would be. We already had this huge stack of films to make, so we figured we better get to it.

When asked to revisit the *House Party* and *Boomerang* experience from a contemporary perspective, Reginald said:

> It's very interesting, there's a split in terms of the audience consensus in retrospect regarding *House Party* and *Boomerang*. *House Party* is a well-liked film generally. White audiences love *House Party* and some do and some don't get *Boomerang*. For Black audiences *Boomerang* is the best thing ever, and they see *House Party* as good. I love *House Party* for several reasons: because I wrote and directed it, it feels the most mine, the most uncompromised. Also I think it is the strongest of my films visually, even though *Boomerang* has far greater production values. Right after the first *House Party* film the studio wanted to make another one right away. I didn't want to become this sort of teen movie filmmaker. The money they offered to do the sequel was equal to or a little less than what they offered us to do the first film. At that point we were getting offers from every other studio in Hollywood. So it was sort of a non-issue.
>    But they had the rights to make sequels, and they did. On the one hand the fact of their (the sequels') success was good, because it estab-

lished the first Black franchise of our generation. Those kinds of precedents are important in the marketplace. Certainly the *House Party* sequels did not remotely go in the direction that I would go. You never say never in terms of a fourth sequel. But it would be highly unlikely that we would get involved in a fourth sequel. The studio can make more *House Party*s if they choose; but I feel like Steven Spielberg and *Jaws*, there was *Jaws* in 3D. You just hope that people remember the original film.

*House Party 2* and *3* concepts were based on the original *House Party* film. See the chapter on George Jackson* and Doug McHenry.* The Hudlins' role was a financial one for the two sequels; they were paid for the use of their original concept.

## Co-Producers

*Bebe's Kids,*** 1992, 74 min., 35mm, color. Directed by Bruce Smith. An animated feature film, featuring the voices of Faizon Love, Nell Carter, the rap music artist Tone Loc, Vanessa Bell Calloway, Wayne Collins and Jonell Green. The film's concept was based on a routine by the comedian Robin Harris (*House Party,*** *Do the Right Thing***). Reginald described the film's genesis:

> *Bebe's Kids* was going to be a live action film starring the late Robin Harris. So when he passed away, we picked something that would be a memorial to his genius. I didn't want to re-cast him, so we decided to do an animated film. We got a young comedian, Faison Love, to do his voice. As a film it is somewhat compromised to me. We had to work in partnership with the movie studio and the animation company. I wanted to do a film 100% true to the spirit of Robin Harris. Half-way through, a decision was made to make it a film for children. That is completely different from, say, the animated television series on the FOX television network *The Simpsons*, which kids love but adults like as well. I wanted to go more in that direction, where you have adult material but it is not objectionable for a young audience. The film reflects that tension between what we wanted and what we accomplished. At the same time, so many parents come up to me and say that their kids refuse to get dressed in the morning unless they watch *Bebe's Kids*. It is the first African American animated feature film. I've spoken to young audiences and I mention my list of films and they shrug, until *Bebe's Kids* is mentioned and then all of a sudden a great cheer goes up. There is unquestionably a power in that movie. It's great to break new territory, and it's good to have something as a memorial so that people will remember the late Robin Harris.

*Boomerang,*** 1992, 35mm, color. Paramount. Produced by Warrington Hudlin and directed by Reginald Hudlin; featuring Eddie Murphy. The film has grossed over $120 million worldwide. It cost $42 million to make—so far the most expensive Black film to date (in comparison, *Malcolm X*** by Spike Lee* cost $39 million). Reginald talked about his experience in making this film:

When we started doing it, I was very pleased to be working with Eddie Murphy. At the outset I thought this was a great movie for him, at this point in his career. To expand him, this film would take him into a Tom Hanks kind of direction. A more romantic, sophisticated leading role that would reflect his age. He had been doing the same character for a long time, and he was anxious to expand and as a fan I wanted to be there. As a result, we seem to have made a movie that has become a classic. The number of people I've met who watch it every Thanksgiving—it's kind of the fallback rental. You know, like, "Oh, let's watch *Boomerang* again." The number of film scripts that are floating around Hollywood that say they want that *Boomerang* type feeling is very flattering. It's funny—when I made the movie, I didn't necessarily see it as a socially political film. It turns out to be a very political film. A number of critics reacted hostilely to the film because it showed a significant number of Black middle-class people who didn't think about White people one way or another. White people weren't a factor in their lives. That was shocking and offensive to these certain critics. In retrospect, I look at that reaction and go, "Wow! That movie was really, really important." You realize after the fact there isn't anything like this. I'm very proud of *Boomerang*.

### Director (Reginald Hudlin)

*The Great White Hype*, 1996, 35mm, color. Stars Samuel Jackson, Damon Wayans, Jeff Goldblum, Jon Lovitt, Jamie Foxx, Cheech Marin, Corbin Bernson, Sally Richardson and John Rhys-Davies. Reginald expressed his thoughts on his latest film:

I was impressed with the magnitude of cast just being on the set every day. It's a pretty incredible collection of people. It is comedy set in the boxing world. It's about a flamboyant boxing promoter (Samuel Jackson) who has a heavyweight champion (Damon Wayans) that is so good that no one goes to see the fights because they know the fight will be over in a few rounds. For the sake of novelty to get the crowds and people excited again, he decides to create a Great White Hope. It's about the hype machine and how the race card is played for fun and profit.

### *Television*

*Cosmic Slop*, 1994, 90 min. A three-part HBO anthology, each part directed separately. Reginald and Warrington Hudlin were also executive producers. The program was hosted by funk music great George (*Parliament-Funkadelic*) Clinton. A Clinton-penned song, *Cosmic Slop*, provided the title for the series.

*Space Traders*. A story of racial conflicts that is set against the background of an alien encounter. Featuring Bertice Berry, Franklin Cover, Robert Guillaume, Casey Kasem, Brock Peters and Roxie Roker. Teleplay by Trey Ellis; based on a short story by Derek Bell; directed by Reginald Hudlin. Reginald described the project's genesis:

I'm a huge science fiction fan, as are many Black people. But the ability to get those $40 million budgets in Hollywood is very difficult. So I said, "Maybe this concept is suitable for television and we could establish its presence and build from there." I'm always on the hunt for good stories. I read the short story by Derek Bell called *Space Traders*, and I said, "We've got to do this." I went to HBO cable network, because I thought they might be interested. The show won two Cable Ace Awards; the segment *Space Traders* won for Best Dramatic Special. Paula Jai Parker, who appeared in *Tang*, won a Cable Ace Award for Best Dramatic Actress. The program got rave reviews. There was a firestorm of controversy, all kinds of people responding very strongly about the material in the shows. So it was a very satisfying production from a creative perspective. We did this albeit with virtually no money but to tell a story that just totally moved people. I'm very happy with it. We're talking with HBO about turning it into a regular series. It's a very edgy series and it's tough to move that forward out there, but we just keep at it. The first one is done, so there is no reason to retreat.

*Tang.* Shows urban destruction set in the not-too-distant future. Featuring Chi McBride and Paula Jai Parker. Teleplay by Kyle Baker; based on a short story by Chester Himes; directed by Kevin Rodney Sullivan.

*The First Commandment.* Shows the clash of nontraditional versus Christian religious beliefs in a Latino neighborhood. Featuring Efrain Figueroa and Nicholas Turturro. Written and directed by Warrington Hudlin.

### Independent Productions

**Reginald** (producer and director):

*Reggie's World of Soul*, 1985

*The Kold Waves*, 1985

*House Party*, 1983 (student version), won Student Academy Award as Best Film (New England region)

**Warrington** (producer and director):

*The Making of "School Daze,"* 1987

*Street Corner Stories*, 1980

*Black at Yale*, 1978

## JOINT AWARDS

Black Filmmakers Hall of Fame, Clarence Muse Youth Award, 1991

Cable Ace Award, *Cosmic Slop: Space Traders*, Best dramatic special, 1995

City of Newark, *House Party*, Outstanding Achievement in Filmmaking, 1990

Nancy Susan Reynolds Award, Center for Population Options, Promoting Responsible Sexual Behavior, 1991

Sundance Film Awards, *House Party*: Best Cinematography, 1989; Filmmakers Award (voted by peers), 1989

Urban League, Award for Outstanding Achievement in Filmmaking, 1992

## REGINALD'S AWARDS

Black America Cinema Society, *House Party*, Outstanding Achievement in Cinematography, 1984

Black Filmmaker Foundation, *House Party* (student version), 1983

Black Filmmaker Foundation, *Reggie's World of Soul*, Outstanding Production, 1985

Black Filmmaker Foundation, *The Kold Waves*, Outstanding Production, 1986; 10th Anniversary Award, 1990

Black Filmmakers Hall of Fame, New Voices New Visions, 1991

## EDUCATION

**Reginald**: Harvard University, B.A., filmmaking

**Warrington**: Yale University, B.A., filmmaking

## SOURCES

Interview with Reginald and Warrington by George Hill and Spencer Moon, February 1991; follow-up interview by Spencer Moon with Reginald, February 1996.

# ALBERT AND ALLEN HUGHES

## BACKGROUND

The Hughes "twenty-something" brothers are fraternal twins who moved to Pomona, California, by age 8 and grew up there. Allen is younger by 9 minutes, heavier and the extrovert; Albert is thinner and quieter. They have a biracial background: Their father is African American and their mother is Armenian. Their mother, Aida, raised them as a single parent. She currently runs a vocational center in Pomona, California. They were interested in filmmaking at an early age. Wanting to encourage them in their creative endeavors, their mother gave them a camera. By the time they were 12 they were making Super 8mm films. By the time they were 14 they were developing serious filmic skills with their editing of pictures, creating sound tracks and editing them, and scoring their films as well.

## TRAINING AND INFLUENCES

Their formal training in media came in high school when Allen took television production classes. They received additional formal training when Allen went to Los Angeles City College and enrolled in its film program. They have gone from an apprenticeship with a "toy" camera and have become journeyman filmmakers. Their admitted cinematic influences include Martin Scorcese, Sergio Leone, Francis Ford Coppola and Brian DePalma. Films that have influenced their work include *Scarface*, *The Untouchables* and *Goodfellas*.

Their film/video work caught the attention of rock video director Tamra Davis. This contact led to their first professional assignment producing and directing a video for Hollywood Records. Within two years, they had directed more than two dozen music videos.

## STYLE

Stylistically, Allen works with the camera and Albert works with the actors. Believing that sound is 50 percent of a film, they work aggressively on sound tracks from effects to music. Cinematically, they have an interest in telling about the underside of life and its effects; they say the violence in their films is put only where they feel it is needed. As the youngest members of the Black cinema renaissance, their perspective is contemporary, has created controversy, is entertaining, has made money and shows all signs of creating an important body of work—all on the basis of their first two feature films.

## FILMOGRAPHY

### Directors/Producers

*Menace II Society*,** 1993, 97 min., 35mm, color, New Line Cinema. Screenplay by Tyger Williams, featuring Larenz Tate, Jada Pinkett, Vonte Sweet and Tyrin Turner. The brothers' first film opened so well at the box office that it expanded from over four hundred theaters to over five hundred theaters after its initial opening-week success. Ryan Williams, the brother of screenwriter Tyger Williams, was the person most responsible for getting Williams and the Hughes brothers together. Ryan had a role in the film as well. Regarding violence in the film, the Hughes brothers say pragmatically, "if people turn their face away from the screen, that's what we want them to do, instead of cheering." Grossed $27 million on a $3 million budget.

### Directors

*Dead Presidents*,** 1995, 121 min., 35mm, color, Hollywood Pictures. Co-story and screenplay by Michael Henry Brown. The original story is based on a short story from the book *Bloods* by Wallace Terry. The book is a fictionalized account of the African American experience in Vietnam. The story is a heist comedy about old, out-of-circulation U.S. currency destined to be burned. The subtext of the film involves issues related to disillusioned Black Vietnam vets and issues of civil rights. Featuring Larenz Tate, Keith David, Freddy Rodriguez, Chris Tucker, N'Bushe Wright and Bokeem Woodbine. Grossed $24 million on a $10 million budget.

### *Television*

*America's Most Wanted*, FOX.

### Student Film

*The Drive-By*, 1988.

### Selected Music Videos

Tupac Shakur, Tone Loc, KRS-1, Too Short, Digital Underground

## BIO-CRITICAL REVIEW

*Dead Presidents.* "Solid storytelling and tight pacing. Reaffirms their ability as film-makers. Shows they can go beyond the limits of the urban street drama."—James Berardinelli, *Internet Movie Database*

———. "They show they can direct with confidence and joy."—Roger Ebert, *Internet Movie Database*

———. "One of the year's great movies. The movie is powerful and accomplished."—Mike Clark, *Internet Movie Database*

*Menace II Society.* "More acutely than any movie before, it gives cinematic expression to the hot-tempered, defiantly nihilistic ethos that ignites gangster rap."—Stephen Holden, *New York Times*

———. "Few recent films have been so honest or so willing to make the audience squirm."—Caryn James, *New York Times*

———. "They're split between fatalism and arrant optimism, and, in that split, their film probably expresses the attitude of their generation more fully than they know."—Peter Rainer, *Los Angeles*

———. "Their direction is mature and the visual style is remarkably accomplished for such young men."—Michael Arago, *San Francisco Weekly*

———. "This graphic portrait of the inner city should strengthen our resolve to bring peace to our troubled streets."—George F. Will, *Los Angeles Times*

## AWARDS

*Menace II Society*
  MTV Movie Awards, Best Picture, 1993

## SOURCES

### Newspapers and Magazines

Ames, Katrine and Danzy Senna. "Twin Killing," *Newsweek*, June 7, 1993, p. 37.
Arago, Michael. "Bleak Violence, Slick Sleaze, Hughes Brothers' *Menace* a Dark Engrossing Triumph," *San Francisco Weekly*, May 26, 1993, p. 40.

Gailbraith, Jane, "A Surprise *Menace* to Box-office Competition," *Los Angeles Times*, June 3, 1993, p. F6.

Giles, Jeff, Mark Miller and Danzy Senna, "A *Menace* Has Hollywood Seeing Double," *Newsweek*, July 19, 1993, p. 52.

Holden, Stephen, "Los Angeles Teenagers Driving under the Gun," *New York Times*, May 26, 1993, p. F8.

James, Caryn, "*Menace II Society* Stakes a Claim to Bleak Turf," *New York Times*, June 13, 1993, p. 24.

Johnson, Quendrith, "Born to Direct the Hughes Brothers," *DGA Magazine* (20), no. 3 (July/August 1995), p. 17–22.

LaSalle, Mick, "*Menace II Society* Twins," *San Francisco Chronicle*, p. E1.

Rainer, Peter, "*Menace*: Message Is in the Madness," *Los Angeles*, May 26, 1993, pp. F1, F5.

Weinraub, Bernard, "Twin Visions: Fighting Violence With Violence," *New York Times*, June 10, 1993, p. 2.

Will, George F. "Therapy From a Sickening Film," *Los Angeles Times*, June 17, 1993, p. 24.

## Other

Berardinelli, James, "*Menace II Society*," Internet Movie Database, 1996.

Clark, Mike, "*Menace II Society*," Internet Movie Database, 1996.

Ebert, Roger, "*Menace II Society*," Internet Movie Database, 1996.

# GEORGE JACKSON AND
# DOUG McHENRY

## BACKGROUND

George Jackson and Doug McHenry are the progenitors of the Black cinema renaissance with their film *Krush Groove*** (1985), which was released a year before Spike Lee* emerged with his film *She's Gotta Have It*** (1986). George and Doug met at a party hosted by Jheryl Busby, president of Motown Records, in early 1980. They found themselves in conversation sharing a common goal: producing feature films. They formed Jackson/McHenry Productions in 1985.

In terms of background, Jackson has an undergraduate degree from an Ivy League school in sociology and was a former studio executive for Indigo Films, hired by company president Richard Pryor at Columbia Pictures. While at Indigo Films with Columbia, Jackson helped Robert Townsend,* Reginald Hudlin* and Roy Campanella II* in their nascent efforts within the Hollywood system. Jackson also had held executive and production positions for Paramount Pictures and Universal Pictures.

McHenry, who has degrees in business and law, had worked at Casablanca Records/Filmworks and at AVCO/Embassy Pictures on the executive level. He was former president of Solar Films, a joint venture between himself and Dick Griffey. Their collaboration included pioneering the development of Black music videos, and the marketing and sales of *Soul City*, the first long-form video compilation that sold in excess of 75,000 units.

George Jackson, the source of the quotes throughout this chapter, was the

George Jackson and Doug McHenry

person speaking for both interviews. He presented the views of their partnership.

## *NEW JACK CITY* AND *HOUSE PARTY 2*

The biggest joy for us was having the audiences respond so positively to each film. What motivates us to make a motion picture is the love of communicating ideas. The films are made from a particular point of view and perspective, African American. The themes in the films, however, are universal. When our audiences embrace the films the way that they have, it is a very rewarding feeling to know that you set out to communicate some ideas and that they were well received by certain people, by the people for whom they were intended. Domestic box office for *New Jack* was right at $50 million in 1991, and we shipped over $20 million in videocassettes, so worldwide we're over $100 million gross for this project. There is enthusiasm for a *New Jack City 2*. The stakes will be a lot bigger, meaning budget and the film itself. The new film will take on an international scope. While we've seen the ravages of drugs on our country, the scope is international in origin. *New Jack City 2* will explore some of the things through the eyes of some of the characters we got to know in the first movie.

## MILESTONES

Were there milestones along the way?

Doug and I have recognized the historical significance of our struggle as African Americans. We have set out to redress the notion that opinionated, articulate, any African American for that matter, can't now work together unless they are relatives. We want to dispel that notion. We are both independent-minded individuals with individual points of view about a lot of things, about most things. But when we set about the task of doing a project we combine our efforts, resources and energy and focus squarely on the common objective. That objective is to create a piece of entertainment that is successful, in spite of our individual wishes. If you look at all the films we've done, they all have a certain amount of edge. They certainly have a point of view that is articulated. They are fairly definitive in how they entertain and educate people.

## NETWORKING

Jackson explained why networking is important.

Wherever we've had an opportunity to help people, we have. What is important to understand is that resources are very scarce. We never take the "crabs in the barrel" [one crab grabs another so neither escapes the barrel] sort of mentality. This attitude seems to affect and infect our community, often. We're very confident in what we have the ability to do. We're not unwilling to share resources. We're not insecure in our ability to get things done in a very competitive environment. We will never make progress as a people unless we continue to help one another. Doug and I are both strong individuals. To the extent that you are strong as an individual, I think we have an obligation to help other people, set examples for other people and show people the way. Whether or not I was ever rewarded for doing that, it doesn't matter. At the end of the day, no matter what they say, the one thing they can't say is that these brothers didn't help out. It is a long and arduous road we have to travel.

## UNIQUENESS

Jackson described what makes them unique as filmmakers.

We have a collaborative partnership. We have a philosophy of edutainment, which we've tried to apply to our films. "Edutainment" is a word I first heard from the rap artist KRS-1, which he used to describe his particular style of rap. It is an attempt to entertain people and at the same time to enlighten them—to give them an education on things and situations to which the audience has no prior context, to have explored the subject in an entertaining way. The whole idea is to make you laugh, to make you angry, but to make you feel. All in the context of thinking at the same time. That's what edutainment is really, for us anyway. In trying to meet that goal and objective, that's what makes our films a little different than anybody's movies. The fact that we collaborate with each other, the fact that we have a common objective, and the fact that we try and meet that objective.

## TELEVISION AND OTHER PROJECTS

Are there television projects in the works?

We have a management company called Elephant Walk Management. We manage Eddie Griffin (*Jason's Lyric* and *The Walking Dead*). Eddie Griffin is now starring with Malcolm Jamal-Warner in a Tri-Star Television and UPN (United Paramount Network) television series called

*Malcolm and Eddie* as a contemporary *Odd Couple*. We manage Matthew McConaghey (*A Time to Kill*, 1996, and *Boys on the Side*, 1995).

In addition, Jackson and McHenry were creators of the *Malcolm and Eddie* television series. They will produce the series as well for fall 1996 airing. They produced over a dozen hours of television prior to this production.
What new projects are you working on?

*New Jack City 2* is still in development. We have two different drafts of *New Jack City 2*.
    The *Family Reunion* project is something in development that we're still trying to get a handle on.

What other new directors are you helping to develop?

Jesse Vaughn, a new young writer/director.

Besides their management company, Elephant Walk Management, Jackson and McHenry have a record label called Jac/Mac Records; Harlem Boys Music and Oaktown Music Boys, music publishing companies; and Slang, a music and hip-hop lifestyle website.
    One of Doug's favorite expressions is that Chinese food is not only for Chinese people, and the same goes for films of African American filmmakers.

## CERTAIN ACTORS

Talk about Allen Payne and Eddie Griffin, who have appeared more than once in your films. Why?

Allen Payne is a fine young dramatic actor who we think has tremendous potential for super-stardom. Eddie Griffin is a continuation of a comedy acting experience started by Redd Foxx and continued by Richard Pryor, Eddie Murphy and Martin Lawrence. We also think Eddie has tremendous star potential.

## ADVICE FOR ASPIRANTS

What can you tell young people interested in the film industry?

You have to be specific about your initial interest. Hold that interest until it becomes second nature. Learn as much as you can about all the other aspects of filmmaking. This is so that you can really appreciate the collaborative nature of film and have a substantial understanding of how films are made. This is so that you can be impactful in all areas of film and thus be a good filmmaker. You have to understand what the gaffers, set designers, production designers and costume designers do. Not just from a perfunctory, mechanical standpoint. You have to understand how it is integrated into the production process and the final outcome, which is the film itself.

## THE FUTURE

What do you hope to accomplish in the future?

We've certainly been fortunate. I think we have a shot. By no stretch of the imagination has our work been completed. As a matter of fact, our work is really just beginning. It is a long road that we have to travel. It is an arduous one. There are many things, worlds and horizons that are yet to be conquered. That more than anything else fuels our motivation, directs our energies and propels our will. It is a fact that we know we have a long way to go. We know that this is just the beginning. Hopefully we are part of the creation and the perpetuation of the Golden Era of African American cinema. That is certainly the objective we have set for ourselves in our work. If we achieve half of what we set out to do, I think that will be a tremendous achievement; but we're not there yet.

## FILMOGRAPHY

### Producers

*Krush Groove*,** 1985, 97 min., 35mm, color. George described the significance of this film by today's standards:

> *Krush Groove* was the first film starring African American rappers to be released by a major studio. We had the honor of working with and learning from Michael Schultz,* who directed the film. He also directed *Disorderlies*, which we produced. This is a seminal film given the fact that hip-hop has emerged as a mainstream aspect of American pop culture. This was a watershed film that ushered in the hip-hop era. The film starred a galaxy of musical stars who have gone on to take their place in hip-hop and pop music culture lore. It has emerged as somewhat of a classic.

The cast included Blair Underwood (who went on to television's *L.A. Law*) in his first feature-film lead role. Musical performers included Sheila E., Run-DMC, The Fat Boys and Kurtis Blow, with cameos by then-rising stars New Edition, Beastie Boys, Bobby Brown, LL Cool J., Dr. Jekyll and Mr. Hyde (Andre Harrell, president of Motown Records, and Alonzo Brown, respectively). The film is a loose adaptation of the real-life story of music producer/entrepreneur Russell Simmons (see the chapter on Stan Lathan*). The cinematographer is Ernest Dickerson, Spike Lee's* favorite cinematographer; this was one of his first feature films as cinematographer. The soundtrack became a popular title on music charts. This fact helped in the marketing and promotion of the film. (Soundtracks have always been an important part of Black cinema. The success of *Shaft* (1971) with its Oscar-winning score was the vanguard of what is now a tradition. Black cinema soundtracks continued to be an equally important part of emerging post-seventies Black cinema, after the success of this film.) Budgeted at $3 million, the film grossed over $15 million.

*Disorderlies*,** 1987, 86 min., 35mm, color. Directed by Michael Schultz. Featuring The Fat Boys, Hollywood veteran Ralph Bellamy, and Troy Beyer. George described the problems they experienced in the making of this film:

> This film was probably a little ahead of its time. What we were trying to do with The Fat Boys was to institutionalize them the same way The Three Stooges became institutionalized. But because of internal problems with the group, we never really got to create the series of pictures that I think would have made them big in the same tradition as The Three Stooges.

*Stalingrad*, 1990, 180 min., 35mm, color. Featuring Powers Boothe, Fernando Allende and Roland Lacey, it was one of the first American/Soviet co-productions in the Gorbachev era.

> This was a co-production between Mosfilms Studios in Russia and Warner Brothers, where we had a deal in a partnership with Quincy Jones and Clarence Avant. It was one of the first co-productions between an American film studio and a Soviet film studio in the contemporary era. It was an epic motion picture that we helped engineer and orchestrate. The film was about the last great siege in a global conflict: the siege in Stalingrad. It has been released in Europe; it has yet to be released in America. It is a narrative film. The finished film was two hours long. There were two different versions. We created an American version. The Soviet version was over three hours long. We were involved in the project from the beginning of 1988 through the beginning of 1989. We spent approximately six weeks in the Soviet Union.

*New Jack City*,** 1991, 97 min., 35mm, color. Directed by Mario Van Peebles.* George described Barry Michael Cooper, the screenwriter for *New Jack City*:

> I read an article in *Spin* magazine several years earlier by him first. He is responsible for creating the phrase "new jack." He wrote the screenplay and created the foundation for what the picture became. I reached out to him and found out we grew up in the same neighborhood and he knew a lot of people in my family. Our paths prior to my contact had never crossed directly. We helped him make the transition from a journalist to a screenwriter. I'm proud of that fact and the work that he did. A lot of people have not given Barry enough credit for creating the subtext of *New Jack City*. The success of the film is

not only a testament to the success of the relationship between Doug, myself and Mario, it is also a testament to helping people. Because in reaching out to help a young writer, we found a tremendous talent in Barry Michael Cooper. He created what *New Jack City* became from a script perspective.

George talked about the milestones in their career:

*New Jack City* and *House Party 2* are the points when we began to infuse our pictures consciously with the theme of edutainment. When we got the opportunity to do *New Jack City*, we knew it was a tremendous opportunity. In having that opportunity, we also felt a great responsibility—not to just create a piece of exploitive entertainment that didn't attempt to shed some light on the underside of the drug subculture, but to explore the trials and tribulations of the people most affected by this situation. The drug dealer is not the most affected by this situation. He benefits the most. The police are not the most affected. There are individual police who are affected, but not the institution of law enforcement. They (drug dealers and police) are the least affected by the drug problem. The people most affected are the users and the victims of the users.

So it is rare that you see in a film that deals with this subject matter the implications of what the bad guys do. You didn't see it in *Scarface* (1983), Al Pacino version; you didn't see it in *The Godfather* (1972). You didn't see any scenes in *The Godfather* where, say, a prostitute was berated or had to live a certain lifestyle as a result of what she was involved in. You didn't see the underside of what racketeering is really all about. Those (*Scarface* and *Godfather*) characters were portrayed in an almost Horatio Alger–type manner. The implications of what they did were not part of the subject matter of the film. I happen to love those films.

As African Americans, since our community is the one that is the most devastated by what drug dealers do, we had a certain ethical responsibility to portray this phenomenon in a different light. When we started developing the script, we recognized that the film was going to be an entertaining film. We did not want to repeat the mistake of the previous generation of films. I'm referring specifically to the films of the Blaxploitation era. Most of those films were not produced by African Americans. They starred African Americans. As a result, the vast majority of them lacked a certain sensitivity to some of the issues that were exploited in the films. We made a conscious decision that we couldn't make that same mistake.

Drugs are something that have had a profound effect on my life. I lost an uncle and a cousin to drug overdoses. The week we started shooting *New Jack City* I lost an uncle who was gunned down by a group of drug dealers. I had two other uncles die of heroin overdoses. So this was an issue that had touched my life in an absolute way, which is death. So this was something that I couldn't take lightly or exploit for the sake of making a buck. It was something I had to give a great deal of thought to.

We collectively took a great deal of time in developing the images and theme that are contained in the film. We worked on the script for two years before we engaged Mario Van Peebles, the director of the film. He came aboard in late 1989, and we started shooting in the spring of 1990. Mario's directing was invaluable, and the story we want to tell is not finished yet.

This is part of the motivation for wanting to do a *New Jack City 2*. Obviously, the success of the first film has a lot to do with it. It would be easy to just do an exploitation send-up of the first film. We're going to take these characters and lay some foundation for their respective motivations, which we did not cover in the first film by way of their background. Then we will take them places that I think will intrigue and again entertain and educate the audience.

In the follow-up interview, his views on *New Jack City* had matured with time:

That film was a historic and ground-breaking picture. Ground-breaking from a box office standpoint. Ground-breaking from the standpoint that it was a traditional American gangster picture done from an African American perspective, created and produced by African Americans. This was a marked departure from the Blaxploitation films of the seventies where you had Black actors starring in them, but behind the cameras there were non–African Americans involved. That picture was really in the tradition of the classic American gangster picture: *The Roaring Twenties* (1939), *Scarface* (1932). It obviously launched the career of an American superstar, Wesley Snipes.

*House Party 3*,** 1994, 94 min., 35mm, color. Directed by Eric Meza. A rarity in Black cinema—a third sequel to an original film concept, *House Party*, by Reginald and Warrington Hudlin.* (Another film that generated two sequels was *Penitentiary* by Jamaa Fanaka.*)

*The Walking Dead*,** 1995, 89 min., 35mm, color. Written and directed by Preston A. Whitmore II. A dramatic rendering of the Black experience in Vietnam. Featuring Joe Morton, Allen Payne, Eddie Griffin, Vonte Sweet and Roger Floyd. George discussed this film:

An important film, again, a departure from the traditional contemporary urban genre that we've come to see. No film prior to this had been made about the Black experience in Vietnam from a Black soldier's perspective. It was a film in which we tried to do something very, very different. It places us (African Americans) in the context of real history. It gives young people an opportunity to see themselves in history and understand that we have made important contributions to history in this country, although they by and large have gone unrecognized and uncelebrated with the exception of Black History Month. This film was an illustration of the positive aspects of the common African American male contribution to the struggle in Vietnam.

*A Thin Line between Love and Hate*, 1996, 35 mm, color. New Line Cinema and Savoy Pictures presents a Jackson-McHenry production in association with You Go Boy! Productions. Executive producer, director, original story and co-author of script, and co-star: Martin Lawrence. (Lawrence was in *House Party 2*\*\* and *Bad Boys*\*\* and is best known for his role as the star of the FOX network series *Martin*.) The film features Lynn Whitfield, Regina King, Bobby Brown, Daryl M. Mitchell, Roger E. Mosley and Della Reese.

> All the films that we have made have been different, in terms of what they are about and where they take place. *A Thin Line between Love and Hate* is directed by and stars Martin Lawrence of FOX network's *Martin* fame. It also marks his feature-film directorial debut. This film is a kind of blue-collar but balanced response to *Waiting to Exhale* (1995), in the sense that *Waiting to Exhale* presented all women as saints and all men as sinners. In our film you have all different kinds of women; you have a class distinction between the men and the women. You have for the first time the mixing of genres in African American cinema, which is difficult to pull off. This movie is a comedic thriller. *Boomerang* (1992) meets *Fatal Attraction* (1987). So that in and of itself is ground-breaking.

Cost less than its $10 million budget; grossed more than $33 million in its first two months of release.

### Producers/Directors

*House Party 2*,\*\* 1991, 97 min., 35mm, color. George described what was important about this film:

> To communicate the value of education. A continuation and a bench-mark establishment of the *House Party* series as a franchise. It was very critical that this film be successful, which it was. This allowed the third film to be done, which then in effect created a *House Party* series. Some of the things that were in this film—the emphasis on education, the emphasis on loyalty, the emphasis on self-determination and pride— were very important underlying themes and messages. These messages were presented in a very entertaining context. Thus it was a real piece of edutainment.

*House Party 2* cost about $4.5 million to make and returned over $17 million gross.

### Producer (George Jackson)/Director (Doug McHenry)

*Jason's Lyric*,\*\* 1994, 120 min., 35mm, color. George's thoughts in hindsight:

> This film is important because it is a marked departure from the tradi-tional urban ghetto picture. It was a love story. The film had universal themes at its core. That picture was successful because it could just as easily have taken place in the Appalachian mountains or in a little village in Italy or on the streets of downtown Tokyo. Those thematic tonalities

resonated with an audience in an extraordinary way and constructed an emotional cord with the audience.

When asked to discuss the encounter with the Motion Picture Association of America over the rating for this film, George was diplomatic:

> Hollywood in general and American media in particular have a very myopic view of African American culture. It's a function of the kind of institutionally racially insensitive society that we live in, where there is a tremendous double standard. What is being sexually explicit for us is commonplace for other people. This film was endemic of that problem, and one in which we had to engage in a fight to protect the integrity of what we were trying to do and not have it tarnished and ghettoized because of that myopic, racially insensitive viewpoint.

In their personal introduction to the video version of this wonderful film, Doug said:

> How many of us have sat around in the comfort of our homes and looked at the 11 o'clock news and said, "Oh my God, another gang-related killing"? We have depersonalized many of the people who are dying in our society. These are real people being killed in our streets. These are mothers and fathers, sons and daughters. *Jason's Lyric* personalizes and brings back to us the essential humanity that links us all.
>
> The soul of the story is the city of Houston. We shot in a place called the Third Ward, which in many respects is the birthplace of the Blues. It's the birthplace of a lot of the cultural rhythms of America. Quite often the poetry of real life is captured in our music. We felt there was an opportunity to capture that same kind of poetry in a film. *Jason's Lyric* is really about the fabric of everyday life.
>
> One of the personal goals I had was the idea of taking a working-class character—not a guy who was rich, not a guy who was extremely poor. But a guy who was just a working stiff, a blue-collar worker. A guy like my father. The fact is, there are more Jasons out there than there are superstar basketball players or members of gangs. But we never get the people that most closely resemble our mothers and our fathers. Very rarely are they in movies. They are the stuff of life. They are the stuff of great stories. Too often we ignore them for the sensational. *Jason's Lyric* is about many things, but most of all I hope the audience will find *Jason's Lyric* is about love, hope and about how to find magic in your life.

This film made about $23 million in domestic box office receipts.

## BIO-CRITICAL REVIEW

*House Party 2.* "Entertaining mix of comedy and music (rap and hip-hop) about the adventure of Kid and pal Play. It works."—Vincent Canby, *New York Times*

————. "Delivers a very important message to young people about the value of education."—George Hill and Spencer Moon, *Blacks in Hollywood*

*New Jack City.* "A timely message on drug trafficking and its devastating impact, especially in the black community. The filmmakers make a good case for legalization; this film could help to create an environment for discussion of this controversial issue."—George Hill and Spencer Moon, *Blacks in Hollywood*

*A Thin Line Between Love and Hate.* "The supposed hero of this movie is the villain, and the villain is the real heroine."—Chris Hewitt, *San Jose Mercury*

## EDUCATION

**George Jackson**: Harvard University, B.A., sociology

**Doug McHenry**: Stanford University, B.A., economics and political science; Harvard University, M.B.A., L.L.B.

## SELECTED AWARDS

**George Jackson**:

Black American Cinema Society Award

Communications Excellence to Black Audiences Award (CEBA)

NAACP Image Award

Star Bright Award for Excellence in Film

**Doug McHenry**:

Cable Ace Award

Communications Excellence to Black Audiences Award (CEBA)

NAACP Image Award

Time-Warner Executive Forum Award

## SELECTED MEMBERSHIPS

**George Jackson**:

American Film Institute, Third Decade

Big Brothers Association

Black Filmmakers Foundation, Advisory Board

Harvard University, Alumni Association

Independent Film Project West

Producers Guild

Project Involve

**Doug McHenry**:

Academy of Motion Picture Arts and Sciences, Academy Awards, Voting Member

Black Entertainment and Sports Lawyers Association

Directors Guild of America

Harvard Law School, Alumni Association

Stanford Alumni Association

State of California Bar

## SOURCES

Interview by George Hill, 1991; follow-up interview by Spencer Moon, February 1996.

### Books

Hill, George, and Spencer Moon. *Blacks in Hollywood: Five Favorable Years, 1987–1991*. Los Angeles: Daystar Publishing, 1991.

### Newspapers

Hewitt, Chris. "Line Veers Between Laughter and Rage," *San Jose Mercury*, April 3, 1996, p. 4.

Taliaferro, A. Jacquie. "McHenry and Jackson Continue Success Story with *A Thin Line between Love and Hate*," *New Bay View*, April 5, 1996, p. 11.

Ashley James

# ASHLEY JAMES

## BACKGROUND

Ashley James is a well-known San Francisco Bay Area filmmaker whose work has received many honors, awards and grants. He is also known because he was president of the Film Arts Foundation (FAF) in San Francisco, one of the largest independent filmmaker organizations in the country. He has continued as a board member since 1984.

James earned a degree in journalism and started working in Hartford, Maine, on the local newspaper. Then he came to the San Francisco Bay Area to get work and entered graduate school, where he developed acumen and a love for filmmaking. By the time he obtained his graduate degree in fine arts, his films were known locally and nationally and his company, Searchlight Films, had established itself as a thriving independent film production facility. His clients over the years have included the Public Broadcasting System, Canadian Broadcasting Corporation, CBS, Apple Computer, Pacific Bell, San Francisco Visitors and Convention Bureau, Westinghouse Corporation, Intel Corporation, Lifetime Cable Network, and Hyundai Computers.

## UNIQUENESS

James described what makes him unique as a filmmaker.

I am particularly interested in African American culture. I want to make films so that people everywhere will be able to look at and appreciate African American culture. Black culture is important to this country; Americans would not be who we are without Black folks. I try to make the Black experience unique. It's not the only thing I do; I do a lot of other things. I also work as a director of photography.

## CURRENT PROJECTS

Right now I'm working on two projects. I am currently producing an hour-long film for public television on Puerto Rican African dance. The film is on a dance style called *bomba*, which is indigenous to Puerto Rico. It was a harbinger of African culture during and after slavery, when Spanish culture dominated the country. A couple of families in Puerto Rico kept the African culture alive through this dance style called *bomba*.

The second project is the second part of a trilogy on gospel music. The series is on Black gospel music in America. The first one in the series is the recently completed film on the Dixie Hummingbirds. The second part is on the great gospel diva Marion Williams. She is from Philadelphia, part of the Philadelphian branch of gospel music. There are two real centers in this country for gospel music: Chicago and Philadelphia. I was fortunate enough to do the first film on the Dixie Hummingbirds, who are based in Philadelphia. Marion Williams died last year.

## CREATING TITLES

James talked about how titles develop for his films.

Titles come out as the film takes on an identity of its own. A lot of the time, the title of a film is embedded someplace in the film itself and it kind of appears. I have a philosophy that at a certain point a film has an identity, and you have to let it speak for itself.

## ADVICE FOR ASPIRANTS

What can you tell young people interested in the business?

You have to have the drive, the brain desire. You have to eat film. You can't let anything stop you. I've been rejected so much in my life by funding organizations, by people who didn't really understand what I was doing, perhaps. I decided a long time ago that every rejection was going to make me push harder. Never give up. When I teach from time to time, I teach filmmaking and cinematography. I tell students that this is the hardest career they could choose. It's expensive, and there is a certain amount of power involved. Money and power are two elements that create an atmosphere of incredible anxiety. If they want to work just as hard and make a lot of money, they should go into law or medicine. You will work just as hard making documentary films, but there is an incredible amount of satisfaction when you're finished with a program and you've touched and affected people's lives. That's what the kind of filmmaking that I do really does. It touches people's lives. There is no greater rush than experiencing that.

## THE FUTURE

What do you hope to accomplish in the future?

Make more films. This is my life's work. I will be doing this until the day I die. I'm intensely interested in African American culture. I want it to be seen by everybody and appreciated by everyone as well. Making films is not a job for me; it's a lifetime's work.

## FILMOGRAPHY

### Producer/Director/Cinematographer

*Duluz*, 1976, 15 min., 16mm and 8mm, b/w.

> This was a film made while I was a student. It was kind of an experiment for me in film technique, a way for me to stretch the boundaries of the narrative experience. You have a beginning, middle and an end, but not necessarily in that order.

*Ancestors*, 1978, 10 min., 16mm, color.

> One of the few nondocumentary films I have made. A personal catharsis film. At the time a lot of family members were dying, and this is a tribute and a way for me to cope with that tragedy. Although it is intensely personal, a lot of people who have seen it can relate to it. It has received wide distribution on the film/poetry circuit. It's still very hard for me to look at that film.

*Zack*, 1980, 10 min., 16mm, color.

> This is a portrait of dancer Zack Thompson. Zack was one of the first characters that I ever produced a film about. He was an incredible performer and character. The bottom line for my films is character. That's what this film is about.

*Tchuba, Means Rain*, 1982, 25 min., 16mm, color.

> The making of this film was our introduction to Cape Verdeans. It deals
> with how they came to the United States and why. Cape Verdeans came
> to the United States of their own free will. They still have strong ties
> to the United States. If you were to go to Cape Verde, you'd see a lot
> of Americans there. A lot of Cape Verdeans go back to Cape Verde to
> retire and collect their pensions.

*American Treasure*, 1984, 30 min., 16mm, color.

> A total act of love. My wife and I were doing research on another film
> on the Cape Verdean community because it lent itself to this idea that
> I have. The idea is that—at the time and certainly it's changed—the
> commonly held notion that Black folks are singular and they are all the
> same. No matter where you are or where you come from. That's what
> a lot of people think of Black folks. Black folks don't think that way
> because they know. You could be from one neighborhood and be totally
> different from somebody else. The perception was that Black folks are
> all the same.
>
> I wanted to make a film on this Black African culture that resided in
> the United States but was totally different from the African American
> experience. These are folks who are Portuguese-Creole. They live in
> what the cultural anthropologists call a cultural isolate in New England.
> They speak their own language; they don't have a lot in common with
> African Americans. They were never slaves. They originally lived off the
> west coast of Africa about four hundred miles off the coast of Senegal
> on an island called Cape Verde. Cape Verdeans are the original Creoles.
> The island was unpopulated when the Portuguese discovered it in the
> fifteenth century. It was kind of the holding place in the middle passage
> for slaves. Cape Verdeans mixed with the Portuguese, whoever came
> through there. It is an archipelago that got its independence in 1975
> from Portugal. The Cape Verdeans are a distinct Black culture; they see
> themselves as distinct.
>
> We were doing research for a film called *Tchuba, Means Rain* (1982).
> We discovered this folk artist who lived in this little studio in New
> Bedford, Massachusetts. He made model ships of the ships that brought
> Cape Verdeans to the United States. They had their own little shipping
> company that brought their people from Africa to the United States.
> People thought this artist was nuts, crazy. He's just eccentric. We con-
> vinced the National Endowment for the Arts to fund this, because we
> saw it as true folk art. Since our film on this artist, he's received a Na-
> tional Heritage Award. He is now in the permanent collection of the
> Smithsonian Institute. He finally has received recognition as an impor-
> tant American folk artist. Because of his work, Cape Verdean culture is
> now really on the map in the United States, specifically in New England.
> But there are Cape Verdeans everyplace.
>
> After the film was completed we had been negotiating with the Whal-
> ing Museum in New Bedford for exhibition of the completed film there,

a very prestigious institution for the tea and sympathy crowd. We ran into flak because they didn't want to seat members of the community at the exhibition. The institution does indeed foster the image of the whaling world; that is, from a European perspective, but we know that some of the best whalers in the world were Africans. The Cape Verdean culture really recognizes that. So instead of having the screening there we had it at the Cape Verdean Veterans Hall, which was a converted firehouse in New Bedford.

I'll never forget the night we went. My father came down, my in-laws were there. We walked up to this place and there were Black folks spilling out into the street, Cape Verdeans. They had never seen anybody pay attention to their culture like this. They were hanging from the rafters, man. It was July; it was about a hundred degrees; the sweat was so thick you could see it in the air. Up came this beautiful old man— Joaquim Miguel Almeida. The mayor came and lambasted the museum for not having the exhibition there. There, for that exhibition, I realized the power of what we were doing. Finally someone was recognizing them; it was an amazing experience. People came from miles around to see this film on this little old man that everyone thought was a town fool. He would go around collecting little pieces of wood for his art and make ships and then give them away.

There are more Cape Verdeans in the United States than there are on Cape Verde. I grew up with Cape Verdeans in New England; they were called Portuguese for a long time, they considered themselves Portuguese. The Cape Verdeans settled around the old sailing ports like New Bedford. They were the whalers that Herman Melville wrote about but didn't have the guts to say they were the great whalers. These were the harpooners, the leaders, really. The Cape Verdeans introduced the ukelele to the Hawaiians, which they never got credit for. They have a four-stringed instrument called the *kavakene*.

*And Still We Dance*, 1988, 60 min., 16mm, color.

I've gotten a kind of reputation as a "song and dance man." Sometimes you are labeled based on what your last film was about. Although I'm drawn to dance and music, I do other films. This was one of the first full-length documentaries on dance. This was a portrait of the San Francisco Ethnic Dance Festival. I was very happy with this work's success. It was picked up by PBS. It is still in distribution. What happens is, when I finish a film I get incredibly depressed. Is that all there is? You have a post-mortem. Dealing with critics—whether they like it or don't like it. I'm generally satisfied with all the films I've made. You put your heart and soul into these, and they kind of go out and they're on their own.

## Director/Cameraman

*Takezo*, 1990, 5 min., video, color.

A rock video for Japan's NHK television network. This is a portrait of a Japanese blues singer. The Japanese are very enamored of American pop culture. I thought it was interesting when the prime minister of Japan made some remarks about Black people, because you have a whole subculture in Japan of young people who adore Black culture in the United States.

*Season of Hope*, 1991, 30 min., video, color.

We produced this program for an organization called the Family Welfare Research Association—a group of sociologists, really. They came to me because they wanted to do a film on crack cocaine. They were under the thesis—and I support this—that Black women especially bore the cross in this whole idea of women, of Black women especially, using drugs and having crack-addicted babies. I wanted to make a film that took that onus off of Black people. Because the truth is, there are more White people in the suburbs using drugs that get away with it than Black people. But you don't see that in the popular press. In the popular press you see Black folks getting arrested. So I made a film, a trilogy, that focused on an African American, Hispanic and a Caucasian woman. Women who were strung out on drugs but recovered because of their children. The film is being distributed by Pyramid Films and is doing very well in distribution. It was made five years ago.

*We Love You Like a Rock*, 1994, 77 min., video, color.

I am happy with this work. We are fielding distribution offers right now. We're also still doing festival circuits with the program. Every piece that I do, whenever I finish, I go back and I look and I see all the flaws that nobody else does. I say, "Oh man, I should have done this a little bit different, or I should have done that a little bit better." Most of the time most people don't see that, because a work stands on its own. I do the best that I can with each piece. Then it has to stand on its own. Then it's its own entity. I'm pretty satisfied with this program. *We Love You Like a Rock* kind of illuminates a certain part of history. People have a short memory, especially in the nineties and the age of technology. People think, well, Black music started on this event, maybe. Or Black culture started this way. Without the Dixie Hummingbirds there wouldn't be the modern rap groups now. As Ira, one of the members of the group, says in the program, he was one of the original rappers. I feel blessed being able to go in and talk with these people and learn about their lives and be able to share that with other people.

### Work-in-Progress

*I've Got a Home in That City up Yonder*, a work-in-progress, is in post-production. This is the third part of the gospel trilogy. This part will be a portrait of New York city grass-roots gospel groups, people in the community and why they perform gospel music. The program deals with the cultural migration of African Americans from the South to the North.

## Producer/Director

*Crisis—AIDS in the Black Community* is a film proposal in progress. This is a film I want to do about the needle exchange program in the San Francisco Bay Area. Although it's about the Bay Area as a focus, AIDS is a major crisis in the African American community. A documentary about the needle exchange program. It is really designed as a jumping-off place, so people can talk about it because the needle exchange program is so controversial. It's the idea of drugs versus combating AIDS, and issues of community ethics versus health issues. I hope I can get some funding for this. I've applied to a few places; we'll see what happens. It's extremely controversial because it's an illegal program in California. Foundations don't want to be seen as supporting something that's illegal. Did you see this morning's *San Francisco Chronicle?* AIDS is killing Black folks, more than any other group combined. It is because of intravenous drug use and unprotected sex.

## BIO-CRITICAL REVIEW

*And Still We Dance.* "The film achieves what is all too rare in films about performances—a rousing, intimate translation to celluloid without self-conscious cinematics."—*Release Print*

*Season of Hope.* "In its straightforward portrayal of struggles . . . it reminds us both of the magnitude of the task and the necessity for believing against hope that it will work out."—Alix Christie, *Oakland Tribune*

*We Love You Like a Rock.* "Modern ethnography at its most accessible—joyous and intimate, with a soundtrack worth marketing right away."—Dennis Harvey, *Variety*

———. "A spirited musical documentary that is rousing and at 77 minutes seems much too short."—Walter V. Addiego, *San Francisco Examiner*

———. "A joyful documentary that works as both a portrait of the legendary "Birds" and a parable about the simple rewards of faith."—Ed Dean, *CityPages*

## AWARDS

Bellvue International Film Festival Award, 1979

Black American Cinema Society Award, 1986

Black Filmmakers Hall of Fame Award, 1978

Chicago International Film Festival, Bronze Hugo, 1991

CINE, Golden Eagle, 1987, 1991, 1992; Golden Eagle, Best Cinematography, 1994

Dance Bay Area, Isadora Duncan Special Achievement in Film Award, 1989

Dance on Camera Festival, Gold Award, Best of Category, 1989

National Educational Film Festival, Golden Apple, Best Performance Film, 1989

San Francisco Advertising Club, Award of Excellence, 1986

San Francisco International Film Festival Award, 1987


## GRANTS

American Film Institute, 1993

Black Filmmakers Hall of Fame, Sidney Poitier Fellowship, 1994

Ford Foundation, 1993

Grants for the Arts, San Francisco Hotel Tax Fund, 1985, 1986, 1988

Massachusetts Foundation for the Arts and Humanities, 1984

National Endowment for the Arts, 1994

National Endowment for the Arts, Folk Arts, 1983, 1984

National Endowment for the Arts, Western States Regional Fellowship in Film, 1991

New York State Council for the Humanities, 1992

Oakland Arts Council Fellowship, 1990

Pennsylvania Council for the Humanities, 1992

Pew Charitable Trust, 1993

Polaroid Foundation, 1982

South Carolina Humanities Council, 1993

Wallace Alexander Gerdbode Foundation, 1990

Zellerbach Family Fund, 1990


## EXHIBITIONS

Boston Children's Museum Folklife Festival, 1985

Broadcast Solo Shows, KQED-TV and KQEC-TV, San Francisco, 1989–1990

Cannes International Film Festival, 1978

Exploratorium, Solo Exhibition, 1989

*From San Francisco* (PBS), national acquisition and broadcast, 1990

*Good Morning America* (ABC), 1985

Kabuki Theater, Solo Exhibition, 1988

Metropolitan Museum of Art Independent Filmmakers Exposition, 1986

Mill Valley Film Festival, 1985

National Endowment for the Arts International Consulate Series, 1987

Pacific Film Archive, 1979

Roxie Theater, Theatrical Run, 1988

San Francisco Cinematheque, 1980, 1983, 1984

San Francisco Film Arts Festival, 1985

San Francisco Museum of Modern Art, Independent Black Filmmakers, 1978
U.C. Theater, Theatrical Run, 1988
University of California Anthropological Film Festival, 1985

## EDUCATION

University of Hartford, Maine, B.A.
San Francisco Art Institute, M.F.A.

## SOURCES

Interview by Spencer Moon, February 1996.

### Newspapers and Magazines

Addiego, Walter V., "We Love You Like a Rock," *San Francisco Examiner*, September 1994, p. B1.
Christie, Alix, "Season of Hope," *Oakland Tribune*, February 15, 1991, p. 12.
Dean, Ed, "We Love You Like a Rock," *CityPages* (Washington, D.C.), October 1994, p. 18.
Harvey, Dennis, "We Love You Like a Rock," *Variety*, November 1994, p. 41.
*Release Print* (San Francisco), "And Still We Dance," June 1989, p. 9.

Avon Kirkland. *Photo courtesy of Donald Jones Photography.*

# AVON KIRKLAND

## BACKGROUND

Avon Kirkland's background includes a Ph.D. in chemistry. One wonders how you go from being a chemist to television producer.

I was a poor student in high school and a very good college student. I won a Woodrow Wilson Fellowship. I was the first Black person in the South to get one. I was a chemistry major and an honors student. My goals initially were to become a doctor. Because I was poor, I decided from a pragmatic perspective to work toward a degree where I could get a well-paying job that would allow me to go to medical school. I was at graduate school at Washington University in St. Louis when my intellectual and social consciousness exploded. I got interested in everything; this was around 1960. I decided not to become a doctor.

I worked after graduate school as an organic research chemist in Chicago. I paid off my school debts. I disliked the conservative culture of the field and the work itself, so I quit the field. My mother thought I was crazy. I worked for a time with a foundation that helped children and libraries. I left Chicago and moved to New York. I wanted to pursue my musical aspirations as a guitarist/singer/vocalist. After realizing it would take too long to prepare to succeed in this field, I wound up joining an educational publishing firm. They designed books and programs that would improve reading and math skills in children.

I was a teacher/trainer/project coordinator for them. I did real well. In two years I became a vice-president and they moved me to Palo Alto, California. The company got overextended financially, and after about two years I decided I didn't like where they were going. I had saved some money, so I quit and opted to take one year off from work.

I watched a lot of television. After a time I began to watch it more seriously. I said, "I think I could do that." I bought a book on script-writing. I wrote some scripts and even got turned down on a script I submitted for *Sanford and Son*. But they said they'd done a show like the one I wrote and would be interested in other scripts on another subject. By then I figured out the place for me was public television. It was a growth industry at the time. Through the local Broadcast Skills Bank, I found out there was a job at KQED-TV, the local PBS affiliate. The job was director of instructional television. As it turned out, I got hired.

I was so interested in the job I did two weeks of research and wrote a proposal on how they could improve their service. I know how to raise money, how to make others see the attraction or appeal in a subject, where to take it and how to present it. I found out later that I was the only applicant with a proposal about how to do the work. This was in 1974. I improved the service there. I started a summer program there that they now do statewide. Mainly, though, I came up with the idea for a series. I originally wanted to adapt already-written children's books for a television series. At that time there was money for this through something called ESAA (Emergency School Aid Act). It was designed for television to improve interracial understanding.

### SERIES PRODUCTION: *UP AND COMING*

While still at KQED-TV I wrote the proposal for the series in early 1977, with the help of a former situation-comedy writer, Ilunga Adell. He is now chief writer on a Nickelodeon situation comedy series. We met through mutual friends and hit it off well. The original idea for the series of producing children's books for television was really beyond the capabilities of KQED-TV. I didn't know much about production. I did feel comfortable with story-telling at the time; I've since learned a lot. Ilunga and I conceived of a series based on two striving Black families, one lower class and one middle class. KQED-TV invested about $10 thousand in the project. They didn't think it would work but liked the job I was doing in instructional television. So they gave me $8 thousand to work up the proposal, and we later got the money back through a grant. That gave me time off from the instructional television job to develop the project idea. We got the proposal written with an assortment of consultants and submitted the proposal, which was competitive at the time; our competition round was a very close round. We got the money. Ilunga wasn't available at the time. He had moved away, so we continued to develop the concept without him. I wound up authoring the concept for the series that we did.

Here we were, funded to do twenty-six half-hour programs, and there was a writers' strike by their guild. The staff was in place and everything. After the strike was over, we got going. Later, KQED-TV was difficult to deal with initially after we got funding. Ilunga came back and became our primary writer. We got started and produced fifteen half-hours. We sent several of our completed shows to PBS. They were delighted and astounded. They said it was good entertainment with a good deal of learning potential for young people, etc. They fed the show to their affiliates at prime time on Thursday evening that first season. We had guest stars like Esther Rolle and Danny Glover. This was his first television production. The week he worked for us he was splitting his time between us and the NBC hit series *Hill Street Blues*, which opened the door for his movie career. Peter Coyote was on before he began to do movies. The daughter of the Wilson family on the show was played by Cindy Herron, who is one-quarter of the popular music group En Vogue. Wolfe Perry, who played the oldest son, went on to a lead role in *White Shadow* (CBS).

### Second Season

So the first season happens and you start work on the second season. Did things go a little more smoothly?

KQED-TV management became more cooperative after PBS called and raved about the show and its quality. We got good national reviews. PBS called one day and asked if we had seen the *Washington Post* that day. We said no. They said Tom Shales, their television critic, doesn't like anything on television this season, but he gave *Up and Coming* a rave review. I have that review framed in my office. The show was described as a breath of fresh air. We got all our money for the second season from the Corporation for Public Broadcasting (CPB) that year, $1.1 million; that was a lot to get from CPB. We got several hundred thousand more from public stations. *Working Women* magazine gave us an award for our portrait of a working woman with the working mother character of our show.

### INDEPENDENT PRODUCTION

How did you make the leap from producer/creator for a television series for public television to your own production company, New Images Productions, Inc.?

I had raised all the money for *Up and Coming*. KQED-TV had gotten several hundred thousand dollars for their overhead. I was burned out. Twenty-five half-hour shows in three years. I had raised all the money; I said, "If I'm going to raise all the money, then I may as well do my own thing." I left KQED-TV on April 28, 1982. In May somebody gave me a public television Request for Proposals. They were looking for programs for young people that dealt with the humanities and history. I had been working on the concept of dramatizing the life of Booker T. Washington. I said there might be an hour-length film on his childhood.

In three weeks I wrote a treatment. Charles Johnson, the novelist, edited it for me. He had worked on the second season of *Up and Coming* as a writer and producer. I recruited the major scholars in the field. I got a production grant without a script. I had to incorporate to get the money. I did it myself, using the Nolo Press book on how to incorporate a company. So within a month of leaving KQED-TV, I had applied for and received my first grant—which, with other small grants we got for the program, was about $500 thousand.

## CHANGE OF FORM

You subsequently produced and directed *Street Soldiers*, a documentary. Why a documentary after your success in the narrative form?

I haven't done the same form since I've been producing. My list of credits is not that long. I started fast with twenty-five original half hour dramas. I did a one-hour children's movie. Then a two-and-a-half-hour docudrama on the Supreme Court. I basically get interested in material. I consider myself a long term OJT (on-the-job-training). The form fits the material. I'm interested in good stories, frankly. I read once that many fiction writers tend to write about the same thing, from one work to the next; ultimately it's about the same thing. The bottom line. All my programs are about Black striving, to find a sense of well-being in a hostile society. But it's all pro-active struggle. This is not anger turned inward. It's a "go get 'em" attitude that has characterized our people for a long time. Now my concerns turn to what we're doing to hurt ourselves. The striving of people like Joe Marshall to get us to take a look at what we're doing.

## DIRECTING

How does it feel to be a director after so many years as a producer/writer?

I feel good. I appreciate how difficult it is to be a producer and director often when we are trying to solve an editorial problem, with me wearing my director's hat at the moment. I was distracted very often by the need for the producer to raise money. I do everything from conceive of these shows and develop them to buying office supplies. I feel good as director because I have more control of what the show becomes. This is a collaborative business, always is, but in drama you have a creator/producer. I've created everything I've done. You have a better chance of getting your vision as director than as script writer and creative producer, which is what I've tended to be.

## BEYOND HOLLYWOOD

Do you think independent production and distribution is any more viable today than when you made *Booker?*

No. It's harder for me because I've tended to depend on public broadcasting resources to support my projects. That money is drying up. I've tended to do specials, programs designed to be what they are and not be a series. PBS is more and more looking for series, documentary series as opposed to documentary specials. There is less and less money available in PBS in general for the kinds of specials I've done. I'm not all that optimistic. Until there is a new political mood in the country, I don't see there being a lot of resources put out there. The consolidation of media entities into media empires suggests less and less. There are places for some good creative ideas within commercial television. I'm going to try to pursue some of those potentials. Some of the premium cable channels are buying independent productions, both documentaries and narrative stories, from independents.

## RENAISSANCE

What do you think of the Black film/video renaissance?

I have no idea where it's going. It will be rare that an independent can fulfill his or her own vision in the development and production of their own program without compromising what they're doing.

## ADVICE FOR ASPIRANTS

What can you tell young people who want to get into the business?

Learn your craft. Read widely and deeply in areas that you're interested in. Write well, organize well, communicate well. The craft and art of production—many of those things can be learned over time by studying the work of the masters. The main difference I find between producers who are really able to move their project forward is their ability to both conceive of and articulate the concept, what it is and why it's good.

## THE FUTURE

What do you hope to accomplish in the future?

I'd like to make more programs, more intelligent and more ambitious programs on the characterization of Black people. I'm very interested in us and in our experience. I have a file drawer full of ideas for shows. I hope I get in a position where I can develop these things without having to do them all myself.

## FILMOGRAPHY

### Creator/Executive Producer

*Up and Coming*, 1980–1982, twenty-five 30-min. episodes, PBS series. Kirkland wrote or co-wrote most of the first season's episodes and one episode of season two. The program focused on the Wilson family. Robert DoQui portrayed Frank Wilson, the father, an independent building contractor. Gamy Taylor portrayed Joyce Wilson, a working mother and an executive at a local bank. The three children were portrayed by Wolfe Perry as the oldest son, Kevin; Cindy Herron as Valerie, the daughter; and Yule Caise as the youngest son, Marcus. This is before the Cosby family program, which resembled it, ran on NBC.

*Booker*, 1984, 60 min. PBS *Wonderworks* series. Dramatic story of the youth of Booker T. Washington, featuring Levar Burton as young Washington. When asked if he was happy with the success of *Booker*, Kirkland replied:

> Very. It's still a good film. *Booker* was the premier work for the now very popular PBS young people's series *Wonderworks*. I have a 9-year-old son in third grade. I just spoke to his class during Black History Month. They were studying, among other things, slavery and they used the film for a presentation to his class. I'm very happy with it. It has just been picked up for home video distribution. It has had very strong distribution in schools. The film also ran on the Disney Channel for two years.

### Executive Producer/Co-Author Screenplay

*Simple Justice*, 1993, 150 min., PBS *American Experience* series. Docudrama on the story of Thurgood Marshall and the landmark Supreme Court decision *Brown v. Board of Education of Topeka, Kansas.*

I first read the book *Simple Justice* by Richard Kluger in 1984. I was blown away. I didn't know anything about the *Brown* decision. I remember I was in high school when the case was resolved and talking to my mother about it. The first third of the book is an excellent history of race relations before the *Brown* case. I acquired an option on the book within about six months of reading it. It had been out awhile and several other people had originally acquired the screen rights to it. I loaned my company five thousand dollars to acquire the screen rights option. The author was not going to sell it to me until he met me. We had a long talk over the phone. After our conversation, he said he thought I understood his intent with the book. So I got the screen rights.

I got a script grant from the National Endowment for the Humanities. I had seen a work produced in the style that I wanted from WGBH-TV. So I called them. Peter Cook and WGBH-TV helped me in the process of putting a proposal together, along with a treatment. I got a $200,000 grant to do a four-part miniseries from the National Endowment for the Humanities. Writers I talked with initially saw the difficulty in writing a script where the Constitution is one of the characters. The writer I eventually hired was George Wolfe, somebody who was recommended by my contacts in the field. By that time we got another $1.5 million from NEH. So we got another writer on board, John McGreevey.

Just as I was getting a handle on the concept with the writers and we were getting comfortable with the concept, ABC made an announcement. They were going to do a four-part production on the same *Brown v. Board of Education* court case starring Sidney Poitier and Burt Lancaster, to be produced, written and directed by George Stevens Jr. The worst day of my life.

The first session of our interview stopped here with this cliff-hanger. I called him back and we concluded our interview.

It took me a few days to recover. I recovered with new determination. What occurred to me was that a commercial program dealing with the *Brown* decision and the Constitution would probably have to be melodramatic to attract a large audience to ABC. I figured they'd distort the story and not really tell it well or truthfully. I thought they would play down Black/White tensions, among other things. I got a copy of the script. I was right. It was clear they had used material from the book that I had bought the rights to. We determined that it is the expression of the facts that are copyrightable, not the facts themselves. Their script had the lawyers from both sides being very nice to each other. As the author of the book (*Simple Justice*), Richard Kluger, said, "You would think that this was a polite debating society." In fact, there were hard feelings on both sides of the case, and most members of the opposition to *Brown* were dyed-in-the-wool racists. In the ABC presentation, all of that was muted.

Eventually I was able to convince my funders and additional funders that our show was more important than ever. We were going to tell the truth. At the same time I was encouraged—by Peter Cook at WGBH-TV in Boston, who had been a project resource before—to think about the project in a shorter version. We started working on a two-hour script at the time and started trading drafts to boil the material down. The *American Experience* series on PBS became very interested in the show through Peter's contacts and decided to contribute $450,000. That gave us legitimacy within the public broadcast system. It gave us 20 percent of what we needed. We already had over a million dollars from NEH; we were able get additional money from the Ford Foundation and the production happened.

Was the response to the ABC program *Separate But Equal* and your *Simple Justice* program what you had expected?

Yes and no. The ABC show was directed and produced by George Stevens Jr. There was an editorial in the *New York Times* by Anthony Lewis, who loved the book (*Simple Justice*) and devoted a column praising the history, the book and *Separate But Equal*. Stevens also won an Emmy for Best Miniseries for the year. Their production aired almost two years before ours was broadcast. We showed the work to the critics who meet twice a year in Los Angeles to review new television programs. The first question I got was, "We've seen *Separate But Equal*; why do we need another show on *Brown?*" My answer was, "At last count there were three productions on *Fisher v. Butafucco*; the *Brown* decision is considered one of the twenty most important events in American history. This was determined by a large group of newspaper editors who were questioned on the matter during the Bicentennial in 1976. So if we can have three programs on *Fisher*, I'm sure the country can stand two on this matter." After the ABC show, we felt it necessary to set the record right. The ABC show pulls its punches.

Were you pleased with the response to your program in particular?

Yes, the show is being distributed by PBS Video. Everything from elementary schools to law schools. We've had a very good response to the use of the program in the classroom. Thurgood Marshall and his wife, I'm told by Thurgood Marshall Jr., enjoyed the program. His son said he was over at the house the night the show was broadcast and his mother and father were in the study watching. He heard a couple of grunts coming from his dad. He thought he knew his dad's grunts, and they sounded positive.

### Producer/Director/Writer

*Street Soldiers,*\*\* 1996, 90 min., video, documentary. The Omega Boys Club (OBC) of San Francisco is an anti-violence, anti-drug program. This documentary tells stories of the members and leaders of the OBC. First, some background on the OBC.

The diagnosis is hood disease. The cure: equal parts of academic director Margaret Norris, providing classes; Wilbur Jiggetts, the surrogate grandfather, a full-time volunteer; the co-director Jack Jaqua, who visits Juvenile Hall three times a week and organizes meetings; and the director, Joe Marshall. Marshall was a 1994 recipient of a MacArthur Fellowship. As part of its outreach, the OBC can regularly be heard in the San Francisco area over a local hip-hop radio station on Sunday nights with its program entitled *Street Soldiers*. OBC's record speaks for itself: The OBC has sent over 150 San Francisco Bay Area youth to college from the mean streets in seven years. In 1996 eight OBC youth are expected to graduate, making a total of thirty college graduates in three years.

In this documentary we follow the lives of Enoch, Kai and Donald, three young Black men who have a date with a destiny yet to be determined. Will they be cured of hood disease, or will it take another victim? In the video program, two of the three are on their way to success. The care and passion of the OBC is conveyed by the filmmakers with a clever device. All three young men are given video cameras to record video diaries. Nothing could be more personal, revealing and at times heart-rending. This is a fine, independently produced program about real solutions to real problems. It doesn't get any better than this.

## AWARDS

*Booker*
Banff Television Festival, Best of Festival, Children, 1985
*Los Angeles Herald Tribune*, Ten Best Television Programs, 1984
National Educational Film Festival, Best Film, Social Science, 1985
Prix Jeuness International Prize, 1986
Writers Guild of America, Best Script, Childrens Program, 1985 (co-author with
    Charles Johnson)
*Simple Justice*
CINE, Golden Eagle, 1993
Houston International Film Festival, Best of Festival, 1993
Humanitas Award, Finalist, 1993
National Education Association, Advancement of Learning through Broadcasting,
    1993
*Up and Coming*
Action of Children's Television, Special Award for Excellence, 1981
American Film Festival, Blue Ribbon, 1981
National Education Association, Best Children's Drama, 1982

## EDUCATION

Clark College, Atlanta, Georgia, B.S., chemistry
Washington University, St. Louis, Missouri, Ph.D., organic chemistry
Woodrow Wilson Fellowship

## SOURCES

Interview by Spencer Moon, May and August 1996.

Stan Lathan

# STAN LATHAN

## BACKGROUND

My life's experience and my point of view are influenced by growing up in Philadelphia. I'm from a working-class family, an extended family of strivers. They were African Americans that did everything they could to pave the way and encourage the children in the family to make the best of their lives, to live out the American dream, to help get all those things that theoretically are promised to us by this so-called democratic system.

As a child I was always pushed to develop self-esteem and to work hard. We were encouraged to go to college. My brother and I were helped to go to college by the family banding together to help us financially—as an example, chicken dinner sales in addition to scholarships we earned. I had a strong background as a child, and that has had a lot to do with my attitude toward my work. This has helped to formulate my point of view.

I was a theater major at Penn State and got my degree in drama. I was involved in theater in the early days of my career. I always wanted to direct; I always wanted to be involved in the formulation and execution of ideas. I was a product of the sixties, where African Americans were involved in examining self-pride and identity. I think all these things have affected my outlook or the kinds of things that I'm interested in.

## EPISODIC TELEVISION

Lathan moved to Hollywood in 1975 and directed episodic television for a decade.

When you look back on a career as it unfolds, you let it because it's a meandering kind of path. I saw *Sanford and Son* as a great opportunity to come out and work with Redd Foxx and as entrée to Los Angeles and Hollywood. I was starting to feel like there really was a way for me to make a living doing this for the rest of my life and that it would grow into something bigger. I didn't know and probably still don't, but I tried to set goals for myself and have been constantly re-evaluating as I go along from year to year what the goal is. *Sanford and Son* was a great experience because it was a hit show and it gave me the kind of credentials I needed to be offered a lot more opportunities.

Over the next few years not only was I able to do *Sanford and Son* but I was able to keep my public television ties. I would go back to the East Coast occasionally and do specials with the likes of Alvin Ailey, Baryshnikov, Martha Graham, Agnes DeMille. These things kept me in touch with the cultural community. I always felt very fortunate that I was able to move between public television, these cultural programs and commercial prime-time kinds of things. It kept me, as an artist and a communicator, sort of primed—in shape, so to speak. Even though I might spend a couple of months working on a special with Alvin Ailey, in five days I could go and do a *Sanford and Son* that twenty times as many people would compliment me on, even African American people. It was obvious to me that commercial television was reaching a lot of people. So I felt it was important to stay in that groove.

I was doing hour-long episodics, so my filmmaking skills were honed. As a result, I know how to move quickly and solve certain production problems; that sort of became second-nature. Those skills that I developed were really fine-tuned during shows like *Hill Street Blues* and *Miami Vice*, so that by the mid-eighties I was very employable in Los Angeles. There was a certain frustration that developed because I was unable to re-crack the feature film area, trying to sell scripts and get some sort of acceptance from the studio filmmaking community. I always felt that if I were going to do anything that was significant, it would be a feature film. But as long as I could direct episodic television, I could make money and a good living—but as an artist I didn't feel like I was being fulfilled.

*Beat Street* came along, but this was a period when I was constantly working on two or three projects—obscure public television projects or commercial television projects. I was really feeling frustrated as a director. *Beat Street* didn't do much to make me feel any better about the work I was doing. I was very busy all the time. I hate to rag on racism and the system, because racism is a factor in our lives as African Americans, period. It exists in the film and television industry. It's very obvious, it is very apparent, because of the kinds of things that are made available to Black directors and writers. [This is also apparent in industry] perceptions of the audience, the kinds of things that the industry likes to disregard, or place[ment of] the Black audience into a certain kind of attitude as far as a demographic is concerned.

I went through some personal crisis where I examined how I was living my life, my personal objectives. You need to do that every once in a while—re-examine, rethink this life that we're leading in order to grow into middle age and retirement with some sense of accomplishment. So it was toward the end of the eighties that I felt like just directing. I consider myself a very skilled and accomplished director who is able to and has worked in all mediums. Maybe what I needed to do was become more of an entrepreneur, to put myself in a position to pass on some of this knowledge and these skills to other directors. Often I had very little control over how these projects were marketed or perceived.

## ENTREPRENEUR

Let me see if I understand correctly: Is SLBG (Simmons, Lathan, Brillstein, Gray) your individual office under the Def Pictures banner and Polygram Entertainment?

OK, let me answer that because that is a perfect segue. Let me just set the table a little bit, you know. When I talk about the late eighties, that was a time when there were other colleagues of mine that were working; we started to feel a certain frustration. A lot of us felt it: George Jackson* of Jackson/McHenry and some other very close friends of Bill Duke,* who knew Spike (Lee).* We had a lot of dialogue and there was a lot of rivalry, but there was certainly this feeling among a group of filmmakers and television makers. The Hudlin brothers* were coming along at the time—filmmakers who had a vision, a dream, an objective. There was never an organization formed to say that we had to do something about this, but I think there was a growing frustration based on the fact that there were more and more of us who had similar needs and experiences.

I was probably one with more commercial experiences than most of the others, but we came out of the same pot and all ended up back together and all had a certain respect for each other. So I realized coming out of the *Beat Street* experience and seeing how a film that had a lot to do with my culture was out of my hands somewhat during the production, and most certainly after we finished it, and how it was marketed—the way it was perceived, the way it was released. I realized that it was necessary for me now as a mature man to think about how to make some adjustments and control a little more. I looked around for ways to make alliances.

I had come to know Russell Simmons, who was in his own music world—the world of rap—making a name for himself and having control of the material and the artists. He had a certain power among the record companies because at a time when they didn't pay much attention to it, he had made sure he maintained contractual control. So when it became the phenomenon that it did, he was already in a position to start to wield some of that power. There were a few others like him, and even Spike was able to do that in the film industry. But they came along at the right time and made the right maneuvers and used their power. Russell and I came together to try to figure out a way to do some things together. We knew there was a huge void in the comedy area for Black entertainers, Black performers. We also knew there were a lot of clubs in various towns and that every town had a Black comedy club—or it did at the time—that filled up on certain nights of the week, or a Black Night at a major club. This undercurrent of performers like Robin Harris in Los Angeles and Dougie Doug in New York had strong followings, loyal fans, and there was some great stuff. There was Martin Lawrence and certainly Steve Harvey; these were guys who were well known among the Black community of club-goers who liked comedy.

So we sold to HBO the idea of putting on a show in the middle of the night that would make that venue available to the late-night HBO audience. It would be totally uncensored in its raw form and would allow the White HBO audience and a large percentage of the Black audience to go to a club they wouldn't go to normally. That was the original concept behind the *Def Comedy Jam* team [who put *Def Comedy Jam* together]. This is the sixth year; we've produced about fifteen shows a year. We're up to about eighty shows. We had no idea what we had, what kind of a phenomenon it would be, but there were two things we made absolutely clear. We realized there might be some archival potential in this. So first of all we partnered with Brillstein/ Gray, the leading comedy managers. They manage a lot of huge White comedy stars and have a production company. I have had an affiliation with them for many years in a lot of my projects. So we partnered with them and struck a deal with HBO whereby we got all the negatives and they gave us the license fee but we totally owned the franchise—lock stock and barrel—which we'd learned from watching some of our counterparts who made a killing in the entertainment business. Russell, of course, had done that with Def Jam Records.

That was probably the first step in us building a *Def Comedy Jam* franchise, which became very profitable because then we were able to send the tour out to various cities as Russell Simmons's *Def Comedy Jam*. We also put his name on it so it would be absolutely identifiable, and we were able to sell tapes and get into merchandising and have total control without having to answer to anyone. We owned these eighty negatives, some of which are classics and some are very predictable. We took a lot of heat because of the material.

As a result of it, a lot of comedians surfaced. Someone said to us once, "Why do you need three hundred comedians?" Cause that's how many we had! Well, why do you need thirty point guards? Maybe Oscar Robertson should have been the only one. But what he did was to open up a door to add to a revolution in basketball and every other field, including music and all the sports. Now in comedy we believe we have certainly opened doors for a lot of very talented actors, writers and now stand-up comedians, because basically stand-up is a fusion of those two things. Some people are a lot better than others—certainly Martin Lawrence, Chris Tucker, Bernie Mac and people like that who have been on *Def Jam*. I'm not saying *Def Jam* is responsible for their success, but it certainly has helped make a lot of Americans aware of their brilliance as performers. And they've gone on to do a lot of other things. It's interesting that this provided inroads so that they could do what they do best, which is where they came from, so to speak.

## ALLIANCES AND PROJECTS

How is the relationship with Polygram going?

Polygram doesn't have anything to do with *Def Comedy Jam*. SLBG is in fact Simmons, Lathan, Brillstein, Gray—a very strong, very positive and nurturing relationship because now it's reciprocal and we have this money-making entity. Because they [Polygram] are a management company and Russell is involved in management as a rap producer, we then formed a management company initially to take advantage of some of the better comedians—those comedians we thought had promise in other areas (writing and acting), so we signed management deals with them. This is something that has been done for years and years by people in the business. In that respect we were able to help develop careers and help build a life in other areas. One of our most successful clients is Bill Bellamy, who is well known in entertainment circles as a host and a great performer. Now we've recently brought on Donna Chavous, a very powerful former Creative Artists Agency agent, to run the management company. Now we're signing a lot of other kinds of clients. The company that started out as a vehicle for *Def Jam* comedians has developed into a thriving management company that is surviving and flourishing on its own, partly due to the perceived success of *DCJ* and partly because of the overwhelming success of *Def Jam* Records in the last ten years and the fact that *DCJ*, Russell and his partners have moved to make a deal from Sony to Polygram—the record company who then approached Russell and myself separately.

Here is our record. Russell has sold millions and millions of records to an urban audience. We have the most successful show on late-night television, period. We're both filmmakers: Russell as producer on *Krush Groove*** (1985) and *Tougher Than Leather*** (1988), and I, of course, have an undeniable background in film and television. We want to start a film company. We believe that the way the studio system seemed to be going—bigger, more expensive films—we wanted to help dispel this myth that low-budget, modestly budgeted films couldn't be made; that films that were urban, African American, couldn't be financially viable. There is a huge market for that. It has been proven over the last few years, not by us but in general.

So our pitch to them (Polygram) was that we want to make modestly budgeted films. Essentially, we want to nail the urban audience but don't want to be limited to it. We are pretty sure that given certain budgets, we would guarantee successful movies. Polygram was all for it. They were thrilled to make a deal with us and to help us start a company, which we called Def Pictures. We were thrilled to be able to get Preston Holmes, one of the leading African American filmmaker/producers. There are very few of us who carry the title of producer. Preston not only has that title but has a very impressive list of credits going back to, as a matter of fact, *Go Tell It on the Mountain*. We worked together on that. He also worked with Spike on many movies, *Malcolm X*** (1992), produced *Posse*** (1993) and *Panther*** (1995) with Mario Van Peebles, which associated with Polygram Movies—so he was already appreciating and understood the Polygram system, which was different from the studio system. So the three of us formed this company, Def Pictures. Right now we're involved in two "go" projects, both of which we are co-producing with other Polygram labels. You understand the label system at Polygram?

Yes, they have individual labels that they market with various kinds of artists and different kinds of styles.

Two of the labels—one is Island Pictures (that's Island Records, of course) and then there's Innerscope Records—just sold to MCA, but then there's Innerscope Pictures. We're co-producing two movies, one with Island and one with Innerscope, both of which will be in production the spring or summer of this year (1996), so both will be in the marketplace by the second quarter of next year. And we're developing a number of projects. We're in business with several young film-makers for films that are going to cost less than $3 million; some will actually cost less than $1 million. We're also developing a couple of pieces that will be in the $7 to $10 million range, and we have a much larger film in development.

Let me explain to you what the development for us is all about. We have a development department, but we're not like a studio. We can't fool around just writing drafts and drafts and drafts. We enter into each deal very carefully with the intention of making the movie, which is one of the reasons why we're co-producing one of these films: We so wanted to make this movie and saw that it was going to be difficult for us to pull it off by ourselves financially. We were able to bring on, to interest, Ted Field and the Innerscope people, who were very anxious to get involved. So now we have a co-production that's going to work very nicely.

## SUCCESS AND DISTRIBUTION

Are you having the success or opportunities for production and distribution that you had hoped for in this relationship?

Distribution will be another hurdle once we get these films made, but absolutely I don't mean to say "hurdle." We do have a great relationship with Gramercy distribution on Polygram. When you talk about success in movie making, in the movie industry, it's very important to understand that the road from a good idea and even a good script to a produced and distributed movie is a long and deceptive one. As I said, we had a script that we loved. It was packaged with great actors and had a good director. Definitely a good idea. Still, because of various reasons—the ability to prove to ourselves and to Polygram that it would do well in domestic, foreign, video and television sales; and running numbers and crunching; and trying to get support from one element as opposed to another element, because supposedly African American movies don't do well in Europe; and so forth—you always have to work around those perceptions in order to garner financial support. You have to have the ability to say, "OK, we can't make it by ourselves. Now let's figure out a way to make it attractive as a co-production to someone else."

The feature film–producing arena is one that requires many skills, not just the artistic skills of a writer. We like to believe that we as a Black company are not sitting around and waiting for some White man to tell us, "Yes, you can do it." And so, when you ask if we are having success, that success is on us, not Polygram. Polygram wants to make movies. Polygram wants to make money from product that is out there. All organizations do. The challenge is to the filmmaker—the producer, if you will—to build in each project an entity that is going to make money for those people. You do it by coming up not only with a great package and a great story but with a plan for how this thing can be structured and then marketed and distributed so that it does make money. I've found that having Preston's expertise as a producer and understanding of finance and distribution and Russell's marketing abilities, we all kind of complement each other. We have a total package of a film company that knows enough about the business of making films and distributing films and about the aesthetics of writing and directing a lovely piece.

## ADVICE FOR ASPIRANTS

What can you tell young people interested in the business?

You need to have filmmaking and craft skills that are already developed. I work on productions and I see assistants and runners, the lowest jobs on the totem pole. Many of them have film degrees, some of them master's degrees in film. It is such a crowded, competitive field here in both the craft areas and in the writing and directing areas; there are so many highly talented people jockeying for position. My advice when I speak to students is this: When you're not in Los Angeles and you're in a local area, you should probably use your energies to establish experience. If you are a filmmaker, do anything you can to get a leg up on the experience factor. You might find yourself stuck in the job as a runner for a couple of years before someone notices or gives you the opportunity to become a set production assistant, which gets you closer to the action. Then there may be a longer period of time before you actually become a second assistant director. Each case is different. I think the key is to understand that it's a highly competitive area, now more than ever.

I do believe the industry has softened a little bit, in that I am seeing more and more young Black directors in local television and network television, and there are more women and Black women and young African Americans since 1992 just on movies and working in television. That's very apparent, working on television. I think the opportunities have widened. The pool of those seeking those opportunities has widened a lot more. So any firepower you can build before you get here will probably go a long way toward helping you find something here, if Hollywood and network television are your goal.

## THE FUTURE

What do you hope to accomplish in the future?

I hope to build SLBG and Def Pictures to the point where we're doing any project that we want to do; to help build an arena for African American writers to flourish and do important and profitable material for film and television.

## RUSSELL SIMMONS

Russell Simmons, who helped produce *Krush Groove* (1985), was instrumental in the soundtrack for the film going gold. His talent pool from Def Jam Records was showcased in the film. Polygram Filmed Entertainment has signed Def Pictures to produce films and soundtracks for Black audiences and people interested in Black culture. Simmons has produced artists, co-produced films and supervised the production of film soundtracks featuring hip-hop music.

## FILMOGRAPHY

*Save the Children*, 1973, 123 min., 35mm, color, Paramount. Produced by Clarance Avant and Matt Robinson. In 1972 in Chicago, Operation PUSH (People United to Save Humanity), an organization founded by Jesse Jackson, produced a Black business exposition, one of the first of its kind. Part of this exposition was a music concert/benefit; a film of the concert was shot for theatrical release as part of the several-day event. Participants in the concert read like a Who's Who of Black entertainment: Cannonball Adderly Quintet, Jerry Butler, the Chi-Lites, the Reverend James Cleveland, Sammy Davis Jr., Roberta Flack, Marvin Gaye (who penned and sings the title song), Isaac Hayes, the Jackson Five, Quincy Jones, Ramsey Lewis, the Main Ingredient, Curtis Mayfield, Gladys Knight and the Pips, the O-Jays, the Staple Singers, the Temptations, Albertina Walker, Nancy Wilson, and Bill Withers, among many others. Their performances in the film, intercut with highlights from the several-day event, produce a concert film that is difficult to rival in terms of a gathering of Black entertainers, let alone the incredible performances. Exposition speakers and attendees included Black leaders and personalities such as Don (Mr. *Soul Train*) Cornelius, actor Ossie Davis, Dick Gregory, Richard (*Shaft*) Roundtree, Smoky Robinson, Boston Celtic basketball great Bill Russell, Betty Shabazz (wife of Malcolm X), Percy Sutton (owner of Innercity Broadcasting), and Berry Gordy (then president and founder of Motown Records). The message of the film and purpose of the benefit/concert and proceeds from the film—to save the children—is still a timely message for the Black community. Stan described the film's production:

> There was a group of people who got together—Quincy Jones, Clarance Avant, Jesse Jackson—to make a documentary as part of a benefit for Jackson's Operation Push organization. We pulled together an amazing array of talent. It was a pretty intense experience. I had been directing a lot of music for television at the time, including *Sesame Street*. This was a musical documentary that allowed me to expand on what I had already developed as a television director. It introduced me to the world of feature films, multi-camera film shooting and technical adventures; it was amazing. It was my first introduction to a lot of the Black stars that over time I came to know personally very well. Those relationships helped me to make the transition from a public television director working in New York and Boston to a director in Hollywood.

*Amazing Grace*,** 1974, 99 min., 35mm, color, United Artists. Featuring Moms Mabley, Rosalind Cash, Moses Gunn, Slappy White and Dolph Sweet. Cameo appearances feature legendary Black film actors Butterfly McQueen and Stepin' Fetchit.

> This was Moms Mabley's only feature film that we put together with my partner at the time and African American writer/producer Matt Robinson. Matt is an expert on the history of Black entertainment. He had the idea to make a movie with Moms Mabley. Moms was a very important American entertainer. She was quite old at the time of the film. We knew this would probably be the last opportunity to do something like this. It was a tribute to early Black film stars who by this time in the seventies had been mostly forgotten and overlooked by the contemporary generation. We did this little comedy for $750,000. We had to stop production while Moms had a pacemaker put in. She came back to finish the film; it was amazing. Moms played a woman called Grace Tisdale Grimes who singlehandedly influenced the election of the race for the mayor of Baltimore.
>
> It was a cute little movie that I enjoyed making. It was my introduction to comedic and dramatic feature filmmaking. I learned a lot on that production, in terms of understanding the filmmaking process.

*Beat Street*,** 1984, 106 min., 35mm, color, Orion Pictures. Co-produced by Harry Belafonte. Featuring Rae Dawn Chong and Guy Davis.

> This film was offered to me by my friend David Picker, who I met when he was at United Artists. That was a pretty intense experience. We really tried to pull off a lot more than our budget and time and a New York winter would allow. But under the circumstances we got it done. Now for a lot of young people, this film—along with *Krush Groove*** (1985) among a certain generation of young people—is my most impressive credit to them.

*Gridlock'd* (co-executive producers Russell Simons and Preston Holmes), 1996, 35mm, 91 min., color. A Gramercy release of a Polygram filmed entertainment presentation of an Interscope Communications production in association with Def Pictures/Webster and Dragon Pictures. Directed/written by Vondie Curtis-Hall. Featuring Tim Roth and Tupac Shakur. Story of jazz musicians trying to kick a heroin habit.

## Made-for-Television Movies

*Child Saver*, 1986, 35mm, color, NBC movie of the week.

> A movie that was brought to me by some television producers. The cast included Alfre Woodard, who I had worked with on *Go Tell It on the Mountain*. So, the main thing that attracted me to work on it was the opportunity to work with her again, because she is such an extraordinary actress.

*Uncle Tom's Cabin*,\*\* 1986, 110 min., 35mm, color, HBO. Based on the legendary novel by Harriet Beecher Stowe. This is the first American sound version of this classic novel. The cast included Avery Brooks, Kate Burton, Bruce Dern, Paula Kelly, Phylicia Rashad, Kathryn Walker, Edward Woodward, Frank Converse, Edward Coe and Albert Hall. Stan said of this production:

> When it was initially brought to me, I toiled with it until I read the original novel. The whole concept of Uncle Tom had taken a bad rap over the years, so when I discussed with the producers the idea of portraying Tom in a very positive light, they were totally all for that. That was one of the reasons they brought it to me. Then we were lucky enough to get Avery Brooks. He brought real dignity to the role. He made Tom the real hero he should have been portrayed as through history. We also scored with Edward Woodward, who portrayed Simon Legree. He was the perfect villain. That was a film where once we got Avery Brooks on board, everybody wanted to do it. White and Black actors wanted to work with Avery because he is so highly regarded among his peers.
>
> It turned out OK, I guess. It was another tough, low-budget movie. We shot in Mississippi on plantations, using actual former slave quarters, under conditions that were very oppressive. We were working in a heat wave and a drought. We would be out there in 110° heat in these cramped slave quarters shooting these scenes. It was a tough, tough shoot. A lot of us got sick; there was this rampant illness going through the crew. There were snakes and bugs. Because it was a television movie, we were on a budget that wasn't changing. It wasn't like we could take more time. We actually cut a lot of scenes that we just didn't have time to shoot.

*Go Tell It on the Mountain*,\*\* 1985, 97 min., 35mm, color, PBS *American Playhouse* series. Based on the highly acclaimed semi-autobiographical first novel by James Baldwin. In a *TV Guide* article written in 1985, at the time of the film's telecast, Baldwin described the process and pain of his first novel. He wrote the book in early draft form at age 12 and finally finished it by age 27. To his amazement, it was published the next year. In his own words,

*Mountain* comes out of the tension between a particular father and a particular son. He gave me myself. I may not always like that self, yet here it is, and here I am, and I would not be here had it not been for him.

The cast included Ruby Dee, Olivia Cole, Paul Winfield, Alfre Woodard, Rosalind Cash, C.C.H. Pounder, Giancarlo Esposito, Linda Hopkins and James Bond III.

The film conveys the coming of age (in a fictionalized version) of the young Baldwin with tremendous grace and articulation. The director says of the film:

> This is one of my favorite experiences as a filmmaker. I was involved early on with two of the producers of this production on the *American Short Story* series for PBS (*Almos' a Man* and *The Sky Is Gray*). It was because of our experience on those that we wanted to tackle something larger. We communicated with James Baldwin; he gave us his blessing. He was very helpful and encouraging. The book is an epic, and to try to adapt it to a television movie, where less than a million dollars was spent, was kind of tough. We were able to pull it off. We had an amazing cast; they all were excited about doing the project, and they all worked a lot harder and for a lot less than they were used to. We shot it in Atlanta and Harlem. It was really a very inspiring experience for me because it did take a strong collaboration on everybody's part.
>
> The real reward came when Baldwin came to the screening and really liked it. We made concessions with the novel to screen adaptation about what to keep and what to lose, and Baldwin felt they were right on. He mentioned several times afterwards that if his work was going to be adapted, this is the way he wanted screen adaptations of his novels done, for people who cared and understood what he was trying to say in his novels. For me, that was one of the highlights of my career.

*Booker,*\*\* 1984, 60 min., 35mm, color, PBS *Wonderworks* series. Produced by Avon Kirkland. Chronicles the boyhood of Booker T. Washington. Featuring Levar Burton of *Roots; Star Trek: The Next Generation*; and *Reading Rainbow* in the title role. Additional cast members included C.C.H. Pounder, Thalmus Rasulala, Shavar Ross, Shelly Duvall and Marian Mercer.

*The Sky Is Gray,*\*\* 1979, 35mm, color, PBS, *American Short Story* series.

*The Trial of the Moke,*\*\* 1978, 35mm, color, PBS, *Theater in America* series.

*Almos' a Man,*\*\* 1977, PBS, 35mm, color, *American Short Story* series.

## Episodic Television

*Alien Nation*, FOX; *Barney Miller*, ABC; *Boone*, NBC; *Breaking Away*, ABC; *Cagney and Lacey*, CBS; *Eight Is Enough*, ABC; *Falcon Crest*, CBS; *Fame*, NBC; *First and Ten*, ABC; *Flamingo Road*, NBC; *Frank's Place*, CBS; *Goodsports*, CBS; *Hill Street Blues*, NBC; *It's Garry Shandling's Show*, HBO; *James at 15*, NBC; *MacGruder and Loud*, ABC; *Miami Vice*, NBC; *Remington Steele, Roc*, FOX; *Sanford and Son*, NBC; *Say*

*Brother*, PBS; *Sesame Street*, PBS; *Shirley*, NBC; *Soul*, PBS; *Teech*, CBS; *That's My Mama*, ABC; *True Colors*, FOX; *Up and Coming*, PBS; *The Waltons*, CBS; *Wonderworks*, PBS.

## Specials and Syndication

*Alvin Ailey Memories and Visions: A Dance Special*, 1973; *Apollo*, 1976; *Black Journal*, 1969–1972; *Broadway Plays Washington*, 1982; *Fall River Legend*: Agnes DeMille's ballet performed by the Royal Winnipeg Ballet Company, produced by CBC and ZDF, West German Television, 1981; *The Greatest Show on Earth*: Trinidad Carnival, 1972; *In Performance at Wolftrap*: eight shows, including concerts by Mikhail Baryshnikov, the Martha Graham Company, the Panovs and the Eliot Field Ballet Company, 1978; *Kennedy Center Tribute to Dr. Martin Luther King Jr.*, 1983; *Don Kirschner's Rock Concert*, 1974–1975; *Muhammad Ali Variety Special*; *Soultrain*, 1980–1981; *V.D. Blues, 1971*; *Flip Wilson Special*.

## Theater

*Riot*, 1968–1969, Boston and on Broadway

## BIO-CRITICAL REVIEW

*Go Tell It on the Mountain*. "Such a cast, such a script, so delicate and subtle a director, found a way to convey, so powerfully, so much that is not stated in the original book."—James Baldwin (author of the novel on which the teleplay is based), *TV Guide*

*Gridlock'd*. "Acting is strong across the board. Tech contributions on this modestly budgeted effort are sharp, and soundtrack is bound to be a winner." "Characters fly high, but *Gridlock'd* stuck in box."—Todd McCarthy, *Variety*, January 20–26, 1997, p. 45.

"Roth and Shakur make a likable enough team, and the sharp humor on the misery of dealing with government agencies is dead on."—Michael Arago, "Tupac's last dance." *San Francisco Weekly*, January 29, 1997, p. 81.

*Uncle Tom's Cabin*. "Above average."—*Leonard Maltin's Movie and Video Guide, 1995*

## SELECTED AWARDS

*Beat Street*
   NAACP Image Award, 1984

*Black Journal*
   Emmy Award, Magazine Programming, 1970

*Booker*
  Black Filmmakers Hall of Fame Award, 1983
  Jamaica Film Festival, Best Picture, 1985

*Color of Friendship*
  NAACP Image Award, 1982

*Go Tell It on the Mountain*
  San Francisco International Film Festival, Best Feature for Television, 1985

*Save the Children*
  Jamaica Film Festival, Best Director, 1974

*The Sky Is Gray*
  American Film Festival, 1980

*The Trial of the Moke*
  Eudora Welty Award, Outstanding Public Television Drama, 1978

*V.D. Blues*
  Christopher Award for Direction, 1972

## EDUCATION

Pennsylvania State University, B.A., theater

Boston University, studied theater

## SOURCES

Interview by Spencer Moon, February 1996.
Baldwin, James. "Belatedly the Fear Turned to Love for His Father." *TV Guide*,
    February 12, 1985, p. 26–29.
Maltin, Leonard, ed. *Leonard Maltin's Movie and Video Guide, 1995*. New York: Pen-
    guin Group, 1995.

# SPIKE LEE

## BACKGROUND

Shelton Jackson Lee got his nickname "Spike" from his mother, who said he was a tough baby. His great-grandfather, a disciple of Booker T. Washington, founded Snow Hill Institute in Alabama. Lee told *Playboy* magazine's Elvis Mitchell in an interview in 1991, "I'm grateful for my parents. Whatever we wanted to do (careerwise), they said okay." Lee studied mass communications in college and got a graduate degree in filmmaking. He is a third-generation graduate of Morehouse College. He directed the coronation for homecoming queen at his college. He shot 8mm films while in college. In fact, Rolanda Watts (of television talk fame) appears in Lee's first student film. In addition to making films, Lee had a radio show on campus and wrote for the school newspaper.

After Morehouse he enrolled in the graduate film program at New York University, where he met Ernest Dickerson, his favorite cinematographer; they were the only two Black students enrolled in the school's film program at that time. Dickerson was the cinematographer for Lee's second graduate-level student film, *Sarah* (1981). Lee's first student film, *The Answer* (1980), caused quite a stir when originally shown. The story is about a Black screenwriter hired to make a multimillion dollar remake of the classic *The Birth of a Nation*. Lee sprinkled his film liberally with clips from the epoch. That fact did not endear him to cinema traditionalists who revered D.W. Griffith, the classic film's director and a father of American cinema. Lee did survive this controversy to get a teaching assistant position at New York University.

He credits his grandmother with getting him financially through Morehouse and New York University and gives her a producing credit in his third student film, *Joe's Bed-Stuy Barbershop: We Cut Heads* (1982). This film won the student Academy Award yet brought no offers of consequence from Hollywood. Lee's next film, shot after graduation in 1984, is called *The Messenger*.

## CINEMATIC INFLUENCES

In the book *Spike Lee's Gotta Have It: Inside Guerrilla Filmmaking* (1987), Lee mentions that his influences from the world of cinema included but were not limited to Jonathan Demme, Martin Scorcese, Carlos Saura, Jean-Luc Godard, George Miller, Steven Spielberg and Akira Kurosawa.

## LOOKING BACK

As today's most well-known Black filmmaker, Spike Lee has helped to generate a renaissance in American Black cinema and television programs. Quite an accomplishment, considering the odds. If someone had told me there would be as many feature films produced by the Hollywood studio system on the Black experience between 1986 and today as there have been, I would have said they were crazy. The question becomes, Will there be continuity? The previous renaissance of the seventies was known later as the Blaxploitation period. It ended because Hollywood said, "no more." As a result, the African American community was still without production companies, studios, financial mechanisms for capital or even a decent network of communication among African American filmmakers. To have the feature film work by African Americans continue without the Hollywood system of financial support is crucial.

Lee started his feature film debut with *She's Gotta Have It* (1986) and has recently released his ninth feature film, *Girl 6* (1996). His tenth is due out before year's end. He started his first feature film without Hollywood support, yet today Island Pictures, Columbia Pictures, Warner Brothers and Universal Pictures have released his films to great international box office success. If anyone will survive the renaissance without Hollywood's support, it will be Lee. In 1991, when the Black media renaissance was peaking, Lee assessed the then-current crop of Black filmmakers. He told *Rolling Stone's* David Breskin, "I'm not begrudging anybody, but we'll find out the contenders from the pretenders."

## TODAY'S FINANCES

Lee has proven that he is a contender, because all the funds for his recent film on the Million Man March (1995) come from the Black community itself. Not a first, but a first in this part of the twentieth century and amidst the Black media renaissance. We hope this is not the last time that the Black bourgeoisie supports art—any art, not just feature films. Give, but do so consciously. The money for Lee's newest film, *Get on the Bus* (1996), comes from individuals such as Wesley Snipes, Danny Glover, Will Smith, Johnnie Cochran, Robert Guillaume and Lee himself. The docudrama feature is budgeted at $2.5 million.

## LEE AS AUTEUR

Lee's films have had a mixed and vocal response from both the Black and White communities. Many Black women find his portrayal of them on screen to be as sexist and stereotypical as that by White filmmakers. The sexually active character of Nola Darling in *She's Gotta Have It*, the sorority women and their treatment by the fraternity men in *School Daze*, the opening credits dance sequence by Rosie Perez in *Do the Right Thing*, the women characters in *Mo' Better Blues*—these are some of the things that have many Black women more than slightly annoyed. Lee has commented on many occasions that he makes his films with a Black audience in mind, but he feels he can't create films that will make all African Americans happy with his work.

What is important to him is an African American perspective on things relating to the media. In the book *Five for Five: The Films of Spike Lee* (1991), for which Lee wrote the introduction, he says as much about the African American perspective.

Black artists in music, theater, dance and other areas of the arts are ever so rarely given serious journalistic criticism by their own. So we got some people who can and do write their butts off from an African American perspective.

The writers in the book are some of America's best, including Toni Cade Bambara, Henry Louis Gates Jr., Nelson George, and Charles Johnson, with an introduction by Melvin Van Peebles.* These writers assess and critique Lee's first five feature films. This book is a unique contemporary critical analysis of the leading Black filmmaker in America today. The photographs are by David Lee, Spike's younger brother.

## FAMILY AND BUSINESS

Spike's father, Bill Lee, a jazz musician in his own right, has created the music for many of Spike's films. Spike's sister Joie Lee, a talented actress, is featured in several of his films. His commitment to family and community is part of the reason he has his offices in Bedford-Stuyvesant. He also owns several buildings there in which he has a retail store, Spike's Joint, to merchandise products that are created to market his films.

Lee has opened Spike's Joint West in Los Angeles; it includes a store and a kiosk. New stores are planned for Atlanta, Boston and Chicago. He has a clothing line (Forty Acres and a Mule Products) and a record label (Musicworks), as well as Forty Acres and a Mule Filmworks.

## DIRECTOR FOR HIRE

Spike Lee has also directed commercials and music videos for artists and athletes such as Michael Jordan, Miles Davis, Branford Marsalis, Anita Baker, Public Enemy, Tracy Chapman and Phyllis Hyman.

## AUTHOR

Not content to write, produce, direct and play leading roles in his films, Lee has also co-authored five books that chronicle the preparations for and making of five of his films from a personal perspective. These books also contain complete scripts for his films. They are titled: *Spike Lee's Gotta Have It: Inside Guerrilla Filmmaking*; *Uplift the Race: the Construction of* School Daze; *Do the Right Thing*; *Mo' Better Blues*; and *By Any Means Necessary: The Trials and Tribulations of the Making of* Malcolm X. All are available in paperback.

## SOCIAL AGENT

In 1990 in a poll conducted by *Black Enterprise*, Lee ranked tenth in terms of who speaks for Black America. In Lee's film *Mo' Better Blues* (1990), two Jewish characters were said by some Jewish groups to be stereotypical in presentation, thus offensive. Lee had to defend himself against charges of anti-Semitism in an article that he wrote for the *New York Times*.

The list of actors who have worked in Lee's films reads like a Who's Who of Hollywood actors: Halle Berry, Tisha Campbell, Giancarlo Esposito, Jasmine Guy, Laurence Fishburne, Samuel Jackson, Martin Lawrence, Rosie Perez, Annabella Sciorra, Wesley Snipes, John Turturro, Denzel Washington and Cynda Williams.

## SELECTED AWARDS

Black Filmmakers Hall of Fame, Clarence Muse Youth Award, 1987

*Gallery of Greats*, Inductee, 1991

*Do the Right Thing*
  Academy Award Nomination, Best Script, 1989

*Joe's Bed-Stuy Barbershop: We Cut Heads*
  Student Academy Award Winner, 1982

*She's Gotta Have It*
  Cannes Film Festival, Prix de la Jeunesse Award, Best New Director, 1987
  Los Angeles Film Critics, New Generation Award, 1987

## EDUCATION

Morehouse College, B.A., communications
New York University, Tisch School of the Arts, M.F.A., film production

## FILMOGRAPHY

### Student Films

*The Answer*, 1980.

*Sarah*, 1981.

*Joe's Bed-Stuy Barbershop: We Cut Heads*, 1982. Lee's love affair with San Francisco began in 1983 when *Joe's Bed-Stuy Barbershop: We Cut Heads* was shown as part of the San Francisco International Film Festival. Across the street from the city bus barn, at a now-defunct restaurant named Josephine's (for Josephine Baker), a reception was held by members of the African American community in Lee's honor. Members of various multicultural media groups attended.

### Producer/Director/Script/Actor

*She's Gotta Have It*,** 1987, 84 min., 35mm, b/w and color, Island Pictures. Featuring Tracy Camilla Johns, Tommy Redmond Hicks, John Canada Terrell and Spike Lee. The film had its U.S. premiere in San Francisco in March 1986 as part of the 29th San Francisco International Film Festival Black Cinema Series, which was co-curated by myself and two other members of the African American community, Elena Featherston and A. Jacques Taliaferro. A representative from Island Pictures came to the premiere at Spike's invitation and subsequently picked up the film for distribution. Spike reflected on his experience in San Francisco in his book *Spike Lee's Gotta Have It: Inside Guerrilla Filmmaking* (1987): "I have to say it was one of the highlights of my life. I had a great time in San Francisco."

The film is guerrilla filmmaking with Black urban/urbane sensibilities. Because of that fact, it does not win friends in the feminist camp. For example, Nola, the lead female character, is too dependent on the male characters and Nola later dreams she is raped by these same characters. Even today, Lee has problems with his depictions of the Black female experience. Part of the way to improve the quantity and quality of Black female images is to give more video cameras to young Black female children. Black women directors say that the more of them there are (and not just in Hollywood), the more their work just by its existence and distribution will influence their male counterparts, both Black and White.

*She's Gotta Have It* was the one film that began the torrent of the Black media renaissance. Made for under $200,000, it grossed nearly $9 million.

*School Daze*,** 1988, 114 min., 35mm, Columbia Pictures. Featuring Laurence Fishburne, Giancarlo Esposito, Tisha Campbell, Joe Seneca, Art Evans, Ossie Davis, Joie Lee, Tyra Farrell, Jasmine Guy and Spike Lee. The film is a musical "dramedy" with a message—not a traditional musical. Lee wanted to integrate music into the movie, and the settings for the musical numbers are realistic. His father, a jazz musician, contributed to the musical score, and his aunt, Consuela Lee Morehead, wrote an original song. The piece, called *Kick It Tigers*, was played for the first time ever by combined marching bands from Morehouse/Spelman, Clark and Morris Brown Colleges. Other musical numbers were written by a variety of pop music groups and artists. In all there are nine musical numbers in this film, which re-creates Lee's days in college.

In *Uplift the Race: The Construction of* School Daze (1988), Ernest Dickerson says Lee is a frustrated musician and that's why he became a cinematographer. He says the instrument Lee plays is the camera.

*Do the Right Thing*,** 1989, 119 min., 35mm, color, Universal Pictures. Featuring Danny Aiello, Ossie Davis, Ruby Dee, Richard Edson, Giancarlo Esposito, Bill Nunn, John Turturro, Joie Lee and Spike Lee. Of all the feature films Lee has produced, directed and co-starred in, this is his strongest work. The film takes current newspaper headline stories and skillfully indicts the growing American system of apartheid. We spend one hot summer day in the community of Bedford/Stuyvesant, New York. Sal's World Famous Pizzeria is the center of personal, family and community confrontations. The last confrontation leads to violence and death. This is as real as American cinema gets. The film confirms that the cutting edge of American culture is still in the African American community in areas of music, dance, sports, art, literature and cinema.

An important issue related to economics was resolved on the set of *Do the Right Thing*. Lee's crew for this film was a mostly union crew. His previous feature films were shot with mostly non-union crews. Because of the paucity of African Americans in the film unions, Lee and his producers received concessions and a significant number of African Americans received opportunities to work on the film and thereby get their union cards.

Lee says in the book *Do the Right Thing* (1989), "It is my most political film to date; at the same time I think it is my most humorous."

*Mo' Better Blues*,** 1990, 127 min., 35mm, color, Universal Pictures. Featuring Denzel Washington, Wesley Snipes, Giancarlo Esposito, Robin Harris, Bill Nunn, John Turturro, Cynda Williams, Joie Lee and Spike Lee. In his book on the making of the film, Lee said, "I was on a mission . . . one look at *Bird*** and *Round Midnight*** told me what not to do." He didn't like either film's portrait of the black jazz musician's experience. His own film, like some jazz music, is an extended improvisation. There are some very nicely done ensemble scenes. The music scenes in the club come alive. The cinematographer for most of Lee's feature films, Ernest Dickerson, describes their process by saying, "We knew we were going to be the first filmmakers in a while to look at jazz from a Black perspective." The characters in the film come to grips with their values and vulnerabilities, and watching this process can be painful for the thoughtful viewer.

*Jungle Fever*,** 1991, 132 min., 35mm, color, Universal Pictures. Featuring Annabella Sciorra, Wesley Snipes, Lonette McKee, Ossie Davis, Ruby Dee, Anthony Quinn and Spike Lee.

*Malcolm X*,** 1992, 201 min., 35mm, color, Warner Brothers. Featuring Denzel Washington, Angela Bassett, Al Freeman Jr., Albert Hall, Delroy Lindo, Theresa Randle, Kate Vernon, Lonette McKee and Spike Lee. The score is by jazz trumpeter Terance Blanchard. The soundtrack features saxophonist Branford Marsalis, the Boys Choir of Harlem, Sir Roland Hanna on piano, Britt Woodman on trombone and several additional outstanding jazz soloists. Lee co-wrote the script with James Baldwin and Arnold Perl.

The dichotomy between the man Malcolm X and the film of his life generated more press than any Black film event in recent memory. It even prompted publication of a book entitled *Malcolm X: In Our Own Image*, wherein prominent individuals from the African American community assess the man and his impact. Included in the book, which was edited by Joe Wood, are opinions from Whoopi Goldberg, Senator Bill Bradley, Justice Thurgood Marshall and Congresswoman Maxine Waters.

This is Lee's most ambitious film, but can any film appropriately tell the story of a now-legendary warrior such as Malcolm X? Positive Black male role models need to be presented in as many ways as possible, but Malcolm X was politically problematic for this country and its conscience. However, before his assassination he adopted what would be called today a universalist philosophy.

Lee says in *By Any Means Necessary: The Trials and Tribulations of the Making of* Malcolm X (1992), "The sixth film we've done in seven years, and frankly, I'm tired, I'm whipped." The film cost $30 million to make; Lee raised $9 million through the Black community from Bill Cosby, Tracy Chapman, Michael Jordan, Oprah Winfrey, Janet Jackson, Magic Johnson and Peggy Cooper-Cafritz. Lee understood that this was a precedent for Black film. In the same book, Lee said of the money from the Black community, "Definitely a historic event, it was a precedent, the world needed to be told, we can do for ourselves." Lee was bold enough to speculate on going directly to the African American community for funds for his next film.

*Crooklyn*,** 1994, 132 min., 35mm, color, Universal Pictures. Featuring Alfre Woodard, Delroy Lindo, Zelda Harris, David Patrick Kelly, Sharif Rashid, TseMach Washington, Carlton Williams, Chris Knowings and Spike Lee. Lee co-wrote the script with Joie Susannah (who also played the role of Aunt Maxine), his sister and Cinque Lee, a younger brother. The budget was $14 million.

*Clockers*,** 1995, 129 min., 35mm, color, Universal Pictures. Featuring Harvey Keitel, Delroy Lindo, John Turturro, Mekhi Phifer, Isiah Washington and Spike Lee. Lee co-wrote the script with Richard Price, the author of the book *Clockers* on which the film is based.

*Girl 6*,** 1996, 109 min., 35mm, Searchlight Pictures. Featuring Theresa Randall; script by Suzan Lori-Parks.

### Executive Producer

*The Drop Squad,*\*\* 1994, directed by Clark Johnson.

*New Jersey Drive,*\*\* 1995, directed by Nick Gomez.

*Tales from the Hood,*\*\* 1995, directed by Rusty Cundieff.

## BIO-CRITICAL REVIEW

"Spike Lee is an exhilarating mix of brilliance and bravado, of artist, businessman and preacher."—Caryn James, *New York Times*

"A controversial figure whose films explore the nature of American racism."—Ephraim Katz, *Film Encyclopedia*

*Clockers.* "What makes *Clockers* so special and so superior to most drug-and-gun potboilers is the skill with which it penetrates its characters."—Edward Guthmann, *San Francisco Chronicle*

————. "Spike Lee has made his most deeply felt, emotionally arresting and socially significant film."—Leonard Quart, *Cineaste*

*Crooklyn.* "So where *Crooklyn* attempts to counter racist assumptions about black identity, it also completely valorizes and upholds sexist and misogynist thinking about gender roles." bell hooks, *Z Magazine*

*Do the Right Thing.* "This authentic success story and uneasy Positive Role Model [Spike Lee] is going to find it increasingly difficult to inveigh against racist limitations."—Thomas Doherty, *Film Quarterly*

————. "The beauty in this film is the frustration of never being sure who did do the right thing."—Jacquie Jones, *Cineaste*

————. "Insights abound in this torch-bearing filmmaker's third feature."—Salim Muwakkil, *Cineaste*

*Jungle Fever.* "Lee's ability to make such strong social statements within the framework of mainstream entertainment has made him the key Black filmmaker in the movie business."—Jack Kroll, *Newsweek*

————. "The most thoughtful, provocative and deeply felt statement on race problems and gender relations to arrive on the screen in a very long time—and the funniest and most entertaining to boot."—David Sterritt, *Christian Science Monitor*

*Malcolm X.* "The complex film is seldom pompous and never ponderous and it has a wonderful story to tell. I can't imagine it being told better."—Herb Caen, *San Francisco Examiner*

————. "It's done with impressive skill and style, sometimes approaches the level of Mr. Lee's best work in the past."—David Sterritt, *Christian Science Monitor*

————. "It shows how one man can change attitudes, and be changed in turn."—Derek Malcolm, *Guardian Weekly*

*Mo' Better Blues.* "An extended riff on the life of a fairly successful jazz musician."—Mick LaSalle, *San Francisco Chronicle*

————. "That meaning of *Mo' Better Blues* does not leave us: You can't do it alone, and more important, you don't have to."—Charles Johnson, *The Films of Spike Lee*

*She's Gotta Have It.* "An entertaining and in spots invigorating first feature; a witty low-budget film."—Vincent Canby, *New York Times*

————. "Serves up homophobic, anti-woman ideas disguised as sexual liberation, and irresponsibility and unfaithfulness as the essence of human relationships."—Robert Allen, "Letters to the Pinkie," *San Francisco Chronicle Examiner Datebook*

## SOURCES

### Books

Katz, Ephraim. *Film Encyclopedia.* New York: HarperCollins, 1994.

Lee, Spike. *Five for Five: The Films of Spike Lee.* New York: Stewart, Tabori and Chang, 1991.

Lee, Spike, with Lisa Jones. *Do the Right Thing.* New York: Simon & Schuster, 1989.

————. *Spike Lee's Gotta Have It: Inside Guerrilla Filmmaking.* New York: Simon & Schuster, 1987.

————. *Uplift the Race: The Construction of* School Daze. New York: Simon & Schuster, 1988.

Lee, Spike, with Ralph Wiley. *By Any Means Necessary: The Trials and Tribulations of the Making of* Malcolm X. New York: Hyperion, 1992.

————. *Mo' Better Blues.* New York: Simon & Schuster, 1990.

### Newspapers and Magazines

Allen, Robert. "Letters to the Pinkie," *San Francisco Chronicle Examiner Datebook*, September 1986, p. 48.

Bell, Alan. "Success with *She's Gotta Have It*," *Los Angeles Sentinel*, November 13, 1986, p. B6.

*Black Enterprise*, August 1990, p. 82.

Breskin, David. "Interview with Spike Lee," *Rolling Stone*, July, 1991, pp. 63–71, 124.

Caen, Herb. "By-line Column," *San Francisco Examiner*, November 24, 1992, p. B1.

Canby, Vincent. "Films for Viewers Who Think For Themselves," *New York Times*, September 7, 1986, p. 27.

Doherty, Thomas. "Do the Right Thing," *Film Quarterly* (43), no. 2 (Winter 1989–90), p. 35–40.

Guthmann, Edward. "Lee's Timely *Clockers*," *San Francisco Chronicle*, September 13, 1995, p. C3.

hooks, bell. "Death and Patriarchy in *Crooklyn*," *Z Magazine*, October 1994, p. 17.

Johnson, Charles, et al. "On Meaning of *Mo' Better Blues*," *The Films of Spike Lee: Five for Five*, Introduction by Spike Lee (New York: Stewart, Tabor and Chang, 1991), p. 117.

Jones, Jacquie. "Critical Symposium on *Do the Right Thing*," *Cineaste* (17), no. 4 (1990).

Kroll, Jack. "Spiking a Fever," *Newsweek*, June 10, 1991, p. 32–39.

LaSalle, Mick. "Spike Lee's One-Note Jazz," *San Francisco Chronicle*, August 3, 1990, pp. E1, E8.

Lee, Spike. "I Am Not an Anti-Semite," *New York Times*, August 22, 1990, p. A23.

Malcolm, Derek. "Sealed with a Loving X," *Guardian Weekly* (U.K.), March 14, 1993, p. 24.

Mitchell, Elvis. "The *Playboy* Interview with Spike Lee," *Playboy*, September 1991, pp. 51–68.

Muwakkil, Salim. "Critical Symposium on *Do the Right Thing*," *Cineaste* (17), no. 4 (1990), p. 9–11.

"People Are Talking about . . . " *Jet*, June 3, 1996, p. 57.

Quart, Leonard. "Spike Lee's *Clockers*: A Lament for the Urban Ghetto," *Cineaste* (22), no. 1 (1996), pp. 7–10.

Sterritt, David. "Lee Follows His Own Tough Act," *Christian Science Monitor*, June 13, 1991, p. B2.

———. "Lee's No-Nonsense *Malcolm X*," *Christian Science Monitor*, August 18, 1992, p. B2.

Wood, Joe. "X Appeal in the Nineties: Talking Back to Malcolm X," *Elle*, November 1992, pp. 128–30.

# LOUIS MASSIAH

## BACKGROUND

I was interested in story-telling, and that was how I became originally interested in film and video production. As a kid growing up, I had jobs in summer theater as a technician. I originally wanted to be a director. I studied physics and astronomy in college. One summer I had a job as a planetarium lecturer. This job was a strange mixture of astronomy and theater. The job was at the Franklin Institute. That job was a way that I could put my interests in science and story-telling together. Often during my summer months while in college I would have two jobs. One summer I worked in the prop shop for the Public Theater and was also working at WNET-TV, public television in New York City. After I got my degree I began working at WNET-TV writing continuity. I wrote all the material for the live breaks between the odd-length programs. Those breaks, usually 3 minutes or less, you would fill with promotional material and other assorted material. Sometimes the breaks would be longer. I began producing science news broadcasts. I would take topical stories like, say, the Nobel Prize and use that extra time to explain what the Nobel Prize was, from a historic perspective. So it might consist of a voiceover, slides and some rough animation; they were little mini-docs. After a year, a programming job opened. I read program proposals that came in, I helped

Louis Massiah. *Photo courtesy of Carlton Jones for Scribe Video Center.*

producers write proposals for funding. It really helped me to understand how you conceptualize a program. I decided I wanted to do more in terms of production. I decided to go to graduate school, not so much for filmmaking but to use media—specifically video—as a way of exploring complex ideas. As an example, to take mathematical equations or other material arcane to the general populace, and create a visual means of explaining it. Not an illustration, but a visual language that one might develop to help people understand complex ideas. Let's say you're trying to explain gravitation to someone who doesn't read a lot; how do you do that? Is there a visual way to convey the precise information in the gravitational equation or the second law of thermodynamics? I was accepted into a very good graduate filmmaking program at MIT. The program was a very good cinema verité documentary program. Reluctantly I began producing more documentaries. After I left MIT in 1982, I traveled to Berlin and India.

## WHYY-TV

Later I got a job at WHYY-TV through a person who had worked at WNET and was now station manager at WHYY-TV in Philadelphia: David Othmer. As a staff producer I was able to produce lots and lots of programs, documentaries and a variety of other programs. In some ways it was nice to have access to wonderful equipment, but to also have a reason to produce. There was a fair amount of leeway as to subjects. I could pitch projects. I might end up producing three or four documentaries a year. I was there about four years or so. As an example, I produced a program on worker self-management, *My Own Boss*. I looked at a number of worker-owned enterprises, some of which were buyouts by employees. One was about mainly Black textile workers in North Carolina. I looked at enterprises where workers organized and bought factories. Similar things were happening in Philadelphia in the supermarkets. A number of the supermarkets in Philadelphia, the employees purchased them. I was really looking at employee self-management.

I produced another program called *Bolt of Lighting* on Isamo Noguchi, the sculptor. This was an interview with footage following the construction of the work itself. I produced six short 5-minute programs on the history of astronomy. A cosmology of various cultures, that series of shorts as a group were called *In the Beginning*. Some examples of the cosmologies presented included the African Dogon cosmology, Western European cosmology, Hindu cosmology, a variety of Native American cosmologies, Mayan cosmology and Chinese cosmology. We talked with scholars in the field, combined with original artwork and other related visual material. I did a portrait of a Negro baseball leaguer, a guy named Judy Johnson, who played for the Pittsburgh Grays and a couple of other teams.

Those were examples of shows I think I did mainly in the first year. I was doing a lot, acting mostly as producer/director. I look at the folks who did *Black Journal,* and the thing that was so wonderful for many of them was having a weekly program format and a deadline, to produce shows regularly. To have a venue and the resources to do that was important. It was an extraordinary opportunity.

## THE SCRIBE VIDEO CENTER

Scribe has a lot of inspirations. When I was getting ready to leave MIT, I realized Philadelphia did not have a media art center where people could have access to equipment. There were exhibition spaces but no places where people could collaborate on projects together. I remember reading about Pearl Bowser and Oliver Franklin and their exhibition of work by Oscar Micheaux,* and I thought wouldn't it be wonderful to have a place where work like that could be shown and archived. I didn't really do what I wanted at MIT, which was to work on a new visual language. I thought, wouldn't it be great to have this lab where I could do that? I began by having meetings, which were workshops, at a place called Brandywine Graphic Workshop, because of its location and the particular neighborhood it was in. I rang their doorbell one day and said what I was interested in doing. Allen Edmonds, who runs that organization, said, "Why don't you use some space here?"

### Scribe Beginnings

In the beginning, we offered free workshops. The state arts agency said it was great, Philadelphia really needs this, the program officer is someone who is very progressive. Why not apply through Brandywine as a fiscal sponsor and try to move forward with this? We did, and we offered a few more workshops. By 1985 we had incorporated. Then a couple of years later we were having a fairly large number of classes and a lot of people coming through. Brandywine was growing and we were growing, so we had to move and find our own space. We moved to our present address on Cypress Street.

It took a while before we had equipment to produce things. By then I was working at WHYY-TV and Scribe was like an evening thing. A lot of it happened out of the trunk of the car of this woman, Sandy Clark, who was working with me. We kept all our supplies and stuff in her trunk. We found out equipment houses would charge very, very low rates if you took equipment at 5 PM and returned it the next day before 10 AM. We would rent really good equipment from equipment houses and use it to teach at night and return it the next morning. That was our equipment, because we didn't have any money to buy equipment.

## Organization Growth

Slowly we began to grow; some local foundations began to support us. We began to produce video at Scribe. The video projects at Scribe are individual projects, but there are also projects that are often collaborative works. One of the collaborative projects I was particularly interested in was a project dealing with housing. The National Union of the Homeless was based in Philadelphia, so we did a number of projects documenting their work. One project we did was called *The Taking of One Liberty Place*, which I shot and put together. This was a high-rise building that was the first skyscraper in Philadelphia. The building was taken over by the National Union of the Homeless as a political, agitprop sort of thing. We documented that, and there were other takeovers that we documented. There was another piece called *Mayday Takeover*. Through the work of Scribe I began to work with other media activists and other public access television groups around the country through Deep Dish, a national public access television network based in New York. I became a board member of Deep Dish, and I coordinated and produced two programs through them. Through the Scribe workshops, individual artists were producing work. We realized that since Scribe was running largely by donations and volunteer efforts, people who had money and access knew about it more than working-class individuals. Because of the scarcity of resources, people in the know were using it as a resource. That was fine; but because it was mostly a volunteer effort, all this volunteer effort was going out to people who might be able to pay for it.

## COMMUNITY VISIONS

We decided to programmatically try to begin reaching a more diverse audience. We began a project called Community Visions.

This was a free project whereby we would solicit community groups around Philadelphia and they would send in a proposal for a video project that they would like to do. They could use video to address a cultural issue or a social issue affecting them. For a ten-month period, one or sometimes two experienced filmmakers would train them on how to use the equipment and then help them produce a videotape. It is an extraordinarily successful model. It is very high in terms of sweat equity, and a lot of labor is involved in making the projects. Community Visions has become a very important part of Scribe as well. We are actually now preparing for round eight of this project. We do about four Community Visions projects a year. They are very labor-intensive. The works are not schlock videos; they are works that have pretty high artistic value. That's one of the goals of the making. It is not a question of the two filmmakers doing everything, using the ideas of the people as the content that they shape. The works are shaped by the groups because they are adults; we're working with adults who are doing community work, and they then are trying to learn video as another form of literacy. That is Scribe in a nutshell. Scribe is my art project. I am director. The day-to-day operation is done by Herbert Peck. I'm a very active board member.

## ADVICE FOR ASPIRANTS

What can you tell young people who want to get into the business?

You have to make work. You have to figure out how to have access to technology, whether it's a camcorder, or through a media arts center, through family or friends, through school. Even before you pick up a camera, think about what it is you want to say, the structure of what you want to say. Think of video and film as storytelling. Spend a lot of time thinking about how your story will unfold. Try to figure out what stories are needed and useful. There is no need to tell stories that are not useful. We need stories that are going to carry us forward. Things that carry us forward can be things that are painful or difficult; sometimes processing that information helps us go forward. If the story is not going to take us to a higher ground, you should think about whether it is really worth the energy to do it. Because there are so many stories that can take us to higher ground.

## BEYOND HOLLYWOOD

Do you think independent production and distribution outside the Hollywood system is a viable artistic and business venture?

It is viable for some people. The problem is, there are thousands of independent filmmakers in the United States. There are not enough venues for screening work publicly. There are not enough venues for distribution. There is not enough access in terms of cable and broadcast. There is a lot of very, very good work being made, and there aren't the venues so people can be compensated for their work. That, to me, is the major work that needs to be done in the independent sector right now. Yes, people need training and access; unless there are venues that support an independent vision, it's a bottleneck. Makers need to be compensated.

## UNIQUENESS

What makes you unique as a filmmaker?

I see commonality not just with filmmakers but with people who see themselves as cultural workers. Whether the particular media they are using is film or painting, dance or writing as a way of dealing with particular needs of the community. That's the context in which I see my work.

## RENAISSANCE

What do you think of the Black film/video renaissance?

A lot of things have come into play. I think changes in technology—definitely the camcorder and the new digital technologies for editing—have been pushing the ability of more people to make work. More and more people understanding that film and video making is an important form of literacy. It's not just African American; it's out there. Part of the way that Hollywood works is by making media precious. One of the problems with the growing independent market is that if the work gets out there, the Hollywood work becomes less precious. So that's really what the struggle is about. Once you increase supply, there's a notion that it's going to hurt a particular kind of product. What Hollywood makes is special and fills a specific need. If there were two theaters in every city that just screened independently made work, I don't think that would close down or effectively hurt Hollywood. Hollywood is not impervious to changes in the media environment; it's reflected in work that's produced, too. I also credit Spike Lee* and Julie Dash,* certainly Marlon Riggs* and Henry Hampton.* There are a lot of important forces out there that have helped to push things forward.

## THE FUTURE

What do you hope to accomplish in the future?

To make more work and to try to tackle the venue issue, even if just in a localized way.

## FILMOGRAPHY

### Producer/Director

*Words and Works: Three Artists from the Studio Museum of Harlem*, 1980, video.

> A portrait of three artists-in-residence at the Studio Museum of Harlem. The artists had a group showing at the University of Massachusetts, Amherst. The visual artists were Louis Delsarte, Candace Hill-Montgomery, Jacquie Holmes. It documents the exhibit and interviews with the artists.

*Miami Journal: The Haitian Refugees*, 1981, 30 min., video.

> I produced a documentary at MIT on the Haitian refugees that aired on local public television in Philadelphia. A 30-minute video documentary that I produced and directed. My mother financed and co-produced it with me. We flew to Miami and shot the program. WHMM-TV public television at Howard University also aired it. It was shown eventually at the market of the Berlin Film Festival.

*The Bombing of Osage Avenue*, 1986, video.

> In 1985 there were hearings into why the city had decided to drop this bomb, which resulted in a neighborhood being burned down and the resulting deaths. The decision was to televise them, and I produced the televised hearings. There were many hours of programming on these hearings. Up until the recent judgment in favor of Ramona Africa, one of the survivors of this event, the police and fire commissioners were found negligent. This was the only other time that a body had found clear culpability and clear evidence of criminal activity. Unfortunately, it had no power to indict. After that, the decision at the station was to re-look at this event and contextualize it. The mass media had described

it as a crisis of Black leadership and to make out the MOVE organization as a horrible group; that was why this had happened. Neither of those two approaches interested me at all. At that time I met Toni Cade Bambara, who had recently moved to Philadelphia. She said I should go ahead and make a program on those events. She said I should look at the bombing in the context of the neighborhood where it happened. She wrote the script and narrated the work.

*Cecil B. Moore*, 1987, 60 min., video. Toni Cade Bambara wrote the script for this work.

> Cecil B. Moore was a Philadelphia civil rights leader. He really led the movement here in Philadelphia. He was head of the local chapter of the NAACP. He was much more radical than the national NAACP leadership, although politically I wouldn't say he was Left. Some of the things he did were reminiscent of the things Fred Hampton did in Chicago, maybe ten years later. He (Moore) was organizing the gangs in Philadelphia. He was turning them into the shock troops of the civil rights effort here in Philadelphia. He was trying to make the NAACP more than a middle-class social organization. He tried to make it much more of an activist grass-roots phenomenon. He was a lawyer. In many ways there are great similarities to Adam Clayton Powell Jr.—in terms of coming from a prominent family and a bon vivant type. He was very articulate, very witty, very quick with his tongue.

*Digging Dinosaurs*, 1987, 30 min., video.

> This was really an assignment, documenting a dinosaur dig. It was being carried out by paleontologists at one of the local institutes here. The dig was in Montana. The piece looked at what goes on, what was entailed in doing a dig, looking at the specific findings. It was really a nature kind of piece. A portion of the work aired on the PBS news program *McNeil-Lehrer Newshour*.

*Eyes on the Prize*, Part II, 1992. (*Eyes on the Prize* was a fourteen-hour series on the civil rights movement and the emerging Black social political consciousness in America from 1955 to 1986. Part I was six programs, Part II was eight programs, each one hour in length. The executive producer was Henry Hampton.*)
   Massiah worked as co-director, co-producer and co-script with Terry Rockefeller on two programs for Part II. Episode entitled *Power*:

> This program looked at three manifestations of Black power. The first section was about the election of Carl Stokes to the mayoralty of Cleveland. The second section looked at the birth of the Black Panther Party in Oakland, California. The third was about the struggle for control of schools in Brooklyn, New York.

Episode entitled *A Nation of Law*:

> This was about the government's reaction to the Black freedom movement, the killing of Fred Hampton in Chicago, COINTELPRO

(Counter Intelligence Program) and their involvement in that. This work was the first program that layed out the evidence about COIN-TELPRO and its effect on the Black political movement. The second section looked at the Attica prison uprising and the suppression by the state government of New York.

*W.E.B. Du Bois: A Biography in Four Voices*, 1996, 114 min., video. Written and narrated by Toni Cade Bambara, Amiri Baraka, Wesley Brown and Thulani Davis.

The distribution includes advanced screenings and fundraising screenings to retire the debt. I thought the project was going to take about two years, and it took a little more than four years. The bills are extraordinary. The formal premiere will be at the Toronto Film Festival in September 1996. It is available for educational and classroom use through California Newsreel. Newsreel offered us an advance against royalties; I don't know if I would have done that if I had not needed the money. Having your work available for educational distribution before it has done other forms of marketing, I'm not sure is the best idea. I needed the money; it does create tension because they want to market the film. If they do that too much, it kills your other potential venues. We've been trying to make it work for both of us. It will be broadcast on the Public Broadcasting System in February 1997. We're trying to get other distribution. The Toronto Film Festival, the largest North American film festival, will be a good leg up and a good way to get the word out about the film.

Why this project?

I had a long-term interest in Du Bois, a pivotal figure in our century. He was someone who because of the McCarthy era and the communist hysteria was erased from popular history in many ways. He was very important, an inspiration to a variety of activists and scholars. It is very important in re-looking at Du Bois's life that we give some foundation to the current era—certainly to the civil rights era and the current era by looking at that span of time between the end of slavery, the beginning of reconstruction and the mid-twentieth-century civil rights movement.

## EDUCATION

Cornell University, B.A. (College Scholar), astronomy and physics

Massachusetts Institute of Technology, M.S.

## SELECTED AWARDS

Pew Fellow, 1994
*W.E.B. Du Bois: A Biography in Four Voices*

San Francisco International Film Festival, Golden Gate Awards, Certificate of Merit, 1996

## SOURCE

Interview by Spencer Moon, August 1996.

Oscar Devereaux Micheaux. *Illustration courtesy of R. Ellis Lee.*

# OSCAR DEVEREAUX MICHEAUX

## BACKGROUND

Oscar Micheaux (1884–1951) was the first great Black filmmaker in America. Black entrepreneurs such as George Johnson and William (Bill) Foster made films before Micheaux; but they did not make as many films as he did, they did not make films for as long as he did, and they did not make films that stand the test of time. Micheaux, a master filmmaker, tells a good story, chooses substance over mundane subjects, knows how to make us laugh and cry.

## ENTREPRENEUR'S SPIRIT

From *The Conquest*, by Oscar Micheaux (1994 [1913]): "One of the greatest tasks in my life has been to convince a certain class of my racial acquaintances that a colored man can be anything."

Micheaux was the fourth son and the fifth child of a family of thirteen. His father, born in Kentucky the son of slaves, became a prosperous farmer. His mother, also born from slaves, wanted more for her children; she wanted to move to Metropolis, Illinois, so her children could attend the local colored school. Micheaux was not fond of farm work, so he was given the job of selling the family produce in town. At age 17 he left home and went to visit one of his older brothers in Chicago who worked as a Pullman porter. Micheaux subsequently got work as a Pullman porter as well. He saved his money and dreamed of creating an opportunity for himself beyond the railroad. He heard about land being made available for homesteads and ranches in the eastern part of South Dakota. When the opportunity presented itself, he bought land there in an all-White community in 1905.

Micheaux married his first wife, Mildred, around 1910. She was the daughter of a minister from Chicago. Because of what is described as interference from her relatives, they divorced within a few years. This episode in Micheaux's life he refashioned and incorporated, along with aspects of his farming experience, into his second novel, *The Homesteader* (1917). Because Micheaux considered this part of his life as a failure, he chose to move on. In addition, there was financial failure owing to mortgaging his home.

Micheaux turned failure into success. He taught himself how to write a novel. His first novel, *The Conquest*, he published himself and sold door-to-door in South Dakota. It was such a success that he was able to finance his first company. Micheaux took the sales acumen of selling vegetables, and his own ideas about what the new Negro was capable of, and in 1918 formed the Micheaux Film and Book Company with offices in Sioux City and Chicago. He sold stock in his new company to White farmers around Sioux City.

## FILM PRODUCTION

This technique of self-promotion was adapted to film production as well. Micheaux's success as a filmmaker was tied to his strong will and confidence. His determination and drive were assisted by his second wife, the actress Alice Bertrand Russell, whom he married in 1929. She helped in the operation of his film company. With the self-made success of his first novel and film, Micheaux went on to create films for three decades.

Those who knew him agreed that Micheaux had a tremendous amount of energy. When he was not making movies, he was busy booking dates for completed films and raising capital for films. He attended other movies to observe how films were produced. He went to live theater looking for new actors, making mental notes for his own productions and later recruiting those actors in whom he was interested.

The key to success for any filmmaker is distribution. Micheaux taught himself not only how to make films but how to distribute them. Over a thirty-year period, no *independent* filmmaker—Black or White—has a record of completed productions that matches Micheaux's.

## INFLUENCES

Influences on Micheaux were the standardbearers of the Negro race of the day. Booker T. Washington and W.E.B. DuBois were his role models. Micheaux was also a serious student of history. He used the work of popular

Black authors of the day. Charles Chestnutt and Paul Laurence Dunbar were inspirations. Other inspirations for his scripts were the words of people such as Marcus Garvey and Harriet Tubman.

## CONTEXT

Micheaux overcame tremendous odds and obstacles to create positive images of Black people. At the time, images from Hollywood and other independent White producers were negative and stereotypical at best. Micheaux employed the best actors he could find. He employed crews of Black and White technicians. His need for capital was the flame that stoked the fires of his desire to produce, distribute and help create new and positive images of his people.

By today's standards, Micheaux's work appears crude and technically lacking. But the context in which he produced his work has to be considered to understand his work more fully. He usually used borrowed sets, equipment and costumes. He shot his short films and features within tight production schedules of a few days; no more than ten or twelve days on a feature. No room for error, no chance for re-takes; often mistakes wound up on the screen. Money played an important part in this. By the standards of his day, Micheaux's budgets were small—usually $10 to $20 thousand. When the funds were depleted, he would take what had been shot and show it to exhibitors and investors to obtain money for production. After he had money, he would go back and shoot some more. The sheer volume, variety and level of quality he did achieve under these circumstances are extraordinary. He produced an average of one feature and one short per year.

## STAR MAKER

Micheaux launched several careers in the process of writing, directing, producing and distributing his own films. He helped launch the careers of Paul Robeson, Leigh Whipper, Ethel Waters, Nina Mae McKinney and Marva Smith, among others.

Micheaux knew how to market his talent. He created Black counterparts to the Hollywood legends. He had the Black Valentino—Lorenzo Tucker; the Sepia Mae West—Bee Freeman; the Negro Harlow—Ethel Moses; the Colored Cagney—Alfred "Slick" Chester.

## CONTEMPORARY FILMMAKER

Micheaux broke ground as an American filmmaker. His films dealt with the issues of the day. *Within Our Gates* (1919) dealt so explicitly with lynching that the Chicago Board of Movie Censors was afraid to approve it for exhibition, for fear of regenerating the riots that had stirred the city during the prior year. In *The Symbol of the Unconquered* (1920), the hero battles the Ku Klux Klan. *House behind the Cedars* (1923) deals with the issue of an interracial marriage; this film was an adaption of the work of Charles W. Chestnutt.

## INDEPENDENT BLACK FILMMAKER

Micheaux's films, all made against the competition and influences of Hollywood, stand as Black lights of hope. They express the basic idea that there is hope in life for Black people. Micheaux's image of Black life is somewhat jaded. He simplifies it to Good versus Evil. Good always wins; life is a struggle, but there is always love.

His characters, played mostly by unpolished actors and performers, press on despite their weaknesses. He keeps each story moving with scenes of northern Black urbanites enjoying nightlife in clubs and cafés, where there were usually an abundance of dancers and singers. Micheaux's films expressed bold Black ideas from a very gray period in U.S. history.

Micheaux managed to create feature-length films catering to mostly Black southern audiences by giving them what they wanted, a view of the northern big cities. They were mostly moral tales, which I'm sure pleased audiences with their cast of all colored players. Micheaux distributed his films himself by driving from town to town showing them in small movie houses. These films, dated in nature but beautiful in essence, are a tribute to early independent Black cinema.

## MICHEAUX REMEMBERED ANNUALLY

*Body and Soul*, a Micheaux classic, featured Paul Robeson. It was a silent work that marked Robeson's first screen appearance. A print of this film was screened at a special ceremony in Hollywood in 1986, when Micheaux was posthumously given a Life Achievement Award by the Directors Guild of America—the only African American so honored. Micheaux later received a star on the Hollywood Walk of Fame.

The Black Filmmakers Hall of Fame, Inc., in Oakland, California, is a group established to honor Blacks in literature, theater, music, film and recordings. It chose Micheaux as the person after whom its annual awards program would be named, the Oscar Micheaux Awards. The Black Filmmakers Hall of Fame has been giving awards to Blacks and creating a Hall of Fame since 1974. Micheaux's career was the seminal influence for aspiring independent Black filmmakers.

## FILMOGRAPHY

### Silent Films

*The Homesteader*, 1918, 35mm. Based on Micheaux's third novel. The story of a Black farmer with a White wife in an all-White community. The film starred Charles Lucas, Iris Hall, Charles S. Moore and Evelyn Preer.

*Within Our Gates*,\*\* 1918, 35mm. The story follows a woman who goes north from the South to raise money for a school for young children. In the film the lynching of a Black man and woman is shown. This created a controversy, which caused the film to be banned in Chicago and widely throughout the South. Because it was banned for many years, a full-length unedited print—or any print at all—was unavailable. Subsequently a print was discovered in the vault of the Spanish Cinematheque. The film was retitled *La Negra* (*The Black Woman*); the titles of this silent film were in Spanish. It has been fully restored and retitled in English and is now available on home video. The film starred Evelyn Preer, Lawrence Chenault and Charles D. Lucas. Since its rediscovery it is now *the* earliest surviving feature film by an African American.

*The Brute*, 1920, 35mm. A young Black woman becomes involved with a gangster who mistreats her. The hero of the film is a boxer. The film starred Sam Langford, Evelyn Preer and A.B. Comathiere.

*Symbol of the Unconquered*, 1920, 35mm. The story of a Black woman passing for White. She goes to claim a family inheritance, gets in trouble and is saved by the hero. The film starred Iris Hall, Lawrence Chenault and Leigh Whipper.

*Deceit* (originally entitled *The Hypocrite*), shot in 1921 and released in 1923, 35mm. This is a film within a film. The story focuses on a film producer trying to get approval from a Censor Board. The film the producer makes is rejected by local ministers even though they have not seen it. The film starred Norman Johnson, Evelyn Preer and A.B. Comathiere. The internal film featured Preer and Johnson as well.

*The Gunsaulus Mystery*, 1921, 35mm. A Black man is falsely accused of the murder of a White woman. Based on a true story from the time. The film starred Lawrence Chenault, Evelyn Preer and Ethel Waters at the beginning of her film career.

*The Dungeon*, 1922, 35mm. A woman is drugged and abducted by a man who has murdered several women in his dungeon. She is saved in the nick of time by her fiancé. The film starred William E. Fountaine, Shingzie Howard, J. Kenneth Goodman and W.B.F. Crowell.

*The Virgin of the Seminole*, 1922, 35mm. An adventure that follows the efforts of a Black Canadian Mounted Policeman to rescue a woman from Native Americans. He receives a reward and the love of the woman. The film starred William E. Fountaine and Shingzie Howard.

*The Ghost of Tolston Manor*, 1922, 35mm. A mystery melodrama. The film starred Andrew Bishop, Lawrence Chenault, Edna Morton and Monte Hawley.

*Uncle Jasper's Will* (originally entitled *Jasper Landry's Will*), 1922, 35mm. A melodrama, sequel to *Within Our Gates* (1918), dealing with the will left by Jasper Landry, a sharecropper who was falsely accused and lynched for the murder of a White plantation owner. The film starred William E. Fountaine and Shingzie Howard.

*The House behind the Cedars*, 1923, 35mm. Based on the book of the same name by Charles Chestnutt (African American author), who wrote the screenplay. The story concerns a Black woman passing for White who falls in love with a White man. Later she returns to her people and marries a Black man. The film starred Shingzie Howard, Lawrence Chenault and Douglas Griffin.

*Birthright,*** 1924 (a sound version was made and released in 1939), 35mm. This is an adaptation of a novel by Thomas S. Stribling, with the script being written by Micheaux. A Black man graduates from Harvard and tries to build a college for his people in the South. Despite obstacles from the Black and White community, he pursues his dream. There is a love story in all this as well. The film starred J. Homer Tutt, Evelyn Preer, Salem Tutt Whitney, Lawrence Chenault and W.B.F. Crowell.

*Body and Soul,*** 1925, 35mm. The film concerns twin brothers—one good, one evil. The evil twin is a womanizing, gambling, hard-drinking minister. The good twin is a young man making his mark in the world as a teacher. Paul Robeson in his screen debut delivered a tour-de-force performance as the twin brothers. The film also starred Julia Theresa Russell and Mercedes Gilbert.

*A Son of Satan*, 1924, 35mm. Sequel to *The Ghost of Tolston Manor* (1922). A melodrama depicting unsavory aspects of Black life. The film starred Andrew Bishop, Lawrence Chenault, Emmett Anthony, Edna Morton and Shingzie Howard.

*The Devil's Disciple*, 1925, 35mm. A melodrama that dealt with White compulsory prostitution (White slavery) in New York City. Cast included Evelyn Preer and Lawrence Chenault.

*The Conjure Woman*, 1926, 35mm. An adaptation of a Charles W. Chestnutt novel of the same title published in 1899. Melodrama. Cast included Evelyn Preer and Percy Verwayen.

*The Spider's Web*, 1926, 35mm. A drama about a young woman from Harlem who wards off the advances of a White man while visiting her aunt in Mississippi. The hero who saves her is a Black Secret Service agent. Later the agent investigates and clears her aunt of a false murder charge in Harlem. The cast included Evelyn Preer, Lorenzo McLane, Edward Thompson and Grace Smythe.

*The Broken Violin*, 1927, 35mm. A melodrama about a child musical prodigy who plays violin. The conflict is with the child's father, who is an alcoholic. The father is killed by a passing truck in retribution for his behavior to his family. The child, now a young woman, later finds success and happiness. The cast included J. Homer Tutt, Ardell Dabney, Alice B. Russell (later Mrs. Oscar Micheaux) and Ethel Smith.

*The Millionaire*, 1927, 35mm. A man makes his fortune in South America. Swindlers try to ply the hero from his fortune with one of their women. The hero avoids their traps and reforms their woman. Cast included Grace Smith, J. Lawrence Criner, Cleo Desmond and Lionel Monagas.

*Marcus Garland*, 1928, 35mm. A melodrama based on the life of Black activist Marcus Garvey, father of the back-to-Africa movement. Cast included Salem Tutt Whitney and Amy Birdsong.

*Dark Princess*, 1928, 35mm. The story may have been based on or suggested by a W.E.B. Du Bois novel by the same title (also 1928). A young medical student goes to Berlin to secure a hospital internship and falls in love with an East Indian princess.

*A Fool's Errand*, 1928, 35mm. This story may have been suggested by or based on Eulalie Spence's one-act play by the same title from 1927. The play won second prize in the National Little Theater Tournament held in 1927 at the Frolic Theater in New York City. A group of nosy neighbors assume that the daughter of a church-member is pregnant and try to force her into marriage.

*Thirty Years Later*, 1928, 35mm. Based on Henry Francis Downing's *The Racial Tangle*. A Black man born of a White mother and Black father is raised as White. The man falls in love with a Black woman. The woman refuses marriage on racial grounds. Once he learns his true heritage, he embraces it and wins his true love. Cast featured William Edmonson, Mabel Kelly, A.B. Comathiere, Ardella Dabney and Gertrude Snelson.

*The Wages of Sin*, 1929, 35mm. A drama about two brothers of opposite moral character. One brother is a hard-working film producer. The other brother is looking for the easy road to success. After their mother's death, the film producer hires his brother to work in his company. The corrupt brother almost destroys his brother's company by spending its money on wine, women and song. The cast included Lorenzo Tucker, William Clayton Jr., Bessie Gibbens, Gertrude Snelson, Ethel Smith and Alice B. Russell.

*When Men Betray*, 1929, 35mm. A re-release of *The Wages of Sin* (1929), revised and retitled in order to satisfy the board of censors.

*Easy Street*, 1930, 35mm. A crime story. Cast included Richard B. Harrison and Alice B. Russell.

### Sound Films

*A Daughter of the Congo*, 1930, 35mm. Adapted from *The American Cavalryman: A Liberian Romance*. Micheaux's first partly sound film. An adventure set in Monrovia, Liberia. A woman is kidnapped from her wealthy family and is brought up by people of the jungle. She is kidnapped again by Arab slave-hunters. Her rescuer is a Black cavalry officer. Cast featured Lorenzo Tucker and Katherine Noisette.

*Darktown Revue* (also known as *Darktown Scandal's Revue*), 1931, 35mm. This is a film version of Irvin C. Miller's nightclub floor shows. The film featured Miller with the Club Alabam Stompers, the Dixie Jubilee Singers, the Harlem Strutters, Sara Martin and Maude Mills.

*The Exile*,** 1931, 35mm. This film is based in part on Micheaux's first film, *The Homesteader* (1918), which was a screen adaptation of his 1917 novel of the same title. Scenes featuring nightclub singing and dancing are added to this sound film. This is the first total sound film by a Black film company. A young man from Chicago breaks off his engagement with his fiancé, who inherits a mansion and turns it into a nightclub to pay for its upkeep. He is not happy with this arrangement. He leaves the big city for the countryside. He moves to South Dakota to develop land, falls in love and pursues the woman he loves. The cast included Stanley Murrell, Eunice

Brooks, A.B. Comathiere, Katherine Noisette, and dancers, singers and musicians from the famed Cotton Club and Connie's Inn. The musical cast included the Blackbirds, Donald Heywood's Band and Leon Harper's Chorines.

*Ten Minutes to Live,*** 1932, 35mm. A mystery/musical built around a threatening note that gives the heroine only "ten minutes to live." The cast included Lawrence Chenault, Willor Lee Guilford and William Clayton Jr.

*Black Magic,* 1932, 35mm. Another nightclub revue.

*Veiled Aristocrats,*** 1932, 35mm. Based on Gertrude Sanborn's novel of the same title (1923), a love story of racial mixing, the color caste system and deception. The film featured Lorenzo Tucker, Laura Bowman and Barrington Guy.

*The Girl from Chicago,*** 1932, 35mm. A remake of Micheaux's silent *The Spider's Web* (1926). The same story as in *The Spider's Web.* This cast featured Carl Mahon, Starr Calloway and Eunice Brooks.

*Phantom of Kenwood,* 1933, 35mm. A mystery melodrama.

*Ten Minutes to Kill,* 1933, 35mm. A mystery melodrama; a re-release of or sequel to *Ten Minutes to Live* (1932).

*Harlem after Midnight,* 1934, 35mm. A drama that depicts the more sensational aspects of life in Harlem. Nightclubs, cabarets and gang activity are depicted. The cast featured Lorenzo Tucker, Dorothy Van Engle, Bee Freeman, Alfred Chester, A.B. Comathiere and Count Le Shine.

*Murder in Harlem*** (original title, *Lem Hawkins' Confession*), 1935, 35mm. A remake of the silent film *The Gunsaulus Mystery* (1921). A woman has an attorney defend her brother, who has been falsely accused of murder. Meanwhile a romance is rekindled between the lawyer and the woman. The cast starred Clarence Brooks, Dorothy Van Engle, Alex Lovejoy, Lionel Mangas, Henrietta Loveless, Bee Freeman, Alice B. Russell, Andrew Bishop and Flournoy Miller.

*Temptation,* 1936, 35mm. A melodrama about a Black female model who becomes entangled with the underworld and extricates herself from a difficult situation. The cast featured Andrew S. Bishop, Ethel Moses, Lorenzo Tucker, Hilda Rogers and Alfred Chester. The nightclub scenes featured the Pope Sisters, the Kit Kat Club Orchestra, Dot and Dash (tap-dancing duo), the Six Sizzlers Orchestra, Taft Rice, Lillian Fitzgerald and Raymond Kallund.

*Underworld,* 1936, 35mm. A gangster film that focuses on a college graduate who gets involved with the underworld. The hero experiences drugs, gambling, prostitution and racketeering. The cast starred Oscar Polk, Bee Freeman, Sol Johnson, Alfred Chester, Ethel Moses, Larry Seymour, Lorenzo Tucker and Angel Gabriel.

*God's Stepchildren,*** 1937, 35mm. Marshall Hyatt (1983) says, "Micheaux's effort is free from stereotypical images and has a more serious story line than many of his early efforts." The story deals with issues of color, especially the subject of a Black person passing as White. The cast featured Alice B. Russell, Jacqueline Lewis, Gloria Press, Ethel Moses, Carman Newsome, Alec Lovejoy and Laura Bowman.

*Swing,*** 1938, 35mm. A musical travelogue. A musician and his girlfriend travel from Birmingham, Alabama, to Harlem. They visit clubs and music spots along the way. The cast featured the Tyler Twins, Cora Green, Hazel Diaz, Carmen Newsome, Dorothy Van Engle, Amanda Rudolph and Alec Lovejoy.

*Birthright*, 1939, 35mm. A remake of Micheaux's silent film of the same title (1924). The story is essentially the same. The cast featured Alec Lovejoy, Laura Bowman, Ethel Moses, Carmen Newsome and George Vessey.

*Lying Lips*,** 1939, 35mm. A nightclub singer is convicted of murder and sentenced to prison. Two Black detectives solve the crime and get the heroine released. The cast included Edna Mae Harris, Carmen Newsome and Robert Earl Jones.

*The Notorious Elinor Lee*,** 1940, 35mm. A gangster's moll is given the assignment to make a boxer throw a fight. She gets to know the boxer and changes her mind. The film starred Edna Mae Harris, Robert Earl Jones, Carmen Newsome, Gladys Williams and Ella Mae Waters.

*The Betrayal*, 1948, 35mm. Drawn from Micheaux's novel *The Wind from Nowhere*. Historian Thomas Cripps (1993) says this film and its release "signaled the end of the race movie era." The story is an interracial romance set in South Dakota. The cast included Leroy Collins, Myra Standon, Verlie Cowam, Harris Gaines, Yvonne Machen and Alice B. Russell.


## BIO-CRITICAL REVIEW

"It is only by constructive criticism, arising from an intelligent understanding of the real problem, however, that the colored producer can succeed in his efforts and produce photoplays, that will not only be a credit to the race, but on a par with those of the white producer."—Oscar Micheaux, "Editorial from the Philadelphia Afro-American," in Henry T. Sampson, *Blacks in Black and White: A Source Book on Black Films*

"A narrow discourse satisfies those who would dismiss the work based on its low production values and Oscar Micheaux's lack of conformity with the rules. The films are dismissed because they don't fit into the Hollywood mode. But so much of his work, particularly the silent productions, have been unavailable until recently. The rediscovery of *Within Our Gates* and *Symbol of the Unconquered*, two highly controversial films in their time (and perhaps even in our time), challenges us to take another look."—*Black Film Review*


## SOURCES

### Books

Bogle, Donald. *Blacks in American Film and Television: An Illustrated Encyclopedia*. New York: Simon & Schuster, 1988.

Cripps, Thomas. *Slow Fade to Black: The Negro in American Film, 1900–1942*. New York: Oxford University Press, 1993.

Fontenet, Chester J., Jr. "Oscar Micheaux, Black Novelist and Film Maker." In Virginia Faulkner and Fred Luebke, eds., *Visions and Refuge: Essays on the Literature of the Great Plains*. Lincoln, NE: University of Nebraska Press, 1982.

Hyatt, Marshall, comp. and ed. *The Afro-American Cinematic Experience: An Annotated Bibliography and Filmography*. Wilmington, DE: Scholarly Resources, 1983.

Micheaux, Oscar. *The Conquest: The Story of a Negro Pioneer*. Lincoln: University of Nebraska Press, 1994. (Originally published in 1913.)

Ogle, Patrick, comp. *Facets African-American Video Guide*. Chicago: Facets Multimedia, 1994.

Peterson, Bernard L., Jr. *Early Black American Playwrights and Dramatic Writers: A Biographical Directory and Catalog of Plays, Films and Broadcasting Scripts*. Westport, CT: Greenwood Press, 1990.

Sampson, Henry T. *Blacks in Black and White: A Source Book on Black Films*. Metuchen, NJ: Scarecrow Press, 1995.

## Other

Black Filmmakers Hall of Fame. Oscar Micheaux Awards Program. Oakland, CA, 1989–1993.

# FLOYD NORMAN AND LEO SULLIVAN

## BACKGROUND

Animation is one of the least visible jobs in the media industry. Leo Sullivan is the second-oldest Black animator in the country. His ideas and talent are as fresh today as when he first started in the industry. He worked for Bob Clampett Productions, first as an animation cel polisher (final step in creation of animated frames) and later as artist/animator. He worked on the original *Beanie and Cecil Show* (1961–1962). He met a kindred spirit in Floyd Norman, the other Black animator in town working at the legendary Disney Studios.

After a decade of work as individual animator/artists, an opportunity presented itself and they formed Vignette Films (now Vignette Multimedia). The opportunity was KIIX-TV in Los Angeles. Although not owned by Blacks, the station employed a number of Black technicians. These individuals got the opportunity to produce the station's logo animation as well as commercials, both live-action and animated. One of their most famous animated logos was the first logo for *Soul Train*, the longest-running Black popular dance program in the country.

Our original interview took place on the occasion of Norman and Sullivan's second Award of Recognition from the Black Filmmakers Hall of Fame in February 1991.

Leo Sullivan

## More Background

### Floyd

It was sort of a dream of mine to have my own studio. It seemed at the time to be darn near impossible for a couple of young Black kids to have their own studio. To me it was just a dream. When I met Leo in 1960 he said, "Why not? Let's do it." I don't think I would have had the guts to even try it.

For us, the only way in the door was the educational market simply because it wasn't a high dollar market at the time and nobody else wanted it. We realized that this was the sixties now and there just wasn't that much material on Black history. That's what we decided to take a shot at. We didn't do it just blindly; we did our own marketing research. We sent a questionnaire out across the country to various school districts. We asked, "If these films existed, would you buy them?" The response was overwhelmingly yes. That got us going.

The first package consisted of four films on famous Black Americans: Booker T. Washington, Paul Laurence Dunbar, George Washington Carver and W. C. Handy. These were designed for educational use, so what the teachers wanted was material 12–14 minutes in length. They did the job in creating that interest in these people. A film can't do it all. The whole idea is to inspire kids, to learn about people and then to go out and read more about them on their own.

At that time the only way to produce, write and direct a film like that was to start your own company. You sure couldn't do it for anyone else. We couldn't get anywhere at the outside studios; you didn't have a shot. This was the sixties. You were lucky if you got a job, much less write or direct.

### Leo

Downstairs we were watching the awards with the young actors and actresses. It's their time. We saw a young Melvin Van Peebles* when he was doing theater, and he later told us about the success he would have with his first feature film, *Sweet Sweetback's Baadasssss Song* (1971), which hadn't come out yet. Now we were looking at his son Mario Van Peebles,* who co-hosted the event and is a young rising filmmaker. It's like a time warp. It's no different than it was for Oscar Micheaux.* Financing is tough. Working as either a producer or director was an issue for us. Now it's about how we are going to make some money. How can you use your talent, bordering on over sixty years experience combined. He would produce, I would direct, we would change roles to get the job done. We did government films, educational films. We did two films for the navy in the late sixties; we produced and directed them and did the animation on them. These films are still used as training films for pilots on refueling aircraft. When the Vietnam War was winding down, we did a film on those river boats they used to go on missions. We shot those in Vallejo. It's as young Mario was saying, it's about survival. By whatever means are necessary. Whether you're doing theatrical films or television. It's still survival, economics. We worked together off and on about fourteen years.

## PHIL MENDEZ

Floyd talked about working with Phil Mendez.

I first met Phil Mendez at the Disney Studios. They literally flew him in, because he was such a great artist, designer and creator. His style was almost perfect for Disney; ironically, he didn't last at Disney. The Disney Studio was going through a change; their creative head, Walt, had died. Phil and a lot of other creative talent left. I worked off and on with Phil. *Kissyfur* was developed as a cartoon short. Leo directed the pilot episode as well as two more episodes. The pilot was used to sell the show to NBC as specials and as a series.

Leo and then Floyd talked about their contribution to *Kissyfur*'s success.

We went to UCLA, Cal Arts, USC—the schools that taught animation—and put the word out that we wanted people who were interested in animation to come over and interview. We felt that based on the ones we picked, based on a kind of standard that we had to select them, we picked the cream of that year's graduating class.

### *Floyd*

Phil passed the job of interviews on to Leo. We were right, these same young people have gone on to create a reputation for themselves as individual animators. All those students we picked then are doing very well for themselves in the profession of animation with their own individual talents.

## COLOR CODING

Leo responded to being called a Black animator.

We're just artists. When we do a job, we do it as a professional. When it comes to doing the job for a production, your color is irrelevant. I would like it if those on the other side would not make color an issue.

Generally it's not an issue. The *Kissyfur* project was Phil's character. The young creative talent we hired and Floyd and I all contributed to the overall look of the work. It was a collaborative effort, as most animation projects are.

Floyd talked about working at Phil's studio.

The vast majority of our employees were White. We were known because we did the project under Phil's studio; it was known in animation circles as the Black animation company. Bill Melendez (creator of the animated *Peanuts* television specials) was not known as the Hispanic studio. Herb Clinton, who ran Format Studios, was not known as the Jewish studio; Hanna-Barbera (*Flintstones, Jetsons*, etc.) was not known as the White studio. They were all professionals doing their work. We resented being called the Black studio. We were just a studio, and I wanted to be regarded as a professional.

### Leo

People responded to it as an issue. Seeing Black people in control was an issue we had to deal with in doing business. We had power. At one point there was an animators' strike by the animators' union, and we were working. During that time our studio and Don Bluth (*Secret of N.I.M.H.*) were the only animation studios working. Our two studios were non-union studios, so that was an issue. We became targets because there were other issues. Black was only just one of them. The I.A.T.S.E. local that covered all the animators was the group on strike.

### Floyd

Our company was a start-up company, and we were hoping to be affiliated with the animators' local. Since we were non-union, we were able to work. When people were out of work and didn't have jobs, that caused a lot of resentment from the other White animators against us. This was in 1982. The strike lasted over six months. It was a bitter strike; there were bad feelings all around after it was over.

### Leo

Speaking on the issue of color, they hire us when we work for these large White companies because we can do the job. Then what kind of pressure does that put the company under, having a Black person be in charge?

### Floyd

Color is always an issue, even though it should have nothing to do with your performance.

Leo talked about working with Bill Cosby on his animated series *Fat Albert* (1968).

> Cosby hired a guy we knew. I was trying to get that job; he got there faster. He was the eventual producer/director of the project. I could never get Floyd on the show because they probably figured one Black person was enough. I worked on the characters and did the first *Fat Albert* special, and did some minimal work on a couple episodes of the eventual series. They said they wanted Black participation, but in reality what they wanted was window dressing. Secretaries and the like. But you know, I had fun; it was an enjoyable project.

### Floyd

> Cosby created the concept and the show, but Leo and the guys in that crew developed that show.

Floyd talked about working on the *Muhammad Ali* animated television series.

> A White friend we knew sold Muhammad Ali and NBC on doing an animated television series on the boxing champion. He called us for our talent and said it wouldn't do any harm to have Black talent. He made a point so that Ali could see that there were some Black artists on the show.

### Leo

> So when you address the issue of color, sometimes it's played to an advantage. Sometimes it's not. Sometimes six guys show up at the employment door and they need six guys. If you're one of the six, they ask, "Can you do it?" You answer, "Yes, I can do it." They say, "Fine." Maybe along the animation line, there is someone who has a problem with that.

## SINCE 1982

### Leo

> I went to the Caribbean. I said, "Why aren't there Black animation companies in the Caribbean?" I went on this great quest in the Caribbean. I got involved in doing commercials for four years, 1983–1988. After that I did fifty-three half-hour programs from 1988 to 1990. I've been managing a studio in Shenzen, China. My job was to oversee all their worldwide clients, including those here in the United States. My

job was to control the production flow through the various departments. There were twenty-three departments. Last year I did one film. We worked on about ten of the Fox network *Peter Pan* animated series shows.

### Floyd

To go in as professionals and see Black-run companies. Instead of "here comes the Black animator," it was good to have it be "here comes the animator" period. You went in just as a professional who did the job, and they hired you because you could do the job. Not because of who or what you were. I liked that. I thought that was great.

### Leo

I would do the Caribbean commercials back in the States. They would hand you half the money. Get on a plane and come back here with the storyboards and the money and do the project. There was an inherent trust. The contracts were usually one page long. It was really a receipt. I liked that. Here are people who just trust you to do the job, with no hidden agenda. You had to deliver. We lost money on some jobs. I always delivered. The down side was the distance, the foreign exchange, not getting the dollar value. The pleasure of having that experience that Floyd was talking about—what is that worth.

## CAPITAL-INTENSIVE WORK

### Floyd

Since Leo and I no longer had the company full-time, I simply worked on animation projects for others. I worked for Disney, for Hanna-Barbera, for various companies doing some writing, some drawing. Doing whatever I could in order to stay in the business. To keep on practicing my craft. I always wanted to do what we did full-time, but we were not able to get financing together to have our own company as we had some years before. Because it required so much more money now than before. Who is going to give you that money? It was tough to get the money back in the sixties. We went to banks with our research. We said, "We've got school districts who say if we produce these films they'll buy them." Even then the banks thought we were crazy.

### Leo

This was before the videocassette market. It didn't exist. What makes it possible for those young people who act and write and direct in films now is that their ideas and talent become viable investments. Once it's on film, they have a market with videocassette where they will make back the investors' capital.

### Floyd

The film business is a high-risk business. A Black film business probably scares the bankers to death. We couldn't find a bank in town that would take us seriously.

## ADVICE FOR ASPIRANTS

They offered suggestions for young people interested in animation as a profession.

### Floyd

Get into it. The time now is better than ever. There is more work than ever. The animation business, because of the additional markets, is booming. We can't even find talent at Disney now where I'm working. If the young person has the ability, it couldn't be better right now.

### Leo

Do it. When I entered the field, there were four or five Black animation artists. Now there are about a hundred and twenty-five or a hundred and thirty Black animation artists in the field. There are very few of them doing an independent animation career, as I am doing. It's too easy to go to the studios and collect those paychecks. Just show up and do the work. I'm the second-oldest Black animator after Floyd. I was always the entrepreneur between the two of us.

## TODAY'S STANDARDS

### Leo

In the animation industry now, they do all the recordings here in the States and the production is farmed out to the Far East. It's a labor-intensive business; labor costs are cheaper in the Far East. Because of that they sell more shows. You're talking about an area of the world where they have almost a hundred thousand people in the animation field; collectively there are only about four thousand here in the United States. Because of the merchandising of toys attendant to the more successful animation series, you realize the international aspects of the business. Black films are very popular in the Far East. I always wondered how Fred Williamson continued to make his films. I realized his work is shown in the international markets.

My work in the Far East gave me exposure to the international aspects of this business. When we think of making a cartoon, it doesn't have to be a Black cartoon. Black filmmakers always have to have the Black experience. They have to make films with Black people in them. So when they do that, what audience are they seeking? The Black audience, the crossover audience. They have a different agenda. I wonder how many of them feel that sometimes they would like to do something other than a Black experience–related film. They can't do it.

## STEREOTYPES

Leo talked about the old Black stereotype cartoons of the past.

I spoke with the artists of those old films, and they defended themselves by saying it was done with a sense of naiveté. In an interview this morning for BET Cable, I explained those things that are stereotypical of a people. The things that you make into humorous characterizations. That's what they did in those days. During the forties, Disney was castigated for Brer Rabbit and Uncle Remus in *Song of the South* (1946).

Styles come and go. If all Black kids have their hair the same, is that a stereotype? I remember when my wife worked in the sixties for a local county job and it was big deal to have a natural hair style. You could get fired. That symbolized something else. See, I've been gone for two years; when I left we were Black Americans, now we're African Americans. I said, "What happened?" You really have to put things in their historical context. If a Black actor gets a job acting and does something that is considered stereotypical as a representation of his/her race, is that good or is that bad?

## CURRENT AND FUTURE PROJECTS

Leo addressed the question of what he is doing today and talked about the future.

I work with Floyd on occasion. We're doing a series of children's films geared toward African American children. I've been in the animation and film business for about thirty-five years. I work in the industry on a freelance basis to keep active in my craft and field. These films I am developing are designed for the special needs of our young people. Positive identification for our people, since the Saturday morning cartoons don't reflect it. If there are Black characters, their contributions are minimized for the sake of the marketing. No one talks about our rich African heritage. The sales reinforce what I always knew. Yeah, they can have the *Power Rangers* and the Disney films. In every Black family there comes a time when they have to sit down and look at who they are. I hope my work can help contribute to that.

## FILMOGRAPHY (LEO SULLIVAN)

### Producer/Director

### *Independent Films*

*Afro-Classic Folk Tales*, Vols. 1 and 2, 30 min.; *Afro-Classic Mother Goose and Other Rhymes*, 30 min.; *Ed and Chester Bible Stories*, Vols. 1 and 2, 30 min.; *Black Profiles*, 48 min. These films are a mix of live action, puppetry, artist illustrations and animation, all in color.

### Timing Director

*Tiny Toons; Tazmania; Animaniacs*, 1991–1992, Warner Brothers Animation Studios.

*The Hulk; Fantastic Four*; and *Ironman*, 1992 to present, New World Entertainment/Marvel.

*Dumb and Dumber*, 1995, Hanna-Barbera.

### CD-ROM Interactive Development

Animation for interactive CDs, 1993 to present, Live Wire Productions.

### Studio Manager

Pacific Rim Animation, 1988–1990. Worked in Hong Kong, Shenzen, and Manila (Philippines). Oversaw all phases of production on animated television shows and theatricals for Thailand, Spain, France, Canada, Australia, Germany, Ireland and the United States. Established layout departments and trained animation personnel.

### Producer

Produced educational, training and public service films, filmstrips and 35mm slides for Bailey Associates, Doubleday Multimedia and Gould. Produced animation television commercials for Jamaica Ltd., Jamaica W.I. Clients included Grace Foods, Shelltox, National Commercial Bank, Desnodes and Geddes Inc., and Royal Bank. 1964–1988.

### Director

*Kissyfur*, 1985. Created by Phil Mendez, the first African American animation artist/ producer to have a Saturday morning cartoon series on a major U.S. television network. Sullivan directed the pilot episode for this animated Saturday morning half-hour cartoon series.

### Animator/Artist

Hanna-Barbera Studios; Filmation Productions; Turn On; Laugh-In; Film Roman Studios; Saban Productions; Bill Cosby's *Fat Albert and the Gang* television special.

## BIO-CRITICAL REVIEW

"As African Americans, they [Floyd and Leo] can be considered pioneers in their field—not simply because they are among the first, but because they are among the best."—*Black Filmmakers Hall of Fame*

## AWARDS

Black Filmmakers Hall of Fame, Inductees (Norman and Sullivan) 1979; Special Tribute, 1991
*Tiny Toons*
    Emmy Award, Leo Sullivan, Timing Director, 1992

## SOURCES

Interview with Floyd Norman and Leo Sullivan by George Hill and Spencer Moon, February 1991; follow-up interview with Leo Sullivan by Spencer Moon, February 1996.
Black Filmmakers Hall of Fame. "Special Tribute." Oakland, CA: Black Filmmakers Hall of Fame, 1991.
Brooks, Tim, and Earle Marsh. *The Complete Directory of Prime Time Network TV Shows, 1946–Present.* New York: Ballantine Books, 1992.
McNeil, Alex. *Total Television including Cable: A Comprehensive Guide to Programming from 1948 to the Present*, 2nd ed. New York: Penguin Books, 1991.

Michelle Parkerson. *Photo courtesy of Leigh H. Mosley.*

# MICHELLE PARKERSON

**BLACK WOMEN FILMMAKERS**

In January 1991, in his introduction of Michelle Parkerson, who was a participant in the symposium entitled "Visions, Views and Values: Filmmakers Discuss Their Craft," Donald Bogle (a noted author and the panel moderator) described the fact that African American women filmmakers have been overlooked in discussions of African American cinema. He described Parkerson as part of a group:

> Black women who are forcing their way through doors that in the past were open only to males, particularly White males. Michelle has given us striking documentaries that really shake up our expectations and make us look at women in a different way. Films that are an open challenge to our assumptions on race and gender. Her films let the subjects speak for themselves.

The symposium was part of a two-day event in Los Angeles marking the *Gallery of Greats* program.

Parkerson herself described the larger context of over sixty (in 1991) professional African American women filmmakers working in independent production nationwide:

> We are breaking down barriers not only of discrimination but of pure invisibility within the industry. My involvement in filmmaking was to

broaden the context of how we define ourselves, to delve into the complexities of identities we all carry. Men, women and African Americans
are not monolithic. My work has focused on African American women
artists and the way that their experiences reflect the larger reality that
we all live as Africans in this country. I want you to be challenged by
what you see, to dialogue across lines where we might not get together
in the same room because we have different ideologies, or different
references, or gender biases, or other biases that go across other racial
and sexual lines. I want to make infotainment or docutainment, to
make documentaries that also give some solid political substance.

## BACKGROUND

Parkerson described her background as a broadcast engineer for seven
years at television stations in Washington, D.C. She felt this brought more
experience of the "how to do it" to her work as a producer/director.

My job and my task and the blessing of my challenge is to challenge
you to talk to each other. Part of the safety that insulates some of the
prejudices, the violence, that sustain us in this neo-slavery is the silences that we surround ourselves with and don't cross those lines.
They're invisible chains, in a sense. I'm out to break silences using a
screen that's either large or small. I'm part of a continuum. My influences have included films like *Sweet Sweetback's Baadasssss Song*, the
politics of the late sixties and early seventies, the Black nationalist
movement, the women's movement, the gay and lesbian movement.
All these concurrent liberation struggles were talking to me about defining your destiny, knowing your history, controlling your body, controlling your political presence in the world. Having power in that way.
Image making is power; this is the process that I try to use. You must
think globally about Black independent film. I'm a piece of a larger
pie.

## FILMMAKING PROJECTS

In our interview conducted during the two-day *Gallery of Greats* program
in 1991, Parkerson spoke candidly and frankly about herself and her work.
She said, "If there is a motif in my documentary work, it's that it represents
the selected experiences of African American women artists." She described
her projects.

Programs about African American women. We (African American
women) are usually making films about ourselves, so I wouldn't say

that I'm unique in that way. Most of us tend to turn the camera on to other Black women and represent our experience through them, because our images have for so long been either absent or denigrated—denigrated to a point of ridicule. Here is a moment where Black women actually have the control to create their own imagery. We're doing that to rectify an absence or to heal the huge psychic wound that's been inflicted on our experience by the media. We take the time to actually value Black women's experiences. We are saying, "this is worth your time to watch and learn."

I don't think that the society at large values us, so the media of that society reflects its own predominant biases, stereotypes and prejudices. Black women are either not of value at all or undervalued in society. My work has been about African American women in the arts, who represent a translation of African culture through whatever art form they produce. They in some way embody a politic that is feminist/womanist in its aggression, in its self-empowerment. Most of these women reference themselves from a womanist-centered base. That's showing that African American women, and women in the diaspora, value themselves regardless of how the society devalues them, how men demote and objectify us and our value. We ourselves have another image, another celebration, another recognition of our achievement and glory and tenacity in the face of all these adversities over time. To quote Maya Angelou, "and still we rise."

Parkerson receives inspiration from networking with other women film-makers, among them Julie Dash* and Ayoka Chenzira.* She talked about having met and being inspired by filmmakers such as Stan Lathan.* She liked his ability to remain employed as a director in film, television and theater. She said, "Every product of his that I've seen has come out so wonderfully."

## Update (1995)

When we spoke again she updated me on her portfolio of films. She spoke about several new projects in the feature film genre.

There are two ideas; the one that I spoke with you originally about is in my pocket and dormant, because I've been processing a lot of things including the Audre Lorde film, in between teaching and other things. I thought this first idea could marinate awhile. What I want to do is kind of heavy, so I can't come out half-stepping. The second feature idea came into my path through Dr. Elizabeth Hadley-Freydberg, an African American woman I met through Don Marbury at the Corporation for Public Broadcasting. She was getting her doctorate at Indiana University. Her thesis was on Bessie Coleman, the first African

American female aviator. She and I have been working on that project. She is now developing the next draft of the script. My interest is the subject. My role will be co-producer and director. Her thesis has been published as a book on Bessie Coleman.

## DISTRIBUTION

I asked whether she has been satisfied with the distribution of her work.

I would say yes, I have been. I look forward to seeing the avenues the Audre Lorde film will travel. Its premier at Sundance was really important. I'm interested to see what will happen with it. Third World Newsreel, the distribution agent, has a political agenda and an impetus in their work that I really support. That's the only way the film could have been made—through an agency like Third World Newsreel.

Distribution of my other work has shifted and changed over time. That's the organic nature of it. When a film first comes out, there is the excitement around it. How a film does ten or twenty years later, how you continue to find audiences, is important.

## EDUCATOR

In addition to filmmaking, Parkerson has been a teacher in media at Howard University, Temple University and the University of Delaware. She emphasizes to her students the need to be prepared. The classes she has taught have been a combination of practicum, theory and historical survey courses in media.

Parkerson has held teaching appointments at Temple University, Northwestern University, Howard University, the Institute for Policy Studies (Media Studies) and the University of Delaware. She has also lectured extensively. Some of the locations have included Yale University, Black American Cinema Tour of India, Princeton University, Berlin Film Festival, National Film Board of Canada, University of California (statewide), Harvard University, Schomberg Center for Research in Black Culture, and the Museum of Modern Art.

## THEATER AND PERFORMANCE

Parkerson has a decade-long history (1984–1995) in theater and performance art. She has worked as a writer, performer, producer and director in theaters in Washington, D.C.; Austin, Texas; Minneapolis, Minnesota; and Philadelphia, Pennsylvania.

## ADVICE FOR ASPIRANTS

There is a way and a process and a formula. The way that you manipulate that formula can mark your success or failure. We are all trying to twist the equation so it works in our favor. They have to be hyperprepared if they are looking for a job in the industry. To be beyond good to get the job in the first place. I try to push them also to step outside of the formulas that they see replicated on television and in movies, to show them that it's the extraordinary that will get them their own business. Build a reputation while they're students. Observe the festivals' process, venues and circuits. There are more venues now than when I began because of home cassette and cable television. There is a place for them to go, but not to imitate what's gone before. Create their own version, voice and vision based on what's past, what's been used. Let's do something fresh. I also want them to see that there are no small jobs in production. More than anything, it's a collective effort.

## THE FUTURE

What do you hope to accomplish as a filmmaker?

To grow in my craft. I really am pursuing directing with a quiet passion. I want to flex my hand as a director. I would like to move into directing feature films. I would like to work with more commercially based programs, even doing game shows. There is the business of earning a living at what you're doing. Doing situation comedies. Directing features that have politically relevant content in terms of race and sexuality and gender.

## FILMOGRAPHY

### Director/Producer/Editor

*Sojourn*, 1973, 10 min., b/w, film. An impressionistic bicycle ride contrasts the activity, tension and problems of an inner-city community with the serenity of nature.

*But Then, She's Betty Carter*, 1980, 60 min., film. In a 1985 interview from *Black Film Review*, Parkerson talked about why she made this film.

> Here's a woman who has hung in there in a business that's very tough. It's male, it's White, and in Betty Carter's case she's devoted to an art form that's not commercial. She's the last of the pure jazz vocalists. Her story was untold. I was surprised to find that out, so I feel very blessed to have been able to put some of her life and her work on film.

*I Remember Betty*, 1987, 10 min., 16mm, comedy.

*Storme: The Lady in the Jewel Box*, 1987, 20 min., film. Parkerson described the pre-production and background of this film in *Black Film Review*:

> The Jewel Box Revue were a troupe of female impersonators and one male impersonator. It was a very, very lavish production with mimes and comedians. It toured the Black theater circuit in the mid-fifties and early sixties. It was on the scale of the Follies Bergère or the Ziegfield Follies—original music, huge production numbers, lavish costumes, everything.

The finished film focused on Storme De Larverie, the biracial master of ceremonies. She was a male impersonator and the only female of the only integrated female impersonation show. It is an intimate portrait of her and a history of this troupe and their place in theater history.

### Producer

*Gotta Make This Journey*, 1983, video, 60 min. Directed by Joseph Camp. Parkerson had worked as production coordinator on the second album of the all-female acappella group Sweet Honey in the Rock; as a result of this relationship and Parkerson's interest in African American women artists, this compelling documentary was produced. The documentary features interviews, concert footage and commentary by Angela Davis and Alice Walker.

### Associate Producer

*It's My Choice: Teen Sexuality*, 1988, 30 min., video.

### Director/Producer

*Urban Odyssey*, 1991, seven 30-min. segments, video. WHMM-TV, Channel 32, Howard University, Washington, D.C. Parkerson described her role on this series.

> It was a great learning process for me—being able to work with the writers and actors, having a window in which to be able to shape the work in collaboration. These were one-person dramas. They presented lives of well-known Washington, D.C., African Americans. We presented their lives in a docudramatic style. We used studio and location sets for the production. These were the first dramatic works for television I had done. This was work where I was commissioned to direct.

### Director/Writer

*Odds and Ends: A New-Age Amazon Fable*, 1993, 30 min., video.

One of the things about living in this independent film life is the challenges that come your way and the kind of challenges you want to put yourself in the way of. This was that for me. I applied and was accepted to the American Film Institute (AFI) directing workshop for women. I was one of 11 women selected out of over 500 applications. I always wanted to take in this experience because I saw how it had shaped the work of Carol Munday Lawrence, Neema Barnette,* Dyan Cannon, Cicely Tyson. The program is about twenty-one years old now. It happens in an eighteen-month cycle. I was part of the eighth cycle. The work was based on an original short story I had written and then adapted for the workshop.

For me this was a wide-open opportunity to throw caution to the wind and not have too heavy a financial investment where it couldn't be a great experiment after all. Apprenticeship in independent film is so rare. You just make movies and hopefully your craft grows and your audience grows; it's very hard. The work has been in several film festivals, national and international. It has been featured on the gay and lesbian film circuit. It was shown on WHYY-TV in Philadelphia on the series *Independent Focus*. It circulates. AFI distributes it. I also get to enter it in festivals. It was a great experience in terms of giving me a taste of what the Hollywood community is about. I got to work with Screen Actors Guild members. I got to do Hollywood-type contracts and work with Hollywood-trained technicians. I got to work at some of the top postproduction houses in Los Angeles.

## Co-Director

*A Litany for Survival: The Audre Lorde Film Project*, 1995, 90 min., 16mm, Third World Newsreel. A documentary portrait of Audre Lorde, a Black, female, warrior, poet, lesbian, mother, educator, activist. One of the most revealing moments in the film occurs when Lorde comes to a personal realization. She has just spent six weeks as a visiting teacher at Tougaloo College in Jackson, Mississippi. Lorde said, "I realized that I could take my art, in the realist way, and make it do what I wanted. Not as propaganda, but as altering feelings and lives. And that in order to do that, I had to be everything I was." Parkerson described the process of making this film.

Ada Griffin invited me back in 1987 to work with her on this project she initiated. She is co-director and producer. It was great to do a documentary feature, because my projects previously had only been hourlong documentaries. I got to see what 90 minutes feels like in terms of information and as a viewing experience. It was great to work with an editor like Holly Fisher, who is an experimental filmmaker in her own right. She brought another kind of interrogation into the life and importance of Audre Lorde's work. The kind of blend of biography, literature and social climates during her lifetime that became a weave in the film—that, I think, is very successful. We shot over an eight-year period and we had a tremendous amount of material to boil down into a feature-length work.

## BIO-CRITICAL REVIEW

*But Then, She's Betty Carter.* "An exciting film from which the audience walks away exhilarated."—Dare Thompson, Kirkland Arts Center

*A Litany for Survival: The Audre Lorde Film Project.* "Lorde's pioneering spirit is revealed by readings of her poetry, through talks she has with her daughter, conversations with her lovers, and discourse with the camera itself."—Karen Carrillo, *Cineaste*

## EDUCATION

Temple University, B.A., communications

## MEMBERSHIPS AND LICENSES

Association of Independent Video and Filmmakers (AIVF)
General Radiotelephone Operators License

## AWARDS AND HONORS

American Film Institute, Directing Workshop for Women (8th Cycle), 1991
Black American Cinema Society, Special Merit Award, 1986
Black American Cinema Tour of Europe, Delegate, 1989
D.C. Commission on the Arts and Humanities, Fellowship, 1989
D.C. Mayors Art Award, 1989
Delta Sigma Theta Sorority, Lillian Award, 1988
*Gallery of Greats*, Inductee, 1991
PBS/Sundance Retreat for Women in Media, 1988
Philadelphia International Film Festival, Leigh Whipper Award, 1985
Rockefeller Foundation Film/Video Fellowship, 1992
*Gotta Make This Journey*
    American Film Festival, Blue Ribbon, 1984
    Emmy Award Nomination, Cultural Affairs Programming, 1984
*A Litany for Survival: The Audre Lorde Film Project*
    Festival International de Creteil Films de Femmes, Prix du Public, 1995
    San Francisco International Film Festival, Audience Award, Best Biography, 1995
*Sojourn*
    Student Oscar, Best Experimental Film, 1973

## SOURCES

Interview and follow-up interview by Spencer Moon, January 1991 and August 1995.
Carrillo, Karen. "A Litany for Survival," review. *Cineaste* (22), no. 2 (1996), pp. 31–32.
*Black Film Review*, no. 3 (May 1985), pp. 2, 8–9.

# GORDON ALEXANDER PARKS SR.

## BACKGROUND

Gordon Parks Sr. was the youngest of fifteen children in a family of farmers. His father also sold kerosene, and his mother did laundry for five dollars a month. As a young man Parks watched four people die, three of them by the gun of the local bigoted sheriff. After his mother died of natural causes, at age 15 Parks was sent to live in Minneapolis with relatives. After getting married and having several children, to support his family he worked as a piano player, busboy and railroad dining car waiter. He also was a member of the Civilian Conservation Corps and later became a professional basketball player. He eventually moved to Chicago, where he took up photography as a hobby. In 1942 he was awarded the first Julius Rosenwald Fellowship in photography and chose to work with Roy Stryker at the Farm Security Administration in Washington, D.C. During World War II he was an Office of War Information correspondent. After the war he again worked with Stryker at Standard Oil Company in New Jersey. During this period he wrote two books on photography and did freelance photography for *Vogue* and *Glamour* magazines.

## *LIFE* MAGAZINE

Parks joined the staff of *Life* magazine in 1948 and worked as a photojournalist there until 1968, doing over three hundred assignments and articles on a wide variety of subjects. He never let himself be ghettoized to covering only Black subjects. He covered sports, fashion, royalty—everything that came along. He felt his coverage of topics such as the Black Muslims and the Black Panthers provided an opportunity for their voice to be heard by the over seven million people who read *Life* magazine weekly, a wider range of people than they might otherwise have reached. Some of his stories on the Black experience were incorporated into his first book, *Born Black*. After Parks left *Life* magazine he was a founder and editorial director of *Essence* magazine.

## FILMMAKING

Around 1964–1965, while covering the production of *Stromboli* by Roberto Rosellini with Ingrid Bergman for *Life* magazine, Parks first began to seriously consider becoming a filmmaker. His friend John Cassavetes kept after him to direct a feature film. Cassavettes helped arrange a meeting between Warner Brothers and Parks, and that meeting led to Parks directing his first feature film, *The Learning Tree* (based on his novel of the same name).

As a filmmaker Parks's imperative has always been to direct as diverse an array of subjects as possible. He feels Black directors owe it to themselves to direct everything and not just Black-themed films; this will broaden their opportunities. A true renaissance man, Parks has written several autobiographies, books of poetry and fiction; has composed ballet and orchestral works; and has written the musical score for several of his feature films.

## MEETING GORDON

Meeting genius in one's lifetime is rare. Twice is a blessing. In the summer of 1984 the Black Filmmakers Hall of Fame of Oakland, California, sponsored a summer workshop for apprentice and journeyman filmmakers. I was fortunate to be a member of that very first summer workshop class. Later, over two more summers, I participated again as a student and eventually as program coordinator. Gordon Parks Sr. was among the filmmaker/instructors that first year; others included William Greaves,* Hugh Robertson* and Avon Kirkland.* Other student filmmakers I met that summer included Ayoka Chenzira* and Michelle Parkerson.*

In the summer workshop, I remember being so excited by Parks and his class that at one point he told me I couldn't ask any more questions, because I was like a machine gun with my questions.

The second time I encountered Parks was in 1990 as part of an arts festival sponsored by various San Francisco arts agencies. I was coordinator for the film/video portion of the festival, and Parks was invited to be part of our program. The program highlighted newly commissioned work by local artists and a screening of Parks's film *Leadbelly* (1976), with Parks present. The

Black Filmmakers Hall of Fame was also instrumental in helping with the screening of the film.

During the festival Parks had two days of scheduled appearances; one was at San Francisco State University (SFSU), where he delivered a lecture demonstration using his film *The Learning Tree* (1969). His technique for the summer workshop and for the SFSU appearance is one I've adapted to my own teaching methods. He read from his novel *The Learning Tree*, then read the shooting script, then screened that same scene from the film and talked about the process and answered questions. It was brilliant. For the SFSU event he did me a great honor when he asked me to read from his novel to an audience of students and teachers. After my reading he gave me a compliment on my interpretation of his work. We then screened his film. My reminiscences of these events I'll always cherish.

## GORDON PARKS JR.

Parks's son, Gordon Jr., became a photographer and feature film director, directing four films: *Aaron and Angela*,** *Superfly*,** *Thomasine and Bushrod*** and *Three the Hard Way*.** Parks Jr. was killed in a plane crash in Africa while scouting locations for a new film. Gordon Sr. and his family suffered a great loss, as did Black movie making as well.

## FILMOGRAPHY

### Director

### *Feature Films*

*The Learning Tree*,** 1969, 107 min., color, Warner Brothers. Parks has described the story as being about a Black youth living in America in a rural environment and how he survived the cruelty of that environment while others did not.

*Shaft*,** 1971, 98 min., color, MGM. A landmark film that helped open Hollywood's doors to Black experience films and Black filmmakers during a turbulent social/political period in American history. The impact of desegregation, civil and social militancy, and the deaths of Martin Luther King Jr. and Malcolm X are part of the background on which the Black-themed films of this period were made. This film was all action and adventure, a new experience for Black audiences of the time.

*Shaft's Big Score*,** 1972, 105 min., color, MGM. A follow-up to *Shaft*, cashing in on the prior film's financial success. Parks wrote, arranged and conducted the film's music score.

*The Super Cops*, 1974, 94 min., color. An attempt by Parks to mainstream himself as a director. The leads in this action film were White actors; Parks wanted to prove that he could direct non-Black-cast films. This film was based on the true story of two New York beat policemen who eventually were made detectives and received many honors and commendations for their work.

*Leadbelly*,** 1976, Paramount. Because of the change in administrative direction at the film studio from the time the film was finished until it was marketed, this film received very limited distribution. Parks met Huddie Ledbetter (a.k.a. Leadbelly) several times before he died. His experience of the man, combined with the availability of producer Marc Merson and a screenplay by Ernest Kinoy, led Parks to agree to direct the film biography of this Black music legend.

An interview that took place on location during the filming of *Leadbelly* was published by *Millimeter* magazine a year after the film was completed and poorly distributed. The author, Roy Campenella II,* wrote in the conclusion of his article, "*Leadbelly* is thus far an example, at the commercial level, of how the present system of motion picture production and distribution restricts the creative vision of filmmakers regarding their work."

*Solomon Northup's Odyssey*** (alternate title, *Half Slave—Half Free*), 1984, 113 min., PBS American Playhouse. Parks wrote the film's music score as well.

### Documentaries

*Flavio*, 1961. A short work about a young boy growing up in the Brazilian slums.

*The World of Piri Thomas*, 1964.

*Diary of a Harlem Family*, 1968.

*Moments without Proper Names*, 1986. An autobiography combining Parks's poetry, prose and music. Parks also wrote the film's music score.

### Other

*Martin*, 1990. A ballet. Parks composed the music and directed the filming of this tribute to Dr. Martin Luther King Jr.

## BIO-CRITICAL REVIEW

"All his films reveal his determination to deal with assertive, sexual black heroes, who struggle to maintain their manhood amid mounting social/political tensions."—Donald Bogle, *Blacks in American Films and Television*

*Leadbelly*. "The film has a classic narrative structure: strong, simple, direct and pointed. In short, it's very much like Leadbelly's own music."—James Monaco, *Cineaste*

*Shaft*. "The film was tough, lean, cool, hip, angry, and in the end even wise."—James Monaco, *American Film Now*

## PUBLICATIONS

*Born Black* (New York: Lippincott, 1971). Autobiography.

*Camera Portraits: Techniques and Principles of Documentary Portraiture*. Photographic techniques.

*A Choice of Weapons* (New York: Harper, 1966). Autobiography.

*Flash Photography*. Photographic techniques.

*Flavio* (New York: Norton, 1978). Photo essay.

*In Love* (New York: Lippincott, 1971). Poems.

*The Learning Tree* (New York: Harper, 1963). Fiction.

*Moments without Proper Names* (New York: Viking, 1975). Poems.

*A Poet and His Camera* (New York: Viking, 1968). Poems with photographs.

*Shannon* (Boston: Little, Brown, 1981). A novel.

*To Smile in Autumn* (New York: Norton, 1979). Poems.

*Voices in the Mirror* (New York: Doubleday, 1990). Autobiography.

*Whispers of Intimate Things* (New York: Viking, 1971). Poems with photographs.


## SELECTED AWARDS

American Society of Magazine Photographers, Photographer of the Year, 1960

Black Filmmakers Hall of Fame, Inductee, 1974

Governor's Medal of Merit, Kansan of the Year, 1985

International Center of Photography, Life Achievement Award, 1990

NAACP Hall of Fame Award, 1984

NAACP Spingarn Medal, 1972

National Conference of Christians and Jews, two awards, 1964

National Medal of Arts, 1988

*A Choice of Weapons*
American Library Association, Notable Book Award, 1966

*Diary of a Harlem Family*
Emmy Award, Best Documentary, 1968

*Flavio*
Christopher Award, Best Biography, 1978

*The Learning Tree*
National Film Registry, Library of Congress, 1989


## SELECTED MEMBERSHIPS

Academy of Motion Picture Arts and Sciences

American Federation of Television and Radio Arts

American Society of Composers, Authors and Publishers

American Society of Magazine Photographers

Authors Guild

Black Academy of Arts and Letters

Directors Guild of America

National Association for the Advancement of Colored People, Lifetime Member

National Association for the Advancement of Colored People, Legal Defense Fund, Board Member

National Association for American Composers and Conductors

Schomberg Center for Research in Black Culture (New York Public Library), Schomberg Society, Board Member

Writers Guild

## SELECTED MUSIC COMPOSITIONS

*Celebrations for Sarah Ross and Andrew Jackson Parks*

*Concerto for Piano and Orchestra*

*Five Piano Sonatas*

*Piano Sonotas for Gordon Jr., Toni, David and Leslie*

*Piece for Cello and Orchestra*

*Run Sister Run* (film score)

*Tree Symphony*

*Work for Piano and Woodwinds*

## SOURCES

### Books

Bogle, Donald. *Blacks in American Film and Television: An Illustrated Encyclopedia*. New York: Simon & Schuster, 1989.

Cloyd, Iris, ed. *Who's Who among Black Americans*. Detroit, MI: Gale Research, 1990.

Famighetti, Robert, ed. *The World Almanac and Book of Facts, 1996*. New York: Funk and Wagnalls, 1991.

Monaco, James. *American Film Now: The People, the Power, the Money, the Movies*. New York: Zoetrope, 1984.

Parks, Gordon, Sr. *A Choice of Weapons*. New York: Harper & Row, 1966.

———. *Voices in the Mirror: An Autobiography*. New York: Doubleday, 1990.

### Newspapers and Magazines

Campanella, Roy, II. *Millimeter* (July 1975).

Monaco, James. "Gordon Parks *Leadbelly*" *Cineaste* (8), no. 2 (1977), p. 40.

Shepard, Thom. "Beyond the 'Black Film': An Interview with Gordon Parks," *Cineaste* (8), no. 2 (1977), p. 38.

# MATTY RICH

## BACKGROUND

Rich is one of the youngest members of the Black cinema renaissance who came straight out of Brooklyn. His debut film marked him as an original talent in contemporary Black cinema. At age 10 he had wanted to make films. He graduated from high school and was accepted to New York University's film writing program. Frustrated with that process, he dropped out after three weeks but learned about the process of creating structure and story. He decided to strike out on his own, with dreams and ambitions of making a feature film. Using credit cards, publicity supplied by WLIB radio in New York and a trailer, he staged a community-based fundraising benefit. It raised $40 thousand. Using this method several times netted another $30 thousand, all of which came directly from the Black community. Then Rich found an ally in filmmaker Jonathan Demme, who helped him contact the Deutchman Company, a supporter of independently made films. With their help and with finishing funds from public broadcasting's *American Playhouse* series, Rich realized a childhood dream—the completion of his first feature film.

I sat down with the 19-year-old Rich in 1991 while he was on a publicity junket for the national distribution of his film *Straight Out of Brooklyn*. The response to Rich and the film prior to San Francisco had been uniformly excellent. We spoke first about the prize he won at the Sundance film festival.

## SUNDANCE AWARD

Rich felt that once he received money from *American Playhouse* for finishing his production, he had already won. But he didn't personally need an award from White society to tell him that he was good; he said he won because from age 17 to 19 he had worked hard to accomplish something. Before receiving the award, the community gave him a big party at the Cotton Club with over twelve hundred Black people from a number of sections of New York City and all over the tri-state area. Many of those Black people had not even seen his movie; they just knew he wanted to do the film. Sundance was an opportunity for the world to see his work, who he was and why he did this film at such a young age. The award meant that outsiders had accepted him.

## PRODUCTION

I asked Rich to describe any memorable production moments.

There was one scene where he said he couldn't take it; he broke down and cried. The crew had never seen him cry before, but he told them to just keep rolling the camera. It was the scene where the father talks in soliloquy to White society about his anger and his failure to achieve the American dream. The actor who portrays the father, George Odum, did that scene in an extraordinarily moving way.

## FUNDRAISING

In terms of raising funds for his film projects, Rich spoke in similes and metaphors. Making this film, he said, was like being in a grocery store; for his next film he wants to be in a supermarket. A little more money would really display his talent. If this movie was a jab, he said, the next one would be a knockout.

## RENAISSANCE

Do you think the current Black film renaissance has a future?

Rich hoped that would be so because, he jokingly said, he wanted a job. In a more serious vein, he thought that black filmmakers should work together. There should not be an elitist attitude toward would-be and aspiring filmmakers; each person should be taken at face value. No one, whether apprentice or journeyman, should be no less important than the next person. We should treat each other as equal individuals.

## UNIQUENESS

Rich felt that he hits home with the problems of the Black male experience. His home environment has shaped the way he looks at the world. Even today, when he goes to the store to buy a magazine they still take a long, hard look at him because he is a Black man. He described himself as a street kid who hasn't changed.

The night before our interview, he spoke to an audience of young people after they had seen his film. He said that what it portrays is someone who is real and understands the anger, frustration and oppression of the Black man and the Black family. That is his special quality. He wants his films to affect people viscerally. He showed me a pair of his overalls covered with sewn-on question marks. The significance, he said, was the question, why? Using characters from his film, he asked why this Black man fights with his family. Rich described Black people being knocked down by society innumerable times. Why do young Black men have to literally work in the streets to make their lives economically better? Why does the mother have to mediate the conflict between father and son? He quoted from the epilogue of his film, "the first things learned are the hardest to forget; traditions pass from one generation to the next." He described the subtext of the film: from the father to the son's oppression, from the son to his son's oppression, on and on ad infinitum. That, he said, is what he brings to cinema.

## YOUNG AUDIENCES AND ASPIRING FILMMAKERS

I asked about the previous evening's screening to young people. What was their response, and what do you tell young people who want to make films?

He described the screening as interesting. Rich said the young audience found it just like the situation in their own homes. One young brother said directly to him, "Matty, tell me what to do." Rich digressed to mention meeting an older brother in his sixties who said, "I see your movie is coming out; I lost one son already to the street, I have another son at home. What can I do?" It hurts him, he said, that he doesn't know the answer to either brother's question.

Rich doesn't want young people to be filmmakers just because he is a filmmaker. The actual filmmaking process is a tool. He described his collection of 250 film books and explained that filmmaking is a mental process. He said he is an actor's director; he hires people who know the technical aspects of filmmaking.

Rich described three qualities for filmmaking: heart, soul and mind. All, he feels, are essential to make films. The actors in his first feature film were dedicated and hungry. For the initial audition, over two thousand people showed up. Filmmaking requires that there be a burning fire in your soul to be an actor or director. It is hard work. From age 10 to 13, he said, everything in his own life involved paying hard dues. He saw his brother get beaten in the streets into a coma. He saw a friend get shot in the head. He saw many Black men in his community be oppressed and give up. The commitment he made to filmmaking takes courage, he said.

Being Black and making films is like having at least five odds against you. If a young White person wants to make films, he or she can go to Yale, get a degree and obtain money to make a film. For a Black person, the commitment to filmmaking has to come from deep inside. Because filmmaking is not a traditional occupation in the Black community, that process and commitment are a difficult road to travel. The goals for aspiring Black filmmakers are hard work, time, dedication and setting aside people and relationships that can distract you from your goals.

Rich said he is no different from any other young person. He hangs out, has a girlfriend, has a nice car and drives down the street with his car radio booming music. Filmmaking is a way to express himself. But it is hard. You need to want it enough to taste it; then you'll get it.

### INFLUENCES

Watching television, specifically *The Brady Bunch*, was an influence. Seeing that family made Rich want to create a real Black family for the screen. His ambition was to make a film that would talk about what the Black man and the Black family goes through. He enjoyed *Raisin in the Sun*\*\* (1961) with Sidney Poitier because of its intense acting and its scrutiny of the Black family on the big screen.

### GREATEST FEAR

Because of the success of his first feature, two Hollywood studios are vying for him to direct his next film with them. His biggest fear is being "eaten alive." Part of it involves going into a system where they don't understand you, a studio where editorial control is not the filmmaker's but the studio's. Although the companies reassure him that they understand he needs artistic freedom to work creatively, he also knows that if someone gives him $15 million they are going to want some input into the making of the film. The film also must meet commercial expectations.

### FILMOGRAPHY

*Straight Out of Brooklyn*, 1991, 91 min., 35mm, color. Goldwyn Studios, PBS *American Playhouse*. Written, directed and produced by Matty Rich. Featuring George T.

Odom, Ann D. Sanders, Lawrence Gilliard Jr., Reana E. Drummond and Mark Malone.

*The Inkwell*, 1994, 35mm, color. Directed by Matty Rich. Featuring Larenz Tate, Joe Morton, Suzanne Douglas and Glynn Turman. Domestic gross is $7.7 million.

## BIO-CRITICAL REVIEW

*The Inkwell*. "He [Rich] has moved into frankly commercial territory and the entertainment values are there. He knows how to tell a story."—Roger Ebert, *Internet Movie Database*

*Straight Out of Brooklyn*. "Teases strong performances from his cast and contributes some sophisticated writing—especially the vivid dialogue."—David Armstrong, *San Francisco Examiner*

———. "One of the most dynamic, honest, proactive films about black life that has ever been attempted."—Judy Stone, *San Francisco Chronicle*

———. "A promising filmmaking debut. Echoes the formal, socially responsible dramas from an earlier era of American filmmaking."—Stephen Holden, *New York Times*

———. "A blunt instrument, but that's one of the reasons it works. Rich doesn't preach or impose rational arguments on an irrational world. He makes the irrationality sing."—John Leland and Lynda Wright, *Newsweek*

## AWARDS

*Straight Out of Brooklyn*
   Sundance Film Festival, Special Jury Award, 1991

## SOURCES

Interview by Spencer Moon, May 1991.

### Newspapers and Magazines

Armstrong, David. "Straight Out of His Childhood," *San Francisco Examiner*, May 3, 1991, p. E2.
Holden, Stephen. "Where the Streets Are Mean and the People Meaner," *New York Times*, May 22, 1991, p. B3.
Leland, John, and Lynda Wright. "Surviving to See a Future," *Newsweek*, May 27, 1991, p. 58.
Stone, Judy. "Young Filmmakers Searing Ghetto Vision," *San Francisco Chronicle*, May 1991, p. F1.

### Other

Ebert, Roger. *Internet Movie Database*, 1996.

Marlon Riggs. *Photo courtesy of Cornelius Moore, Estate of Marlon Riggs.*

# MARLON RIGGS

In the San Francisco Bay Area, Marlon Riggs (1957–1994) became the most well-known independent filmmaker through forces that opposed him and his work because of its partial government funding. As a Black gay filmmaker/activist, Riggs had steered a course that took more than courage of convictions. His life and work exemplified the ideals of strength and integrity.

## BACKGROUND

Riggs was reared in the deep South. Later he moved because of his father's work in the military. He attended school in Germany for a time while his father was stationed there. After high school he attended Harvard and majored in history. During his senior year he decided to become a documentary filmmaker.

In 1991 a two-hour interview with Riggs was aired on *The Creative Mind*, a series of television documentary interviews with creative individuals in the San Francisco Bay Area. Riggs talked about wanting to communicate all that he was learning, with his Ivy League education, about notions of race and identity. He decided that filmmaking was the way to best communicate his knowledge to the rest of the world. To learn his craft, after receiving his undergraduate degree he worked for a year at a television station. Because he was a Harvard-educated Black man and because of the passion of his inquiry into how things worked, people thought he wanted to take over the television station. Being naive to the politics of television, at age 21 and frustrated he decided to apply to the Graduate School of Journalism at the University of California, Berkeley. Part of the degree requirements involved producing a documentary for the thesis.

Riggs produced and directed a documentary on the blues scene in the adjacent city of Oakland. That program was *Long Train Running: The Story of the Oakland Blues* (1982). His success with this work defined the spirit with which he would produce other programs. His goal as a trained journalist was to get others to tell him their stories and for him to convey that from an objective perspective. Riggs felt that this objectivity and its lack of passion prevented journalists from using their subjective passion to better tell their stories. He undertook producing the documentary on blues with tremendous passion, and this became a modus operandi that he would continue to use in telling stories that he felt passionate about.

## EARLY WORK

One of my first encounters with Riggs and his work was at an early fundraiser for his second film (*Ethnic Notions*, 1987) to receive national and international visibility. The room where he screened this work-in-progress was small, the audience was attentive and his presentation afterwards drew rapt attention. The clip, his rap and his one-page handout on how the audience could help indicated that this was one very "together" independent filmmaker. His handout described having received a challenge grant from the California Council for the Humanities in the amount of $29 thousand, and it enumerated the many ways the audience could help in his efforts. The handout said at the end, "With your continued help, we're assured of success." Riggs created his successes the old-fashioned way: He earned them. *Ethnic Notions* ultimately garnered a national Emmy. Its mix of interviews, images of stereotypical ethnic representation, and performance were outstanding.

## NATIONAL RECOGNITION

*Tongues Untied* (1989), a video-poem about the African American gay experience, became Riggs's most well-known and most controversial work. He received a few thousand dollars from the Western Region Media Fellowship, a re-granting agency of the National Endowment for the Arts. Because this was federal government money, the political right wing cited the film as an example of the need to censor, control and monitor the funding of art that relates to unpopular ideas.

Riggs said in *The Creative Mind* interview that he saw the historic antecedent of this kind of documentary filmmaking and emulated it. He referred to fathers of independent documentary filmmaking, such as Robert Flaherty, as people with lyric, poetic and photography backgrounds, that infused their work with a unique quality. These historic filmmakers created much more than information but something that spoke to the heart of humanity. Riggs wanted to communicate about a voiceless and seemingly invisible group, Black gay men. He considered the visual style for this work as being much like we talk—metaphors, condensed ideas that expand on closer examination, encoded expressions. Poetry was the language of speaking, especially the colorful and poetic language of African Americans. For example, rap music as a genre emerged from Black street talk.

Riggs did not think his program contained shocking images. He knew that his original audience, Black gay men, would not be shocked by his images or ideas. Only the wider populace, with its notions of propriety and the Judeo-Christian ethic, found it shocking. Riggs said he wanted to affirm, explore, acknowledge and show the truth of the Black gay experience. He did not intend to shock the popular press and the general public. Riggs *did* see as obscene the exploitation, degradation, deliberate distortion and falsification of people's humanity. The positive responses from a wider audience, who related to the work's sense of solitude and the denial of one's true self because of distortions, were affirming to him. Self-acceptance and self-love are some of the keys to understanding the motivations and power of this work to speak to mass audiences.

In the interview, Riggs said he felt it was important to affirm that he was a Black gay man with HIV. He also felt that as a social/political activist he should affirm his humanity against those who would oppose and oppress him. He spoke about having communion with self as artist, communion with the wider audience, connecting with the past and history of other life-affirming artists such as Langston Hughes and James Baldwin. He spoke very profoundly of an artist's history living after the artist's death—prophetic and unsettling when seen today in the aftermath of his death by HIV infection.

## ACTIVISM

A three-day conference was held at the Studio Museum in Harlem in 1991. Part of an ongoing Discussions in Contemporary Culture Series, this conference was conceived by Michele Wallace. Participants presented their ideas under an assortment of topics related to Black culture. Riggs was part of a panel on Gender, Sexuality, and Black Images in Popular Culture. He spoke about his role as defined by society:

> I am typically called upon to speak on matters of race and sexuality in queer media; race and sexuality in Black culture; race and sexuality in Western cinema. I have become the Race and Sexuality Resident Expert.

Riggs was a filmmaker and activist. His activism led him to participate and speak at that conference. In 1988 in a Senate hearing of the communications subcommittee, as reported by *The Independent*, Riggs spoke about the role and circumstances of independent filmmakers:

> I am here to describe what it's like to be a smaller independent producer in America. In a word, dismal.

## CORNELIUS MOORE ON MARLON RIGGS

Cornelius Moore was a friend of Marlon Riggs and is the executor of his estate.

> There's clearly a break in his approach to dealing with the form of the work after *Ethnic Notions*. In *Tongues Untied* he got away from this documentary voice that he was schooled in. Because he was very ill and that made him realize the urgency of what he was doing, he needed to speak from his gut. You see this evolution in his work, even though clearly he got elected to being this voice of Black gay men. As an example, in *Black Is . . . Black Ain't*, sexuality is a recurring motif in his later work. He was looking at other aspects in the dialogue about gender, color and class that made people uncomfortable. He is saying to look at these differences and deal with them. His death unfortunately left the potential for dealing with these issues unchallenged. There were really different aspects to Marlon that were difficult and hard. There was a side to Marlon that also liked to go dancing.

Riggs was outspoken and articulate. He blazed a contemporary trail for independent and African American filmmakers. A documentary on his life entitled *I Shall Not Be Removed: The Life of Marlon Riggs* (1996, 57 min.) was produced by Karen Everett, one of his former students. Riggs was a professor at the University of California, Berkeley, in the Graduate School of Journalism.

## FILMOGRAPHY

*Long Train Running: The Story of the Oakland Blues Project,*** 1982, 60 min., video. This work looks at blues historic antecedents but focuses on contemporary artists at the then-emerging club called Eli's Mile High Club. This club, its artists and the music produced there have since become institutions in the Oakland area. Riggs's documentary captures the blues and its cultural, social and political implications. Riggs saw this work as a way to communicate something of Black history to large audiences.

*Ethnic Notions,*** 1987, 56 min., video, documentary. This work started with a collection of Black icons in popular culture. Later, a written thesis was produced by the collector of the icons, Jan Faulkner. The program is a history of the Black image from a political, social and cultural perspective. It makes use of cultural icons, cartoons, song lyrics, ads for products, performance and interviews with social scientists and others to explain how ethnic notions of Black people have developed.

*Tongues Untied,*** 1989, 60 min., video, documentary. In the book *Blacks in Hollywood* (1991), in the section on television programs, a review of *Tongues Untied* was written:

> Riggs has created a very personal statement about the nature of being Black and homosexual in America. He comments, as a Black man, on being a second-class citizen, "When you add being a homosexual, you have painted yourself into a corner as far as some people are concerned. In our country today, to be Black and admit homosexuality creates enormous tension." This videotape, supported in part by government funding, has the moral right beating the drum of censorship and decrying the waste of tax dollars on programs like this. It is because Riggs has fashioned a work with such conviction, care and using government funds that there is controversy. Some Public Broadcasting System stations deliberately omitted it from their program schedule as part of its nationwide broadcast premiere. Time will be the final arbiter for the American psychosexual self and our ability not to let differences, whether racial or sexual, divide man figuratively and literally against himself.

*Affirmations,*** 1990, 10 min., color, video. This tape addresses issues related to the Black gay dichotomy and duality. Included in the work are the experiences of a young Black gay male and his first homosexual experience. There are also scenes from an African American Day Parade in Harlem. In the parade we see the Black gay contingent confronted and booed by members of the Black community. Some of the marching Black gay activists included members of the Gay Men of African Descent and the Minority Task Force on AIDS.

*Color Adjustment,*** 1991, 87 min., video, documentary. An uncompromising look at the nature of television and its impact in creating lasting images of African Americans that have shaped popular perceptions of Blackness itself.

*Anthem,*** 1991, 9 min., color, video. An experimental montage of voices, images and music. Some of the images include the American flag, the Black Nationalist flag, men kissing and making love, a bright red rose, a crucifix, African warriors, drag queens, Essex Hemphill reciting poetry and men dancing.

*Non, Je Ne Regrette Rien (No Regret),*** 1992, 38 min., color, video, documentary. A film about Black gay men dealing with AIDS. Through poetry, songs and a montage of images with the personal testimonials of people with AIDS, the viewer is drawn inexorably into their lives. The men discuss the stigma, family reactions, the Black church's reaction, the Black community's reaction, the shame, the transformations, and coming out after forty years for one man. In these honest and revealing individual stories, a very intimate and personal face is put on the impact of the ravaging AIDS epidemic.

*Black Is . . . Black Ain't,*** 1994, 87 min., color, video. Riggs's last, most personal and most powerful work. He himself is the focus of this work. Riggs says, "the work is a personal journey through identity." It is about being Black, gay, HIV-positive, death and dying. The viewer sees Riggs being sick with HIV in the hospital. He gives us a T-cell count and tells us his weight. He describes how this project is his way of dealing with AIDS. Commentary is included from Cornel West, Essex Hemphill, Angela Davis, Michelle Wallace and Maulana Karanga on Black contemporary psychosocial issues. At one point Riggs says he wants to pass on something people can use to grow in their own lives. He wants us to have faith in each other, and against all odds we will all come through. God bless Marlon Riggs.

## BIO-CRITICAL REVIEW

"Marlon Riggs should be remembered as a talent and tireless artist whose own personal and professional spirit inspired courage in others."—Patricia Turner, *Humanities*

*Color Adjustment.* "Of all the ways television impacts our lives, none is more dramatic than race relations. No film has told this story better than *Color Adjustment*."—Nicholas Johnson, former Federal Communications Commission member

―――. "A fascinating reminder of how far television and American society have come . . . and how far both have to go."—William Raspberry, syndicated columnist

*Ethnic Notions.* "It's nothing short of astounding."—*New York Post*

―――. "A superb video handling the critical issue of racism sensitively but objectively."—Alvin Poussaint, Harvard University

―――. "An invaluable aid for American culture, Afro-American history and U.S. history survey courses."—*Journal of American History*

All of the above quotes are from the *California Newsreel* catalogue.

## EDUCATION

Harvard University, B.A., history

University of California, Berkeley, Graduate School of Journalism, M.A.

## SELECTED AWARDS

Riggs has personally won more than two dozen awards and commendations for his art and humanity.

*Color Adjustment*

  Black International Cinema, Berlin, 1992
  Columbia School of Journalism, DuPont Award, 1991
  George Polk Award, 1992

Organization of American Historians, Erik Barnouw Award, 1992
San Francisco International Film Festival, Golden Gate Award, 1992

*Ethnic Notions*
American Film and Video Festival, Red Ribbon, 1989
Black Filmmaker Foundation, Nomination, 1988
Emmy Award, Best Documentary, 1989
NAACP Image Award, Nomination, 1988
Newark Black Film Festival, 1987

*Long Train Running: The Story of the Oakland Blues Project*
American Film Institute, National Video Festival, First Prize, 1982

*Tongues Untied*
Berlin International Film Festival (2 awards), 1990
Black Gay and Lesbian Leadership Forum (2 awards), 1991
National Black Programming Consortium (2 awards), 1991

## SOURCES

Cornelius Moore, executor of Marlon Riggs's estate.

### Books

Hill, George, and Spencer Moon. *Blacks in Hollywood*. Los Angeles: Daystar Press, 1991.
Wallace, Michele (and Gina Dent, ed.). *Black Popular Culture*: Unleash the Queen *by Marlon Riggs*. Seattle: Bay Press, 1992.

### Other

Turner, Patricia. "Marlon Riggs, Independent Producer," *Humanities* (16), no. 3 (Summer 1994), pp. 1–2.
*The Independent* (11), no. 5 (June 1988), p. 37.
*The Creative Mind*. Video documentary, KQED-TV San Francisco, 1991.
A two-hour conversation with Marlon Riggs. 120 min.
*California Newsreel* catalogue. San Francisco: California Newsreel, 1993.

# HUGH ROBERTSON

## BACKGROUND

Hugh Robertson (1932–1988) was born in the United States to parents who were from Trinidad. At age 17 he was introduced to film business as a can carrier for Seaboard Studios in New York City. He learned editing and television through his stint in the Army Signal Corps during World War II. When Robertson returned to New York, he applied for a film editor's union card but was denied membership for over a decade simply because of his color. Robertson continued to study his craft; he attended the New York Institute for Motion Pictures and the University of Paris (Sorbonne), and he studied acting with Elia Kazan and the Negro Actors Guild. He got his union card with the I.A.T.S.E. Motion Picture Editors Local 771 in 1960.

## FEATURE EDITING AND A BIG BREAK

Robertson studied editing with Carl Lerner and Dede Allen. Once given the opportunity, he worked as an editor on many feature films and continued to work as an editor on television programs. He worked his editing magic on the film *Shaft*\*\* (1971) and helped to launch the Black cinema explosion of the seventies. His work on *Shaft* became the standard by which Black cinema of the period was measured from an editing perspective.

His big break was as senior editor on the critically acclaimed *Midnight Cowboy*\*\* (1969), for which he was nominated for both the British and American Oscar. In fact, he is the first and only Black American to be nominated for the Oscar as a film editor. He and the director, John Schlesinger (who is British), made a bet after Robertson's two nominations as to whether or not he would win the Oscar. Robertson lost the American Oscar but won the British Oscar for editing, becoming the first Black American to do so. He took his loss in stride, moved to the next level and began to direct first commercials and later feature films and episodic television.

## MEETING HUGH

I first met Hugh Robertson as a student during the summer of 1984, when independent Black filmmakers from all over the United States gathered. About two dozen independent Black filmmakers were the students (I was among this group), and there were nine instructors (Hugh among them). The instructors were a Who's Who of filmmaking: Gordon Parks,* Carroll Ballard, William Greaves,* Topper Carew, Lonnie Elder III, Avon Kirkland,* Michael Schultz,* Stan Lathan,* Louis Peterson, Booker Bradshaw and Hugh. I later worked with Hugh as a coordinator for the same program, in the summer of 1986. Hugh again was in the role of instructor.

In 1987 I worked with two dozen other independent black filmmakers, technicians, producers and writers to do a special tribute, premier and retrospective of Robertson's film work. I was fortunate to receive Hugh's insights as a master craftsman and a unique individual. His sense of humor and wisdom are a cherished memory.

## FILMOGRAPHY

### Associate Editor (Selected Work)

*The Fugitive Kind*, 1959, 135 min.; *Harvey Middleman, Fireman*, 1965, 75 min.; *Lillith*, 1964, 114 min.; *The Miracle Worker*, 1962, 107 min.; *Odds Against Tomorrow*, 1959, 95 min.; *Twelve Angry Men*, 1957, 95 min.

### Editor

*Franklin Delano Roosevelt*, ABC, 1970. *Midnight Cowboy*, 1969, 113 min.; *Shaft*, 1971, 100 min.

### Director

### *Feature Films*

*Melinda*,** 1972, 109 min., 35mm, color, MGM. An assignment that came as a direct result of Robertson's work on the film *Shaft*. His contract for editing *Shaft* stipulated that MGM give him an opportunity to direct. *Melinda* was produced by former football great Purvis Atkins; script by Lonnie Elder III, edited by Paul Evans and music by Jerry Butler and Jerry Peters.

*Bim*, 1976, 104 min., 35mm, Parker Street Productions. The second feature film Robertson directed was produced by his own production company, Sharc Productions, Ltd. He produced *Bim* in Trinidad, where his parents were born. He was able to assemble the island's only fully equipped production facility and work with local actors and technicians.

*Bim* recounts the life of an East Indian in Trinidad. The abandoned son of a murdered labor leader, Bim pulls himself up to continue his father's work. The story follows the young Bim from foster home to runaway and, later, street hoodlum. His rise from underworld thug to labor leader is a brutal ascendancy. Although the portrait is presented very dispassionately, the passions of Bim are abundant and volatile. This gritty portrait makes clear that colonialism is part of the equation of grim reality we experience. The work ends much the way it began, with violence—part of what colonial corruption has wrought on people all over the world.

*Obeah*, 1987, 110 min., 35mm, Parker Street Productions. One of the most interesting glimpses of the religious practices of Trinidad. During the forties and later in the seventies there was a wave of Hollywood films on voodoo. They are mere pablum compared with this film. It is authentic in detail, and it is engrossing to see what mighty forces, when summoned by a priestess, are capable of doing. Belief on the part of the viewer is left to the imagination. The forces portrayed in *Obeah* are mighty and transcend the inaccurate picture given thus far by other films on the subject. The story of two lovers whose romance is impeded by voodoo seems incidental to the picture of voodoo and its rites, rituals and practices. Definitely not for the squeamish. Graphic without being gratuitous.

### Episodic Television

*Love American Style*, ABC; *Roll Out*, CBS

### Television Specials

*Dream on Monkey Mountain*, PBS; *And Beautiful II; The Great American Dream Machine*, PBS; *Black Music in America: From Then till Now*, PBS

## BIO-CRITICAL REVIEW

*Melinda.* "*Melinda* represented a new wave in the black film cycle that attempted to respond to the backlash from the black community against the blaxploitation syndrome."—George Hill and James Robert Parish, *Black Action Films*

————. "That there are not resemblances to other recent slick sex-and-violence films but the differences, there is no actual gunplay, the love relationship is three-dimensional, there are positive anti-drugs and pro-community messages within. You can enjoy this film simply as a diversion, but you'll also be impressed by its heavier aspects."—James P. Murray, *Encore*

*Obeah.* "An intriguing drama. Robertson treats the beliefs of these African descendants with as much respect as that paid to others who believe that wine and the communion wafer represent the blood and the body of Jesus."—Judy Stone, *San Francisco Chronicle*

## AWARDS

Black Filmmakers Hall of Fame, Inductee, 1982

*And Beautiful II*
   Emmy Award
   Los Angeles Black Media Coalition, Outstanding Technical Achievement Award,
      Spencer Williams Pioneer Award, 1987
*Midnight Cowboy*
   British Academy of Film and Television Arts Award, Editing, 1969
   Oscar Nomination, Editing, 1969

## SOURCES

### Books

Hill, George, and James Robert Parish. *Black Action Films.* Jefferson, NC: McFarland,
      1989.

### Other

Black Filmmakers Hall of Fame. *Program Catalogue.* Oakland, CA: 1982.
Los Angeles Black Media Coalition. *Program Catalogue*, Outstanding Technical
      Achievement Award. Los Angeles: 1987.
Murray, James P. "Perspectives on Black Film." *Encore*, October 1972, p. 30.
Stone, Judy. "A Bad Spell for Lovers." *San Francisco Chronicle*, October 1987, p. E9.
Williams, John. "Hugh Robertson, 1932–1988." *The Independent*, May 1988, p. 7.
Williams, John. "Film Pioneer Dies in Los Angeles." *Black Film Review* (3), no. 4
      (Fall 1987), p. 9.

# MICHAEL SCHULTZ

## BACKGROUND

Michael Schultz has a career of directing films for the big screen and the small screen that defies category. He transferred from the University of Wisconsin to Marquette University to become involved in the theater arts program. In 1964 he moved to New York and found work as an assistant stage manager and actor. He appeared in two productions of the American Place Theater; Frank Langella and Roscoe Lee Browne were fellow actors there. He began directing theater in 1966 at Princeton. Soon his work came to the attention of Douglas Turner Ward, artistic director of the newly formed Negro Ensemble Company (NEC). Schultz was hired as a staff director for NEC's 1967–1968 season. By 1969 he had begun to direct projects outside NEC, and his Broadway debut production *Does a Tiger Wear a Necktie?* (1969) earned him a Tony award nomination for Best Director. That same play was also the Broadway debut for actor Al Pacino, who won a Tony award and co-starred in the production with Hal Holbrook. Schultz's theater career spanned more than a decade.

## MEETING MICHAEL SCHULTZ

No matter what kind of film you want to make, Michael Schultz had already directed one like it. With the exception of Oscar Micheaux,* no Black director has directed more feature films and more television movies

Michael Schultz

than Schultz. His goal from the beginning was always to direct interesting and challenging films. He has succeeded.

When I met Schultz I was struck by his piercing green eyes. He spoke to our group of apprentice and journeyman filmmakers about his career on a hot summer day in 1985 on the campus of the University of California, Berkeley. The weekend seminar was organized by the Black Filmmakers Hall of Fame of Oakland, California.

## GETTING THE DOOR OPEN

We listened that day to what Schultz and Stan Lathan* told us about directing in Hollywood, and later they answered our every question. Schultz said his success in Broadway theater as a director and actor opened the door to Hollywood. He got work first at Universal Studios directing episodic television. He talked about how he moved to Los Angeles and got an office and a phone. He would call all over town introducing himself as Michael Schultz, a new director in town looking for work. When he went to appointments and people saw him in person with his sandy-colored hair, striking creole features and piercing green eyes, they usually were speechless for a moment. His biracial heritage opened many a door initially.

Once through the door, Schultz created more success than many have. The courage of his convictions and his talent are a testament to not being pigeonholed as a director. His career has been longer than that of most Black directors, and certainly more diverse in terms of variety of material.

In the book *Creative Differences: Profiles of Hollywood Dissidents* (1978), Schultz is quoted as saying, "Every artist, no matter how devoted he is, wants to reach the greatest number of people. The trick is to avoid reaching them with a diluted product." Schultz also made another valid point: "Underneath it all there has to be a realization that when you put out powerful images, you're going to generate powerful, positive people" (Noel, 1991).

## FILMOGRAPHY

### Director

All 35mm and color.

*Together for Days*, 1973, Kelly-Jordan Productions.

*Honeybaby, Honeybaby*, 1974, Olas Company. Marked Diane Sands's last screen role before her untimely death.

*Cooley High*,** 1975, 107 min., American International. A story that is more than the sum of its parts. Young Black teens are out to have fun and meet girls. Positively rendered Black images during a time when there was a dearth of positive Black images. The cast included Lawrence Hilton Jacobs, Garrett Morris, Corin Rogers and Glynn Turman. The film was shot in twenty-five days; it was made for a modest $750,000 and grossed over $13 million.

The television show *What's Happening* (1976), a Black sitcom, was a spin-off using some of the characters from the film.

*Car Wash*,** 1976, 97 min., Universal Pictures. Featuring Richard Pryor, Bill Duke,* Ivan Dixon,* Antonio Fargas, the Pointer Sisters, George Carlin, Irwin Corey, Franklin Ajaye, Garrett Morris, Clarence Muse and Danny DeVito. Grossed over $14 million.

*Which Way Is Up?*,** 1977, 94 min., Universal Pictures. The film takes on serious social and political issues and still is a very good comedy vehicle for Richard Pryor. Luis Valdez, Daniel Valdez and other members of the famed El Teatro Campesino theater group were part of the ensemble cast. They participated in portions of the story that dealt with Latin migrant workers and issues related to agribusiness and labor. Featuring Margaret Avery, Julie Dorman, Lonette McKee, Richard Pryor, Dolph Sweet and Morgan Woodward. Co-written by novelist Cecil Brown (*The Lives and Loves of Mr. Jiveass Nigger*). Grossed $19 million on a budget of $3 million.

*Greased Lightning*,** 1977, 96 min., Warner Brothers. A biographical film on the life of the first Black stock car auto racer, Wendell Scott. This film and *Which Way Is Up?* show Richard Pryor at his acting and cinematic best. These two films represent some of the best efforts of Hollywood Black cinema. *Greased Lightning* featured Beau Bridges, Pam Grier, Cleavon Little, Vincent Gardenia, Richie Havens and former congressman Julian Bond. Co-written by the godfather of modern Black cinema, Melvin Van Peebles.* Wendell Scott acted as technical advisor.

*Sgt. Pepper's Lonely Hearts Club Band*,** 1978, 111 min., Universal. Featuring George Burns, Peter Frampton, Sandy Farina, the Gibbs Brothers (Barry, Maurice and Robin), Steve Martin, Donald Pleasance and Billy Preston. Music by John Lennon and Paul McCartney. Produced by music impresario Robert Stigwood. In 1978, Schultz's budget of $12.5 million was the largest ever at the time for a Black director.

*Scavenger Hunt*,** 1979, 116 min. Featuring Richard Benjamin, James Coco, Scatman Crothers, Ruth Gordon, Roddy McDowell, Robert Morley, Cleavon Little, Richard Mulligan, Tony Randall, Cloris Leachman, Dirk Benedict, Vincent Price, Avery Schrieber and Arnold Schwarzenegger.

*Carbon Copy*,** 1981, 92 min., Avco-Embassy. The story of a White businessman who discovers to his surprise that he has a Black son. George Segal, Denzel Washington, Jack Warden, Paul Winfield, Susan Saint James and Tom Poston are featured.

*The Last Dragon*,** 1985, 109 min., Tri-Star Pictures. Starring Taimak and Vanity. A young man interested in kung-fu falls in love and has adventures like a latter-day Hercules. Soundtrack provided by Motown Records. Grossed $33 million.

*Krush Groove*,** 1985, 97 min., Warner Brothers. Schultz also acted as co-producer with George Jackson* and Doug McHenry.* The cast included Blair Underwood. Musical performers included Sheila E, Run-DMC, The Fat Boys and Kurtis Blow, with cameos by rising stars New Edition, Beastie Boys, Bobby Brown, LL Cool J and Dr. Jekyll & Mr. Hyde. The film is a loose adaptation of the real-life story of music producer/entrepreneur Russell Simmons, who also acted as associate producer on the film. For more on Simmons, see the chapter on Stan Lathan.* The cinematographer was Ernest Dickerson, a favorite of Spike Lee's.*

*Disorderlies*,** 1987, 86 min. The rap group The Fat Boys were the stars of this comedy: Mark Morales, Darren Robinson and Damon Wimbley. Troy Beyer and Linda Hopkins, the empress of the blues, were also featured. Pop artist/musician Ray Parker Jr. had a bit part.

*Livin' Large*,** 1991, 96 min., Samuel Goldwyn. A brother gets an opportunity to advance from the street to being a television reporter in a heartbeat. A Dorian Gray–like story. The more successful the hero becomes, the whiter he gets figuratively and literally. A funny spoof of today's buppies (Black upwardly mobile professionals). Featured are T.C. Carson, Lisa Arrindell, Blanche Baker, Nathaniel Hall and Julia Campbell.

### Television Movies

*Benny's Place*, 1982, CBS. Louis Gossett Jr., David Harris, Anna Marie Horsford, Cicely Tyson and Michael Wright are featured.

*For Us the Living: The Meadgar Evers Story*, 1983, PBS. A dramatic rendering of the political life and times of the assassinated Mississippi civil rights leader Meadger Evers. The cast is excellent with Margaret Avery, Roscoe Lee Browne, Irene Cara, Howard Rollins Jr. and Paul Winfield.

*The Jerk, Too*, 1984, NBC. Executive producer was Steve Martin, who was the star of the theatrical film on which this television movie was based (*The Jerk*,** 1979). The premise of a White boy adopted by a Black family is still the same. The tele-film follows the hero, Navin Johnson, as he tries to attend a friend's wedding in Los Angeles.

*The Spirit*, 1987.

*Timestalkers*, 1987. Featuring William Devane, Lauren Hutton, John Ratzenberger, Forrest Tucker, Klaus Kinski, Tracey Walter and James Avery.

*Rock 'n' Roll Mom*, 1988.

*Tarzan in Manhattan*, 1989. Certainly not the last Tarzan film to be made. There have been approximately 42 other films on this mythic jungle-bunny. Featuring Joe Lara, Joe Seneca, Tony Curtis, Kim Crosby and Jan-Michael Vincent.

*Jury Duty: The Comedy* (alternate title, *The Great American Sex Scandal*), 1990.

*Day-O*, 1992.

*Young Indiana Jones and the Hollywood Follies*, 1994.

### Episodic Television

*Baretta*, ABC; *Movin' On*, NBC; *The Rockford Files*, NBC; *Starsky and Hutch*, ABC; *Toma*, ABC.

### Television Specials

*Ebony/Jet Showcase*, 1986, synd.

*Fade Out: The Erosion of Black Images in the Media*, 1984, documentary, PBS.

*Ceremonies in Dark Old Men*, 1971, ABC. A tele-film based on a play by Lonnie Elder III. The cast from the Negro Ensemble Company theater group features Douglas

Turner Ward, Glynn Turman, Rosalind Cash, Robert Hooks and Godfrey Cambridge.

*To Be Young, Gifted and Black*, 1971, 90 min., PBS. A tele-film of a successful off-Broadway production.

### Unsold Pilots

*Change at 125th Street*, 1974, CBS.

*Hammer Slammer and Slade*, 1989, ABC. Produced and written by Keenan Ivory Wayans.* A television version of his film *I'm Gonna' Get You Sucka*** (1988).

### Independent Production

*Earth, Wind and Fire in Concert*, 1982, 60 min. A concert film of a pop group; later licensed to HBO cable, under the banner of Schultz's Crystalite Productions, Inc. Produced by Michael and Gloria Schultz.

### Theater

Director for the world-renowned Negro Ensemble Company (NEC) and the Eugene O'Neill Memorial Theater productions.

*The Poison Tree*, 1973

*Thoughts*, 1973

*The Three Sisters*, 1973

*Operation Sidewinder*, 1970, written by Sam Shepard and staged for the Lincoln Center.

*Woyzeck*, 1970

*Dream on Monkey Mountain*, 1971, NEC, staged in Los Angeles.

*Every Night When the Sun Goes Down*, 1969

*The Reckoning*, 1969, NEC

*God Is a (guess what?)*, 1969, NEC

*Does a Tiger Wear a Necktie?* 1969 (Broadway debut)

*Kongi's Harvest*, 1968, NEC

*Song of the Lusitanian Bogey*, 1968, NEC

*Waiting for Godot*, 1968, American Place Theater


## BIO-CRITICAL REVIEW

"A painter of word pictures that uplift the audience."—Angela Noel, Black Filmmakers Hall of Fame, Program Catalogue

"His is a talent that shouldn't be underestimated. Schultz's films get seen."—James Monaco, *American Film Now: The People, the Power, the Money, the Movies*

*Car Wash.* "A more radical departure from narrative conventions than any recent Hollywood film, Black or White."—James Monaco, *American Film Now: The People, the Power, the Money, the Movies*

*Cooley High.* "A landmark movie, one of the year's most important and heartening pictures, that shows what the black film can be when creative talents are given an opportunity free of the strong sex and violence requirements of the exploitation formulae."—Kevin Thomas, *Los Angeles Times*

*Greased Lightning.* "Effective for the good-humored manner in which the story is presented. There is not a more likable movie currently on view."—Richard Schickel, *Time*

———. "It's about real social relations, real tensions, real lives. An example of how to make mass movies without insulting your audience."—Pat Aufderheide, *Cineaste*

*Livin' Large.* "Some good performances elicited under Schultz's always amiable direction."—Nelson George, *Blackface: Reflections on African-Americans and the Movies*

———. "Pic has a loose, comfortable spirit that serves it well as a comedy vehicle."—Amy Dawes, *Variety*

## EDUCATION

Attended University of Wisconsin, Marquette, Wisconsin, studied theater arts

## SELECTED AWARDS

Black Filmmakers Hall of Fame, Inductee, 1991

*Car Wash*
    Cannes Film Festival, Best Music; Superior Technique; 1977

*Ceremonies in Dark Old Men*
    Christopher Award, 1971

*Does a Tiger Wear a Necktie?*
    Tony Award Nomination, Best Director, 1969

## SOURCES

### Books

Bogle, Donald. *Blacks in American Film and Television: An Illustrated Encyclopedia.* New York: Simon & Schuster, 1989.
Cloyd, Iris, ed. *Who's Who among Black Americans.* New York: Gale Research, 1990.
George, Nelson. *Blackface: Reflections on African Americans and the Movies.* New York: HarperCollins, 1994.
Katz, Ephraim. *The Film Encyclopedia.* New York: HarperCollins, 1994.
Kendell, Stephen D. *New Jack Cinema: Hollywood's African-American Filmmakers.* Silver Springs, MD: J.L. Denser, 1994.

Maltin, Leonard, ed. *Leonard Maltin's Movie and Video Guide, 1995*. New York: Penguin Group, 1995.

McNeil, Alex. *Total Television Including Cable: A Comprehensive Guide to Programming from 1948 to the Present*. New York: Penguin Books, 1991.

Monaco, James. *American Film Now: The People, the Power, the Money, the Movies*. New York: Zoetrope, 1984.

Singer, Michael, comp. and ed. *Film Directors: A Complete Guide*. Beverly Hills, CA: Lone Eagle Publishing, 1985.

Terrace, Vincent. *Encyclopedia of Television: Series Pilots and Specials. Volume Two, 1974–1984; Volume Three, 1937–1984*. New York: Zoetrope, 1986.

Zheutlin, Barbara, and David Talbot. *Creative Differences: Profiles of Hollywood Dissidents*. Boston: South End Press, 1978.

### Newspapers and Magazines

Aufderheide, Pat. "Michael Schultz," *Cineaste* (8), no. 2, p. 32.

Dawes, Amy. "Livin' Large," *Variety*, August 23, 1991, p. 48.

Jackson, Elizabeth. "Living Large," *Black Film Review* (7) no. 1, p. 21.

Noel, Angela. "Michael Schultz," Black Filmmakers Hall of Fame, Program Catalogue, 1991, p. 12.

Schickel, Richard. "Greased Lightning," *Time*, August 15, 1977, p. 42.

Thomas, Kevin. "Cooley High," *Los Angeles Times*, July 13, 1975, p. C4.

### Other

*Internet Movie Database*, Biloxi: University of Mississippi, 1996.

# JACKIE SHEARER

## BACKGROUND

Jackie Shearer (1946–1993) was a pioneering woman filmmaker whose untimely death ended a promising and accomplished career. Her film credits are in her given name of Jacqueline, but personally and in professional film circles she was always known as Jackie.

She attended Boston public schools and graduated from the Girl's Latin School in 1964. After college, her first job was designing a U.S. history curriculum focusing on African Americans for the Educational Development Center (EDC). In the fall of 1969 Jackie got a job at Urban Planning Aid (UPA), a nonprofit agency providing technical support to community organizations. The group produced videotapes, slide-tape shows, silk-screened posters, pamphlets, brochures and a community newspaper feature service. She used mass media to contribute to the growth of a radical movement. Over the next three years she made slide shows and videos about tenants' rights and tenants' unions, trained community activists in the use of video equipment and public access cable television, and organized conferences about alternative community-based media, both visual and print. Working with the tenant self-management group at the Bromley Heath housing project in Jamaica Plain, she directed her first dramatic video.

After she left UPA she began to produce a weekly African American public affairs show for WBCN radio. In 1974 she became an associate producer of *Third World* and other public affairs programs on WCVB-TV, the ABC affiliate in Boston. Somewhat by accident, she found herself at the founding meeting of Boston Newsreel, a film production and screening group that saw and used media as a tool for social change. In Newsreel, she continued learning and teaching herself how to make films. During this time she also worked with the Newsreel group to prepare public service announcements for organizing efforts, including an early announcement about the Nestle's infant formula boycott campaign.

When the intransigence of the Boston School Committee toward black parents' demands for quality education exploded into the school busing crisis of the mid-seventies, Jackie looked for a way to respond in film. With Terry Signaigo and Mary Tiseo, she formed Walnut Films and plunged into fundraising and research for the film she eventually directed, *A Minor Altercation* (1976). This was her first independently produced film.

Shearer was helpful to other independent filmmakers. She mentored people of color, Black people and Black women. She would offer information on fundraising, even on how to direct crews. She was astutely aware of the problems faced by women and other people of color. Shearer managed to incorporate her social and political views into her career and work.

**PEERS**

One of her last efforts to promote independent filmmakers was as Board chair and president of the Independent Television Service. Shearer was part of a wave of women filmmakers that emerged in the late seventies. Her peers included Michelle Parkerson,* Ayoka Chenzira,* and Julie Dash.* These women, by their own tenacity and hard work, broke down barriers of invisibility.

**MEETING JACKIE: AVAILABLE VISIONS CONFERENCE**

I met Jackie in the summer of 1992 in Geyserville, California. We were part of the Available Visions: Improving Distribution of African-American Independent Film and Video conference. She was the invited keynote speaker. Other participants included the conference organizers, filmmakers, distributors, educators and advocates for improving distribution of independent African American film and video. My impressions were that Jackie was forthright and honest. Her keynote speech set the tone for this historic and important event.

Some of her remarks to the Available Visions conference are included here, as a lasting tribute to her memory and spirit. A friend of Jackie's has commented to me that Jackie's words when speaking in public were carefully and honestly chosen.

> I am very happy to be here with you, but a little bit scared. Usually when I speak it's in academia. I adjust my attitude up a few notches,

put on intellectual armor, murmur a mantra of my SAT score and hope for the best. But this time I'm at the Marketplace, not the Academy. Instead of feeling intimidated but superior, I feel intimidated and out of my league.

I've always respected the ability to survive in the business world as a particularly evolved set of knowledge, talent and skills that I don't have. I call my remarks *Random Notes of a Homeless Filmmaker*. Those of you who know me think I refer to my recent nomadic existence, but I'm waxing metaphorical here. If I had a home, there would be a codified body of work that my individual work belongs to. If I had a home, when I ask my local video store owner for documentaries, he would understand what I had just said. If I had a home, my local library would have more choices than *Eyes on the Prize* and mediocre Hollywood fare.

I came to production from distribution. I was a member of the Boston Newsreel Collective in the late sixties. Boston Newsreel was not a strong production center like New York Newsreel or San Francisco Newsreel were. (Author's note: Today these two organizations are known as Third World Newsreel and California Newsreel, respectively.) But what we did do was distribute and exhibit films. I conducted a lot of community screenings, led a lot of discussions and saw people open up and make connections with the images they saw. It became clear to me that film had no potential merit gathering dust on the shelf. It was only in interaction with an audience that it had power. This is a very simple-minded truth but one that is still stunning to me in its significance and consequences. So a long-standing cornerstone of my understanding about media is that the production of a piece is not finished until and unless it plays to its audience.

I have seen independent filmmakers successfully distribute their own work, but always with a lot more effort than I feel I can spare from the work I feel I'm better at. I have my own personal theory that good filmmakers are not good businesspeople; I know there are too many expectations for this to be true, but still it comforts me. So until this year, that was my education on distribution—absolutely vital but a total drag. Either you put your fate in someone else's hand and take what comes, or you put aside your own creative agenda to become a salesperson and office worker. Of course I do things, and I have reasons for doing things, but my thinking about myself professionally and my work occurs in a funny myopic frame, absent history, background and context. I invent every wheel I try to set in motion.

Thanks to Pearl Bowser I know about Oscar Micheaux,* but I'm fuzzier about what happened in the sixties and seventies and eighties besides what I directly experienced myself or just happen to know about. I have no home as a filmmaker. Spike Lee* and John Singleton* have a home: Hollywood. Madeline Anderson* has a home: public television. Where am I? Once again, in the margins between the cracks. I think I have lots of company, but it's hard to get an overview from the margins.

African American independent film. Who, what, where, when, why, how can we see it? All very interesting and important questions whose answers will constitute my home. Why am I bringing this to you? Because I think that the task of constructing my home falls to you. It's in the distribution that the production comes full circle. I know what my intentions were, but you may see more clearly what I have achieved. I make my films with an audience in mind, but you are the ones with the skills and the knowledge to bring the two together.

Isn't it traditionally at the point of distribution that the product gets handled and molded into a saleable commodity? Here's a clipping from the *New York Times* business pages about a commercial tie-in: "Coca-Cola Backs Spike Lee's *Malcolm X*." Maybe in an alternative vision, distribution becomes the stage where the product that we create becomes contextualized. It looks to me that this process is in your vested interests. If there is an identified body of work, African American Independent Media, won't it be easier for you to sell? This is meant to be an action-oriented, hands-on, concrete, strategizing kind of session. In that spirit, let me offer a project for your consideration. What about an African American Independent Film Infomercial? Clicking the remote in the wee hours of the morning, I have been held spellbound by Dionne Warwick and friends offering spontaneous testimonials about their buddies' skin care system. I was overjoyed that Cher and the girls found the answer to their hair crises through the revolutionary products of her hairdresser. I can personally attest to the draw of this kind of programming. What would it take to realize this vision? On one hand, not much—a tastefully decorated living room set, a few celebrities to kick it around and testify about the films they saw that changed their lives, some clips to screen at appropriate intervals. But when it comes time for the on-screen display of an 800 number and information on how to order, that's when the work that we will have begun here this weekend will come into play. Who wants to work with me on this?

### After-Conference Report

The conference was a success in no small part due to Shearer's convictions in her opening remarks. The Conference Report from which her remarks are excerpted was widely disseminated. Activities in the independent African American film/video field were invigorated. Alliances in the diaspora and

Africa flourished, and new alliances between U.S. Black and diaspora film-makers were formed.

## FILMOGRAPHY

### Producer/Director

*A Minor Altercation*, 1976, 30 min. Two adolescent girls get into a fight at school and are suspended. The incident is the focal point for an examination of racial attitudes within both girls' families as well as institutional racism in school.

Shearer was quoted as saying, "Film is the most potent force in the world today because it works on the emotional level. Since television is the transmitter of American popular culture, I intend to use techniques, already accepted by the public, to express a political idea" (quoted in Bowser and Harris, *Independent Black American Cinema: 1920–1980*, 1981).

*Your Way or Mine*, 1977. Distributed by Blackside, Inc. Two 20-minute training films for labor arbitrators.

*The Unemployment Test*, 1978. Distributed by Blackside, Inc. A 20-minute nationally broadcast public film.

*Easy Street*, 1979. Distributed by Blackside, Inc. A 30-minute vocational education film on health matters.

### Director

*The Road to Recovery*, 1979. Distributed by Blackside, Inc. A 20-minute training film for disaster relief workers.

*Choices*, 1987. Two 45-minute instructional media productions for middle management training.

### Producer/Director/Writer

*Yes, We Can*, 1981. Distributed by Blackside, Inc. A 30-minute high school job training recruitment film.

*The Incident Report*, 1984. Distributed by Fanlight Productions. A 30-minute training film on nursing home abuse prevention.

*We Can Win*, 1986. A 15-minute promotional video for the Center for Constitutional Rights.

*Eyes on the Prize, Part II*, 1990, PBS. Shearer worked on two segments, each 60 minutes.

*The Promised Land*, 1990. Distributed by Blackside, Inc. The story of Martin Luther King's radicalization, death and legacy.

*The Keys to the Kingdom*, 1990. Distributed by Blackside, Inc. Documents Boston school desegregation and affirmative action.

*The Massachusetts 54th Colored Infantry,* 1991, 56 min. Distributed by PBS. Shown on PBS as part of the third season of the *American Experience* series. Blacks in the North fight slavery in the Union army. Presents facts on which the film *Glory\*\** (1990) was based. This documentary is informative, essential and a must-see.

## BIO-CRITICAL REVIEW

*A Minor Altercation.* "A superior film that achieves exactly what it was designed to do—stimulate discussion which focuses on the feelings, attitudes, perceptions, and fears about race that underlie open racial conflict in school situations."—*Independent Black American Cinema: 1920–1980*

## EDUCATION

Brandeis University, B.A., American history

## MEMBERSHIPS

Academy of Motion Picture Arts and Sciences

Boston Film and Video Festival

Corporation for Public Broadcasting

Massachusetts Foundation for Humanities and Public Policy

National Endowment for the Humanities

New York Foundation for the Arts

New York State Council for the Humanities

## SOURCES

### Magazines

Sandler, Kathe. "In Memory of Jacqueline Shearer." *Black Film Review* (8), no. 1 (1993), pp. 43–44.
Zeinabu, irene Davis. "Jackie Shearer: 1946–1993." *The Independent: Film and Video Monthly* (17), no. 2 (March 1994), pp. 9–11.

### Other

*Available Visions: Improving Distribution of African-American Independent Film and Video Conference Report.* Geyserville, CA: AVCC, 1992.
Bowser, Pearl, and Valerie Harris, eds. *A Minor Altercation: Independent Black American Cinema: 1920–1980.* Program notes. New York: New York State Council on the Arts, 1981.

Additional notes were taken from the Boston Memorial to Jackie at the African Meeting House, December 4, 1993.

Jackie's papers are at the Schomburg Center for Research in Black Culture, New York City Public Library.

Friends of Jackie Shearer who helped with this chapter: Nancy Falk, Janet Axelrod, Cornelius Moore.

# JOHN SINGLETON

## BACKGROUND

At age 9 John Singleton saw the film *Star Wars* and was so taken with it that he decided he wanted to be a filmmaker. During high school he kept journals and began to develop his skills as a writer. After graduating from high school he enrolled in the filmic writing program at the University of Southern California (USC). Before graduating from college he had signed with one of Hollywood's largest talent agencies, Creative Artists Agency (CAA). This happened because he was a script reader for Columbia Pictures as part of his senior-year internship. After reading many bad scripts, he mentioned and then passed along a couple of his own scripts to his boss at Columbia. His boss sent his scripts to CAA, and they were so impressed they signed Singleton to a management contract. An African American vice president at Columbia, Stephanie Allain, mentored Singleton and helped him secure a contract for a three-picture deal with Columbia.

## WRITING, DIRECTING, AND THE INDUSTRY

The following discussion is from an interview conducted by George Hill in 1991 while *Boyz N The Hood* was in post-production, prior to its nationwide release.

Singleton said he had only produced 8mm short subjects at USC. He began to find his writing voice in high school while writing for the school paper, which included writing film reviews. *Boyz* was a vision he had since the age of 13. It is about people he grew up with. Singleton considers himself a writer first; he is a director to protect his vision. The original vision starts on the page, but it can be changed by the time it reaches the screen.

Singleton said he worked hard, went to film school and looked forward to making films. While at USC he won three awards for his screenplays; the Jack Nicholson Award in screenwriting included $8 thousand prize money for tuition. Singleton felt the feature film process was better than he anticipated, and he said he was taken as a serious filmmaker right away.

Singleton reflected that no matter what age you are, you need to be able to tell a good story. One problem with the industry as a whole, whether Black or White filmmaker, is the power of good writing. To be a great director, you have to have a good sense of story. Writers have that intuitively. He sees that his uniqueness to filmmaking is good, well-rounded characters, definite plot, the diaspora of cinema as art as well as entertainment. He sees Spike Lee's* films as both artistic and entertaining. He wants other Black filmmakers to understand the artistic side of filmmaking as well as the entertainment side. Black filmmakers need to have Black audiences for their films, coming away with some things to think about.

When asked to talk about how other young people should prepare for work in the industry, Singleton was quick to answer: Learn how to write good screenplays, learn how to tell a story. He attributed his current success with Columbia Pictures to his writing abilities. One influence on Singleton as a writer was the Pulitzer Prize–winning playwright August Wilson. Singleton added that the focus for young people should not be about the limelight, but about the work. He also added that there is plenty of room for good technicians. Remember, not everyone can direct or star in movies. The industry needs level-headed people who are "about the work." There is plenty of room for everybody. There are hundreds of jobs pertaining to the film business; not any one of them is exclusive.

Prior to the production of *Boyz*, African American author Nelson George met Singleton. George felt that he was part of a new wave of Black filmmakers with an important message to deliver. Singleton's self-confidence and vision made George realize that "The hip-hop age of Black cinema was under way" (George, 1994).

### AFTER *BOYZ* OPENED

Singleton was interviewed on *Live from L.A. with Tanya Hart* (BET Cable). In describing the significance of a clip from the film that was shown, he said that the scenes of the two sibling brothers who fight each other is a metaphor for Black-on-Black violence. Black people should not fight each other. The film is about the erosion of the Black family over the last thirty years. Now we have a whole population of young men who only have Black females as parents in the family. Singleton does not think women can teach a young boy how to be a man. A woman can only teach the young boy her perception of what a man should be.

It was important to make his first film about his neighborhood because no one had ever done that. No one had done it the way he did it.

When asked to describe how someone so young had achieved success in Hollywood so quickly, he was candid. Singleton felt his success with Columbia Pictures was because his images and ideas leap off the page and because of the single-mindedness he had from his days in film school. At that time he talked over and over again about the films he wanted to do. He practiced pitching his film ideas over and over again, to classmates, even to brothers in the 'hood in front of the 7-Eleven store. He felt if you can pitch an idea to anybody, you can pitch it to a studio head.

Because the film's portrayal of Los Angeles police was very frank, he was asked to explain why he did so. Singleton recalled at age 10 having police pull handguns on him and a friend. The friend had returned from Disneyland with a toy gun. He and his friend were running around as kids do, and the police saw them and pulled up. The police believed it was a real weapon and drew their own weapons on them.

## CANNES

At a special screening of *Boyz* at the Cannes Film Festival, Singleton talked about the French response to the film. He said they loved the film; they gave him a standing ovation after it was screened. (The film was shown with subtitles for the French audience.) Singleton felt the film festival circuit is important to gain respect in the international market. It is also a good way to see the level of market interest in your film. The festival adds prestige to films. Singleton described it candidly as "pissing with the big dogs."

## SPIKE LEE

Singleton was 18 years old when he met Spike Lee at the Los Angeles premiere of *She's Gotta Have It***\*\*** (1986). Singleton was two weeks away from starting film school. He introduced himself to Lee and talked to him; their conversation made a strong impression on Singleton. That night, with the new typewriter he had gotten in preparation for college, he wrote Lee a letter telling how much he appreciated the film. At Cannes, Lee was there and they had dinner. Lee said he still had the letter. Singleton said he felt honored. Lee told him the story of having done the same to Ossie Davis, writing to him and saying that Lee was going to work with Davis some day. The circle continues. Singleton later wrote that he learned three things from Spike: "Stay Black, make good films, Stay Black" (*Essence*, November 1991).

## ICE CUBE

Ice Cube appeared with Singleton on the *Live from L.A. with Tanya Hart* and talked about his role in *Boyz*. Cube talked specifically about his preparation for the part of Doughboy in the film. Cube said the character was developed by adding some personal experience, some things from some of the guys he grew up with. As a person, Cube felt he could relate to everybody in the movie. The film was a slice of his own neighborhood. Reading the script got him interested for the first time in acting in films. He hadn't been interested in doing films previously, because he would not have control— unlike making records, where he was in control. He had met Singleton several years earlier at a Los Angeles rally held by the Nation of Islam that featured Minister Louis Farrakhan (the rally was called Save the Family). Singleton told Cube about the movie, and he shined it on. But once he read the script, he felt the part was really one he could do.

### Singleton on Ice Cube

Singleton explained that he chose Ice Cube for his film because he came from Los Angeles and his music reflected the Los Angeles experience. Singleton wanted to pick people who wouldn't distract from the focus of the film.

## VIOLENCE SURROUNDING *BOYZ*

After *Boyz* opened, there were several incidents of violence in and around theaters where the film was shown. Singleton was quick to respond. He said the violence was not a reflection of the film, but a reflection of the condition of African American existence. The condition of over 450 years of subjugation is really a continuation of the divide-and-conquer rule. He felt that the most dangerous Uncle Tom is a brother that would pose a threat to another brother. We must come together as a people because there are so many forces that are already working against Black people. Singleton can't turn his back on the violence because the people perpetuating the violence are his brothers and cousins, figuratively speaking.

## FILMOGRAPHY

### Producer/Director/Writer

*Boyz N The Hood,*** 1991, 107 min., 35mm, color, Columbia Pictures. Featuring rapper Ice Cube, whose song *Boyz N The Hood* inspired the film's director to use it as his film title. Additional key performers were Laurence Fishburne, Cuba Gooding

Jr., Nia Long, Angela Bassett, Morris Chestnut and Tyra Farrell.

The film made over $56 million in domestic box office receipts and over $100 million worldwide. The film cost $6 million for production. That's a 16:1 profit-to-cost ratio on a first feature film. The film had a 38-day production schedule and was shot on location in south central Los Angeles. It features a mostly Black cast with a large Black production crew as well. Singleton said, "The audience will be able to see the direction that characters take when there is an absence or presence of fathers in their lives" ("New Crop of Black Filmmakers," 1991).

Singleton became the youngest person nominated for an Academy Award and the *first* African American nominated for Academy Awards in the Best Director and Best Screenplay categories.

*Poetic Justice,*** 1993, 110 min., 35mm, color, Columbia Pictures. Singleton started writing this film while editing *Boyz*. He saw this film as a contrasting work to his freshman film effort. Whereas *Boyz* dealt primarily with issues of the African American male in contemporary society, for his second film he wanted to focus on the contemporary African American female. He felt it was important to tell the story of Black female experiences. The story is about a young woman named Justice who writes poetry (thus the title of the film). Janet Jackson of pop music fame plays the role of Justice. Her male romantic counterpoint, Lucky, is played by another pop musician, rap artist Tupac Shakur. The poetry Justice writes and recites in voiceover throughout the film is written by one of America's pre-eminent poets, Maya Angelou. Angelou also has a small part in the film. The film made $27 million in domestic box office receipts.

*Higher Learning*, 1995, 127 min., 35mm, Columbia Pictures. Featuring Laurence Fishburne, Omar Epps, Ice Cube, Tyra Banks, Kristy Swanson, Michael Rappaport, Jennifer Connally, Regina King and Jason Wiles. The story takes place at the fictional Columbus College. "The film is trying to tell everybody to wake up, look around and understand what we're doing to each other. It's just telling everybody to open up their eyes" (Evans 1995), Singleton said prior to the film's release. It earned over $24 million in domestic box office receipts.

## Director

### Music Videos

Michael Jackson, *Remember the Time*. The video featured Jackson, Eddie Murphy, black supermodel Iman and basketball great Magic Johnson.

## BIO-CRITICAL REVIEW

*Boyz N The Hood*. "Great narrative storytelling that captured the trials and choices young black men are confronted with. A feeling of wholeness to *Boyz*, as it tried to embrace several African-American impulses—ghettocentricity, nationalism, moralism."—Nelson George, *Blackface: Reflections on African-Americans and the Movies*

———. "A work that is exemplary. Does not pander to its audience. New and dynamic, socially realistic cinema."—George Hill and Spencer Moon, *Blacks in Hollywood: Five Favorable Years, 1987–1991*

*Higher Learning.* "A brilliant, powerful film with an important social message. Singleton's writing and direction along with fine performances by the cast make this a must-see film. *Higher Learning* rates an A."—Martin Evans, *Los Angeles Sentinel*

————. "Singleton remains a fluid filmmaker who works well with actors. His skill is evident. He may not be there yet, but he is on the road."—Kenneth Turan, *Los Angeles Times*

*Poetic Justice.* "Singleton goes far afield and delivers a love story, told largely from a woman's perspective. Demonstrates that Singleton is more than a one-shot wonder."—Edward Guthmann, *San Francisco Chronicle*

————. "Jackson and Shakur make an appealing enough couple. You can't miss the sense of this artist [Singleton] beginning to test his wings, reaching up from the dirty streets to touch the sky."—Scott Rosenberg, *San Francisco Examiner*

## EDUCATION

University of Southern California, B.A., filmic writing

## AWARDS

*Boyz N The Hood*
  Academy Award Nomination, Best Director, 1991
  Academy Award Nomination, Best Screenplay, 1991
  NAACP Image Award, Best Picture, Best Director, Best Screenplay, 1991
  New York Film Critics Award, Best New Director, 1991
  Writers Guild of America, Best Original Screenplay, Nominee, 1991

Singleton also received three University of Southern California awards for script writing. Two are Jack Nicholson Awards 1987 and 1988: Best Feature Length Screenplay, and Scholarship Award, 1987; The third is the Robert Riskin Award for Humanitarian Writing, 1989. The awards were for various scripts including *Boyz N The Hood.*

## PUBLICATIONS

John Singleton and Veronica Chambers, *Poetic Justice: Filmmaking South Central Style* (New York: Bantam Doubleday Dell, 1993).

## SOURCES

Interview by George Hill, April 1991.

## Books

George, Nelson. *Blackface: Reflections on African Americans and the Movies*. New York: HarperCollins, 1994.

Hill, George, and Spencer Moon. *Blacks in Hollywood: Five Favorable Years, 1987–1991*. Los Angeles: Daystar Publishing, 1991.

Kendell, Stephen D. *New Jack Cinema*. Silver Springs, MD: J.L. Denser, 1994.

Singleton, John, and Veronica Chambers. *Poetic Justice: Filmmaking South Central Style*. New York: Bantam Doubleday Dell, 1993.


## Magazines and Newspapers

Evans, Martin, "Higher Learning," *Los Angeles Sentinel*, January 7, 1995, pp. 32–33.

Guthmann, Edward, "Singleton, Jane Make Poetry." *San Francisco Chronicle*, January 10, 1995, pp. C1, C8.

"New Crop of Black Filmmakers Find Box Office Success." *Jet* (80), no. 15, July 29, 1991, p. 23.

Rosenberg, Scott, "Singleton's Talent Budding Not in Full Bloom." *San Francisco Examiner*, July 11, 1993, pp. D1, D5.

Turan, Kenneth, "L.A. Boyz Life." *Los Angeles Times*, January 10, 1995, pp. F1, F16.

Singleton, John, "With Spike." *Essence*, November 1991, pp. 64, 112.


## Television

*Live from L.A. with Tanya Hart* (BET Cable), September 1991.

*Screen Scene* (BET Cable), July 1991.

Arlando C. Smith

# ARLANDO C. SMITH

## BACKGROUND

When your work as a director for television is seen by literally almost a billion people, you know you've reached the Himalayas of television. When Arlando Smith was in Iowa learning his craft by directing children's programming for a local PBS station, he never imagined audiences all over the globe would one day see his work. But in 1990 he was the international director for the Goodwill Games, an awesome responsibility. He directed a crew of over one thousand production, engineering and technical personnel in a series of international broadcasts that reached nearly one billion people. More than sixty nations were reached by these Games over a two-week period; over twenty-five hundred athletes competed in twenty-one major sports events.

How do you come to direct this kind of event? Smith worked as stage manager and as associate director for a plethora of local and national productions over many years. This included a twelve-year period as stage manager for the Academy Awards broadcast, always one of the biggest live shows of the year in television. He felt his stint as stage manager and later as assistant director taught him his craft. He also described having worked as technical consultant in the production of *Live from L.A. with Tanya Hart* (BET Cable). He helped develop the show from concept to air. This included supervision of the design of the entire visual presentation of the show.

## GOODWILL GAMES

When asked to describe the highlight of his work on the Goodwill Games, he commented:

> I think the highlight was the fact that what I was doing was going to the entire world. I felt very proud about it. I'm one of the few directors who can do live television. It was a pleasant experience, and I'm very proud that they asked me to do it.

## EMMY WIN

Regarding the Emmy he won for his work on the Olympics two years earlier, he said:

> I was more surprised when I won it. The award was given in New York, and one of the producers called me in Los Angeles and said, "You won, you won," so that was quite a surprise. I said, "You're kidding!" He said, "No, I'm not." I said, "Oh, great!" I was very elated.

For the Olympics he worked essentially as director of the studio segments that preceded the live events. These segments were hosted by Bryant Gumbel (*Today*), with whom he had worked previously in the series *Games People Play*.

## DIRECTING

We asked him to describe how he works as a director for television in Hollywood.

> When I do situation comedies, I do them as if they were live shows. I don't worry about fixing it later. I direct and have the crew shoot so I get maximum coverage. I plan my work ahead so I can work quickly and efficiently.

This is a major consideration in Hollywood. Because of his expertise and ability, Smith has worked with four Black executive producers in Hollywood: Topper Carew, *Bustin' Loose* (synd.); Robert Guillaume, *Robert Guillaume Show* (ABC); Scooey Mitchell, *13 East* (NBC); and Michael Moye, *Married with Children* (FOX).

## PROTÉGÉE

He spoke with pride about a new protégée:

I was able to bring in a black female as my assistant director on the Goodwill Games—Lynn Harris, who also worked as my relief director, a high point in her career as well. She and I are essentially becoming a team. She did a recent pilot, *The Grudge Match*, with me and will go with me if it goes into production. She has done her homework in Washington, D.C., television production. She was prepared to come here. This is why I felt very comfortable in using her. She directed a lot of multiple camera stuff back there, so I knew that she knew what was going on in the control room.

## UNIQUENESS

He told us what makes him unique as a director:

Overall I'm very efficient, very fast; I go for the interesting camera shots, plus technically understand how everything works. When I prepare the show to shoot it, I set it up so I don't waste time later in production. Ninety-five percent of what I plan usually works later in production. A lot of directors don't understand how television works. I've had experience on all levels of television production. I have directed essentially all different formats of television—situation comedies, news, sports, game shows, pageants, variety, awards shows. Most people specialize in one area. I do them all. Every show I do, I'm excited about it.

## ADVICE FOR ASPIRANTS

He gave us his suggestions to current and aspiring stage managers, assistant directors and students:

I firmly believe that if you want to be in the business, you start in a small market. Because that's where you get your hands-on experience. So that you really learn the ins and outs of the business. I think that's really important. You have to be prepared. Preparedness comes out in the long run. Longevity comes when you can handle essentially any situation, when it's nothing new to you. I had six years of directing when I became a stage manager and assistant director in Hollywood. The thing I had to learn when I came to Los Angeles working in situation comedies was directing comedy; sitcoms were a completely different animal to me. Directors should start as stage managers and then become assistant directors. Then they understand and are not very impatient in the booth, saying, "Well, why isn't this or that happening?" Because you know what the process is.

## THE FUTURE

We discussed his aspirations for the future:

I would like to do a drama, but right now I'm very happy. I like doing the "multiple camera live" or "live to tape"; that's really what I like to do. I would like to do features, but it takes so long. I prefer fast-paced stuff. That's exciting to me; that's where the adrenaline goes for me.

## FILMOGRAPHY

### Director

### *Episodic Television*

*Bustin' Loose*, MCA, synd.; *Games People Play*, NBC; *Generations*, NBC; *Robert Guillaume Show*, ABC; *Homeroom*, ABC; *It's Your Move*, NBC; *The Jeffersons*, CBS; *Married with Children*, FOX; *My Brother and Me*, Nickelodeon; *NBC Nightly News, Sportsworld*, NBC; *227*, NBC; *13 East*, NBC; *She's the Sheriff*, Lorimar, synd.; *What's Happening Now*, Columbia, synd.

### *Television Specials*

*Summer Olympics*, NBC; *Goodwill Games*, TBS; *Alvin Goes Back to School*, NBC; *American Dream Festival*, NBC; *National Football League and National Hockey League*, FOX. Smith has worked as coordinating director for FOX network feeds to affiliates and studio segments since 1994.

## WORK

Since 1993, Smith has been an adjunct faculty member at the University of Southern California. He instructs the following courses: "Directing Multiple-Camera Situation Comedy," and "Introduction to Multiple-Camera Production."

## AWARDS

*Summer Olympics*
Emmy Award, Sports Programming, 1988

*227*
Luminas Award, Directing, 1985

## SOURCES

Interview by George Hill and Spencer Moon, January 1991; follow-up interview, Spencer Moon, June 1995.

# ROBERT TOWNSEND

## BACKGROUND

Robert Townsend's ambitions led him to join a theater group of Black actors in his hometown. At age 16 he was the youngest member of a group called EXBAG (Experimental Black Actors Guild). Additional experience and training came in the Second City improvisation group. (Second City is most famous for providing many of the cast members of the original *Saturday Night Live* television program.) Townsend started college in Chicago at Illinois State University. His talent earned him work in two feature films being shot in the area. The first was *Cooley High*** (1975), directed by Michael Schultz.* Schultz saw Townsend performing in local theater, liked what he saw and offered him a small role in the film. The second role was in another film shot in Chicago, *Willie and Phil* (1980). Townsend later moved to New Jersey to continue his undergraduate study at Hunter College. While in New Jersey he also commuted to New York to study and work with the Negro Ensemble Company. Townsend's talent landed him work within the first week of being in New York. He obtained a recurring role on a public television series, *Watch Your Mouth*, as an aristocratic African prince. His penchant for comedy brought him work in nightclubs doing stand-up, sometimes alongside Eddie Murphy. They both auditioned for *Saturday Night Live*, and Murphy got the job. Townsend continued his training as an actor and studied with Stella Adler.

Townsend acted as an extra in films; had bit parts in *Mahogany* (1975) and *The Wiz* (1978); acted off-Broadway with Ruby Dee and Ossie Davis in a play entitled *Take It from the Top*; and did commercials. His work on national television commercials enabled him to buy video equipment, which he used to record himself practicing his craft.

In 1982 Townsend moved to Los Angeles and landed a role in the feature film *Streets of Fire* (1984). His movie roles enabled him to learn more about the filmmaking process and its techniques. He began to save money. Then he took a bigger gamble than his move to New York: He used a variety of credit cards and his savings and invested the money in his first feature film. Acting was always a means to an end for Townsend; in 1987, one year after Spike Lee* burst on the Hollywood and American scene with *She's Gotta Have It** (1986), Townsend produced, directed, co-wrote and featured in his debut film, *Hollywood Shuffle* (1987).

As a writer of films, Townsend wants to entertain, amuse and provide a message. His inspiration comes from people like Oscar Micheaux,* whose courage and independence fueled his own courage during an even more difficult period for African American filmmakers. Townsend felt if Micheaux could deal with the odds of his day, then he (Townsend) could do it. Townsend also found inspiration in the talent and work of Melvin Van Peebles,* Francis Ford Coppola, Elia Kazan and screenwriter Budd Schulberg. Townsend sees his comedy style as a mix of Richard Pryor and Bill Cosby.

## FILMOGRAPHY

### Writer/Actor/Director

*Hollywood Shuffle,** 1987, 35mm, color, Samuel Goldwyn. Written by Townsend and Keenan Ivory Wayans.* A satire on the experience of Black actors in a Hollywood system that treats them with disdain. Through a variety of scenes we see one Bobby Taylor (Townsend) go through the maze of cattle-call type auditions. Taylor's fantasies of playing roles usually reserved for White actors provide some funny parodies: a Black action hero, a Black detective, Black movie critics à la Siskel and Ebert, and even a tale of the South and Reconstruction. The comedy is funny and incisive; it takes the sting out of what must surely be a bleak and depressing experience for Black talent in Hollywood, trying to find work that isn't stereotypical in nature and substance. A primer for aspiring Black actors.

### Director

*Eddie Murphy Raw,** 1988, 35mm, color. Shot during a series of New York City comedy concerts by Murphy. Ernest Dickerson (*Juice,** 1992) was director of cinematography using six Panavision cameras. Murphy asked Townsend to direct this concert film because of their friendship formed earlier through shared times in comedy clubs. This film grossed $50 million.

*The Five Heartbeats,*\*\* 1991, 121 min., 35mm, color, 20th Century Fox. Written by Townsend and Keenan Ivory Wayans.\* The film is an obvious labor of love. Townsend spent time talking with Black male pop vocal groups as part of his research. He spoke with members of The Dells, who have a four-decade history of music making. Their story, and the story of survival against the odds of groups like The Temptations and The Four Tops, are part of the inspiration for this musical dramedy.

The story follows The Five Heartbeats, who are seen over several decades in their rise from amateur talent shows and many months doing one-night road shows to making records and winning fame and fortune. The cast included Diahann Carroll, Harold Nicholas (of the Nicholas Brothers), Troy Beyer, Michael Wright, Chuck Patterson, Leon, Harry J. Lennix, Tico Wells and John Canada Terrell, along with Townsend himself. The soundtrack is a tuneful homage to the soulful sounds of Black music of the sixties.

The film barely made back its original $10 million budget. Stephen Kendell in *New Jack Cinema* (1994) cites a recurring problem with Black-cast films: "The box-office failure of the film because of a poor marketing campaign."

*Meteor Man,*\*\* 1993, 100 min., 35mm, color, MGM. The intent of this film was to present inner-city children with a Black superhero. The film's content and intent are of historic importance because this type of film had not been done before specifically for young Black audiences. Townsend's message is ultimately about the importance of self-reliance. The film featured Townsend as the everyman superhero. The featured supporting cast included Marla Gibbs, Eddie Griffen, Robert Guillaume, James Earl Jones and Bill Cosby.

### Television

*The Parent-Hood.* Over thirty episodes of this half-hour sitcom have been produced since 1995. It has been the number-one rated program for the WB (Warner Bros.) network since it premiered. Townsend is executive producer, creator and star. The series is about two Black parents trying to raise two children in the nineties. The series is an outgrowth of Townsend's own home life (he is married with two children).

### Director/Writer/Producer

*Townsend Television,* FOX. A sketch comedy series, a hodgepodge of ideas that included satire, drama, musical variety and Black music artists such as Ice Cube and James Brown.

*Partners in Crime,* HBO. A sketch comedy series.

### Actor

#### Selected Films

*The Mighty Quinn,* 1988; *Ratboy,* 1986; *American Flyers,* 1985; *A Soldier's Story,* 1984; *Streets of Fire,* 1982; *Willie and Phil,* 1980; *Cooley High,* 1976.

### Selected Television Roles

*Uptown Comedy Express*, HBO, 1986; Rodney Dangerfield's *It's Not Easy Being Me*, HBO, 1987; *Showtime's Comic of the Month*, Showtime, 1989; *An Evening at The Improv*, A&E Cable, 1990. This list does not include several national commercials in which Townsend has been featured.

## BIO-CRITICAL REVIEW

*Eddie Murphy Raw.* "Be prepared to laugh. *Raw* gets a B."—Alan Bell, *Los Angeles Sentinel*

*The Five Heartbeats.* "It's too joyful and heartfelt to fault."—Arion Berger, *Los Angeles Weekly*

————. "Charm, rhythm and good-naturedness that is hard to resist."—Jeff Menell, *Hollywood Reporter*

————. "A rich, textured portrait of Black music-making in the sixties."—Alan Bell, *Los Angeles Sentinel*

————. "Conveys an obvious love of its material and a fundamental sweetness and sincerity."—Janet Maslin, *New York Times*

*Hollywood Shuffle.* "An irreverent, hilarious look at Hollywood moviemaking from an aspiring black actor's point of view."—Cynthia Griffen, *Wave Newspapers*

————. "Will be topical for quite a while."—*Crow*

*Meteor Man.* "Undeniably earnest, it is hard to hate."—Alex Patterson, *Eye Weekly*

## EDUCATION

Hunter College, New York, B.A., drama

## SOURCES

### Books

Harris, Erich Leon. *African American Screen Writers Now: Conversations with Hollywood's Black Pack.* Los Angeles: Silman-James Press, 1996.
Kendell, Stephen D. *New Jack Cinema.* Silver Springs, MD: J.L. Denser, 1994.

### Newspapers and Magazines

Bell, Alan. "*Five Heartbeats,*" *Los Angeles Sentinel*, April 11, 1991, p. B6.
————. "*Hollywood Shuffle,*" *Los Angeles Sentinel*, December 31, 1987, p. B10.
Berger, Arion. "High Five," *Los Angeles Weekly*, April 11, 1991, p. 25.
Griffen, Cynthia. "*Hollywood Shuffle,*" *Wave Newspapers* (Los Angeles), June 1987, p. 17.

*"Hollywood Shuffle," Crow*, no. 25 (July 1988), p. 15.
Menell, Jeff. *"The Five Heartbeats," Hollywood Reporter*, March 25, 1991, p. 49.
Patterson, Alex. *"Meteor Man," Eye Weekly* (Toronto), May 12, 1993, p. 32.

## Other

*Internet Movie Database*, Biloxi: University of Mississippi, 1996.

# MARIO VAN PEEBLES

## BACKGROUND

Mario Van Peebles describes his parents in the book *Panther: A Pictorial History of the Black Panthers and the Story behind the Film* (1995): "two non-conformist, nonmaterialistic, interracial, avant-garde, crazy-ass parents who made an in-your-face art of kicking down almost any racist or sexist barriers placed before them." Mario traveled the world as a young child, from Mexico (where he was born) to Morocco, Amsterdam and Paris.

Mario grew up in Europe, but his family eventually settled in the San Francisco Bay Area. Young Mario was acting by age 8, making his debut in a local production of *A Thousand Clowns*. As a young teen he made his screen debut in his father's ground-breaking film *Sweet Sweetback's Baadasssss Song*** (1971). His German-born mother taught him her avocation, photography. Taking his photography skills, and using self-portraits and his natural good looks and personality, Mario worked as a model for the famous Ford Agency. His father instilled in him early the need to know the business side of show business. An economics degree led him for a time to work in the office of New York City mayor Edward Koch as a budget analyst. After studying acting with Stella Adler, the pull of show business eventually saw him take to the boards off-Broadway. His turns in theater led to film roles as actor; later, working with his father on a variety of projects in theater, film and television, he eventually landed in the director's chair for both film and television.

## FILM DIRECTING

His debut as film director was very auspicious. *New Jack City*\*\* created a firestorm of controversy within the first week of its opening. There was violence attendant to several of its nationwide screenings. The violence led to the usual chicken-and-egg routine: Do films with violence cause violence, or is it inherent in a violent society? The net result was widespread publicity surrounding the film and its content and intent.

In a *New York Times* Op-Ed page, Mario and Melvin Van Peebles\* exchanged letters to each other regarding this violence and its implications for African American films and filmmakers working through the Hollywood system. Melvin put the whole thing in perspective with his usual sage wisdom. His own film, *Sweet Sweetback's Baadasssss Song*, originally could not find distribution. When Melvin himself put the film in two theaters (one in Detroit and one in Atlanta) and people bought tickets in droves, Hollywood came knocking. They came for the love of money. As Melvin adroitly puts it, "Hollywood isn't as much black and white as it is ultra-green" (Van Peebles 1995). Despite bad publicity, the film *New Jack City* became an international box office hit.

Mario not only knows from whence he came but is very clear about where he's going. He said in an *EM* magazine article (1995), "As a director I've made the films I have to make. As an actor I've made the films I want to make." Pretty clear thinking, but you'd expect no less from the son of the now-legendary Black film maven Melvin Van Peebles. In their various projects together as father and son, Mario puts things in proper perspective when he says, "I'm dealing with the person who changed my diapers. We're two different filmmakers, but I think that is healthy" (Van Peebles and Van Peebles 1990). In the book *No Identity Crisis* (1990), Mario says of his father, "His method of working is a revelation from which I have gained many valuable lessons."

## HIS FATHER HONORED

Mario was present with his mother for the Directors Guild of America African American Steering Committee salute to his father and his contributions to cinema at a special event in Los Angeles in March 1996.

## FILMOGRAPHY

### Scriptwriter

*Identity Crisis*,\*\* 1991, 98 min., 35mm, color, Academy Entertainment Release. This film managed to somehow escape. No distributor could be found for its theatrical release, so Melvin (who directed and produced the film) found a video distributor. The film is billed as an action comedy: the low-impact variety of action and the silly, funny, bizarre and outrageous school of comedy.

The story is about one Chilly D (played by Mario), a street hustler who manages to get involved in the fashion and design business through a mix-up. Yves, a fashion designer, is in financial trouble with his fashion house; his brother and some Middle Eastern businessmen want to wrest control from him. Chilly D is always a day late and a dollar short with his street cons. By accident Chilly D, while escaping from some street toughs he has crossed, manages to fall a couple of stories and survive. When he wakes up he has assumed the identity of Yves, who is dead by now from the handiwork of his brother and his thuggies. Given the inevitable mix-up of Mario as Yves, and then with blows to the head and sometimes back as Chilly D, you have your identity crisis.

### Director

*New Jack City*,** 1991, 97 min., 35mm, color, Warner Brothers. Produced by George Jackson* and Doug McHenry.* Produced for $8.5 million; shot in the Bronx and Harlem. The film grossed over $100 million worldwide including videocassette sales. *New Jack City* opened in over eight hundred theaters; two dropped out after violence attendant to several openings during its first week of release. Another sixty picked it up after the violence.

*Posse*,** 1992, 110 min., 35mm, color, Polygram Pictures. Featuring Mario Van Peebles, Stephen Baldwin, Charles Lane, Tiny Lister Jr., Big Daddy Kane, Tone Loc, Richard Jordan, Billy Zane and Blair Underwood, with cameos by Melvin Van Peebles,* Isaac Hayes, Pam Grier, Woody Strode, Robert Hooks and Nipsey Russell. Mario was executive producer of the film's soundtrack and wrote one of the songs performed by the artist Vesta, who is also featured in the film. The film grossed over $20 million.

*Panther*, 1995, 123 min., 35mm, color, Gramercy Pictures. Budget was $9.5 million. The dramatic retelling of the story of the Black Panther Party. Revolutionaries, gangsters, gun possession advocates before the militia movements, community activists, victims—the Panthers were all of those things and none of them. This film adds to the mystery, mystique, legend and folk-hero status they achieved. When Melvin completed the novel on which the film is based, young Mario offered his praise and support. When Mario the director got the opportunity, he knew this story was one he wanted to tell on film.

### *Episodic Television*

*21 Jump Street*, FOX; *Top of the Hill*, CBS; *Wiseguy*, CBS; *Sonny Spoon*, NBC.

In *Sonny Spoon*, Mario starred as a private detective with a mastery of many disguises. His father, Melvin, later joined the short-lived series as—what else—his dad in the series. The series producer, Stephen Cannell, let Mario work as director for several episodes. "Shows us how a Black street hustler who has gone to college uses his brain and not brawn to solve his cases" (Hill and Moon, *Blacks in Hollywood*, 1991).

### Television Special

*Malcolm Takes a Shot*, CBS After-School Special.

### Actor (Selected Roles)

### Films

*Solo*, 1996, made in association with Van Peebles Films *Highlander III*,** 1995; *Gunmen*,** 1994, Mario also served as executive soundtrack album producer; *Posse*,** 1994; *New Jack City*,** 1991; *Identity Crisis*,** 1991; *Jaws: The Revenge*,** 1987; *Heartbreak Ridge*,** 1986, Mario wrote and performed three songs on the film's soundtrack; *Exterminator II*,** 1984; *Rappin'*,** 1985, Mario wrote eight songs for this film; *Sweet Sweetback's Baadasssss Song*,** 1971; *Sonny Spoon*, 1989.

### Television

*Stomping at the Savoy*, CBS; *Full Eclipse*, HBO; *Triumph of the Heart: The Ricky Bell Story*, CBS; *In the Line of Duty: Street War*, NBC; *Third and Oak: The Pool Hall*, A&E Cable; *The Child Saver*, NBC; *The Emperor Jones*, PBS; *L.A. Law*, NBC; *Essence*, synd., co-host; *Children of the Night*, CBS.

## BIO-CRITICAL REVIEW

*New Jack City.* "A shrewdly designed, produced, directed and marketed piece of commercial filmmaking."—Nelson George, *Blackface: Reflections on African Americans and the Movies*

————. "First-time director Mario Van Peebles and cameraman Francis Kenny have done wonders with this material, making it almost enjoyable."—Alan Bell, *Los Angeles Sentinel*

————. "This movie may say more about the uneven distribution of wealth in America than the last five years of the Congressional Record."—John Powers, *Los Angeles Weekly*

*Posse.* "A direct, straightforward and entertaining story of people fighting for autonomy and the dream of a better life."—Mick LaSalle, *San Francisco Chronicle*

————. "It never loses its grinning good humor, its revisionist drive, its shoot-the-works spirit."—Michael Wilmington, *Los Angeles Times*

————. "It's nice to see real-life black cowboys materialized in reel-life."—David Armstrong, *San Francisco Examiner*

————. "Part entertainment, part history lesson."—Janet Maslin, *New York Times*

## PUBLICATIONS

Mario Van Peebles, Ula Y. Taylor and J. Tarika Lewis, *Panther: A Pictorial History of the Black Panthers and the Story behind the Film*. Prologue by Melvin Van Peebles (New York: New Market Press, 1995).

Mario Van Peebles and Melvin Van Peebles, *No Identity Crisis: A Father and Son's Own Story of Working Together* (New York: Simon & Schuster, 1990).

## EDUCATION

Columbia University, B.A., economics

## SELECTED AWARDS

*Children of the Night*
  Bronze Halo Award, 1986
*Heartbreak Ridge*
  NAACP Image Award, 1987
*Malcolm Takes a Shot*
  Directors Guild of America, Nomination, Best Dramatic Show, Daytime, 1990
*Posse*
  Black Academy Award Nominees Dinner, Special Recognition Award, Director/
  Actor, 1990
*Third and Oak: The Pool Hall*
  Ace Award Nomination, Best Actor, 1993

## SOURCES

### Books

George, Nelson. *Blackface: Reflections on African Americans and the Movies.* New York: HarperCollins, 1994.
Hill, George, and Spencer Moon. *Blacks in Hollywood: Five Favorable Years, 1987–1991.* Los Angeles: Daystar Press, 1991.
Katz, Ephraim. *The Film Encyclopedia.* New York: HarperCollins, 1994.
McNeil, Alex. *Total Television Including Cable.* New York: Penguin Books, 1991.
Van Peebles, Mario, and Melvin Van Peebles. *No Identity Crisis: A Father and Son's Own Story of Working Together.* New York: Simon & Schuster, 1990.
Van Peebles, Mario, Ula Y. Taylor and J. Tarika Lewis. *Panther: A Pictorial History of the Black Panthers and the Story behind the Film.* Prologue by Melvin Van Peebles. New York: New Market Press, 1995.

### Newspapers and Magazines

Armstrong, David. "*Posse* Saddled with Conventions," *San Francisco Examiner*, May 5, 1993, p. C3.
Bell, Alan. "*New Jack City* Blaxploitation Film," *Los Angeles Sentinel*, March 14, 1991, p. B9.

LaSalle, Mick. "Mario Van Peebles *Boyz N* the Range," *San Francisco Chronicle*, March 14, 1993, p. D4.

Maslin, Janet. "Where Often Is Heard a Discouraging Word," *New York Times*, May 14, 1993, p. C3.

———. "Cop vs. Crack as Done by Mario Van Peebles," *New York Times*, March 8, 1996, p. C6.

Powers, John. "Old Pulp in New Bottles," *Los Angeles Weekly*, March 8, 1991, p. 27.

Wilmington, Michael. "*Posse*: A New Take on the Old West," *Los Angeles Times*, March 14, 1993, pp. F1, F15.

"Mario Van Peebles: Top-Notch Actor-Director in Hollywood," *EM* (Chicago), August 1995, p. 64.

"Mario Van Peebles Stars in Action Adventure 'Solo'," *Jet* (Chicago), August 26, 1996, p. 32.

"For 'New Jack City,' It's the Same Old Story," *New York Times*, March 31, 1991, p. B3.

# MELVIN VAN PEEBLES

## BACKGROUND

The elder Van Peebles, Melvin, has been referred to by *Intellectual Digest* as "umbrageous" and by *Cineaste* magazine as "a Badass Gent and a resistance fighter." He calls himself the godfather of independent Black cinema during the modern era. He was the first Black director to work in Hollywood with his first Hollywood-financed film, *Watermelon Man*** (1970).

## GALLERY OF GREATS

Our initial interview took place in Los Angeles in 1990. Van Peebles and ten other independent Black filmmakers were being inducted into the *Gallery of Greats* series produced by Miller Brewing Company. This series of portraits joins a group of other Blacks in America and the world who have contributed to Black survival and society as a whole. The *Gallery of Greats* program began in 1974. Calendars and other items with portraits on them are sold, and proceeds go to the Thurgood Marshall Education Fund. In 1990, the first group of independent Black filmmakers was so honored. Van Peebles was candid:

> The advantage of the calendar is the audience it reaches. Many times the accolades are among peers, but your work is really for the man on the street. The calendar reaches those people. I've been buying these calendars for years. This is super.

Melvin Van Peebles. *Photo courtesy of Shelley R. Bonus.*

When asked whether he was surprised when he received this honor, he replied:

> Yes and no, if they were going to do one about Black filmmakers. Even to myself it is quite obvious that I have a very pivotal role in the modern Black film industry. Sorta' the James Brown of filmmaking. I'm all for it—not for personal reasons, but it is very important that we see history. Without history we make those same mistakes over and over. In terms of filmmaking, I could not be more gratified at the reception I've received at the hands of the other young Black film-makers. Not that it's for myself per se, but them being aware of the steps and struggle that were made. I remember when I made *Water-melon Man*, I hired Mantan Moreland (Black actor in the thirties to fifties in Hollywood). A guy who had long been forgotten. It was a great opportunity.
>
> The young filmmakers have understood the trajectory. Understood what *Story of a Three Day Pass* (1967), *Watermelon Man* (1970) and *Sweet Sweetback* . . . (1971) did. It's phenomenal, so it's very pleasant.

## TALKING TO THE NEXT GENERATION

When asked what his interaction has been with young Black filmmakers, he said:

> They've called, some of them many times, seeking advice when they were moving in the business and wanted to get a straight answer.

He went on to talk about how his role in modern independent Black cinema is recognized by the man in the street.

> I was stopped by a young Black writer. He said, "You don't know me, but I just wanted to say you inspired me to get into the business. I'm writing scripts and commercials." I think mainly what happened is they saw that someone who was very close to their cultural base had done it. I was in despair as I thought the message of *Sweetback* . . . —that you could do it yourself—had been lost. But it turns out my peers didn't believe what they saw. The next two generations—that included the Hudlin brothers,* Spike Lee,* Charles Lane and St. Claire Bourne*—tell me they saw *Sweetback* . . . and said, "Man, that film made me want to make movies." They saw that you could do it before they were taught you couldn't do it. It shows me how important the positive image of someone else doing it is. Especially how important it is that it happens at a very early age.

I'm very political, you understand. I don't see anything outside of its political, historic context. Take my first feature, *Story of a Three Day Pass* (1967). I think of that film as the wedge I was able to drive as the French delegate to the San Francisco International Film Festival to gain entry into Hollywood. Ninety percent of my feelings about my films have nothing to do with the artistic or creative part of them at all. *Watermelon Man*, for example, was the first time a Black director had directed a film in Hollywood. Ossie Davis and Gordon Parks entered the Hollywood system about that same time, but their films were shot on location, not in Hollywood. I think of the unions I made break color lines and hire minorities. I've never had the luxury to look at my films as art. I was on a different quest. *Sweetback* . . . proved that there was a Black audience. The film possibilities without any input from the White power structure. I don't divorce any of my work from politics.

The film that established Melvin as a power to be reckoned with was *Sweet Sweetback's Baadasssss Song* (1971). It was the first contemporary Black film to reach mass audiences and achieve financial success without financial backing from major Hollywood sources. It was independently distributed originally.

## RENAISSANCE MAN

In addition to *Panther* the book and film, Van Peebles has released an album of music (1995). This is his eighth album, and the first in almost twenty years. The album, entitled *Ghetto Gothic*, in a *Rolling Stone* review is called

Strangely beautiful, hipster funk from an irrefutable font of cool. Melvin waxes deep, randy and blue. The craftsman earns his keep through his expertise, but the artist invents his job.

*Brer Soul* (A&M, 1967) was Melvin's first album. According to Timothy White of *Billboard*, it has historic importance because of its musical content, which "presaged rap music."

Besides music, Van Peebles continues his work in theater. He had a one-man performance on Broadway in 1991. He felt his first play, *Ain't Supposed to Die a Natural Death*—which he wrote, produced, directed, scored and acted in—did for legitimate theater what *Sweetback* . . . did for film.

He became the first Black commodities exchange broker on the New York Stock Exchange in 1983 and for several years was senior partner in Van

Peebles & Hayes Municipal Securities, an investment banking firm. He describes this in his book *Bold Money* (1986).

He is candid on his many successes:

> Somebody once asked me, "Melvin, how did you get to the top?" It was simple: Nobody would let me in at the bottom.

The Museum of Modern Art in New York City and the Sundance Film Institute have held major retrospectives of Melvin's feature films. While in Los Angeles for the *Gallery of Greats* calendar, he accepted a cameo appearance in Charles Lane's film *True Identity*** (1991). Lane was also part of the *Gallery of Greats* calendar.

## ON MARIO

When asked how he felt about his son Mario's involvement in film, he said he was absolutely proud of his son. "He's not borrowing money from me." They have worked together on numerous projects, including eighteen episodes of a game show called *Family Figures* (BET Cable).

## FILMOGRAPHY

### Producer/Director

*Sunlight*, 1958, short subject, 8mm.

*Three Pickup Men for Herrick*, 1958, short subject, 8mm.

Melvin made several other short films in 1958 with Allen Willis.*

### Producer/Director/Original Story/Script

*Story of a Three Day Pass*,** 1967, 35mm, b/w, Sigma III—A Filmways Company. Van Peebles began his career in serious filmmaking with this film. It was based on his original story (published in French) and shot in France. At the invitation of the then director of the San Francisco International Film Festival, Albert Johnson, Melvin (an American) came to San Francisco as a French film delegate. The film is an examination of interracial romance from a Black perspective.

Quite different from *Guess Who's Coming to Dinner?* (1967), this is an open and comic portrayal of two people who are caught up in their own racial fantasies and those of society. In three days they almost come to see each other as real people, if that's possible in a three-day love affair. The woman resolves her feelings about their separation by becoming sick. The man just falls back to earth, with his comic book in hand, back at the barracks letting time go by. No moral or social indignation here, just two people affected by society and injustice but willing to go on from their shared experiences, a bit wiser. A poignant work, honest and very funny.

### Director/Music Score

*Watermelon Man,*** 1970, 100 min., 35mm, Columbia. The film created history, with Melvin being the first Black feature-film director in Hollywood. The script, by Herman Raucher, follows a bigoted White man who through a freak accident becomes Black. The film stars Godfrey Cambridge, one of the Black community's first comics-turned-actors of the modern era who achieved some degree of success prior to the Eddie Murphy phenomenon. The film has appearances by two other notable Black actors: Mantan Moreland, who featured in films from the thirties, and D'Urville Martin, a star and director of films later in the Black cinema wave of the seventies.

### Director/Script/Music Score/Actor (Lead)

*Sweet Sweetback's Baadasssss Song,* 1971, 97 min., 35mm, Cinemation Releasing. Melvin also wrote a book on the making of this film. *Sweet Sweetback* . . . was the first bona fide financial success in independent Black cinema in the modern era. Production costs were $500,000. It grossed over $4 million in domestic rentals. It set off the Black cinema wave of the seventies, with other films such as *Shaft* and *Cotton Comes to Harlem* by Gordon Parks* and Ossie Davis, respectively.

### Co-Author

*Greased Lightning,*** 1977, 35mm. A feature film starring Richard Pryor; directed by Michael Schultz.*

### Producer/Director/Script/Actor

*Don't Play Us Cheap,* 1972, 95 min., 35mm, no distributor. Melvin's third feature film was a film version of his play by the same name, a successful Broadway production. He wrote, directed and was featured in both the film and the play. The film was screened in festivals and had some limited theatrical exhibitions but never received distribution.

### Producer/Director/Actor

*Identity Crisis,* 1991, 98 min., 35mm, color, Academy Entertainment Release. Written by and starring Mario Van Peebles* as Chilly D. Melvin described the problem of getting distribution for this film. He could not strike a deal that he was happy with for distribution through normal Hollywood channels, so to get it into the market at all he distributed the work through the video market.

*Vroom, Vroom, Vroom,* 1993, 35mm. A short subject; an experimental fantasy film.

## Co-Producer/Script

*Panther,*** 1995, 35mm. Co-produced by Preston Holmes, Mario Van Peebles and Melvin Van Peebles; directed by Mario Van Peebles; Gramercy Pictures. The story of the rise of the Black Panther Party. It is based on Melvin's novel *Panthers*.

> The response was very expected. I expected the response that the novel, on which it is based, got as well. Outside the United States it won three prizes in the Locarno Film Festival in Switzerland. It won the Young People's Prize, the Silver Leopard (the second Prize Overall) and the Religious Award for its humanity. People who have control of the mainstream mass media in the United States did not see this film as representing the public sentiment. I feel pretty well received despite that response. In Europe they were not asked to give up their fairy tales, because they had no fairy tales on various of these issues. It could be much more easily absorbed for the reality that it portrayed.

## Author

### Television

*Just an Old Sweet Song*, 1976, 78 min., color, ABC. Van Peebles wrote the teleplay only.

*Sophisticated Gents*, 1981, 200 min., color, NBC. Van Peebles was also an associate producer on the program. He wrote the teleplay based on John A. Williams's novel *The Junior Bachelor Society*. The television miniseries featured an excellent mostly Black cast, including Robert Hooks, Dick Anthony Williams, Paul Winfield, Rosalind Cash, Janet Du'Bois, Beah Richards, Alfre Woodard, Ron O'Neal, Raymond St. Jacques, Thalmus Rasulala, Rosie Grier, Bernie Casey, Denise Nicholas, Janet MacLachan and Melvin Van Peebles. The music was by jazz great Benny Golson and featured a song written by Melvin Van Peebles.

*The Day They Came to Arrest the Book*, 1989, color, CBS. Van Peebles wrote the script only. An examination of censorship issues.

*Down Home*, CBS *Split Second*, HBO.

## Actor

### Film

*O.C. and Stiggs*, 1987; *Jaws the Revenge*, 1987, Melvin co-starred with son Mario; *True Identity*, 1991; *Boomerang*, 1992; *Posse*, 1993; *Last Action Hero*, 1994; *Terminal Velocity*, 1994; *Fist of the North Star*, 1995, *Panther*, 1995.

### Television

*Dream On*, NBC; *Heat of the Night*, NBC; *Sophisticated Gents*, NBC; *Wonderworks: Taking Care of Terrific*, PBS; *Sonny Spoon*, 1989, NBC.

The *Sonny Spoon* series featured Mario Van Peebles as a private investigator named

Sonny Spoon. He occasionally wrote and directed some episodes. Melvin occasionally played Sonny Spoon's father on the show.

### *Plays*

Van Peebles also wrote, produced, directed and scored music for these works.

*Ain't Supposed to Die a Natural Death*, 1971. The subject is life on ghetto streets; a musical.

*Don't Play Us Cheap*, 1972. A comedy about life in Harlem that featured gospel and blues idioms.

*Kickin' the Science*. A one-man show off-Broadway.

*Out There by Your Lonesome*, 1973. A one-man tour.

*Bodybags*, 1981. Director only.

*Waltz of the Stork*, 1982. Featuring his son, Mario Van Peebles.

*Champeen*, 1983.


## BIO-CRITICAL REVIEW

*Sweet Sweetback's Baadasssss Song.* "*Sweetback's* unitary drama is so existentially rooted that it is difficult to see how his anger can work politically. He (Van Peebles) adds that Sweetback himself is a role model, one of the first. Sweetback teaches the lesson of survival. . . . These protagonists triumph in the history of black film because they are rooted in reality."—James Monaco, *American Film Now: Updated*

———. "We're appalled at the filth, degradation, distortion and almost total negativism of "Sweet-back . . ." both as a movie and social statement to black people."—James P. Murray, *Black Creation*


## PUBLICATIONS

Includes some French titles, many translated to English.

*Ain't Supposed to Die a Natural Death* (New York: Bantam, 1973). A play.

*Un Americain en efer* (*The True American: A Folk Fable*) (New York: Editions Denoel, 1976). A novel.

*A Bear for the FBI* (New York: Pocket, 1969). A novel.

*Bold Money* (New York: Warner Books, 1986). A business-world guide to the ins and outs of options trading.

*Le Chinois du XIV* (Paris: Le Gardenet, 1966). Short stories.

*Don't Play Us Cheap; A Harlem Party* (New York: Bantam, 1973). Basis of play.

*La Fête à Harlem* (Paris: Martineu, 1967). A novel.

*Just an Old Sweet Song*, 1976. A novel.

*The Making of "Sweet Sweetback's Baadasssss Song"* (New York: Lancer Books, 1971). Adapted from the film.

*No Identity Crisis*. Co-authored with son Mario (New York: Simon & Schuster, 1990). On the making of the film *Identity Crisis*.

*Un Ours pour le F.B.I.* (*A Bear for the FBI*) (Paris: Bouchet-Chalet, 1964). A novel.

*Panther* (New York: Thunder's Mouth Press, 1995). Basis of the film *Panther*.

*La Permission* (*Story of a Three Day Pass*) (Paris, 1967). A novel; 1967 film is based on this story.

## ALBUMS

*Brer' Soul* (A&M), 1967

*Watermelon Man* (soundtrack) (Colgems), 1968

*Ain't Supposed to Die a Natural Death* (A&M), 1969

*Serious As a Heart Attack* (A&M), 1971

*Sweet Sweetback's Baadasssss Song* (soundtrack) (Stax), 1971

*Don't Play Us Cheap* (cast album) (Stax), 1973

*What The. . . . #*!% You Mean, I Can't Sing* (Atlantic), 1974

*Ghetto Gothic* (Capitol), 1995

## SINGLES

*The Apple Stretching*

*Greased Lightning*

*Identity Crisis*

*La permission*

*Like It Like Dat*

*My Love Belongs to You*

*Spanish Dream*

*That Same Old Raggedy Song*

## SELECTED AWARDS

AUDELCO Award, *Champeen*, 1983

Black Filmmakers Hall of Fame, Inductee, 1976

Directors Guild, Life Achievement Award, 1996

*Gallery of Greats*, Inductee, 1991

Hofstra University, Honorary Doctorate in Humane Letters, 1994

Los Angeles Black Media Coalition, Outstanding Technical Achievement, 1988

*Ain't Supposed to Die a Natural Death*
   Tony Award Nomination, 1971

*The Day They Came to Arrest the Book*
  Emmy Award, 1989
  Humanitas Award, 1989

*Don't Play Us Cheap*
  Belgian Film Festival, First Prize, 1972
  Tony Award Nomination, 1972

*Watermelon Man*
  NAACP Image Award, Score, 1970

## EDUCATION

Ohio Wesleyan University, B.A., English

## SOURCES

Interview by George Hill and Spencer Moon, January 1991; follow-up interview, Spencer Moon, September 1995.

### Books

Bogle, Donald. *Blacks in American Film and Television: An Illustrated Encyclopedia*. New York: Simon & Schuster, 1989.

Guerrero, Ed. *Framing Blackness: The African American Image in Film*. Philadelphia: Temple University Press, 1993.

Monaco, James. *American Film Now: Updated*. New York: Zoetrope, 1984.

Reid, Mark A. *Redefining Black Film*. Berkeley: University of California Press, 1993.

Yearwood, Gladstone L. *Towards a Theory of Black Cinema Aesthetic*. Columbus: Ohio University Press, 1982.

### Newspapers and Magazines

Botto, Louis. "Work in Progress." *Intellectual Digest*, August 1992, pp. 6–10.

Evans, Paul. "Rollin and Tumblin': Short Reviews. Ghetto Gothic." *Rolling Stone*, April 6, 1995, p. 68.

Jaehne, Karen. "Melvin Van Peebles: The Baadasssss Gent." *Cineaste* (18), no. 1 (1990), pp. 4–8.

White, Timothy. "Rap Roots: The Story of Brer Soul." *Billboard*, July 11, 1992, p. 34.

# MARK WARREN III

## BACKGROUND

Mark Warren proved that it could be done. Just as Jester Harrison says that he and Stepin' Fetchit had to prove that Blacks could act in the thirties, Warren proved that Blacks could direct by winning an Emmy in the 1970–1971 season of *Laugh-In*. An Emmy win for directing did not occur again until 1986, when it was won by Georg Stanford Brown. It is a fact that Blacks have starred in four times as many television situation comedies as drama series. Blacks have been in television comedies for over four decades. Black directors have directed scores of episodic situation comedy, but Warren remains the sole African American to be nominated for directing comedy.

He was born in Kentucky. He got his early exposure to media production in the Marines while stationed at the U.S. Embassy in Ottawa, Canada. He worked part-time at a local radio station as a disc jockey. He later proposed a musical variety show to the founders of a new Canadian television station. They didn't accept the show idea, but they hired Mark after his discharge from the service. He moved steadily up the ladder with the Canadian production company, learning to do every job connected with broadcast television. His mentor was a producer on staff, Paddy Simpson. Paddy had achieved success in Canadian television as a producer of specials featuring many Black stars. Paddy and Mark worked on specials featuring Harry Belafonte, Duke Ellington and Sammy Davis Jr. During Mark's six years with CTV (Canadian Public Television) and later CBC (Canadian Broadcasting

Corporation), he developed a lifelong friendship with Sammy Davis Jr. They later did a number of shows together in the United States and in Mexico. Mark went on to produce and direct other Canadian programs, including *In Person*, a musical variety show that became Canada's third most popular program at that time.

## TELEVISION PRODUCTION IN HOLLYWOOD

In an interview done in Los Angeles in 1991, Mark spoke about his career in television and in Hollywood. In 1968 the call went out in Hollywood to find as many Black production staff as possible. The producers George Schlatter and Ed Friendly had been contracted by NBC to produce a number of Black music and comedy specials. They decided to staff the programs with as many Black people as possible to add to the production values and to the shows' authenticity. Mark was invited to Los Angeles to talk with Schlatter and Friendly. His first assignment for them involved directing the musical variety special *Soul* (1968). Mark described *Soul* as a black version of *Laugh-In*, only more music-oriented. Hosted by Lou Rawls with the orchestra of H.P. Barnum, it also featured Redd Foxx, Nipsey Russell and other comics. He described it as a fast-paced musical comedy special.

Mark talked about his reluctance to leave the niche and artistic freedom he had carved in Canadian television. His friend Sammy Davis Jr. persuaded him to come down and do the show. He took a leave of absence from his contract with CBC just to do that one show. The next program he directed in America was *T.C.B. with Diana Ross & the Supremes* (1968). This musical variety special chronicled Motown Records' move from Detroit to Los Angeles. It was also one of the first nationally televised showcases for the Supremes as they made the transition to Diana Ross & the Supremes.

After successfully completing this special, Mark was asked by Schlatter and Friendly to direct a pilot for a possible new series. It was entitled *Turn On* (1968). In *The Complete Directory of Prime Time TV Shows: 1946–Present*, 4th. ed., the authors Tim Brooks and Earle Marsh contend *Turn On* is remembered as one of the most famous one-telecast fiascoes in the history of television. It was publicized as the second coming of *Laugh-In* and even had the same executive producer, George Schlatter. They add that because the show's content was considered off-color (as in bad taste), it "[l]ed many ABC affiliates to refuse to carry it after the first telecast, and Bristol-Meyers dropped sponsorship. It was canceled." The producers felt so bad that they offered Mark a job as director of their hit show *Laugh-In*. Their belief in

Mark was based on their regard for his talent. Schlatter and Friendly spoke about Mark in *Ebony* magazine in 1971: "He's a cool cat. No panic. He knows what he wants and he knows how to get it."

## *LAUGH-IN*

When asked what his thoughts were on winning an Emmy for *Laugh-In*, he said:

> When I was nominated, it became a reality. Before that I never thought about winning awards. Just to be nominated, as so many people have said before me, is indeed enough of an honor. But as it got closer to the date, I did start thinking about it a lot. But I had no feelings of winning. I do recall when I was there in that room and they did call my name, people said that my feet never touched the ground between the table and the podium. Tim Kiley, a friend and fellow nominee in that same category, came over and offered me the first congratulations, which I thought was special. Because I had admired his work for some time, too.

## AFTER *LAUGH-IN*

After winning an Emmy in the second year of his three-year tenure with *Laugh-In*, Mark left the show of his own accord. He wanted to pursue other directing assignments. He directed a special called *Cotton Club '75*, which starred Mr. "Old Black Magic" himself—Billy Daniels (who had his own television show in 1952 on ABC)—and the world-renowned dancers the Nicholas Brothers. Mark worked with Bill Cosby and helped him achieve some of his early fame on *The New Bill Cosby Show*, which as a variety show-case had an ensemble cast that included the dancer Lola Folana; the show's music was provided by the Quincy Jones Orchestra. Mark later directed episodes of the series *Get Christie Love* featuring Teresa Graves. Teresa and Mark had worked together on *Laugh-In*, where she was a former cast member and show regular. This was Mark's first direction of series television (other than variety shows) under a contract he had with Universal Studios. Mark described people's reactions to the show as misguided. He said the show was "Something too many people took serious, I think." Asked what he meant by this, he said, "It was a parody, it was fun, a cartoon. This was not *Police Woman*. *I'm Gonna Get You Sucka*' is a closer comparison. It was designed to be funny, it's entertainment."

## VARIETY AND COLOR

Mark talked about his preference and love for doing musical variety specials as a director over other types of directing assignments, because of his music background as a former disc jockey and his love of music as an amateur musician. "I like variety." Of the many shows he has directed, besides the body of work he did with Sammy Davis Jr., he especially liked working on *Laugh-In* and *The New Bill Cosby Show*. When questioned about the racial environment in which he worked, Mark said, "I never put 'Black director' on my resume, I just put 'director.' They found out I was Black when I won an Emmy." He didn't direct more features during the Black cinema wave of the seventies because "Nobody asked me. When they did, you were typed as to what you could direct. I was not interested in doing some of the kinds of films that were being done at that time. I felt that I had to be able to take my parents to films I made. Directing television gave me other options at the time. . . . It is difficult to say what kind of director I am, by my own design."

## ADVICE FOR ASPIRANTS

He has suggestions for young people:

Observe every aspect of the industry from an intern's perspective. Take whatever job you can get. Take your time to find something to shoot at. For people who want to be directors, get some product in hand that shows what you do. If it's television, you have to work at the local level—out of the bigger markets like New York, Los Angeles or Chicago, but at smaller market stations. If you want to make features, then just do it, within the constraints of the independent filmmaking level. Create your own package, but smaller.

## THE FUTURE

When we spoke again, I asked him what he would like to accomplish in the future.

I want to keep working. What I'm really distressed about, though, is that I don't see more young African Americans getting into television. Especially the creative side. In 1972 when I won my Emmy for directing *Rowan & Martin's Laugh-In*, I'm still the only Black director in 1995 to have won this award. Does that say something. The numbers are not as they should be. Of those who are working, their work is very good. I want to see more young African Americans come into directing, producing and writing. Since we last spoke I found out I was the first African American television director in the Directors Guild. Gordon Parks* was the first African American director in the Guild, by a month. I have been busy, working. Besides my three grown children, I now have a granddaughter and a grandson, and I'm very proud.

## FILMOGRAPHY

### Director

*Come Back Charleston Blue,*** 1972, 100 min., 35mm, color, Warner Brothers. Release of a Samuel Goldwyn Jr. production. Based on the novel *The Heat's On* by Chester Himes. This film is a sequel to the popular 1970 film *Cotton Comes to Harlem*, which was also based on a Himes novel of the same name. The two main characters, "Gravedigger" Jones and "Coffin" Ed Johnson, are played by Godfrey Cambridge and Raymond St. Jacques—stars of the earlier film.

Mark says that part of the original impetus for him to come to the United States was to direct feature films. He worked with Samuel Goldwyn Jr. in casting, writing and developing *Cotton Comes to Harlem* (1970). Because he was not a well-known feature film director, he lost the opportunity to direct *Cotton . . .* ; but he was later deemed well enough known to direct the sequel.

*Crunch*, 1981, 90 min., 35mm, Canadian feature. Distributed and produced by Astro-Belvue & Pathe/Avco-Embassy. A high school football comedy.

### Episodic Television

*The Apollo Comedy Hour*, synd., over 60 episodes since 1991; *Baby I'm Back*, CBS; *Barney Miller*, ABC; *Benson*, ABC; *Big City Comedy*, NBC/CTV; *Burns & Schrieber Comedy Hour*, ABC; *Cher*, CBS; *The Diahann Carroll Show*, CBS; *Don Kirschner's Rock Concert*, synd.; *Dick Clark Presents the Rock and Roll Years*, ABC; *Dinah and Her New Best Friends*, CBS; *Dukes of Hazzard*, CBS; *Fish*, ABC; *Get Christie Love*, ABC; *Joey & Dad*, CBS; *The New Bill Cosby Show*, CBS; *Rowan & Martin's Laugh-In*, NBC; *Sammy & Co.: Starring Sammy Davis Jr. On the Road*, synd.; *Sanford & Son*, NBC; *Snow Job*, CTV; *Turn On*, ABC; *What's Happening*, ABC; *The Wolfman Jack Show*, CBS.

### Television Specials

*An Only Son*, CBS; *And Beautiful: Starring Redd Foxx & Wilt Chamberlin*, synd.; *Black Achievement Awards*, CBS; *The Best on Record (Grammy Awards)*, NBC; *Beverly Sills & Friends*, CBS; *Big City Comedy*, synd.; *Cotton Club '75*, NBC; *Cotton Club Revue*, NBC; *Family Night* (Nancy Wilson in a holiday variety special, 2 hours), synd. since 1991; *The 5th Annual Rhythm & Blues Awards: Hosted by Flip Wilson*, synd.; *The 1983 Billboard Salute to Rhythm & Blues: Hosted by Robert Guilliaume*, synd.; *Funny Side of Sports*, CBS; *The Now Sam: Starring Sammy Davis Jr.*, synd.; *Komedy Tonight*, CBS; *Sammy Davis Jr. Live from Acapulco*, HBO; *Soul*, ABC; *Stellar Awards Show* (gospel music industry awards of recognition, 2 hours), synd. special, 1996; *Sneak Peak Preview*,

ABC; *T.C.B. with Diana Ross & The Supremes*, NBC; *Traveling On*, CBS; *Two in a Box: Starring Shields & Yarnell*, synd.; *The Wacky World of Comedy*, NBC.

### Theater

*Selma*, Huntington, Hartford.

*Alice and the Mad Hatter*, Toronto.


## BIO-CRITICAL REVIEW

*Come Back Charleston Blue.* "The movie has been photographed lovingly on location in Harlem, and shows this is a place of beauty and ugliness, pride and corruption, community-building and drug pushing, all side by side. Sometimes this makes the movie seem a little schizo. . . . [The film] [d]oesn't feel a necessity to present us with still another black superman."—Roger Ebert, *Chicago Sun Times*, quoted in George Hill and James Robert Parrish, *Black Action Films*


## WORK

Mark Warren has been a guest speaker at Kentucky State University, Crenshaw High School in Los Angeles, and the Arts Center, Los Angeles. He has taught various classes: Directors Guild of America, Los Angeles, "Directing the Situation Comedy Workshop"; the Crossroads Academy, "Acting for the Camera"; the Golden State Schools, "Television Direction and Production"; and the University of Southern California, "Multiple-Camera Television Production."


## AWARDS

*Get Christie Love*
    LAPD Commendation for Achievement and Service, 1974/75

*The New Bill Cosby Show*
    NAACP Image Award, Directing, 1972/73

*Rowan & Martin's Laugh-In*
    Emmy Award, Directing, Comedy Series, 1970/71


## SOURCES

Interview by George Hill and Spencer Moon, January 1991; follow-up interview, November 1995 by Spencer Moon.


### Books

Brooks, Tim, and Earle Marsh. *The Complete Directory of Prime Time TV Shows: 1946–Present*, 4th ed. New York: Ballantine Books, 1988.

Hill, George, and James Robert Parish. *Black Action Films.* Jefferson, NC: McFarland 1989.


## Other

"TV's Black Skyrocket: Mark Warren becomes Director of *Laugh-In* in Less than Two Years." *Ebony*, November 1971, pp. 112–20.

# THE WAYANS FAMILY: KEENAN IVORY, DAMON, SHAWN, AND MARLON

## BACKGROUND

Hollywood of late has seen a rash of siblings working successfully in the system: the Coen brothers (Ethan and Joel), the Baldwins (Billy, Stephen, Alec, Daniel), the Carradines (Robert, David, Keith), the Keaches (Stacy, James), the Quaids (Randy, Dennis). The historic precedent was set by the success of the Barrymores (Ethel, John, Lionel). The African American community has the Harrises (Wendell,* Hobart*), the Hudlins (Reginald,* Warrington*), the Hughes (Allen,* Albert*).

The family that tops them all in terms of talent to burn is the Wayans (Keenan Ivory, Damon, Shawn, Marlon). There are a total of ten children in the Wayans family. They exploded onto the national scene with the television program *In Living Color* in 1990. Shawn and Marlon now have their own successful television series, *The Wayans Brothers*. Can't touch them.

## KEENAN IVORY WAYANS

Because of the success of *In Living Color*, Keenan as creator and executive producer was the focus of a lot of attention. In 1990 on *Inside the Comedy Mind*, a television series that focused on interviews with comedians, Keenan was interviewed by the host and producer of the series—the legendary comedian/actor Alan King. King introduced Keenan by reading a comment from a critic who described *In Living Color* as fresh, progressive and street-smart.

Keenan described their household as one where comedy was always supported; they were always allowed to be funny. Comedy was something they could never get in trouble for in the house. As kids they made jokes about their mother and father, who had senses of humor. At a young age he was exposed to Richard Pryor on television. Keenan decided he was going to be a comedian at age 7 while watching *The Della Reese Show* when Richard Pryor was on. Pryor's routines were things that Keenan had done, and his experiences were the same as Pryor's routines. Keenan connected with Pryor and his comedy. Keenan knew that was what he wanted to do, but he didn't tell anyone. He went to college to please everyone else and because he didn't know how to become a comedian. He would do stories and characters on the college campus square for his fellow classmates.

One of his classmates told him about the Improv in New York City, saying he should check it out the next time he went home because people like Richard Pryor had started there. The light bulb went on. The next time Keenan went home he wrote some material, went to the club and stood in line to go on stage. He bombed, but it wasn't the laughter he sought. When he was on stage the lights were on him and he had the attention of the audience. He was doing what he wanted to do. The energy was very good. It was like a dream had come true for him in that moment. He knew that patience was what he needed; he had to work to make himself better as a comedian. He went back later and watched the seasoned comedians work.

Keenan felt the key to comedy is translating your stories to a group of people that you don't know. He feels that the first several minutes you're on stage is when you establish your comedy; after that, the audience will be supportive and laugh. He learned how to do that by studying other people. He studies people. He loves people. He never travels incognito, because he feels that by letting people approach him it is a source of material. He feeds off of that.

## ROBERT TOWNSEND

Keenan met Robert Townsend* in line while auditioning for the Improv. Townsend was the only other Black face in the crowd. They just chatted as one brother to another. The next day Keenan was walking down Broadway and saw Robert coming out of a peep show looking inconspicuous. Keenan thought it would be funny to bust him. Townsend got defensive and said he didn't know anything about an Improv. Later in their comedy and acting careers, after they had both moved to Los Angeles, their relationship developed in Hollywood to the extent that they exchanged information and ideas on acting and comedy clubs. This relationship led to the film *Hollywood Shuffle*** (1987). After the success of *Hollywood Shuffle* Keenan wanted to get more exposure for his talent, so he decided to do *I'm Gonna Get You Sucka'*** (1989).

## BLACK CINEMA OF THE SEVENTIES

The film *I'm Gonna Get You Sucka'* was an homage to Black cinema of the seventies. Keenan said he lived on those films as a kid. He and his brothers and sisters would go to the theaters on the weekend, pay a dollar, see three movies and spend the day in the theater. He saw all those films in their heyday. Keenan does not think Black cinema of the seventies should be castigated for its overt and sometimes multiple episodes of violence. The term "Blaxploitation" came to represent any and all Black-cast films, but any genre contains elements of good and bad. He compares the genre of horror and an Alfred Hitchcock film with, say, a *Friday the 13th* film. He sees that a formula is used to exploit a popular genre or style. *Shaft* he saw as a monumental film. Its firsts for depicting a Black man with strength, integrity and sexuality were groundbreaking. Gordon Parks Sr.* opened doors for Black directors. Isaac Hayes got an Academy Award for his work in scoring the film, a first. Those were great accomplishments. In an attempt to eliminate the negative aspects of Black cinema of the seventies, people overreacted. The result was abandonment of the good films as part of a wholesale effort for change.

## SUCCESS AND WEEKLY TELEVISION: *IN LIVING COLOR*

An opportunity presented itself when Fox network executives came to him saying they wanted him to create a television show, one that he wanted to do. Keenan saw it as an opportunity to make an impact and do something substantive in the field of comedy. He considered his historic antecedents, *Saturday Night Live* and *Laugh-In*, as the irreverent shows of their decade. He felt that in each decade some show would be counter to the political mindset of the country, especially where the political climate is conservative. *In Living Color* was that show of the nineties. With its irreverent, urban point of view, the program had a street sensibility. Keenan described it as hip-hop comedy, a style of comedy that had been brewing with the work of people like Robert Townsend and had percolated to the surface with *Hollywood Shuffle* and *In Living Color*. Just as rap music became mainstream, so had his style of comedy. What made *In Living Color* different from other shows was its different ethnic mix; being something new that people had not seen before gave it its edge.

Finally, Keenan said a contemporary influence on his comedy (besides

Richard Pryor) was Eddie Murphy. Watching Murphy taught him to be fearless with his comedy; that, he said, is Murphy's magic.

### More about *In Living Color*

An interview was conducted with Keenan and other cast members during their second season of *In Living Color*; the interview aired on *Screen Scene* (BET Cable).

Sometimes in rehearsal they would not use all the lines from the script; that way, it would still be fresh when performed. Everyone associated with the show wanted to challenge themselves and come up with new ideas, so they would constantly play around and joke on the set and feed off of each other. They didn't self-censor; they would go as far as they could and then let the network censors do their job. The cast was having a good time doing what they were doing. D.J. rap master S.W.1, Shawn Wayans, joined the cast during the second season with Kim, Damon and Keenan.

### EMMY AWARD

On winning an Emmy award for *In Living Color*, Keenan said frankly, "Just a surprise we actually got it; I didn't think the television academy would be as hip as that." Wayans defends the sharp satire, wit and parody of *In Living Color*: "I want the show to have intelligence to it, but I always want it to be raw funny."

### DAMON WAYANS

In an interview by Terry Gross of National Public Radio, Damon spoke about his aspirations. They spoke just prior to his first HBO comedy special in 1989.

Damon described himself as a very quiet and shy kid. He watched everything, and nothing escaped his eyes. He used to do impressions of people who came to visit his family after they left.

Damon tries to stay in touch with the people he grew up with, because he thinks it's important. He thinks he defied the odds, given that as a kid he got into a lot of trouble by trying to be "one of the guys." There wasn't much to do because all the community centers in his neighborhood had been closed. So the kids invented their own games, like take the money and run. He and his friend did things for fun that were against the law. His father finally told him one day not to call home if he ever got into trouble, because he wasn't coming to get him.

### Acting Career

Damon feels that Hollywood is very limited in its perspective of African American actors. He is sure that he would never win an Oscar as a street character because that is what Hollywood sees him as anyway. He wants to do things that are a stretch to himself and to America; he will have to write those roles himself, he feels. White writers have a hard time writing for Black actors because they label the roles or parts as Black. They write the characters with stereotypical street idioms and when you read it, he says, it makes you nauseous. He doesn't mind roles where they write it and then let him bring the Blackness to it. When they write it Black, then generally he feels those roles are not for him.

## SELECTED AWARDS

### Keenan:
Black Filmmakers Hall of Fame, Clarence Muse Youth Award, 1990
*In Living Color*
   Emmy Award, Outstanding Variety, Music or Comedy Series, 1990

## FILMOGRAPHY: KEENAN

### Producer/Director

*I'm Gonna Get You Sucka',*** 1988, 35mm.
   The host of *Fresh Air* on National Public Radio, Terry Gross, queried both Keenan and Damon Wayans. The program aired in 1995 and was a repeat broadcast of separate interviews conducted in 1989 about their comedy and influences.
   Keenan described the film as a story about a character named Jack Spade, who comes home from the army after ten years. Jack finds that his brother has been killed from an overdose of gold chains. Jack decides to do something about it. He rounds up all his old heroes and they go after Mr. Big, who is a big gold distributor in town.
   Keenan approached Isaac Hayes, Jim Brown and Bernie Casey for the film, and they all got involved because they were enthusiastic about the film and thought the script was funny. They saw it as a chance to have fun making fun of themselves in parody.
   The film grossed over $19 million with a $3 million budget.
*Low Down Dirty Shame*, 1994.
*Don't Be a Menace to South Central while Drinking Your Juice in the Hood*, 1996.

### Writer

*Hollywood Shuffle*, 1987; *Eddie Murphy, Raw*, 1987; *The Five Heartbeats*, 1991.

### Actor

#### *Television*

*For Love and Honor*, NBC; *Partners in Crime*, HBO.

#### *Films*

*Star 80*, 1983; *Hollywood Shuffle*, 1987; *I'm Gonna Get You Sucka'*, 1988; *Low Down Dirty Shame*, 1994; *Don't Be a Menace to South Central while Drinking Your Juice in the Hood*, 1996; *The Glimmer Man*, 1996.

### Producer/Writer/Performer/Creator

*In Living Color*, FOX

## FILMOGRAPHY: DAMON

### Producer/Writer

*Mo' Money*, 1992; *Major Payne*, 1994; *Blankman*, 1994.

### Actor

#### *Television*

*Saturday Night Live*, NBC; *Partners in Crime II*, HBO; *One Night Stand*, HBO; *In Living Color*, FOX.

#### *Films*

*Beverly Hills Cop*, 1984; *Hollywood Shuffle*, 1987; *Roxanne*, 1987; *Punchline*, 1988; *I'm Gonna Get You Sucka'*, 1988; *Colors*, 1988; *Earth Girls Are Easy*, 1989; *The Last Boy Scout*, 1991; *Mo' Money*, 1992; *Major Payne*, 1994; *Blankman*, 1994; *The Great White Hype*, 1996; *Celtic Pride*, 1996; *Bulletproof*, 1996.

## FILMOGRAPHY: SHAWN

### Producer

*The Wayans Brothers*, WB Network.

### Actor

#### *Television*

*The Wayans Brothers*, WB Network; *In Living Color*, FOX.

### Films

*Don't Be a Menace to South Central while Drinking Your Juice in the Hood*, 1996; *I'm Gonna Get You Sucka'*, 1988.

## FILMOGRAPHY: MARLON

### Producer

*The Wayans Brothers*, WB Network.

### Actor

### Television

*The Wayans Brothers*, WB Network; *In Living Color*, FOX.

### Films

*Don't Be a Menace to South Central while Drinking Your Juice in the Hood*, 1996; *Mo' Money*, 1992; *I'm Gonna Get You Sucka'*, 1988.

## SOURCES

### Books

McNeil, Alex. *Total Television Including Cable*. New York: Penguin Books, 1991.
Parish, James Robert. *Today's Black Hollywood*. New York: Windsor Publishing, 1995.

### Newspapers and Magazines

Bates, Karen Grigsby. "Keenan Ivory Wayans: TV Comedy Innovator." *Emerge*, January 1991, p. 42.
Rense, Rip. "Color Blind." *Emmy: The Magazine of the Academy of Television Arts and Sciences* (13), no. 1 (February 1991), p. 33–37.

### Other

*Fresh Air* (National Public Radio), July 21, 1995.
*Inside the Comedy Mind* (Comedy Central Cable), May 1990.
Press Release (FOX Broadcasting), 1991.
*Screen Scene* (BET Cable), July 1992.

Spencer Williams. *Illustration courtesy of R. Ellis Lee.*

# SPENCER WILLIAMS JR.

## BACKGROUND

Spencer Williams (1893–1969) will be remembered by many people for a role that today is considered politically incorrect. He was Amos Brown of the old *Amos N' Andy* (1951–1953) television series. What should be remembered is that he not only opened doors for today's current and aspiring Black filmmakers, but he was a pioneer of Black cinema. Williams had a long career that spanned from silent films to the advent of television.

Williams drifted to New York City and managed to land a job as Oscar Hammerstein's call boy. This job gave him his first stage experience. While in New York he also became friends with Bert Williams, a veteran Black comedian and star of the Ziegfield Follies. Williams learned the art of comedy from Bert Williams. Eventually Williams even managed to record a vocal duet with Lonnie Johnson. The song *It Feels So Good* was released on Okeh Records.

Williams spent time in the armed services and then attended the University of Minnesota. He migrated south after graduation. Al Christie of Paramount Studios sent a company south for location shots, and they wound up hiring the former World War I veteran Williams. He worked first as a technician and even helped to install some of the first sound equipment in a Hollywood studio. Later he was given the assignment to write continuity for Christie Comedies, the earliest of the Black talkies. Many scripts were comedic stories written by Octavus Roy Cohen during the twenties. Cohen's work was steeped in southern lore because he was from Birmingham, Alabama. Williams found the balance in re-drafting the material to include more authentic Negro nuances. He wrote for mainstream films as well as race movies.

Williams's acting career began as his writing career had, with the Christie Comedies. He appeared in an assortment of films where his role was more than just a stereotype: among others, *The Melancholy Dame, Oft in the Silly Night, The Lady Fare, Music Hath Charms* and *The Framing of the Shrew*. All were comedy shorts. Williams's sense of craft, from continuity and script writing to acting, by now enabled him to create roles that displayed his own wit and charm. Over time he moved to other roles in the major studios. He also found work in all-Black films and, finally, television.

## DIRECTING

He directed his first film in 1928, and he secured financing for two of his films from White backers. Those two films, *Go Down Death* and *Blood of Jesus*, presented as serious an analysis of the Black religious experience as has been seen in a fiction film to date. Like that of Oscar Micheaux,* a significant amount of Williams's work as director is available on home video.

Williams was an activist as well. His efforts to write and act honest Black roles were the start. Williams met with Earl J. Morris, a black civic leader, in 1939 to discuss demands for a national Negro censor for the film industry. Their meeting was fuel for the fire ignited many years later by Walter White and the NAACP that resulted in boosts for some Black actors' sagging careers. Positive Black films were at least green-lighted, though few reached the screen. By 1952, when Williams was in the stereotypical role on *Amos N' Andy*, the NAACP was largely responsible for its early demise on television.

Williams moved to Tulsa, Oklahoma, and apparently had given up his film career by the end of the forties. While there, he taught photography and radio to veterans. He heard about the call for actors for the proposed television version of the long-running and successful radio program *Amos N' Andy*. The production was being mounted by the Hal Roach Studios in Culver City, California.

Williams's career as a technician, writer, actor and director spanned over forty years in films and television.

## FILMOGRAPHY

### Writer/Actor/Director

*Tenderfoot*, 1928; *Melancholy Dame*, 1929; *The Widow's Bite*, 1929; *The Georgia Rose*, 1930; *The Virginia Judge*, 1930.

*Blood of Jesus,*** 1941. A husband of small religious faith accidentally kills his pious wife. He agonizes and discovers his own faith. The wife on the journey to the next world chooses God over the Devil and is given life again. She sees her repentant husband, and all is well that ends well. Another serious effort to broach the Black religious experience, specifically the Southern Baptist tradition. Cast included Cathryn Caviness, Eddie DeBuse, Alva Fuller, Rogeinia Goldwaithe, Reather Hardeman, James Jones, Frank McClennan, Juanita Riley, the Heavenly Choir and Spencer Williams Jr.

*Go Down Death,*** 1944. A story inspired by a James Weldon Johnson poem of the same title. A unique look at the Black religious heritage. The film features Myra Hemmings as the almost angelic and also tragic preacher Sister Caroline. The images include some startling shots of a Sunday School picture of Jesus dripping with blood as it hangs above a sick woman's bed. The film also features Spencer Williams Jr., the Heavenly Choir, and Jimmy Green's Orchestra.

*Of One Blood,* 1944. Williams used religious themes one final time. He himself appeared in the film as a deaf mute who is in reality an undercover FBI agent.

*Dirtie Gertie from Harlem, U.S.A.,*** 1946. Loosely based on a W. Somerset Maugham story, *Rain.* A showgirl leaves her boyfriend and flees to Trinidad, where, finding work again, she gets involved with her boss. But her boyfriend shows up to spoil things. The cast features Francine Everett, Don Wilson, Katherine Moore, Alfred Hawkins, David Boykin, Lee Lewis, Inez Newell, "Piano" Frank, John King, Shelly Ross, Hugh Watson, Don Gilbert and Spencer Williams Jr. in a bit part as an Old Hager woman.

*The Girl in Room Twenty,*** 1946. A girl from smalltown U.S.A. moves to New York City to become a "singer." Of course, she gets a rude awakening. The film features Geraldine Brock, July Jones and Spencer Williams Jr.

*Juke Joint,*** 1946. Two aspiring actors arrive in Hollywood with twenty-five cents between them. Their luck holds, and they convince a woman to take them on as boarders. The film is a musical romp. The cast starred July Jones, Inex Newell, Melody Duncan, Katherine Moore, Leonard Duncan, Dauphine Moore, Red Calhoun's Orchestra and the Jitterbug Johnnies and Spencer Williams Jr.

*Beale Street Mama,* 1947. One of Williams's last films, it shows the mark of a filmmaker who had in some way let the times pass him by. The story featured Williams and July Jones as street sweepers who find a bag of money but try to parlay it into setting themselves up in the numbers business. The images were so stereotypical that at its Los Angeles debut it was nearly closed, but one of the actors in the film pleaded with the audience to let it go on. Members of a local Interracial Film and Radio Guild were ready to protest its opening. The social climate had turned from Black people being willing to accept stereotyped images of themselves.

### Writer/Actor

*Bronze Buckaroo,*** 1938. The first all-Black-cast Western musical in the tradition of Roy Rogers and Gene Autry. Herb Jeffries is the romantic lead: the riding, roping, fighting and singing hero Bob Blake. Blake and his sidekick, Dusty, set out to avenge the murder of his father by the bad guys. Cast featured Jeffries as the first Black singing cowboy with Lucius Brooks, Artie Young, Flourney E. Miller, Clarence Brooks and Spencer Williams Jr. as a villain.

*Harlem Rides the Range,*** 1939. The success of *Bronze Buckaroo* generated this film. The girlfriend of Herb Jeffries, the singing cowboy, has a radium mine. They try to outwit the villains who are trying to swindle her out of the mine. The cast featured Lucius Brooks, Clarence Brooks, Artie Young and Spencer Williams Jr. The story was written by Flourney E. Miller and Spencer Williams Jr.

*Harlem on the Prairie,*** 1939. Herb Jeffries as a singing cowboy again, with Mantan Moreland as his comic sidekick. The cast featured Flourney E. Miller, Connie Harris and Spencer Williams Jr.

*Two Gun Man from Harlem,*** 1939. A preacher travels to the Old West. No fool, he comes packing with his six-shooters. This Western featured Herb Jeffries, Margaret Whitten, Mantan Moreland and Spencer Williams Jr.

*Son of Ingagi,*** 1940. The first all-Black-cast horror film. The story follows hidden gold and involves a kidnapping. The script is from an original short story by Spencer Williams Jr. entitled *House of Horror.* The cast featured Laura Bowman, Zack Williams (no relation), Alfred Grant, Daisy Bufford and the Four Toppers with Spencer Williams Jr. Ingagi, the ape-man monster of this film, was originally introduced to audiences ten years earlier in a film from Congo Pictures Limited.

### Writer/Director

*Marching On,*** 1943. A docudrama on the all-Black 25th Infantry. We see segregation, as well as patriotism by Black men at war who are ready to die for a country that did not want them to have their inalienable rights. Originally used as propaganda for the war effort. Later in the fifties, additional footage of dancing girls was added to release it as a full-length feature film, *Where's My Man To-Nite?*

### BIO-CRITICAL REVIEW

"Williams has been all but forgotten as an actor and major filmmaker who contributed to the black race movies of the thirties and forties."—*San Francisco Chronicle*

*Blood of Jesus.* "The greatest religious film ever done in America. A powerful, directly uttered folktale about guilt, atonement, and a wonderful visit to hell."—Ken Adams, quoted in "Program Notes," Wexner Center for the Visual Arts

*Go Down Death.* "Because of it being a retelling of the James Weldon Johnson poem which has its roots in the folk sermon and folk drama, the [story] manages to cement the cross-generic relationship between African American ritual expressions through the medium of film."—From "Program Notes," Wexner Center for the Visual Arts

### EDUCATION

University of Minnesota, B.A., history

# SOURCES

## Books

Bogle, Donald. *Blacks in American Film and Television: An Illustrated Encyclopedia*. New York: Simon & Schuster, 1988.

Brooks, Tim, and Earle Marsh. *The Complete Directory to Prime Time Network TV Shows: 1946–Present*. New York: Ballantine Books, 1988.

Cripps, Thomas. *Slow Fade to Black: The Negro in American Film, 1900–1942*. New York: Oxford University Press, 1993.

Hyatt, Marshall, comp. and ed. *The Afro-American Cinematic Experience: An Annotated Bibliography and Filmography*. Wilmington, DE: Scholarly Resources, 1983.

Kisch, John, and Edward Mapp. *A Separate Cinema: Fifty Years of Black Cast Posters*. New York: Farrar, Straus and Giroux, 1992.

Ogle, Patrick, comp. *Facets African-American Video Guide*. Chicago: Facets Multimedia, 1994.

Sampson, Henry T. *Blacks in Black and White: A Source Book on Black Films*. Metuchen, NJ: Scarecrow Press, 1995.

## Other

Stanley, John. "'30s, '40s, 'Race' Movies: Lost Slice of Black Life." *San Francisco Chronicle*, October 7, 1990, pp. 34–36.

Wexner Center for the Visual Arts. Program notes for Spencer Williams Retrospective. Cleveland, OH: 1989.

Allen Willis

# ALLEN WILLIS

**BACKGROUND**

Allen Willis has the distinction of being the dean of African American film-makers in the San Francisco Bay Area. Those who know the rich history of the area's independent filmmaking community acknowledge him as a founding father. He worked for the San Francisco public broadcasting station KQED-TV from 1963 to 1983 and was one of the first African American news and documentary cinematographers in the Bay Area. He worked with young Melvin Van Peebles* when he lived in the area and was a cable car operator and nascent filmmaker.

Once we sat down for the interview, Willis just started talking about himself and his life as a filmmaker. My questions came almost as an interruption to his stream-of-consciousness thoughts on filmmaking.

I consider myself a filmmaker; at least I want to be called a filmmaker. When I started making films in the fifties and sixties it was an expression of an attitude that was very much anti-Hollywood. We were interested in doing intimate and close documentaries about the Black experience. I got interested in filmmaking initially as part of the avant garde movement in San Francisco in the fifties. The movement was centered around the Museum of Fine Arts in San Francisco. At that time I met Melvin Van Peebles. He was a cable car conductor. He was looking around for something to do creatively. He eventually did a picture book on cable car conductors. He then wanted to do a film; in fact, he did make several impressionistic films at that time. He left the area eventually with his films and went to New York. Later he went to Europe. I didn't see him again until he came back with his film *Story of a Three Day Pass*. It was shown here at the San Francisco International Film Festival.

## UNIQUENESS

When asked to describe what makes him unique as a filmmaker, he answered:

My philosophy is that Hollywood is not the ultimate in filmmaking in one's career. You can make a lot of money and become well known working in that system. I think ultimately that system has a corrupting influence on the filmmaker. I always made mostly documentary and experimental type films. I was trying to do films that I consider very intimate. I was influenced by the concept of cinema verité, where in documentaries you try to get the exact moment of your subjects, the exact essence. That's not Hollywood. People like Fred Wiseman have made careers of doing just cinema verité films. I was interested in the great filmmakers of the time, filmmakers like the Maysles (Albert and David) brothers. I came under the influence of films by people like Robert Flaherty while in school. I liked the work of other documentary filmmakers like Pare Lorenz.

## FILM VERSUS VIDEO

The aesthetics of production were discussed.

Film has greater flexibility and takes longer. Video is cheaper and easier to work with, especially if you don't have a lot of money. Editing is a different aesthetic between film and video. Some people use video for preliminary work and then work later in film.

## MEMORABLE EXPERIENCES

Considering his varied career, I wanted to know about some memorable experiences. When asked, he laughed and told me a few.

Maya Angelou. I did a piece with her called *Blues Black Blues*; she wrote, produced and directed it. I shot a lot of it for her. It was a thirteen-week television series that aired here locally. Working with her was a memorable experience.

Melvin Van Peebles almost burned my house down when we shot his short subject *The Boy*. We had a little set in my basement and we torched it, and the fire got out of hand and it almost burned my house down. That was memorable.

At KQED-TV a program called *Profile Bay Area*. The host, Caspar Weinberger (former secretary of defense), had this weekly program. Anyway, several hundred members of the (San Francisco) Hunters Point (a mostly Black section of the city then and still today) community came into the studio and occupied his program while it was on the air live. A dialogue took place with him and the community members. The dialogue went on for the full day and night. This was all on the air. He called and had members of the financial community come in; these were his friends. They made a lot of promises that were never fulfilled. He won a Peabody with that show. And he didn't do a damn thing; he was just there. Members of the community called in and wanted to send the police, and the station management said no, don't do that. I was part of the studio crew. This happened in the days when anybody could come to the station and just walk in. This is before they had security guards like they do now.

## ADVICE FOR ASPIRANTS

What do you tell young aspiring filmmakers?

Each person has to decide first on their own what they want to do. Whatever you want to do in filmmaking, you should try to do it the best that you can. I know in Hollywood no one has the final say except the guys that put the money up. Distribution is critical. If you want to go to Hollywood, be prepared to deal with that system, lumps and all. But if you want to break new ground, then that's another approach altogether. Orson Welles got smashed by Hollywood. He tried to do a film in the forties on Brazil featuring Black people, and he had very little success in Hollywood after that.

I think African American filmmakers have to set themselves up as part of the American civilization, but as something distinctive in that civilization. The influence African Americans have had on American popular culture and the language—there is no question about that. Because of the nature of this civilization as Americans and as a distinctive element of the American civilization. If we dig into our own history, we can find exceptional personalities and stories of those people who have made tremendous contributions to this country.

Most Black people work hard for a living. We should break the mold of stereotypes. Our history is so rich and so important, we should focus on that. Some Black filmmakers are perpetuating a stereotype. Our traditions are rich. As an example, rap has been around since the twenties. I encouraged Melvin van Peebles; I don't take any credit for what he did. I worked with Tony Batten, who went to New York and made a lot of television. My films inspired other filmmakers from our community.

## SELECTED FILMOGRAPHY

### Co-Producer/Cinematographer/Editor

*Have You Sold a Dozen Roses?* 1950, 16mm, color. An original poem by Lawrence Ferlinghetti with an original soundtrack and a poetic montage of words, music and images.

*Commute*, 1956, 16mm, b/w. A poetic study of rush hour in San Francisco in the fifties.

*The Psychedelic Experience*, 1969, 16mm. Timothy Leary's commentary about people who used drugs at that time. Music by Ravi Shankar and Alla Rahka.

### Cinematographer/Editor

*The Wedding; The Pickup Truck; The Boy;* 1949–1953. Three short films directed and produced in collaboration with Melvin Van Peebles.*

*Annie Lee Ritchie*, 1963, 16mm.

> The reason I did this film was that I had heard that this woman had been kicked out of her home because of urban redevelopment. I wanted to talk to her to find out what happened. I wanted to know what she was feeling about it. She told me her story. She was one of hundreds of thousands who were removed from their homes nationally because of urban redevelopment. She was being removed so that our current rapid transit system could use the land that her home was on. She came to California in the twenties and was living in a home that she had bought and paid for, and now she had no home. She couldn't buy a place to live in with the money that she received for her home. At the end of the film she said she hoped the rapid transit system had as many problems as they gave her. That statement proved to be prophetic. The mass transit system did have a lot of problems initially.

This work became a segment for the larger work entitled *The Great California Land Grab*, 1973.

*Drugs in the Tenderloin*, 1967, 16mm. A documentary about people of the darker side of life. Shot mostly at night. A testament to the lives of people ravaged by drugs and alcohol abuse. The filmic treatment is humanistic and nonjudgmental.

*Stagger Lee,*\*\* 1970, 16mm, 15 min., b/w. A documentary on Black Panther leader Bobby Seale during an incarceration in the San Francisco county jail.

*The Great California Land Grab*, 1973, 16mm. A documentary on the changing social environment that became the California of the late twentieth century.

*Para-Psychology*, 1974, 16mm. A documentary on psychic Uri Geller and the para-psychology movement of the times.

### Cinematographer

*Spirit in the Dark*, 1971, 16mm.

*1001 Days*, 1974, 16mm, color. A documentary on returning prisoners-of-war from Vietnam.

### Producer/Director/Cinematographer

*The Other America,*\*\* 1967, 50 min., 16mm, b/w. In 1967 Dr. Martin Luther King addresses an audience at Stanford University. He criticizes the social economics of the time. He discusses the social system that hides the secret of two Americas, the haves and the have-nots. He has never been more eloquent in his biting, incisive social critique of America. In viewing this film we realize the tremendous loss of social conscience that King's assassination brought.

### Producer/Director/Cinematographer/Editor

*Can You Hear Me?*\*\* 1975, 30 min., 16mm, color. Music by Merl Saunders and Rafael Garrett. A blend of the Black oral tradition expressed by young people (age 8 to 18) in their own poetry, songs and games. A look into the young Black mind juxtaposed with a visually poetic treatment of environmental influences on their lives. A sometimes bleak scrutiny of the urban existence and its effects on young minds. Features eloquent young people who really have a deep understanding of their lives in America, East Oakland, California.

### Co-Producer/Director/Cinematographer

*There Is a There There*, 1975, 60 min., 16mm, color. A documentary on noted writer/social critic/educator Ishmael Reed and the city where he resides: Oakland, California.

### Co-Producer/Cinematographer

*Hurrah for Anything*, 1982, 30 min., 16mm. A documentary on poet-painter Kenneth Patchen, who was considered an innovator with his use of words and images on canvas. He was one of the first poets to recite his verse to live jazz music. A remarkable artist whose life influenced many other artists and lovers of originality and talent.

### Producer/Director/Cameraman

*Love on the Rocks*, 1986, video. A video and photo collage from Willis's experiences finding rocks painted with graffiti slogans on the shores of Lake Michigan and in Oakland, California.

*Karla*, 1992, video. A documentary on a day in the life of an African American Flamenco dancer, Karla Populus. Set in the cabarets of San Francisco, especially the Latin district called the Mission. Willis said, "I thought she was a very interesting woman. She went to Spain and fell in love with Flamenco dancing. I think she is an exceptional dancer." The film documents the development of her career.

*San Francisco Beat: 1970–1993*, 1994, video. Beat poet masters Allen Ginsberg, Lawrence Ferlinghetti and Michael McClure talk about the guru of the beat movement, Jack Kerouac. Ginsberg recites Kerouac's verse and does a Buddhist chant.

### BIO-CRITICAL REVIEW

*Can You Hear Me?* "One of the unknown geniuses of the documentary film. A film of moving words and clear but flowing images."—*Newsreel*

*Hurrah for Anything.* "A remarkable half-hour documentary."—Calvin Ahlgren, *San Francisco Examiner and Chronicle*

*The Other America.* "The film touches on a number of topics, making it a useful sociological, historical and oratorical tool."—*Video Rating Guide for Libraries*

*Stagger Lee.* "A remarkable interview worthy of a national award. Remarkable for the sheer humanity which [Bobby] Seale projected. The filmmaker-editor was KQED's talented Allen Willis."—Ralph J. Gleason, *San Francisco Chronicle*

### EDUCATION

Bowie Normal College, Bowie, Maryland, B.A.

California School of Fine Arts (now the San Francisco Art Institute), M.F.A.

### AWARDS AND HONORS

Black Filmmakers Hall of Fame Tribute, 1983

East Bay Media Center Tribute, Berkeley, California, 1989

Proclamation from the City of Berkeley, California, 1989

San Francisco Museum of Modern Art, recognition for his historic and important contributions to Bay Area Filmmaking as a Black pioneer, 1980

*Can You Hear Me?*
  Emmy Award Nomination, Best Documentary Programming, 1975

*Drugs in the Tenderloin*
  National Educational Television Award for Excellence, 1967

*The Great California Land Grab*
  DuPont–Columbia University Journalism Award, 1973

*Newsroom* (KQED-TV, studio camera, cinematographer, editor)
  Peabody Award, 1974

*1001 Days*
  Emmy Award, 1974

*Para-Psychology*
  Emmy Award Nomination, Best Documentary Programming, 1972

*The Psychedelic Experience*
  National Educational Television Award, 1965

*Spirit in the Dark*
  Emmy Award, Outstanding Achievement, Special Programming, 1971

## FESTIVALS

Berkeley Video Festival, 1991–1995

Edinburgh Film Festival, 1975

Mill Valley Film Festival, 1994

San Francisco Film Festival, 1984

## MEMBERSHIPS

Advisory Board, East Bay Media Center

## SOURCES

Interview by Spencer Moon, May 1992.

### Newspapers and Magazines

Ahlgren, Calvin. "Hurrah for a Poet's Universal Spirit." *San Francisco Examiner and Chronicle*, July 25, 1982, pp. 46, 48.
"Can You Hear Me?" *Newsreel* Catalogue (San Francisco), 1976–1978, p. 37.
Gleason, Ralph J. "On the Town; You Don't Tell Jokes No More." *San Francisco Chronicle*, April 10, 1970, p. 46.
"The Other America." *Video Rating Guide for Libraries*, Summer 1990, p. 43.

## Other

Mel Vapour, East Bay Media Center, Allen Willis' films and records representative.

# APPENDIX

Filmmakers whose work can be ordered directly from them and other resources:

St. Clair Bourne
310 Water Street
Guilford, CT 06437
203–453–9943
203–453–9949 (Fax)

Ayoka Chenzira
Red Carnelian Films
107 Lexington Avenue
Brooklyn, NY 11238–1411
718–622–5092
718–622–1174 Fax

Francee Covington Productions
1533 Eddy Street
San Francisco, CA 94115
415–775–3200

William Greaves
230 West 55th Street, #26D
New York, NY 10019
800–874–8314
212–315–0027 Fax

Henry Hampton
Blackside, Inc.
486 Shawmut Avenue
Boston, MA 02118–3320
617–536–6900
617–536–1732 Fax

Hobart Harris
969 Duncan Street
San Francisco, CA 94131–1800
415–206–4649
415–206–5484 Fax

Wendell Harris
1632 Kensington Avenue
Flint, MI 49503–2775
810–232–3732

Ashley James
Searchlight Films
30 Berry
San Francisco, CA 94107
415–543–1254

Avon Kirkland
New Images Productions
2600 Tenth Street
Berkeley, CA 94710
510–548–1790

Louis Massiah
1507 N. 16th Street
Philadelphia, PA
215–763–1900
215–763–1903 Fax

Leo D. Sullivan
Vignette Multimedia
1283 S. La Brea Avenue, #159
Los Angeles, CA 90019
212–939–4174
212–939–2762 Fax

Marlon Riggs's work is distributed by:
California Newsreel
149 Ninth Street
San Francisco, CA 94103
415–621–6196

and

Frameline
346 9th Street
San Francisco, CA 94103
415–703–8650
415–861–1404 Fax

Allen Willis's work can be ordered from:
East Bay Media Center
2054 University, Suite 203
Berkeley, CA 94704–1059
510–843–3699
510–843–3379 Fax

Other resources:

Facets Video
1517 West Fullerton Avenue
Chicago, IL 60614
800-331-6197

Spencer Moon
766½ Hayes Street
San Francisco, CA 94102-4132
800-615-6290

Third World Newsreel
335 West 38th Street, 5th Floor
New York, NY 10018
212–947–9277

Women Make Movies
462 Broadway, Suite 500
New York, NY 10013
212–925–0606

# SELECTED BIBLIOGRAPHY

Bogle, Donald. *Blacks in American Film and Television: An Illustrated Encyclopedia*. New York: Simon & Schuster, 1989.
———. *Toms, Coons, Mulattoes, Mammies and Bucks: An Interpretive History of Blacks in American Films*. New York: Continuum, 1989.
Brooks, Tim, and Earle Marsh. *The Complete Directory of Primetime TV Shows: 1946–Present*. New York: Random House, 1992.
Cham, Mbye B., and Claire Andrade-Watkins, eds. *Blackframes: Critical Perspectives on Black Independent Cinema*. Cambridge, MA: MIT Press, 1988.
Cripps, Thomas. *Making Movies Black: The Hollywood Message Movie from World War II to the Civil Rights Era*. New York: Oxford University Press, 1993.
George, Nelson. *Blackface: Reflections on African Americans and the Movies*. New York: HarperCollins, 1994.
Guerrero, Ed. *Framing Blackness: The African American Image in Film*. Philadelphia: Temple University Press, 1993.
Harris, Erich Leon. *African American Screen Writers Now: Conversations with Hollywood's Black Pack*. Los Angeles: Silman-James Press, 1996.
Hill, George. *Ebony Images: Black Americans and Television*. Los Angeles: Daystar, 1986.
Hill, George, and Sylvia Saverson Hill. *Blacks on Television: A Selectively Annotated Bibliography*. Metuchen, NJ: Scarecrow Press, 1985.
Hill, George, and Spencer Moon. *Blacks in Hollywood: Five Favorable Years, 1987–1991*. Los Angeles: Daystar, 1991.
Hill, George, Lorraine Raglin, and Robert Davenport. *African-American Television Experience: A Researcher's Bibliography of Scholarly Writings*. Los Angeles: Daystar, 1987.

Hill, George, Lorraine Raglin, and Charles Floyd Johnson. *Black Women in Television: An Illustrated History and Bibliography*. New York: Garland Publishing, 1990.

Hyatt, Marshall, comp. and ed. *The Afro-American Cinematic Experience: An Annotated Bibliography and Filmography*. Wilmington, DE: Scholarly Resources, 1983.

Katz, Ephraim. *The Film Encyclopedia*. New York: HarperCollins, 1994.

Kendell, Stephen D. *New Jack Cinema: Hollywood's African-American Filmmakers*. Silver Springs, MD: J.L. Denser, 1994.

Keyser, Lester J., and Andre H. Ruszkowski. *The Cinema of Sidney Poitier*. New York: A.S. Barnes, 1980.

Klotman, Phyllis Rauch. *Screenplays of the African American Experience*. Bloomington: Indiana University Press, 1991.

Maltin, Leonard, ed. *Leonard Maltin's Movie and Video Guide, 1995*. New York: Penguin Group, 1995.

McNeil, Alex. *Total Television Including Cable: A Comprehensive Guide to Programming from 1948 to the Present*. New York: Penguin, 1991.

Null, Gary. *Black Hollywood: From 1970 to Today*. New York: Carol Publishing Group, 1993.

Ogle, Patrick, comp. *Facets African-American Video Guide*. Chicago: Facets Multimedia/Academy Chicago Publishers, 1994.

Reid, Mark A. *Redefining Black Film*. Berkeley: University of California Press, 1993.

Rhines, Jesse Algeron. *Black Film/White Money*. New Brunswick, NJ: Rutgers University Press, 1996.

Sampson, Henry T. *Blacks in Black and White: A Source Book on Black Films*. Metuchen, NJ: Scarecrow Press, 1995.

Time-Life Books, eds. *African-American Voices of Triumph: Creative Fire, A Tradition of African Art, Filmmaking, Music, Literature, Visual Arts*. Alexandria, VA: Time-Life Books, 1994.

Yearwood, Gladstone L., ed. *Black Cinema Aesthetics: Issues in Independent Black Filmmaking*. Athens: Afro-American Studies, Ohio University, 1982.

# INDEX